T0305131

# *Business Cycles*

# *Business Cycles*

## History, Theory and Investment Reality

### Third Edition

**Lars Tvede**

John Wiley & Sons, Ltd

*Other Wiley Editorial Offices*

Wiley have other editorial offices in the USA, Germany, Australia, Singapore and Canada.

Wiley also publishes its books in a variety of electronic formats. Some content that
appears in print may not be available in electronic books.

*Library of Congress Cataloging-in-Publication Data*
Tvede, Lars, 1957-
    Business cycles : history, theory and investment reality / Lars Tvede.—
3rd ed.
        p. cm.
    Includes bibliographical references and index.
    ISBN-13: 978-0-470-01806-4
    ISBN-10: 0-470-01806-2
    1. Business cycles.   2. Economics—History.   3. Economists.   I. Title.
HB3714.T84 2006
338.5'42–dc22

                                                                                2006005379

*British Library Cataloguing in Publication Data*

A catalogue record for this book is available from the British Library

ISBN 13 978-0-470-01806-4 (HB)
ISBN 10 0-470-01806-2 (HB)

Typeset in 10/12 Palatino by SNP Best-set Typesetter Ltd., Hong Kong
Printed and bound in Great Britain by TJ International Ltd, Padstow, Cornwall, UK
This book is printed on acid-free paper responsibly manufactured from sustainable
forestry in which at least two trees are planted for each one used for paper production.

# Contents

# List of Figures and Tables

# Preface

Canton Zug is the smallest of the Swiss cantons, but even with its tiny size it has everything you would associate with Switzerland. Wooden farmhouses are scattered all over its hillsides, and the sounds of cowbells are never far away. During summer, most houses are decorated with beautiful flowers.

The canton is located at the edge of the Alps. It has great views of the peaks of Mount Rigi and Mount Pilatus to the south, and if you go into the hills you may spot the famous peaks of Jungfrau and Eiger to the west. Rivers from the mountains lead down to the local lake, Zugerzee, and on the eastern side of this lake lies the old town of Zug. Founded in the 11th century, it has old wooden houses, narrow streets, romantic churches, remains of the defensive wall and towers, and a tiny harbor for the boats on the lake.

## Four Seasons

The place changes a lot over the year. During the long, warm summer it bustles with life. The many small outdoor cafes are full of happy people, and there are festivals, open markets, concerts and sometimes great fireworks over the lake. The first sign that the summer is about to end is always the same: thunderstorms. You will first see silent lightning far away – not just a few flashes, but hundreds. Then it will roll closer and closer. As it approaches, the silence will be replaced by a vague rumbling, and then, as it reaches Zug itself, by loud booms as each flash of lightning hits the lake or the hillsides. Then the wind, then rain, and then it is all over. A period of dull and foggy weather follows after the autumn. One day it will clear up, and as you look up at the snow-covered mountains, you know that winter has come.

It was on one of those clear and frosty winter days at the start of 1998 that I walked down Bahnhofstrasse to have lunch with Jorgen Chidekel, my friend and partner (since 2005). We like to meet in a restaurant in the central square to talk about things; 'things' meaning mainly the state of the world economy and the prospects for the financial markets. Jorgen is a hedge fund manager, and he lives and breathes these markets. We ordered our meal before I asked as usual:

"So how are things?"

"Still very unsettled. This is a giant crash unfolding," he said. "The Russian stock market is falling like a rock. Although they have a population of 150 million they now have a smaller economy than Switzerland."

"Smaller than Switzerland?"

"That is right. The valuation of Russia's entire stock market is about equal to a few American Internet companies. And the Asia-Pacific region is of course a mess. There are places where it looks like they were trying to build a new Manhattan. Now they are standing completely empty. It is the familiar old business cycles at work again."

We went further into the details of the crash and theories of business cycles as we had our lunch, and after the coffee we left together. As we were saying goodbye outside the restaurant I asked him what he would recommend doing. "It's a crash, you know. A big one. Wait a while," he said. It was freezing cold and his breath froze in the air in little puffs as he spoke. Finally, he broke into a big smile as he finished, "But the weather's lovely." And then we grinned at each other and left.

As I watched him head towards his office I imagined how all those little puffs of frozen speech would be floating along Bahnhofstrasse with their frozen message, "It's a crash, you know. A big one," and how one of them might perhaps shortly turn the corner into Rigistrasse and mingle with all the other puffs issuing from all the other worried businesspeople. Or perhaps they would carry all the way down to the lakeside, drifting past the boats, "It's a crash, you know . . . But the weather's lovely."

When I came home that evening I kept my coat on and went into the garden, where I sat in a garden chair under a tree. It was pitch dark and snowing slightly. I had always enjoyed the quiet winter nights where tiny snowflakes fell gently around me, sometimes, as on this night, from a seemingly clear sky. Far away I could see the lights from the ski-sport hotel high up at the top of Mount Pilatus, and below me were the navigation lights of a tour ship, which appeared to glide majestically over the lake. It was magical.

My thoughts returned to the lunch when we had spoken of business cycles. I had seen so many otherwise skilled businessmen lose every penny because they were blind-sided by recessions. Even economic experts found the subject hard – how many could say that they *really* understood it? When there was a slump, many believed that we would never recover, while when there was a boom, some thought it would last forever. The problem of business cycles was complex. I wondered about when this phenomenon had started. Surely there weren't any business cycles in the Stone Age. So, did they start with the crash of 1929? No, long before that. At the time of Adam Smith, perhaps? No, further back still. Then I thought that it was probably with the introduction of paper money into the European market economy that the phenomenon really had become important.

It was a man named John Law that had introduced paper money into Europe. This had stimulated the development of a very large credit market. The credit market had been of enormous significance in creating the phenomenon of the business cycle. So *that* was perhaps where this phenomenon really became important.

I thought about John Law. Had he really been aware what it was that he was setting in motion? Probably not. How could he? I tried to visualize him. What had he looked like in the old engravings that I had seen? He was certainly tall. A picture began to take shape in my mind's eye – the profile of a tall, slim man. Since it was the time of the Sun King, his shoes would appear rather feminine, with lots of decoration. I closed my eyes and leant back in my garden chair – now the picture became sharper – John Law. I saw in my mind's eye a confident, proud young man standing in the morning sunlight, one hand on his back. It must have been in a park because there were trees in the background. Some distance away, looking at him, stood a little knot of men dressed in the same, funny Renaissance style of clothing. But John Law remained to one side, lost in deep concentration. I could see his head very clearly now, and noticed that small beads of sweat were running down his face. He seemed quite unaware of them and his gaze remained fixed on a certain point. What he was looking at so fixedly was another man. He stared intensely. And then I saw that he reached quickly for something . . .

# Disclaimer

All reasonable efforts have been made to trace copyright owners of third party material included in this book. In the event of any omission of acknowledgement, copyright owners are invited to contact the Professional and Trade Division at John Wiley & Sons Ltd so that they can be acknowledged in future editions of the book or request that such material be removed from future editions.

# Part I

## The Discovery of Business Cycles

Men often stumble over the truth, but most manage to pick themselves up and hurry off as if nothing had happened.

*Winston Churchill*

*Chapter* **1**

# Gambling Man

John Law, I have always felt, is in a class by himself.

*Joseph Schumpeter*

A sword. He was standing there with a sword in his hand. Soon he would be engaged in something frightening. He would be duelling with John Wilson, the 23-year-old son of one of the town's leading families. John Wilson's carriage was arriving now, and the duel would start unless Wilson had changed his mind and called the whole thing off. But why had John Law accepted the duel? Why risk death at this young age – and for something so stupid? He could just have excused himself, bowed out; he could have walked away from the problem. Or he could simply have disappeared from London for a while, until everything was forgiven and forgotten. But John Law wasn't that kind of person. Just as he always reached out when he saw an opportunity, he also confronted the problems he met. And now, when the problem was that John Wilson had challenged him to a duel, Law was ready to fight his battle.

## THE GAMING HOUSES OF LONDON

John Law was well spoken and well dressed. Although scarred by small-pox, his face looked intelligent, and he was exceptionally tall (1.80 meters, or 6 feet), good looking and charming. To the girls in his hometown of Edinburgh, he had been known as "beau Law". From the age of 14 to 17 he had been taught banking at his father's counting house, and he had demonstrated an extraordinary talent for mathematics during these years. When the father died in 1688, he had left his 17-year-old son the revenues from his banking and goldsmith activities. John Law had seemed to have every opportunity before him in Edinburgh, but he had wanted more out of life than what the little town could offer. Much more in fact.

So he had decided to leave Scotland to go to London. Once settled in London, he had soon begun frequenting the gaming houses to put his talent for the study of numbers into use. And it had worked. After some time he had gained a considerable amount of money. Soon this handsome young Scotsman had become well known and admired, not the least among the ladies. Life had really been fun!

But, slowly and insensibly, John Law turned into an irrecoverable gambler. Gradually, he started to play with larger and larger amounts, until one day he met his Nemesis: he lost so much in a game that he was forced to mortgage his estate to pay the accounts.

Then, in the same year, he had been so stupid as to accept the duel against Mr Wilson – all because of a slight flirtation with his girlfriend. John Law was now 26 years old, and maybe he was going to die.


## ON THE RUN


The duel was short and rough. Wilson left his carriage, approached John Law and drew his sword. And then John Law made a single, defensive lunge with a speed that completely took Wilson by surprise. John Wilson fell to the ground moments later; deadly wounded. But before the day was over, the police came to arrest Law, and soon after his apprehension he was charged with murder. His case was heard, together with 26 others, at a three-day hearing, where he was not allowed to have a defense lawyer or to give testimony. His only defense was a written statement, which was read aloud to the court. The verdicts came out on the third day. Most of the defendants, 21 to be exact, would have their hands burn-marked because they had stolen. One person would be exiled, and five would be hanged. One of the five was a rapist, three were forgers. The last of these five was John Law.

Fortunately, the sentence was later commuted to a fine, as the verdict was changed from murder to manslaughter. Upset about this, Mr Wilson's brother lodged an appeal, and with the case still pending, Law was detained in prison. But before the appeal was tested, John Law managed to escape – there are no records on how. An advertisement calling for his apprehension that appeared in the *Gazette*, described him in this way:

> Captain John Law, a Scotchman, aged twenty-six; a very tall, black, lean man; well shaped, above six feet high, with large pock-holes in his face; big nosed, and speaking broad and loud.

As this description fitted rather badly with reality, there was speculation that this had actually been drawn up to facilitate his escape. Whether true or not, the fact was that somehow he managed to escape from England across the Channel to the Continent.

## A NEW KIND OF MONEY

John Law traveled around in Europe for years, typically spending his mornings studying finance, trade and the monetary and banking affairs of the countries he visited; the nights were spent at local gaming houses. He had learned a lot from his early losses at the gaming tables and had now studied as many pamphlets as he could about statistical probability (which had been described by, among others, Galileo, Pascal and Bernoulli). When Law visited Amsterdam, he also speculated on the stock exchange. It was probably in the year 1700, when he was 29 years old, that he sailed back over the Channel and returned to Edinburgh. There, he started promoting an idea that he had developed through his travels in Europe and in which he believed deeply: if a country was to prosper, it needed *paper money*. Paper money, he thought, would facilitate trade much more than the traditional gold or silver currency. In 1705, he published a pamphlet entitled *Money and Trade Considered with a Proposal for Supplying the Nation with Money*. It began as follows:

> There are several Proposals offer'd to Remedy the Difficulties the Nation is under from the great Scarcity of Money. That a right Judgment may be made, which will be most Safe, Advantageous and Practicable; It seems Necessary, 1. That the Nature of Money be inquired into, and why Silver was us'd as Money preferable to other Goods. 2. That Trade be considered, and how far Money affects Trade. 3. That the Measures have been us'd for preserving and Increasing Money, and these now propos'd be examin'd.

The pamphlet was promoted quite well, and posters summarizing the proposal were put up in many places. It was well written, using arguments that were clear and comprehensible. In explaining the difference between price and value, he wrote, for instance, that:

> Water is of great use, yet of little Value; Because the Quantity of Water is much greater than the Demand for it. Diamonds are of little use, yet of great Value, because the Demand for Diamonds is much greater, than the Quantity of them.

And then about paper money:

> Money is not the value for which Goods are exchanged, but the Value by which they are Exchanged: The use of Money is to buy Goods, and Silver while Money is of no other use.

Scotland was in a recession at the time, and he believed that he understood the problem. It was about money. The pamphlet introduced an expression that hadn't been used before: "demand for money". Law attempted to demonstrate to the readers that the supply of money was too low and the interest rates on money therefore too high. The solution would be to increase the supply of money. An expansion of the money supply would lead to lower interest rates, he claimed, and it would not lead to inflation as long as the country operated at full production capacity.

He made another suggestion: the establishment of a "landbank" in Scotland. This bank should issue notes up to an amount that should never exceed the value of the land belonging to the state. Buyers of the notes should receive interest and have the option to convert their notes into land at a specific time. This new scheme would have two advantages:

- It would relieve the nation of the burden of buying more and more precious metal to supply coins that matched the growth of the economy
- It would make it easier for the country to manage the amount of money in circulation, so as to match the fluctuating needs of the country

The proposal was very well written and generated a lot of excitement, but it was also controversial. Critics ridiculed it, and referred to it as the "sand-bank", suggesting that it would "wreck the vessel of the state". Others supported the idea, however, and eventually it was debated seriously in Parliament. But that was as far as it went; a majority of the members turned it down. Disappointed with this, and with the fact that he was unable to obtain a pardon for his manslaughter at the courts in England (England and Scotland were two different countries at the time), he returned to the Continent. There, he resumed his former occupation: the games. As years went by, he became well known for his skills in gambling houses throughout the capitals of Europe. He was more experienced and careful now, and he became very rich.

John Law went on like this for 14 years, playing in Flanders, Holland, Germany, Hungary, Italy and France. In many places, Law was thought to be a bad influence on young people, and he was in fact expelled for that reason from Venice and Genoa. He also gained some enemies because he now was so good at probability calculations that he kept winning at the gaming tables, and because he kept running away with ladies that were sometimes affiliated with other men. One day he met a lady called Katherine Seigneur, who was married, and who came to like him so much that she eventually ran away from her husband and escaped with Law to Italy. They would later have children together. But he also made influential friends in high places. Among these was the French Duke of Orleans, Philippe d'Orleans, who, like Law, was very handsome, extremely rich and influential, rather charming, and even more of a womanizer than Law himself.

Meanwhile, the paper money idea kept nagging in the back of John Law's head. You needed paper credit to get Europe to prosper; of that he was sure. It was probably in 1708 that he suggested a landbank scheme to the comptroller at the French court. The proposition was turned down. After this he tried in Italy, and was turned down again.

## A Minor Problem

But history is odd; sometimes it is the strangest coincidences that decide the fate of nations. When the extravagant "Sun King", Louis XIV, died in 1715, the French throne was left to an heir only 7 years old. Here, Law's friend Philippe d'Orleans entered the scene: being uncle to the young king, he took control of the government. Unlike Law, the Duke had very little understanding of banking and high finance, but unlike any other head of state in Europe, he seriously considered Law's ideas.

It was not an easy job that the Duke had taken upon himself. The finances of France were in a shambles after the disastrous regime of the spendthrift Louis XIV, who had been more interested in jewelry and palaces than in balancing budgets. These were the key figures of the state:

| | |
|---|---|
| National debt: | 2000 million livres |
| Annual revenue: | 145 million livres |
| Annual expenses before interest payments: | 142 million livres |
| Surplus before interest payments | 3 million livres |

It is not particularly good when your national debt is almost 14 times as big as your annual tax revenue. This debt of two billion was owed largely to about forty private financiers, who were also in charge of tax collection, and the implications were truly horrible, because the annual

**Figure 1.1**   John Law of Lauriston, murderer, womanizer, promoter, investor, millionaire, gambler, pamphleteer – and father of central banking. Reproduced by permission of The Mary Evans Picture Library.

interest payment on this debt was 90 million, equal to 4.5%. How can you pay 90 million in interest if your budget surplus *before interest payments* is 3 million? The Duke of Noailles, who was newly appointed head of financial counsel, later summarized what he found with these words:

> We found the estate of our Crown given up, the revenues of the state practically annihilated by an infinity of charges and settlements, ordinary taxation eaten up in advance, arrears of all kinds accumulated through the years, a multitude of notes, ordinances, and allocations anticipated of so many different kinds which mount up to such considerable sums that one can hardly calculate them.

The Duc de Saint-Simon would later write in his memoirs:

Nobody could any longer pay, because nobody was paid . . .

So what could the Duke of Orleans do? The five standard options of ancient Europe seemed to be the following:

- Declare national bankruptcy
- Raise taxes dramatically
- "Clip" the coins (call in all coins and exchange them for new ones containing less precious metal)
- Sell privileges of monopoly for, for instance, all the trade within a given commodity or colonial area
- Confiscate possessions of corrupt state employees

The Duke chose a combination of clipping and confiscating. He called in all coins to the Mint, banned their use, and gave in return new coins with only 80% of the precious metal in the old ones. But this was a very unpopular move; moreover, the total contribution to the state finances was only approximately 70 million livres.

The Duke also promised any citizen 20% of the fines and confiscations if he could give information leading to conviction of corrupt state employees. This initiative was received with delight by the long-suppressed people, and soon the courts were working at high speed. The government confiscated 180 million livres, out of which – it turned out – the Duke used about 100 million to give special grants to new employees. The total account now looked like this:

| | |
|---|---|
| Revenue from clipping: | 70 million livres |
| Revenue from confiscations: | <u>80 million livres</u> |
| = Total revenue: | 150 million livres |

By using two of his options, the Duke had recovered the equivalent of only 7.5% of the national debt, or less than two years' interest payments. He was unable to do much more by his own initiative; he was neither very competent nor energetic (except with the ladies). John Law, on the other hand, was sharp as a knife, and Philippe d'Orleans knew it. In 1716, the year after the Duke had taken the reins of the country, the Duke met with Law to discuss the options. John Law, who was now 44 years old and extremely wealthy, repeated what he had said so many times before: to prosper, you needed paper money, and this paper money should be hard currency: no depreciations; no clipping. He proposed that they set up a bank to administer the royal revenues, which should issue notes entirely backed by either metal or land, in other words a modified land-bank. The Duke said yes!

## INTO THE UNKNOWN

On May 5, 1716, the bank was founded under the name "Law & Company". It had an assured activity from the outset, as it was declared that all taxes should be paid in notes issued by Law & Co. – France was now introducing paper money.

The capital of Law & Company was 6 million livres. If you wanted to purchase its shares, you had to pay 25% with coins and the rest with "billets d'état". This was a *very* smart move. Billets d'état were the bonds which Louis XIV had issued to finance his vast excesses. These were now regarded as junk bonds and were trading at 21.5 while they had originally been sold at 100. Table 1.1 outlines the scenario.

The reason that the effective interest rate was so high (and the market price of the bonds so low) was, of course, that people were afraid of national bankruptcy. But there was a potential way out: if the government could somehow buy back its own junk bonds at the current, low market price, then it could, in effect, reduce its debt from 2000 million (the price it had sold them for) to 430 million (the current market price). And it could do it without really hurting anyone! If by doing so, it could restore confidence, the state would, in principle, be able to reduce its interest payments to, say, 4.5% of 430 million livres by issuing new bonds. The new interest rate burden would be only around 19 million livres/annum.

**Table 1.1**   French government finances in 1716.

| | |
|---|---|
| *Seen from the Government's point of view* | |
| Outstanding billets d'état (nominal value): | 2000 million livres |
| Interest rate: | 4.5% |
| Annual interest payments: | 90 million livres |
| | |
| *Seen from the investor's point of view* | |
| Outstanding billets d'état (market value): | 430 million livres |
| Effective interest rate $(90 * 100/421)$: | 18% |
| Annual interest receivables: | 90 million livres |

### UNTYING THE KNOT

The problem was how to coax 2000 million livres worth of junk bonds back to the state without raising their market price. If people really thought Philippe d'Orleans could get out of his squeeze, then they would surely bid the bonds up, and his scheme would defeat itself. It was a small part of this problem that John Law solved by inviting people to pay for shares in Law & Company exclusively with government bonds.

At this stage, Law's "debt-for-equity swap" (as we would now call it) was very small in proportion to the remaining national debt of 1850 million livres. The issue of the Law & Company bank shares brought back only billets d'état worth 75% of six million, totalling 4.5 million livres – nothing compared to the 2000 million. But Law had his next move ready. He did three things:

- He made his notes payable "at sight". This meant that you could walk into Law & Company on any day you pleased, present your Law & Company notes and get the full amount back in coins
- He made his notes payable in original coin. If the government resorted to clipping coins (as so often before), John Law would still pay back the original amount of metal
- He declared publicly that any banker who issued notes without backing them with sufficient security "deserved death"

The result: the new paper money was accepted as hard currency and was, from the outset, traded at 101 – that is, with a premium of 1% when compared to coins of the same nominal value. Within a short time, this presence of a reliable means of exchange began to stimulate trading: business got better, and demand for notes rose by the day. Soon, Law & Company was able to open new affiliates in Lyons, Rochelle, Tours, Amiens and Orleans. One year later, in 1717, the price (in coins) of Law's paper money had risen to 115.

This was when John Law made his third strategic move, which was even more brilliant than the first two. He proposed that the government of France should make a new debt-for-equity swap on a scale which could eventually absorb *all* remaining billets d'état. The Duke should agree to the establishment of a company which was granted monopoly for trading with two colonial areas, which France had claimed for herself in 1684: the Mississippi River and the State of Louisiana. When the equity was to be sold to the public, people should pay with billets d'état, and the national debt would disappear. The Duke was excited, and preparations for this new "Mississippi scheme" began.

Meanwhile, the Duke turned his interest to Law's bank. By now it was no longer to be regarded as an experiment; it was an established success. He decided to bolster it further with a number of new privileges, including the sole right to refine gold and silver. And then he agreed to what he had not been willing to do from the start: he renamed it "Banque Royale". The bank was now clearly under his control, and he could do with it whatever he pleased. What he did was based on four observations:

• People had gained confidence in paper money
• Paper money was a pain-free way for the government to borrow
• As paper money traded at a premium, it was apparently in short supply
• Paper money seemed to bring prosperity

Well then, why not print more paper money? If people bought the bank notes for coins, he could spend that coin! So he instructed the bank to print 1000 million livres worth of notes – more than 16 times as much as it had done before. As the chancellor, D'Aguessau, disagreed with this, he was immediately replaced by the more loyal D'Argenson. John Law was horrified.

## ON WITH THE MISSISSIPPI SCHEME

Meanwhile, John Law was about to launch his Mississippi scheme. At the beginning of 1719, the privileges of the new Mississippi Company were expanded so they now included:

• Exclusive trading rights for the Mississippi River, the state of Louisiana, China, East India and South America
• A nine-year monopoly on minting the royal coinage
• The right to act as the national tax collector for nine years
• A monopoly for trading tobacco

In addition to this, the Mississippi Company was given all possessions of the Senegal Company, the China Company and, not least, the French East India Company. With the latter under control, the new giant was expected to challenge the almighty British East India Co.

Given all these privileges, it was not difficult to think that the company should make enormous profits. It was named "Compagnie des Indes" and a new public issue of 25 million livres worth of shares was announced – an issue that would raise the total equity to 125 million livres. John Law declared that he expected the shares to be honored by a total dividend of 50 million livres – equal to a 40% annual return on the investment. But the offer was really much better than that, since you could pay with the Sun King's junk bonds. The calculation was as follows, if you wanted to buy, for example, 1 million livres worth of shares:

| | |
|---|---|
| Nominal share price: | 1.0 million livres |
| Expected annual dividend: | 0.4 million livres |
| Bought with 1 million livres nominal billets d'état at rate 0.2: | 0.2 million livres |

Real yield on investment (0.2∗200/0.2) = 200%! So you could apparently expect a real return of about 200% per annum! 200%!!! Applications to buy the stock poured in immediately and the issue was oversubscribed in no time. As the staff needed several weeks to produce a list of the new subscribers, John Law was unable during this time to tell the names of the shareholders. This waiting period had a dramatic psychological effect. A crowd of people started gathering in front of Rue de Quincampoix from early morning to late evening to hear the result. Soon this crowd numbered thousands and filled the whole street. And it was not a usual crowd. It included dukes, counts and marquises; all eager to make a killing. When the list finally appeared, it was clear that the issue had been oversubscribed at least six times. In the free market, prices of the stocks soared to 5000 livres, or 10 times the subscription price. Law and the Duke of Orleans decided to take advantage of this excitement and make a new issue of 1500 million livres, 12 times as large as the first two.

## THE GREAT BOOM

That issue really ought to have worried the investors. Consider this: they paid with junk bonds, and no new capital – only the interest – was injected into the company. But the profits per share were now diluted 13 times as the capital was increased correspondingly.

But the public didn't worry, and the giant issue was oversubscribed three times. And then something very strange happened: although only four years had passed since France had been in the deepest despair, the entire country now started to virtually boil over in joy and happiness. Prices on any luxury item began rising and the production of rich laces, silks, broad-cloth and velvets increased many-fold. Artisans' wages rose four-fold, unemployment fell, and new houses were built everywhere. As everybody watched prices rise, everybody rushed to buy, to invest and to hoard before prices went even higher.

In Paris, the pot was boiling more than anywhere else. It was estimated that the population of the capital increased during this period by 305 000 inhabitants. Often, the streets were so crowded with new carriages that nobody was able to move. And the city imported art, furniture and ornaments from all over the world as never before; not only for the aristocracy, but now also for a new middle class. People who had bought stocks on margin suddenly found that a few thousand livres could grow to more than a million. Soon, a new word was added to the French vocabulary: "millionaires". The greatest benefit was, however, for the aristocracy. This included John Law, who was a friend of the Irish émigré Richard Cantillon – one of the most successful bankers in Paris. Law, Richard Cantillon and his brother Bernard bought 16 square leagues of land in Mississippi and enlisted around 100 settlers to prospect for gold and grow tobacco there. Bernard left shortly after on a slave ship with his settlers, but as he arrived, he found the environment much more hostile than it had been portrayed in the salons of Paris – three-quarters of his men died from disease and Indian attacks within the next four years.

Such stories took time to reach home, however, and the speculative fever in Paris showed no signs of abating. Many a bourgeois family, which, during the preceding depression, had been severely squeezed, was now saved by speculation in the Compagnie des Indes stock. One of these was the Duke of Bourbon, who made so much money in his stock transactions that he could rebuild his residence in Chantilly in a style of incredible magnificence. His speculation also enabled him to import 150 selected racing horses from England and to buy up an enormous amount of land. Many other members of the bourgeoisie made it big, but one of the largest players was Law's friend and co-investor Richard Cantillon, who accumulated massive amounts of shares while the prices were still good.

## Occasional Tremors

Stock trading is rarely a one-way street; even the wildest bull market has its setbacks. And so indeed had the shares of Compagnie des Indes. On more than one occasion they fell sharply within a few days, enough to wipe out many a margin-trader. During such an occasion, M. de Chirac, a physician, went to see a lady who was feeling ill. Chirac wasn't feeling too well himself: he had bought Indian stocks which had been falling drastically for several days. So, when he took the lady's pulse, his mind was on the stock market. Musingly, he said:

"It falls! It falls! Good God! It falls continually!"

Panicky, the lady stumbled to reach the bell while she cried:

"Oh, M. de Chirac, I am dying! I am dying! It falls! It falls! It falls!"

Astonished, Chirac asked the lady to what she was referring.

"My pulse! My pulse! . . . ," she answered, ". . . I must be dying!"

Fortunately, M. de Chirac was able to calm the lady by explaining that he had been referring to the India stock price, not to her pulse.


## Law Gets Rather Popular

As the bull market continued, something strange happened outside John Law's house in Rue de Quincampoix: the entire street was transformed into a stock exchange filled with speculators scalping the price movements of Compagnie des Indes. Stock-jobbers and brokers rented any house they could get in the street, at prices 12–16 times over the usual, and even bars and restaurants were transformed into trading houses. Together with the speculators and the money came the thieves and swindlers. It was not unusual for a troop of soldiers to be sent to clear the Rue de Quincampoix at night.

Eventually, the noise and the crowd became too much for John Law, who found a new residence in the spacious Place Vendome. But he couldn't move away from the people, because in their eyes he was the epicenter from which all activity generated. To them he was greater than any king had ever been; the greatest financial genius, the man who had single-handedly created the new prosperity of a nation. The aristocracy bribed Law's servants with large amounts to get an audience with him. Whenever he drove in his carriage, a royal troop of horses had to ride before to clear the street of admirers. And the speculators and the stock-brokers had to know every move he made. As Saint-Simon noted in his memoirs:

Law, besieged by applicants and aspirants, saw his door forced, his windows entered from his garden, while some of them came tumbling from the chimney of his office.

And the Duchess of Orleans:

Law is so run after that he has no rest, day or night. A duchess kissed his hands before everyone, and if a duchess kisses his hands, what parts of him would ordinary ladies kiss?

So, like bees moving with their queen, the crowd moved with John Law. Soon, booths and tents were erected all over the square in front of his home, and Place Vendome was transformed into a hectic marketplace; a marketplace where not only stocks and bonds were traded, but where any kind of business took place. And the noise was even worse than it had ever been in Rue de Quincampoix. The Duke received complaints about this new mess; not least from the chancellor, whose court was situated on the same square: because of the noise it had become impossible for him to hear the advocates. John Law agreed to look for a new solution and bought Hotel de Soissons, which had a large garden to the back. At the same time, a verdict was published that forbade stock-trading in any other place than in that garden. The crowd moved once again, and more than 500 tents and pavilions were erected behind the hotel. At this time, anyone and everyone in Paris seemed to be speculating in the India stock, which was in an accelerating bull market. The story goes that the sober Abbe Terrason and his equally sober and intellectual friend M. de la Motte had congratulated each other that neither of them took part in the public madness. A few days later, however, la Motte fell into temptation and went to buy some India stock. But as he was entering Hotel de Soissons, who did he meet coming out from the building? The Abbe, of course, who had just bought at the market. For a long time after that episode, both of them avoided the subject of speculation during their frequent philosophical discussions.

Meanwhile, the Duke was printing still more notes through Banque Royale. Why shouldn't he? Wasn't it evident that the money printing had made the country prosper? And if so, why not print more? Money was simply like oil to the economic machinery, wasn't it? The more oil, the better the machinery worked! And the better for the stock market too. The shares of the Mississippi Company had appreciated from their initial price of 150 to no less than 8000. This was the day that a speculator taken ill sent his servant to sell 250 shares because he had heard of this fantastic price. When the waiter came to the market, he saw that the price was in fact even better, and sold at no less than 10 000, which was 67 times the original issue price – an amazing rise of 6700%. When he came back, he gave his master the expected revenue of 4 million. Then he went to his room, packed his things, as well as the remaining 0.5 million, and left the country as fast as he could.

But then, one day in early 1720, something quite strange happened. A man appeared in front of Banque Royale with two carriages containing an enormous pile of notes. And he was angry. Very angry . . .

# Chapter 2

# Cash Payment

Down he went over the sharp rocks, and the water with him. He was clashed to pieces in his bark; but the waters, maddened and turned to a foam by the rough descent, only boiled and bubbled for a time and then flowed again as smoothly as ever. Just so it was with Law and the French people. He was the boatman and they were the waters.

*Charles Mackay*

Prince de Conti believed he had a good reason to be angry. He had wanted to buy some fresh India shares, but Law had prevented him. That arrogant Scottish bastard! Rejecting *him*! So here he was in front of the bank, with his two carriages filled with notes. He walked through the door.

"Voila, monsieurs! Your notes, which are 'payable at sight'. Now, do you see them? Well then, hand over the coins!"

The bank handed them over, filling his two carriages with coins. When the Duke heard about the event, he was plainly shocked and simply ordered de Conti to refund two-thirds of the metal. Just like that. It so happened that the public didn't like de Conti and so blamed him for this unreasonable act. But nevertheless, the event had an important effect: a small seed of doubt had been sown in people's minds. What if a lot of other people wanted to change their notes? What if everybody wanted to change their notes – would there be enough gold to do it? What if *I* want to change my notes?!

During the next few months some of the more astute speculators started to take their profits, and the share prices started dropping after having briefly touched the 10000 level. Two brothers, Bourdon and La Richardiere, began quietly to present their notes in Banque Royale and change them to coins in small quantities at a time. They also started buying up silver and jewelry, which, together with the coins, they secretly sent to Holland and England. Vermallet, a successful stocktrader, also sold out and packed 1 million livres worth of gold and silver coins in his carriage. He covered it with hay and cow-dung, disguised himself in peasant's clothes and drove to Belgium. While many people left the country, those who stayed started to hoard metal coins as distrust in notes mounted. Coins were either hidden under people's mattresses or exported: the French money circulation was slowing down.

What the Duke did in this situation was not smart. First, he revalued notes by 5% vis-à-vis coins. Obviously, the point was to regain the psychological initiative, but as it had no effect on the capital flight, he revalued by a further 5% – again with no effect. In February 1720, he prohibited the use of coins altogether. No person in France was allowed to have in his possession more than 500 livres worth of coins, under risk of fines and confiscation. It was also forbidden to buy silver, precious stones and jewelry. Anybody who gave information leading to confiscation of such tangible valuables would receive half the value – paid in notes, of course. And then, lastly, the Duke printed 1500 million livres worth of notes between February 1st and the end of May, increasing the total paper money supply to 2600 million livres. The point of all this was obviously to force people to use notes again, but it didn't work. The economy began to contract, and fear took over. What was to become of France in the future? Who was to blame?

John Law. John Law was to blame. Wasn't it him who cooked up this paper money idea in the first place? And what about his Mississippi scheme? What could you do there other than getting eaten by mosquitoes or killed by Indians? Was India stock in reality worth any more than Banque Royale notes? Was it? Better sell the stuff! The stock price collapsed, and with it, over half a million people lost money, and thousands of investors went broke. When people lost their money, they couldn't pay other people. The chain reaction was merciless, and something had to be done to convince the shareholders that Compagnie des Indes was in fact getting in gear. The remedy was simple: the poorest wretches and criminals in Paris were conscripted to be sent to New Orleans to dig for gold for the company. More than 6000 "pouvres" joined the scheme, and processions of these people thronged through the streets of Paris, ready to be sent to the port, from where they could sail to America. At first, people liked the project: six thousand is a lot of workers. If they could find gold, it would surely get the company going. And if you made new coins out of that gold, this might even get France up and running again. For a short while, Compagnie des Indes rallied at the stock market.

**Figure 2.1** Philippe d'Orleans. It was under this man's rule that France introduced its first paper money and experienced a fantastic boom, and then a disastrous depression. The experience of Banque Royale gave the word "bank" such a bad name in France, that most French banks even today are called anything else, such as "caisee", "crédit", "société", or "comptoir".

## WHERE IS THE GOLD?

But something odd happened: most of the people that were parading never left the country. Two out of three simply sold their new clothes and tools and returned to their homes even before reaching the boats. Better poor in Paris than digging gold in New Orleans. The Mississippi ventures were clearly not what people had hoped, and Law and his friend Richard Cantillon, the now 23-year-old super-banker, gave up hope of making any money on the land they had bought there. Cantillon took that in stride, though, because he was now engaged in making his second killing. Unlike so many others, he had actually concluded early on that a depreciation of the French currency was inevitable when they printed too much money, so he had taken out loans fixed to the French currency while placing the proceeds in Sterling. Law heard about this, and legend has it that he went to Cantillon's office and told him:

"If we were in England we would be able to talk and reach an agreement, but in France, as you know, I can tell you that you will be in the Bastille this evening if you do not give me your word that you will leave the country in 48 hours."

That sounded like pretty good advice, so Cantillon sold his entire portfolio, and netted a gain to around 20 million livres, which was a truly enormous amount. And then he left rather quickly.

Meanwhile, the Compagnie des Indes shares continued their fall, and the Duke was getting desperate. It appeared that the more the Duke did to make people abolish the use of coins, the more they seemed to want them. He decided to merge Banque Royale with Compagnie des Indes, hoping one would bolster the other. It didn't work. At the beginning of May, he finally called in an emergency council attended by John Law and all the ministers. First point on the agenda: 2600 livres worth of notes were circulating, each officially redeemable in gold and silver coins. The actual amount of coins was less than half of that, and many of them were hidden under people's mattresses (a habit for which Frenchmen were notorious centuries after). The council chose to devalue the notes by half, effective from the 21st of May. But this was simply too much for the French people. With unrest mounting and the threat of a revolt, the edict was canceled just one week later – the 27th of May. That was also the day when Banque Royale suspended payments in metal and John Law was dismissed from the ministry.

The same night, however, the Duke sent for Law, who entered the royal palace through a secret door. The Duke did everything he could to console Law and expressed how unfair it seemed that he should become the subject of such hatred from the public. Two days later, he invited him to the Opera, where Law appeared with Katherine and their children so that everyone could see the family and the Duke together. But this was nearly fatal for Law. As his carriage arrived at his house afterwards, a mob attacked it with stones. Only the fact that the coachman quickly passed the gates, which the servants slammed after them, saved Law from being lynched. Horrified by this, the Duke sent a detachment of Swiss guards to be stationed at Law's house night and day. But even so, Law did not feel safe. After a short while he moved to the Royal Palace, where he could enjoy the same protection as the Duke.

The Duke was now in full retreat. To help clean up the mess, he decided to call in D'Aguessau, the chancellor whom he had dismissed two years earlier. To persuade him to come to the rescue, he sent Law in a post-chaise to meet him. D'Aguessau agreed and returned with Law, and shortly after, on the 1st of June, the edict against free possession of coins was abolished. At the same time, 25 million livres worth of new notes, backed by the revenues of the city of Paris, were issued. And on the 10th of June, Banque Royale was reopened, prepared to change notes into metal again. But not into the usual metal: part of the payment was now in copper!

## Heavy Metal

There have been many bull markets in copper through history, but this one was unique. During the following months, there was a permanent crowd in front of the bank, as everyone wanted to change their notes to piles of copper, which they dragged away, sweating. On several occasions the crowd was so great that someone was squeezed to death. On the 9th of July, soldiers closed the gates to ease the pressure, and the people outside started throwing stones. A soldier fired back, killing one person and wounding another. Eight days later, 15 were killed under the pressure. Furiously, the crowd put three of the dead on stretchers and marched to the gardens of Palais Royale. Here, they found John Law's carriage and broke it to pieces.

The Council had to find new ways. Their next emergency remedy was to bolster the Compagnie des Indes further by extending its trading privileges, so that it had a monopoly on all maritime trade out of France. But this meant that thousands of independent merchants would lose their business, and petition after petition was presented to Parliament to complain. Parliament refused to approve the matter. The Duke became so furious that he sent the parliament and all its members into exile in the remote Pontoise. In order not to appear defeated, the Members of Parliament decided to engage in demonstrative extravagance. Every night they held a great ball for the ladies, and each day they resorted to card games and other diversions.

On the 15th of August, a new edict was imposed on the poor Frenchmen: all notes for sums between 1000 and 10000 livres could not pass unless used to buy annuities, to place money in bank accounts or to pay instalments on Compagnie des Indes shares. In October, many of the privileges were taken away from the Compagnie des Indes, and all notes deprived of value. Stockholders were obliged to deposit their shares with the Company, and those who had agreed to buy new shares were forced to purchase them at almost 30 times the current market rate. As many tried to avoid this horrendous punishment by leaving the country, orders were sent to all border posts to detain anybody trying to get out until it was clarified whether they had ordered purchases of Compagnie des Indes shares. Those who got out anyway were sentenced to death in absentia.

---

### HOW THE FRENCH MONEY SUPPLY DECLINED IN 1720

The effective money supply in France declined for three main reasons:

- *Capital flight.* People took gold and silver coins out of the country
- *Decrease in the turnover (velocity) of money.* People hoarded coins because they didn't trust paper money, and perhaps later on because of restrictions regarding how many coins each individual could keep. These restrictions probably encouraged people to keep as many coins as possible
- *Reduction in bank credit.* The edict imposing that all notes for sums between 1000 and 10000 livres could only be used to buy bonds, Compagnie des Indes shares and place money in bank accounts reduced the effective money supply

A modern economist would probably have suggested abandoning the gold standard, encouraging increased lending, reducing interest rates, increasing public spending, cutting taxes and letting Compagnie des Indes print more money to buy bonds.

---

John Law was now living a life in terror. The most hated man in France, he could only leave his royal refuge either incognito or with a powerful escort. He requested permission to move to one of his country estates, a dispensation the Duke was more than happy to grant. A few days later, he received from the Duke a kind letter, in which he was given permission to leave France when he pleased. The Duke also offered him whatever amount of money he might want, an offer which he respectfully declined. Then, at the age of 49, five years after the adventure had begun, he left for Venice, taking with him only a large diamond.

The phenomena that John Law witnessed in France were spectacular, but they were not unique. While the great speculation mania played out in France, something quite similar was brewing in England. Just as in France, the English Government had been embarrassed by the growth of a huge public debt. The device to solve this problem had been quite like that in France. A firm named "The South Sea Company" had taken over the obligation of payments of the national debt and had, in return, been granted the monopoly on trade with South America. A number of share issues had been gobbled up by an eager public and the price of these shares had been bid up to prices ten times the nominal value (a period which would later be dubbed "the South Sea Bubble"), even though there was little evidence that any South Sea trading was going to materialize (as we shall see later, 90 years were to pass before it actually did). One of the largest early buyers was none other than Richard Cantillon. In June, 1720, the South Sea Company stock had peaked (Figure 2.2), and during

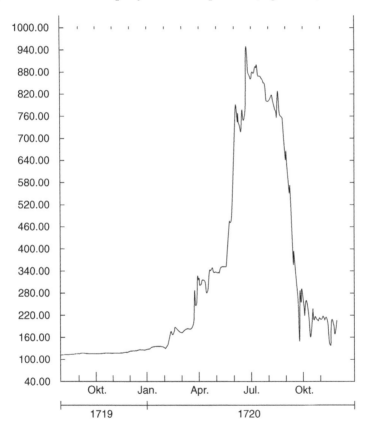

**Figure 2.2** The South Sea Company stock price 1719–1720. The "South Sea Bubble" had started before Compagnie des Indes collapsed in France. Sources from those years indicate that it was largely money going out of the French adventure that flowed to England and contributed to the late stages of this new bubble. Richard Cantillon managed to buy early and sell before the collapse in both cases. Previously published in Business Cycles: From John Law to the Internet Crash, Second Edition, by Lars Tvede, Routledge, London, 2001.

the next three months it fell by no less than 85%, under conditions resembling the meltdown in France.

Many investors in the South Sea Company had used borrowed funds to pay for their shares, and as their price collapsed, they couldn't honour their obligations. This created fear of bank collapses and resulted in a run on many financial institutions, leading to a wave of defaults.

## END GAME

While the English bubble burst, the man behind French paper money, John Law, still lived in Venice. He maintained for a long time the hope of being called back to help the French government re-establish a sound credit system, but as the Duke died in 1723, he lost all hope. For the rest of his life, he supported himself through gambling. Several times he had to pawn his diamond, but each time he won enough to be able to recover it. Finally, in 1729, he died in Venice, 58 years of age and very poor.

And the English South Sea Company? It was finally dissolved in 1855 and its shares converted to bonds. During its 140 years of existence, the company had never engaged in any significant trade in the South Seas. Cantillon had bought when the prices were cheap and had sold out before the meltdown.

*Chapter* **3**

# The Dream Team of Money

The age of chivalry is gone. That of sophisters, economists and calculators has succeeded; and the glory of Europe is extinguished forever.

*Edmund Burke*

The year the Duke of Orleans died and John Law gave up all hope of being invited back to France, was also the year Margaret Smith from Kirkcaldy, a small town some 15 kilometers from Law's hometown of Edinburgh, expected her first child. She was a single mother; her husband had died just a few months before the baby was born.

The baby turned out to be a boy, and on the 5th of June 1723, he was given the name Adam. His childhood was peaceful, disturbed only by an incident in which, at the age of two, he was kidnapped by a gang of gypsies, but quickly recovered. As the boy grew up, Margaret Smith noticed that he showed a keen interest in the society around him. Although Kirkcaldy was a small place with only 1500 inhabitants, there was quite a lot to look at. The town had extensive commerce, and ships from many places berthed close to the houses. The boy loved to sit on cliffs by the sea, overlooking the ships coming in and out.

## YEARS OF TRANSITION

England had a fairly well-established regime of paper money at that time, and it was (unlike the French) working pretty well. Means of payment included not only gold and silver coins, but also notes issued by the Bank of England or other banks, as well as promissory notes and inland bills.

In addition to the coins, notes and inland bills, interest-bearing papers, such as Exchequer bills and East India bonds, were also in circulation – albeit with a lower turnover. The Master of the Mint was no less than Isaac Newton, who had been appointed to the job in 1696. When still young, Newton had noticed that not only governments could use the idea of "clipping" coins – many citizens did it too. Some would put a pile of coins in a sack, shake it thoroughly and then collect the dust. Others would, more rudely, cut off a slice around the edge before they passed them on. To prevent this, Newton had suggested that coins should be given a milled edge, so that it would be easy to detect if they had been clipped.

At this time, the Industrial Revolution was already in its infancy, and conditions were getting ripe for an economic boom. First of all, the British navy was quickly conquering new markets where British products could be sold. Secondly, an "agricultural revolution" had already started in the countryside, as farms were becoming larger and more productive. This process released manpower: more and more young people traveled to the cities to look for jobs, to study or to set up new business ventures. Most would travel to London, which at the time had somewhere between 500 000 and 750 000 inhabitants. Others chose the next largest town, Bristol, with 43 000 inhabitants. And still others moved to Norwich (36 000 inhabitants), Liverpool (22 000), Manchester (20 000), Salford (20 000), Birmingham (20 000) and other centers of commerce.

## AN UNUSUAL PERSONALITY

Back in Kirkcaldy, our young friend Adam Smith had finished his basic school education at the age of 17, and then he too decided to move. He bade his mother Margaret goodbye, saddled his horse, and rode the more than 500 kilometers of dirt roads to Oxford, where he had been enlisted at the university (Figure 3.1). While the 17-year-old John Law had been an aspiring man of the world when in 1688 he had headed for the London gaming houses, this can hardly be said about Adam Smith. He was, in fact, one of the most absent-minded students that ever entered the doors of Oxford University. When preparing tea, people would not be surprised to see him put his buttered bread into the pot and then complain over the taste of the tea. When he had a romantic attachment to a girl, he could be at a party without discovering her presence. And often, people would see him speaking to himself. But when Adam Smith seemed to forget everything around him, it was not because his mind was lost. It was because it was focused on something else.

**Figure 3.1**  Map of England and Scotland when Adam Smith moved to Oxford. Smith was born in Kirkcaldy, studied in Oxford and taught in Glasgow. John Law was born in Edinburgh and Thornton and Ricardo in London. Previously published in Business Cycles: From John Law to the Internet Crash, Second Edition, by Lars Tvede, Routledge, London, 2001.

He could concentrate. He also had a great capacity for expressing himself. He could spend an evening at a social gathering dwelling in his own thoughts, but once anybody caught his attention by a direct question or a provocative statement, he would start talking as if he were giving a lecture on the subject. He could pursue the question on and on and become completely lost in its details, until people regretted that they ever involved him in the debate, or indeed met him.

Adam Smith found the lectures in Oxford rather uninteresting and most of what he actually learnt came out of his own, independent reading. He completed his Oxford education and returned home in 1750, where he was appointed to the Chair of Logic at Glasgow University, and in 1752 to the Chair of Moral Philosophy. During these years, trade was gradually developing along the Clyde River, and this contributed to the development of new local industries. Adam Smith followed the developments in business with great interest, and was quite happy with his job at the university.

## Sympathy and Self-Interest

One of Adam Smith's ambitions was to develop a theory of ethics derived from man's natural instincts and feelings, rather than from artificial doctrines. He believed that every man had a basic desire to be accepted by others, to receive their "sympathy." To obtain this sympathy, man (in his own self-interest) would try to behave in a manner which people would respect and admire. A sense of ethics would thus develop; a conscience, which would filter his thoughts before turning them into actions, omitting those that would not command the sympathy of others. So ethics was a question not of utility, not of benevolence or moral doctrine, but actually of self-interest.

He saw economic progress of society in the same light and concluded that economies were driven by individual pursuits of self interest, and that any attempt to suppress the individual would consequently suppress the economy as a whole. In 1755, he wrote a paper in which he explained:

> Little else is required to carry a state to the highest degree of opulence from the lowest degree of barbarism, but peace, low taxes, and tolerable administration of justice; all the rest being brought about by the natural course of things. All governments which thwart this natural course, which force things into another channel, or which endeavour to arrest the progress of society at a particular point, are unnatural, and to support themselves are obliged to be oppressive and tyrannical.

In 1759 he published his first book, *Theory of Moral Sentiments*, which became very popular in Scotland. It also ensured him a job as personal tutor to the Duke of Buccleuch, who agreed to pay him twice the university salary plus expenses if Smith would join him on a two-and-a-half-year study tour in Europe. Smith agreed, and one day in 1764, he found himself on a sailing boat heading for the French side of the Channel.

## Meeting Quesnay

France had long since overcome the crises of the Duke, John Law and the Mississippi scheme, and was now competing with Britain for colonial dominance. It also had a growing intellectual elite. During his stay, Smith met with many of these, including Quesnay, who was 29 years older. Quesnay had many powerful friends and was, in fact, personal physician to Louis XV, the former child king whom Philippe d'Orleans had represented during the days of John Law.

A part of Quesnay's inspiration came from Richard Cantillon. Cantillon had died in 1734, extremely rich after his triple killings in France and English finance markets, when his house in London was burned down by his cook. Among the 37-year-old millionaire's possessions that his descendants found was a manuscript for a book which they later published. This book, *Essai sur la Nature du Commerce en General*, contained an analysis of many economic phenomena. Seen in retrospect, by far the most important among these were his theories of money supply, velocity of money and capital markets. Cantillon had understood how the effective money supply was influenced not only by how much money was floating around, but also by its *velocity*; by how fast money shifted hands:

> To some degree, an acceleration, or a higher velocity of money circulation, will have a similar effect as an increase in the supply of money.

This worked both ways. If, as he had witnessed during the Mississippi panic, people started hoarding money, the effect was equivalent to a fall in the money supply. Money had to change hands; otherwise it could not grease the market machinery and depression would ensue.

Although Quesnay was inspired by Cantillon, he also contributed with path-breaking thoughts of his own, and managed indeed to set a footprint so strong that the economist Joseph Schumpeter 200 years later would describe him as one of the four most important economists that had ever lived. One of his major contributions was his so-called "tableau economique," a table showing how a given amount of money released into society turned into a flow. It would not flow forever, however, as each receiver of money on average would save a portion before spending the rest. In this way he demonstrated that the impact of the release of new liquidity into society was larger than the nominal amount released. So the physiocrats understood that capital was essentially a series of advances, and that income would flow and would, in a sense, multiply in that process. Everybody regarded Quesnay as the informal leader of the popular "physiocrat" movement, which had invented a popular slogan:

> Laissez faire, laissez passer

They opposed the French mercantilist tradition of state intervention and nationalist protectionism, and they believed in the abolition of monopolies, trade barriers and privileges. They also advocated individualism and the concept of "natural law"; that the laws of society should reflect laws that were natural to man. The name of the movement meant just that, in fact: it meant "Rule of Nature." The physiocrats also thought that the individual was a better judge of his own best interest than the state could ever be. And they preached the full respect of private property.

## PASSING THE TIME

Adam Smith listened, was skeptical, but also interested. Apparently he was not very busy, because in his first year in France, he began, as he later expressed it, "to write a book in order to pass away the time." He stayed in France until 1766, when he returned to Scotland with the first part of the manuscript for his book. Little could he know that these pieces of paper in his luggage would eventually become part of a book which economists would praise as:

> ". . . the most successful not only of all books about economics but, with the possible exception of Darwin's *Origin of Species*, of all scientific books that have appeared to this day." (J. Schumpeter in 1954)

or

> ". . . in its ultimate results probably the most important book that has ever been written." (T.H. Buckle in 1872)

But he did know that he wanted to work very thoroughly with the manuscript. That same year, when he was 43 years of age, he bought a house by the beach in Kirkcaldy where he planned to continue the work.

## TAKE-OFF

During the 1750s, more and more businessmen in England were beginning to use primitive machines. Most often, small industries could be found scattered around on the hillsides, where streaming water could drive the machines. Others were driven by fossil energy. In Smith's hometown, you could find collieries, salt-pans and a nailery. One of his close friends, James Oswald, had another nailery outside the town, but still within walking distance from Smith's home. Here, scrap iron was imported from the Continent, while coal could be found almost at the

**Figure 3.2**  Adam Smith. Like the French physiocrats, Smith believed the economy would correct itself if left alone. His work became the foundation of English Classical Economics, which can be traced from Ricardo through Mill and Marshall to Pigou.

factory's doorstep. Later, Smith would refer to his experiences from these small factories when explaining the keys to industrial progress. Three years after his return, two important technological inventions appeared in his country. One was the "waterframe," a new spinning machine designed by Arkwright, which improved productivity in the cotton industry dramatically. But even more significant was the first steam engine, which was patented by one of Adam Smith's close friends, James Watt. These and other inventions were the origin of industries in areas with coal supplies (Table 3.1).

The machines had two dramatic effects. One was that more could be produced per input of capital. The other was that it was necessary to plan further in advance: to build a new industrial factory plant was very different from ordering the goods at a number of small family workshops. The profit potential had become larger, but so had the uncertainty; there was the risk that the market might change before a planned factory could be put to use. Nobody could know for sure how this development would influence the workings of the economy, but it surely had to mean *something*!?

**Table 3.1** Innovations leading to the Industrial Revolution. Source: Mager, 1987.

| Year | Innovation | Industry |
|------|------------|----------|
| 1709 | Coke-smelting process | Iron and steel |
| 1733 | Flying shuttle | Textiles |
| 1761 | Manchester–Worsley Canal | Water transport |
| 1764 | Spinning Jenny | Textiles |
| 1769 | Steam engine | All industries |
| 1769 | Waterframe for spinning | Textiles |
| 1776 | Four-course rotation of crops | Agriculture |
| 1776 | Steam blast for smelting iron | Iron and steel |
| 1779 | The spinning "mule" | Textiles |
| 1784 | Reverberate furnace with "pudding process" | Iron and steel |
| 1785 | Power loom | Textiles |

## THE MASTERPIECE

While the local capitalists were busy setting up factories with the new machines, Adam Smith used up a lot of feather pens from 1766 to 1773 as he now concentrated entirely on his manuscript. When it was finally finished, it had become huge. Spanning five volumes, *An Enquiry into the Nature and Causes of the Wealth of Nations* (commonly abbreviated to *The Wealth of Nation*) gave its readers an overall description of the mechanics of the capitalist economy, which was far more comprehensive than the theories in Cantillon's book. In the first volume, Smith set out to describe what he saw as the major reason why the economic output of some countries grew: division of labor. Division of labor explained the dramatic rise in productivity and the "invention of all those machines." Rather than assuming some theoretical, rational man, Smith typically would illustrate his points through real examples which he knew first hand (once, while explaining a theory of division of labor in a tannery, he got so absorbed with his subject that he fell in the tanning pit). He illustrated his theory about division of labor by describing, not a tannery, but a pin factory which he had once visited. Here, ten workers produced a total of 48 000 pins a day.

> But if they had all worked separately and independently, and without any of them having been educated to this peculiar business, they certainly could not each of them have made twenty, perhaps not one pin in a day . . .

As division of labor was the prime source of wealth of a nation, he advocated free trade to facilitate the international division of labor. *The Wealth of Nations* continued to analyze, among other subjects, price mechanisms, where prices were described as fluctuating around a "natural" or "equilibrium" price. Other chapters dealt with wages, profits, time-risks undertaken by entrepreneurs, interest, rent, capital and taxation. As regards the role of the state, he recommended this to be minimized:

> I have never known much good done by those who affected to trade for the public good.

The public sector should never interfere with the market, he thought, but should concentrate on protection of its citizens, on general justice and on certain specific tasks such as education, transportation and regulation of paper credit.

## THE INVISIBLE HAND

The most important part of Smith's work, however, was not his partial analysis (of which most was correct); but the fact that he deduced a crucial underlying principle: *freedom was the most efficient economic model.* The capitalist economy would work best, he concluded, if you let every individual be the judge of his own interest, and if you relied on the forces of self-interest:

> He intends only his own gain, and he is in this, as in many other cases, led by an invisible hand to promote an end which is no part of his intention.

And:

> The desire of bettering our condition comes from us in the womb, and never leaves us till we go to the grave.

Over and over, he repeated this message in various contexts:

> It is not from the benevolence of the butcher, the brewer, or the baker, that we expect our dinner, but from their regard to their own interest. We address ourselves, not to their humanity, but to their self-love, and never talk to them of our own necessities but of their advantages.

That Smith stated this principle so emphatically did not mean that he envisaged a free market economy as a utopian paradise. He thought that employers would always try to squeeze labor wages, merchants try to eliminate competition, producers conspire to raise prices, workers be bored, and some would always remain poor. But overall the system would grow rapidly and an "invisible hand" – the market forces – would swiftly correct any deviations from this path of growth.

The book was a masterpiece. No-one had ever come as close to describing how economies worked as he did. It became very influential, and Members of Parliament started referring to it during their speeches. In 1782, one of Smith's admirers, Lord Shelburne, was elected Prime Minister. Shelburne sought Smith's advice on a number of issues and once wrote:

> I owe to a journey I made with Mr Smith from Edinburgh to London the difference between light and darkness through the best part of my life.

When Smith was in London, he often stayed with Shelburne, and through him and other Members of Parliament, he maintained an increasing influence on the debate of the day, in spite of his occasionally strange behavior. When given a piece of paper to sign, Smith, absorbed in his own thoughts, might carefully copy another man's signature already there – instead of writing his own. People chose to forgive.

## A BRIGHT YOUNG BANKER

One of his admirers in Parliament was a remarkable man named Henry Thornton, who had been elected to the House of Commons at the age of 22. Born in 1760, he had joined his father's counting house when 18 years old (as John Law had done 93 years before). The boy had been surprised to see how his father conducted his business, trading in every commodity that moved – wheat, tobacco or whatever. This lack of focus didn't impress Henry, and as any ambitious youngster, he was also quite dissatisfied with his salary. At age 24 he left in order to work in a bank called "Down & Free." He did an excellent job there, and the young Member of Parliament was soon invited to be a partner in what was subsequently called "Down, Thornton & Free."

But banking in England was not always easy. It was fairly common, for example, that banks tried to set up organized runs against each other. Another serious problem for the credit system was bad communication. If the population in any local region smelled economic danger, then they

**Figure 3.3** Henry Thornton. "The father of central banking" was born in 1760, at the beginning of the Industrial Revolution. Thornton was known among his contemporaries not only as a successful banker, but also as public advisor, and for giving away, as a rule, six-sevenths of his annual income to charity.

would bring their bills to their local "country bank" for payment in coins. If the bank was afraid of running short of metal, it would quickly send for more from its correspondent bank in London. And if sufficient amounts of coins did not arrive in time, panic would break out, and people would start a run on other local banks. As dispatches were sent for more metal in London, the London banks would start feeling the pain too, and panic might spread in the capital and even beyond the borders.

Such a process could be started by something as simple as bad roads. Most of them were made of clay, which turned into thick mud whenever it rained. After the snow had melted in springtime, they were often in such bad shape that their surfaces had to be leveled by ploughs drawn by up to ten horses. In most places the roads were full of holes due to the common practice of transporting coal and other hardware strapped to the sides of pack-horses. And the stagecoaches were clumsy, with heavy wheels and no springs.

Sending for dispatches was also expensive. Between 1700 and 1750, the British Parliament had passed 400 road acts allowing erection of gates and collection of tolls on the highways. And these were the times when famous gentlemen-thieves such as Dick Turpin, Claude Duval, Jonathan Wild and Jack Shephard would hide in the woods, ready to attack any passing traveler, not the least, of course, a carriage full of metal coins from some London correspondent bank!

## COMMERCIAL DISTRESS

As a banker, Thornton had noticed that whenever you had enjoyed a few years of relative prosperity, a panic was apparently unavoidable. When he looked back through his century, he could see that England had had economic crises in the following years: 1702, 1705, 1711–12, 1715–16, 1718–21, 1726–27, 1729, 1734, 1739–41, 1744–45, 1747, 1752–55, 1762, 1765–69, 1773–74, 1778–81, 1784 and 1788–1791. Each of these 18 times, the economy had pulled itself out on its own, and most of the time had reached a higher plateau on the revival. But each time, it had only been a few years before a new crisis ensued and everything would crash again.

In the years after the crisis in 1788–1789, business had been booming; however, a phenomenal number of new country banks had been created and the emission of new notes of bills had expanded. But in 1792, trade and manufacture started to level. In November, the stock market experienced a sharp break and the currency started to slide. In February, France declared war against England, and in March, there were runs on a number of country banks which sent couriers to London for coins – but this time the London banks were just as squeezed. So was Thornton's bank, which had grown to be one of London's largest. Thornton later wrote:

> In the year 1793, a season of great commercial distress, we experienced greater difficulties than most other banks in consequence of the sudden reduction of very large sums which we had held at interest for some very considerable banks.

The crisis was solved when the Bank of England decided to issue five million pounds worth of new bills to stimulate the economy. During the preceding crisis of 1783, the bank had stopped a capital flight through reduction of money supply – by limiting the amount of paper credit, thus forcing money rates up. Now, it proved that it could halt an internal crisis by doing just the opposite. Apparently they were beginning to learn.

## LAISSEZ FAIRE – OU NON?

Money supply swelled after the new issue, and Thornton's bank survived. But it was probably this crisis which drew his mind to the theory of credit. Why did these financial crises occur? What could be done to stop them? Should one leave it to Professor Smith's invisible hand or should one –

like the Bank of England had just done – intervene? Thornton had little literature to turn to (a list of the books in his library written after his death mentions only six titles about economics, one of which was *The Wealth of Nations*). He had to base his reason on common sense and experience. But while Thornton was thinking about the problem of instability, the economy continued to challenge. Just two years after the last crisis, a new one started, this time even more severe. As a result of a panic, the gold reserves of the Bank of England suddenly fell from five million pounds to 1.25 million, and on the last day of the year, the Bank decided to introduce rationing of payments in metal. The effects of this were disastrous. During the next month, panic spread even further and an increasing number of merchants and banks closed. On February 26th, 1797, the Bank of England threw in the towel and suspended payments altogether. This, of course, was a great defeat.

### IF PHILIPPE D'ORLEANS HAD KNOWN THIS . . .

The following day, the House of Commons set down a committee to investigate the causes of the problem, and one day later, the House of Lords instigated a similar committee. The first of these two committees called in 19 witnesses, the latter 16. Both called in Henry Thornton, who seems to have been the only representative of the private London bankers in the hearings.

His evidence was amazing. As he spoke, you could sense that Thornton had a remarkable understanding of the nature of banking. He clearly spelled out the responsibilities of the Bank of England and gave a detailed introduction to the instruments that ought to be in the central bankers' toolbox. In retrospect, we know at least part of the reason for the accuracy of his statements: during evenings and weekends he had embarked on a book manuscript about the nature of that very subject. This book, which is still regarded as one of the great classics in the history of economics, was published in 1802 under the title *An Enquiry into the Nature and Effects of the Paper Credits in Great Britain* (commonly abbreviated to *Paper Credit of Great Britain*). It was one of those rare books that was far better than contemporary works, yet was at first underrated because it never emphasized how new and original it really was. Many of the principles explained in it are still regarded as essential in credit (or monetary) theory, and today Thornton is often described as the "father of central banking" – a title which John Law would have aspired to, had Philippe d'Orleans not made his scheme go berserk.

John Law had described the concept of "demand for money", and Thornton followed the same thinking – treating all the different means of credit as one total. Today, any economist will routinely speak of "money supply" defined as some aggregate. "M2", for instance, consists of "notes and coinage, checking accounts of private persons and companies, and other accounts, including small-time saving deposits," but before Thornton, the analytical practice was to focus on each source of liquidity individually. Thornton thus created a powerful tool to observe interactions between the volume of money (liquidity), velocity of money (which we remember from Cantillon) and interest rates. Here are some of his observations:

- A high interest rate will prevent capital flight or even attract liquidity to the country
- A high interest rate will persuade people to part with their cash by putting it in bank accounts. By maintaining a high rate, the central bank can thus reduce velocity, suck up money and consequently dampen activity. Low rates, in contrast, will increase money supply and stimulate activity
- The public expectation of future inflation will influence present interest rates. If people fear future inflation, present rates will be correspondingly higher
- An unintended contraction of credit can lead to an economic depression. On the other hand, too large an expansion of credit (through increased lending) can lead to overheating of the economy. An increase in the money supply will therefore lead to increased inflation, if or when the economy is fully employed. If it is underemployed, it might lead only to increased growth

It was a pity for the French people that their leader after the Sun King, the Duke of Orleans, hadn't known about these rules, because if he had, then he surely wouldn't have wrecked John Law's ingenious schemes by printing far too much paper money.

## A Credit Trap

Thornton explained that if you increased money supply by, say, reducing interest rates below expected profit rates in the business community, this would lead to a higher level of borrowing and, subsequently, of business activity (Thornton mentioned the early phases of John Law's scheme in

France as an example). But then he added a very important observation: given increased activity, society would be able to absorb more money. Every increase in money supply would afterwards seem justified, as long as ensuing growth in activity could follow suit – until you reached full employment. This was crucial as *it could lead the central banker to expand the money supply much too far without seeing the danger before it was too late.* The system was, in other words, unstable – more credit seemed (deceptively) to justify more credit, and less credit seemed to justify less. The idea of such inherent instability was, of course, very different from Adam Smith's invisible hand concept, and indicated that the economy might have the ability to lead itself off track (because of positive feedback) as well as back on track (negative feedback). There was not one invisible hand, but two! It is debatable if Thornton's book contained the world's first business cycle theory, and most would say it didn't. But it certainly came close.

## SAY'S LAW

Meanwhile, Adam Smith's book was also spreading beyond England's borders. One of its readers was Jean Babtiste Say, a French businessman who had picked it up in 1788. Say had invested in new technology and ran a French cotton spinning industry. Being very busy, he had little time to write himself, but eventually, in 1803, he published his own book, *Traite d'economie Politique*. This book was, in many ways, a condensation and clarification of what Smith had written 26 years before, but the structure and argumentation was clearer. However, it also contained some new ideas, one of which brought him fame: the "Law of Markets", or, later, "Say's Law."

So what was that about? Well, Say did business himself, and he had also spoken with many other businessmen about a general observation: the easy part in business seemed to be to make the products. The harder part was to get them sold. So, obviously they could ask a very reasonable question: why can't we run society in a way so that we can always sell our stuff? Why can't there be enough money for people to buy whatever industry has the capacity to make? If we can't sell everything we can make, can't society just give people more money or something? Good question!

Unfortunately, Say's answer didn't provide a patent solution to that problem. His first simple postulate was that supply creates its own demand:

It is worth while to remark, that a product is no sooner created, than it, from that instant, affords a market for other products to the full extent of its own value. When the producer has put the finishing hand to his product, he is most anxious to sell it immediately, lest its value should diminish in his hands. Nor is he less anxious to dispose of the money he may get for it; for the value of money is also perishable. But the only way of getting rid of money is in the purchase of some product or other. Thus the mere circumstance of creation of one product immediately opens a vent for other products.

This sounded quite logical, of course, but it didn't explain why his business friends found it so hard to get their products sold. Say did, however, have an answer to that:

A glut can take place only when there are too many means of production applied to one kind of product and not enough to another.

So that was the answer to their question. And just to make it clear – money was not the problem. The money needed for the transactions was there, and at the end of the day, people were really exchanging one product for another. At least, that's how he saw it.

Say's Law was important in the sense that it explained that you could enhance long-term economic growth simply by stimulating supply, and also why it wouldn't make sense to fight unemployment by letting people work less hours per week – again in the long term. It was also broadly appealing because it could be used as a basis for arguments from both sides of the political spectrum. The right wing could say: let's stimulate demand, and then money will trickle down and create supply. The left, on the other hand, could say: let's give the common man more money; this will stimulate supply.

So far so good. But when it came to understanding economic instability, his law was a bit of a diversion, because while it did remove some potential misunderstanding of what happens over the long term, it ignored completely a number of short-term complications. And because of that it can be rudely argued that understanding of business fluctuations might have evolved a bit faster if no-one had ever heard of Jean Baptiste Say.

## DAVID RICARDO

South America was finally opening up to British merchants in 1809, and a wave of optimism ensued (the event that the South Sea Company could have used 90 years earlier). This led to a large increase in the British money supply, and shortly after, the currency started to slide relative to gold, giving Great Britain an inflation problem. Then, in August, September and October 1809, three articles criticizing the policy of the Bank of England appeared in *The Chronicle*; soon after, a related article was published in *The Edinburgh Review* under the headline: "The High Price of Bullion, a Proof of the Depreciation of Bank Notes." The author was an acquaintance of Thornton, a 37-year-old London stockbroker and financier. His name was David Ricardo.

It was an academic debut. He had received a very basic education in school and had joined his father's stock brokerage business when only 14 years old. Since then, he had established his own brokerage business where he primarily traded government securities. His motto, which has since been adopted by thousands of traders, was:

Cut losses, let profits run.

Following this rule (and presumably a number of others), he had become extremely wealthy. Until he reached the age of 27, it had not occurred to him that he should ever spend time on economic theory. Why should he – economic reality worked just fine with him! But in 1799, while he was at a holiday resort, he had come across *The Wealth of Nations* and had been really fascinated. "Someday . . . ," he had thought, ". . . I just might consider throwing in my own hat." In 1808 he had met a struggling journalist, James Mill, who had the same interest in general economics as Ricardo. Unlike Ricardo, Mill had a formal university training, which he had received at Edinburgh University (where Smith had taught). Ricardo and Mill began taking long walks together, on which they discussed politics and economy, and Mill began to suggest that Ricardo should contribute to the young discipline. This was what happened when Ricardo published his articles.

Ricardo's article in *The Edinburgh Review* contained 17 specific references to Thornton and 13 to Adam Smith. His conclusion was that the cause of the depreciation of the currency was the over-issuing of notes, and not – as Thornton had claimed – excessive imports due to bad harvest and war expenditures. His recommendation was that England should return immediately to the gold standard, which had been abandoned in 1797. When in 1810 the "Bullion Committee" was established to clarify the roots of the problem, Thornton, who was a member of the committee, yielded to Ricardo's conclusion. It is a curious fact that the publication of the committee's report was to lead very nearly to Thornton's own bankruptcy: a panic followed its publication and Thornton had to slip a word to one of his friends that Down, Thornton & Free could use a few time deposits fast. Fortunately, he had many faithful friends, and enough money was deposited to save his bank. Ricardo, in turn, had been squeezed by inflation and stood to benefit from a return to the gold standard.

In 1816 the debate resumed, and Ricardo published *Proposals for an Economical and Secure Currency*, in which he again suggested that England return to the gold standard; not by using gold coins, but by requiring the Bank of England to change paper money to gold on demand – just like Law & Company had done from the outset. Such a system would be self-stabilizing, he thought, for the following reasons:

- If the Bank of England issued too much paper, it would have to import gold to back it . . .
- . . . a process which in itself would reduce the money supply and diminish the Bank of England's potential for issuing new bills

Thornton disagreed. He did not think any monetary system could be self stabilizing, and therefore the Bank of England should – and could – actively manage the money supply. And he believed that fluctuations in money supply would not only affect prices, but also economic activity. In 1820, a plan much similar to what Ricardo had proposed was tried. It led to a drastic fall in prices and a disastrous recession, so it was abandoned again shortly after. The winner of this debate was clearly Thornton, not Ricardo. However, at this point, exactly 100 years after the failure of John Law's scheme, the economy still seemed extremely unstable, and it seemed that paper money wasn't the only cause of economic instability.

## THE DREAM TEAM OF MONEY

It is interesting to note how well the first economists were connected at a time when transportation was difficult and international communities were few by today's standards. Law was a business partner of Cantillon, and Quesnay worked, like Law, for the Royal French Court as doctor for the successor to the Duke of Orleans. Quesnay met Smith, who was a friend of Thornton, who again was a friend of Ricardo.

Four of these remarkable men, John Law, Richard Cantillon, François Quesnay and Henry Thornton, managed together to describe a good deal of what is worth knowing about money and credit. So, as surprising as it may sound, we owe much of our knowledge about money to a dream team consisting of a Scottish murderer, philanderer and gambler, an Irish hard core speculator, an English banker and a French doctor. These four formed one of the greatest dream teams in economics.

### WHAT THEY ARE MAINLY REMEMBERED FOR

Some of the strongest, lasting successes of the economists mentioned in this chapter are:

- François Quesnay: his "tableau economique" and the concept of "laissez faire"
- Richard Cantillon: understanding of the effects of the "velocity of money"
- Adam Smith: the significance and efficiency of the pursuit of self-interest. The damaging effects of protectionism in all its forms
- Henry Thornton: "The father of central banking." The courses and effects of fluctuations in aggregate money supply. How interest rates drive saving rates, money supply, exchange rates and international liquidity flows. How changes in money supply have an initial effect on growth, followed by a later impact on inflation. The potential beneficial effects of active central bank intervention. Why central bankers may go along for too long during booms
- Jean Babtiste Say: the fact that supply can create its own demand
- David Ricardo: the importance of calculating marginal effects in economic theory

*Chapter* **4**

# The Napoleon of Finance

Nicholas Biddle is the Napoleon of Finance. He is twice as great as Henry Clay, twice and a half as great as Daniel Webster – and eight times as great as Martin van Buren.

The Herald, *March 30, 1837*

Ricardo's friend James Mill maintained his interest in economics through-out his life. The two friends and a number of other distinguished men founded the "Political Economy Club," about which the economist Jevons later wrote:

Whether its continued existence be due to the excellence of its monthly dinners – in respect of which the club does not seem to study economy – or to the economical debates which follow each dinner, I will not attempt to decide.

Much of James Mill's work was devoted to promoting Ricardo's ideas, but he also dealt with economic theories and questions of his own. One of these was "the grand practical problem to find means to limit the number of births" – a problem which he saw as a major threat given limited food supply. Mill should know from first-hand observation: Ricardo had been the third of 17 children and Mill himself was the father of nine.

## A RATHER BRIGHT KID

One of these nine children was John Stuart, who was born in 1802. John showed signs of exceptional intelligence at a very early age, and it didn't take long before James thought he was ready for a formal education. When the little boy reached the age of three, he was taught Greek and arithmetic. He learned Latin at the age of eight, and soon after geometry, algebra, chemistry and physics. John taught him logic at 12, and the year after he was introduced to political economy, which James considered the most difficult of the subjects. One of the ways in which James taught him economics was by taking walks (like he had done with Ricardo), in which he gave his son lectures on different aspects of economy – mainly in the way that Ricardo had described it. Every morning, John had to deliver a complete, written report about what his father had said the day before. These reports were afterwards used as a draft for *Elements of Political Economy*, which was published in 1819. This was quite a remarkable effort considering that the author, John, was only 13 years old at the time!

Four years after his son had published this book, James considered his job done, and his son well prepared for the world. The 17-year-old boy joined the East India Company. This gave him an extremely useful insight into private business and public affairs, and it did not prevent him from writing and studying during his free time. When John Stuart Mill reached 20, he had published seven major articles about economics, politics and law, and edited a book about philosophy. Judging from his works, it seems that philosophy was his major interest, but yet in sheer numbers of pages written, economy ended up being his largest subject.

## INHERENT INSTABILITY

His best contribution to economic theory was written during his 23rd and 24th years (but not published until many years later). The title was *Essays on Some Unsettled Questions of Political Economy*. One of the essays was an analysis of Say's Law. Say's notion that supply creates its own demand would hold in a simple barter economy, Mill claimed, but not necessarily if money was used as a medium, because people could save up the proceeds from their sales, so that supply did not *always* create equal demand. Swings in general confidence could trigger imbalances between supply and demand.

During the following years he published a number of other articles about economics. In 1826, he wrote *Paper Currency and Commercial Distress*, in which he introduced the concept of "competitive investment." His idea covered the problem in which a market suddenly expanded; perhaps because of a technological invention. Businessmen might then overestimate how big a piece of the pie they could normally get:

Everyone calculating upon being before all his competitors provides himself with as large a stock as he thinks that the market will take off; not reflecting that others, like himself, are adding to the supply, not calculating upon the fall of price which must take place as soon as this increasing quantity is brought to the market. This deficiency is soon changed into an excess.

In this way, a temporary excess of demand of a specific item could soon after lead to the opposite: a temporary excess of supply. In the same article, he introduced a distinction between "professional traders" and "speculators," the first basing their behavior on long-term economic analysis, the latter on short-term price trends:

The few who watch prospectively the signs of future supply and demand, anticipating a great rise of price, make considerable purchases. These purchases produce a considerable immediate rise; and this in turn tempts many, who look no further than to the immediate turn of the market, to purchase in expectation of a still greater advance.

This meant a vicious circle, which could easily explain why booms could get completely off track, as with the Mississippi scheme and the South Sea Company. And as would happen again 11 years after his book came out.

## THE CRASH OF 1837

It happened in 1837, and it became as excellent an illustration of Mill's theories as anyone could ask for (although few would). To tell this story, we need to introduce five distinguished Americans, each of whom played their part:

- Andrew Jackson, President of the United States from 1828 to 1836, and a man who didn't trust paper money very much
- Martin van Buren, President of the United States after Jackson (in 1836–1840)
- Nicholas Biddle, President of Second Bank of America until 1836: extremely gifted but no friend of President Jackson
- Philip Hone, investor, fairly rich until 1837. After that? Not rich at all
- James Gordon Bennet, editor of the *The Herald* and capable of writing incredible prose

Let's begin. Andrew Jackson, the first President in our story, was a prosperous politician with an authoritarian mindset, firm principles and a very bad temper. He would frequently enter into brawls and had once killed a man in a duel for insulting his wife. He had, however, also been a general in the war of 1812, where he led the defeat of the British in New Orleans; a victory that became his platform to enter politics. One of his first big battles in politics was against the central bank, the so-called "Second Bank of America."

The leader of the bank was Nicholas Biddle, a genius who had completed all studies necessary for a degree at the University of Pennsylvania at the age of, well, 13. The two men hated and fought each other, but when Jackson became President, it was Biddle who had most cause to fear the other. With good reason: Jackson had appointed a Dutchman, Martin van Buren, as Vice President, and told him, "The bank is trying to kill me, but *I will kill it!*" And then he closed Biddle's bank down. Simple as that.

One reason that Andrew Jackson didn't like Mr Biddle and his bank was that he didn't think much of paper money. Paper money was not real, he thought, and it created speculation and all sorts of distortions. He actually had a point there. The total currency in circulation had risen from just 59 million in 1832 to 140 million in 1836 – a huge gain of 137% in just four years. This was an alarming number, but it became even more worrying when you looked beneath the surface. Much of the liquidity was created by start-up banks with little or no reserve capital. And what was all this money used for? New industry? No, most of it had gone into real estate speculation. Before, America had a central bank. Now it didn't.

## AN INTERESTING DIARY

This is where we meet the third character in our story, the wealthy speculator Mr Philip Hone. This gentleman investor, who lived in New York, deserves our attention not only because he became a typical victim of what was to follow, but also because he wrote a daily diary, which still exists. So let's open it, turn some pages, and read his mind on March 12, 1836:

> Everything in New York is at an exorbitant price. Rents have risen 50% for the next year. I have sold my house, it is true, for a large sum; but where to go I don't know. Lots two miles from the City Hall are worth $8000 or $10000. Even in the eleventh ward, towards the East River,

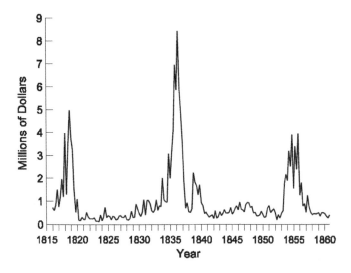

**Figure 4.1**   Receipts from sales of public lands in USA, quarterly 1816–1860. Source: Smith and Cole, 1935. This illustration is discussed in Peter Rousseau's *Jacksonian Monetary Policy, Specie Flow, and the Panic of 1837*, which was published in 2001. It shows a very strong, slow cycle.

where they sold two or three years ago for $2000 or $3000, they are now held at $4000 or $5000.

He had reason to moan. The rapid increases in real estate prices were not confined to New York (Figure 4.1); land values in Chicago had grown from 156 000 dollars in 1833 to no less than 10 million in 1836 – an incredible increase of 6400% in just three years. Just imagine. 6400%. In three years!

So there were real reasons why President Jackson should be concerned, and in July he issued an edict whereby buyers of land in most cases had to pay with gold or silver. No more real estate speculation with paper money! He had another issue to deal with though; a more pleasant one: the state had an increasing fiscal surplus. Jackson proposed to reduce tariffs to rebalance the budget, but Congress voted for distributing surplus money to the individual states instead. So what would that mean? Well, they would withdraw tranches totaling nine million dollars from major New York banks every three months and send them to the individual states, starting January 2nd, 1837. The major New York banks didn't like that idea very much.

Our friend Mr Hone had, meanwhile, managed to find a new plot of land at the corner of Broadway and Great Jones Street for 15 000 dollars. It wasn't cheap at all, but at least he could afford it, and he now commenced the construction of a new house on the plot. And then he left for Europe.

Perhaps he shouldn't have. When he returned he found the mood in the city completely changed, and not for the better. Here is his entry from November 12th:

> Hard times. There has been for some time past a severe pressure for money, which continues, and I feel the effects of it. Stocks have fallen very much . . . The price of houses and lots is not much lower nominally, but there are no sales, there is no money to pay for it, and nobody wants bonds and mortgages which cannot be converted into cash . . .

This was still before the planned distribution of government money, but that came soon enough. On January 2nd, 1937, the Treasury withdrew the first tranche of $9 million from the major banks. Panic and a series of bankruptcies followed almost within days, and there were soon riots on the street. Real estate prices went into a vicious circle of forced selling, banks went under, and numerous businesses too. On March 4th, Mr Hone had to make a very sad entry in his diary:

> This is a dark and melancholy day in the annals of my family. Brown & Hone stopped payments to-day, and called a meeting of their creditors. My eldest son has lost the capital I gave him, and I am implicated as endorser to them for a fearful amount.

There had been a presidential election while this happened, and many were now hoping that the new president, Martin van Buren, would take a more favorable attitude to paper credit, but those hopes were soon shattered. President Jackson had stated in his farewell address that:

> "The corporations which create paper money cannot be relied upon to keep the circulating medium uniform in amount."

However, van Buren said nothing at all about the subject in his inauguration speech. Not a word about the financial crisis that was brewing. Nothing!

Real estate was now impossible to sell unless at heavily discounted prices, and stock markets drifted downwards through January and February. James Gordon Bennet, our editor of *The Herald*, demonstrated his way with words in his editorial from one day in March, 1837:

The United States was never in such a perilous condition as they are at this moment. We are in the midst of a commercial panic which threatens to break up all business of society – to ruin whole states – to lay waste large districts – to sweep half our banking institutions from the land – to excite the most inflammable passions, and to create revulsions that will retard the country for years.

This sounded desperate, but such was indeed the mood. Somebody had to take action, and Hone and his friends got the idea to contact Mr Biddle, the former head of the central bank. Biddle arrived and started coordinating meetings and giving suggestions and instructions. Money was released from here and there and a glimmer of hope was felt. Bennet wrote a new editorial:

Nicholas Biddle is the Napoleon of Finance. He is twice as great as Henry Clay, twice and a half as great as Daniel Webster – and eight times as great as Martin van Buren.

It's not nice to realize that your greatness is just one-eighth of your opponent's, so the President can't have liked this sentence. Nor the way the editorial continued:

Nicholas Biddle walks around the streets like a spirit from heaven – saying to the hurricane of commerce, "peace" – and telling the storm of speculation "be still". He is the genius – the impersonation of the calm summer morning.

Be that as it may, while our Napoleon of Finance might have been a formidable man, he didn't run a central bank any more and couldn't print money. Nor could he persuade the President to change his course. The government withdrew a second tranche of nine million dollars from the major banks on April 1st and the panic spread further. Major runs began at the start of May, and a bank holiday was declared on May 10th to give the financial community some breathing space. It didn't help much. The meltdown continued and unemployment soared to over 20% in the Northwest as the bubble unwound. Chicago land that had fetched $11 000 in 1836 fell, and continued to fall, until it could be bought for just $100 in 1840. As land prices fell, the speculators that had bought large tracts and stacked them out in smaller plots realized one by one that there just weren't any buyers. Eventually, the plots were merged again and converted back into farm land so that they at least could generate a bit of current income. It was only in 1842, five years after the collapse, that real estate prices in most parts of the country finally reached their bottom.

## MEANWHILE IN LONDON

While all of this was happening, our British genius-economist John Stuart Mill was continuing in his job at the India Office. He had, in 1835, also been appointed editor of the *London Review*, and worked now on various essays, which would subsequently be incorporated into his major works. It was also in this year that his friend, Thomas Carlyle, asked him to review a single 800-page draft manuscript about the French Revolution. Mill read a bit one evening and became very drowsy, and as he then slept, his maid came to light up the fireplace – unfortunately using Carlyle's manuscript! Carlyle would afterwards pretend to forgive Mill, and after some hesitation write the whole thing all over again. Carlyle's book was published in 1837 and when he asked Mill to make a public review of it, it wasn't much of a surprise that it was *really* positive.

During the same year, Mill read *Philosophy of the Inductive Sciences*, as well as an important work about history and philosophy by William Whewells, and he reread *Preliminary Discourse on the Study of Natural Philosophy* by the famous astronomer Wilhelm Herschel. Various bits and pieces in these works gave Mill the inspiration for much of his later manuscripts. He decided in 1845 to pull the strings together in a major work, which he would call *The Principles of Political Economy with some of their Applications to Social Philosophy* (or *The Principles of Political Economy* for short). He had been thinking about the subject for years, but when it came to actually writing it, he made something of a record in speed writing. He completed the work, all 971 pages (it was, in fact, five volumes), stuffed with detail and, in many cases, novel analysis, in just 18 months. In these volumes, which became international classics, he related velocity of money – Richard Cantillon's old concept – with the general upswing and speculation.

The year 1848 was interesting for Mill, since his book got published, and it was also interesting for several other distinguished gentlemen. There was Lord Overstone, for instance – England's most successful banker at the time. Overstone had an analytical mind and thought that crisis was a recurring phenomenon with its own, inner dynamics. One day he had a conversation with Walter Bagehot, the chief editor of *The Economist*, and Bagehot quoted him later on for describing the different phases of the boom–bust cycle as follows:

Quiescence, improvement, confidence, prosperity, excitement, overtrading, convulsion, pressure, stagnation, ending again in quiescence.

If we say that Thornton had come close to creating the first business cycle theory, then it's also fair to say that Overstone came close to being the first to define them. But he was a practical man, and he had for some time been concerned about the ability of the Bank of England to halt a severe banking crisis and panic. As a skilled banker, he followed these markets very closely and tried to predict danger. During the fall of 1845, he had begun to sense that such a situation was evolving, so he sat down to write about it to his good friend G.W. Norman. It was not that Overstone thought that a crash was imminent, but the early warning signs were definitely there: "We have no crash at present . . . ," he wrote, ". . . only a slight premonitory movement in the ground under our feet." He was right: the crash came in 1847 – exactly ten years after the previous one.

---

### How the Central Bank Could "Increase the Money Supply"

Central banks were by the mid 19th century aware of three important ways to create money:

- Buy bonds (and pay with money). This had a direct effect (the injection of money) and an indirect effect (bond prices went up so that interest rates went down, which encouraged more private borrowing)
- Reduce the interest rates that the central bank offered to the private banks (discount rates). This encouraged banks to borrow from the central bank so that they could increase their private lending
- Reduce the reserve ratio requirements for the private banks. Lower reserve requirements enabled the private banks to increase their lending

*Chapter* **5**

# Jay and the Phantom Gold

Some people get so rich they lose all respect for humanity. That's how rich I want to be.

*Rita Rudner*

It is always hard to establish the reasons why a period of overinvestment results in a crash rather than a smooth correction, but it seems that the critical factor in England in 1847 was the use of instalment payments for railroad shares. It was common at the time to sell shares in such a way that buyers only had to make initial instalments to start with, and then perhaps hope that they could sell the shares again at a profit before the next instalments were due. A series of these new instalments, totalling approximately 6.5 million pounds, was due in January 1847. And many had difficulties paying them. The full-blown crisis broke out during the summer, and 22 British companies defaulted during August, followed by 47 in September and 82 in October. It didn't take long before the crisis spread beyond the British borders to Holland, Belgium, New York and Germany.

## KARL MARX

The year 1847 was interesting for a young gentleman named Karl Heinrich Marx, who was born in a little Prussian town called Trier on May 5th, 1818. He had grown up in a traditional middle class environment and later on managed to get accepted into the prestigious Berlin University. His specialty at the university became philosophy, and after leaving Berlin, he took a doctor's degree at Jena University. In 1842, when he was 24 years of age, he got a job as an editor at *Reinische Zeitung*. This was all very fine until, just five months later, the newspaper got banned by the government. After this frustrating beginning to his career he moved to Paris, where he worked as a journalist for several magazines – until he got expelled from France two years later. So here was a young man who had studied philosophy at what was generally considered the finest university in the world. And then, when he wanted to write about his ideas, society wouldn't let him!

He became bitter and a radical critic of religion, Negroes, Jews (although he himself was a Jew), and in particular of capitalists and capitalist society. He then involved himself in the organization of the Communist League – a radical movement that wanted workers to take control over business and the state. Karl Marx aimed to show that a capitalist economy was unfair and seriously flawed, and that it should be replaced by a socialist/communist system. The workers should therefore get mobilized as soon as possible and then, when the time was ripe, strike and take control.

The difficult question was to decide *when* the time was ripe, and this was where the crash of 1847 fitted in, because it had triggered some exciting events. There had been several communist uprisings across Europe, and although they had all been crushed, they did indicate something to him: it had clearly been an economic crisis that had led to the attempted revolutions, and it would probably be new crises that would trigger the next attempt. He took an ambitious approach: he would not only show that one system (capitalism) was flawed and the other (communism) was better, but he would also provide a road map for how the transition would take place. It would be triggered by one of the frequent economic crises. So he decided to analyze why there were regular economic crises in market economies.

While he thought about the issue, the kettle started to overheat again. The 1850s brought new waves of speculation in railroad stocks, as well as in wheat (England), land (USA) and heavy industries (Continental Europe). In 1857, exactly ten years after the last crisis, The New York branch of Ohio Life Assurance Trust Company suspended its payments. Soon, a chain reaction started and the railroad stocks went into free fall.

This triggered an incredible burst of energy from Karl Marx. It was happening again! He had to get his theory down on paper and published! Within six months he wrote the first drafts of what would eventually become his classic suite of books, *Das Kapital* ("Capital"). Here he described what he himself called "in every respect the most important law of modern political economy." The process that he described may be summarized as follows:

- Booms are often created by technical innovations
- The effect of technical innovations is that capitalists employ more capital (machines, etc.) and fewer people (workers) in the production process
- It is the people who create the value, and since the ratio of people to capital is falling, the ratio of profits will fall as well

He concluded, "The rate of profits falls not because the worker is exploited less, but because altogether less labor is employed in relation to the capital employed." Subsequent experience has shown that it is the other way around, but he carried on stating that decreased profit rates would lead to increased indebtedness until the final collapse would come and the communists would take over. He got the latter part right. Communists did in fact take over, and rule most of the world during much of the following century.

Karl Marx is still remembered as a contributor to business cycle theory, not because of what he concluded or predicted about cycles (which was largely meaningless), but because of how he approached the problem. He was one of the first authors to attempt to provide a systematic theory of how crises and depressions could develop in a capitalist economy.

## GOLDEN OPPORTUNITY

A new crisis started in 1864 in France and spread to England and Italy two years later. This time, the objects of speculation were wool, shipping and various kinds of new enterprise. However, this was nothing compared to the nightmare that was waiting around the corner: the most devastating, international depression of the 19th century. The financial crash that preceded it started in 1873, which was the year when John Stuart Mill died.

It is difficult to identify which events were the real precursors of the crash of 1873, but if we start in 1869, we will be sure not to miss any part of this rather amazing story. At that time, there was a lively market at the New York Stock Exchange Gold Room. People said that dealers traded gold in this room, but as gold was essentially the international currency (most of the European countries were now on the gold standard), what was really traded was dollars: if you bought gold, you paid with dollars. If the price of gold (as measured in dollars) went up, it really meant that the international price of dollars went down.

Two of the most active traders in the Gold Room were Jay Gould and Jim Fisk. Jim Fisk was fat, happy and charming, and an able salesman. But he was often like a bull in a china shop. Jay Gould was an astute, cynical speculator who had been trained at Erie Lake Railroad, where he had met Jim Fisk. Gould, who had made a lot of money on booming railroad stocks (which he still owned), was not a particularly nice person. He once stated that:

> "In a Republican district I was a Republican. In a Democratic district I was a Democrat. And in a doubtful district, I was Doubtful. But I was always for Erie."

And at another time:

> "I can hire one half of the working class to kill the other half."

Now he decided to try to execute an incredible plan which could add even further to his wealth: he would buy up gold to depress the exchange rate of the dollar. But not just a little gold; a huge amount. As the dollar fell, this would increase America's exports (giving more business to the railways) and it would also stimulate American inflation – reducing the debt burden on his railways.

**Figure 5.1** Jay Gould. Gould became one of the most hated traders in the history of the American stock exchange.

At that time, there was some 115 million dollars worth of gold in America, of which 100 million was locked up in the vaults of the Treasury. As the margin requirements were extremely slack, Gould could buy 10 million dollars worth of gold on future contracts by putting up only 50 000 dollars of his own, as long as people believed in his general creditworthiness. But before he started, he had to take some precautions – just in case President Grant should decide to sell some of the Treasury's gold and thus force its price down. His solution was to cultivate a friendship with Grant's former brother-in-law, Abel Gorbin, who should introduce him to the President. This eventually happened on Fisk's steamboat, where Gould tried to find out what Grant's reaction to a rise in the gold price would be. The meeting didn't turn out to Gould's full satisfaction, however, as Grant apparently had no clear idea about how he would react to a gold craze.

On September 16, Gould asked Gorbin if he could send the President a letter explaining why it would be wrong to sell gold until the grain crops had been moved. After the letter was finished, they sent a messenger with the train to Pittsburgh. As the messenger arrived just after midnight, he hired horses and rode all night to Washington, where he finally found President Grant playing croquet on his lawn. The messenger handed over the letter and asked if there was a reply. "No, nothing," the President answered, whereafter the messenger returned to Pittsburgh to send a telegraph with the short message:

Delivered all right

But something went wrong under transmission: the telegram, which was received by Gould and Gorbin, said something quite different. It said:

Delivered. All right

Seeing this, Gould decided to move. After promising Gorbin a free trading line of 1.5 million dollars, he started to buy gold. He bought in the free market at a price around 135 dollars, and gradually the price started to edge upwards. On September 22, a day when Fisk was leading the charge of the trading room, the price closed at 141.5. That evening, Gould visited Gorbin, who had some very disturbing news: he had just received a letter from Grant, who expressed his dissatisfaction with the fall of the dollar, implying that he might start selling gold from the Treasury.

Through the assistance of Gorbin, Gould met with the President again, and this time at a public party, where everybody could see them together.

Gould tried to convince the President that a rise in the dollar price would do great damage to exports and should at least be postponed until large, pending export orders had been cleared. After this brief meeting, he began trying to convince everybody else that the President had promised to back him all the way. Then he took a deep breath and resumed buying.

## THE GREATEST RAID . . .

He entrusted most of the business to the broker Henry Smith, who recruited a number of others, who again recruited others to make a total of probably 50 or 60. Together they bought up gold until they had sucked up almost all the metal on the market. And when there was no more gold left, he kept buying through forward contracts until he had 40 million dollars worth of gold contracts in addition to his 15 million worth of cash gold. During this process, the price rose to 146 dollars – which meant that single-handedly, he had managed to force down the dollar by almost 8%.

But then something odd happened. For some reason, the price stuck at 146, as if somebody else was selling large amounts at that specific price, or as if somebody knew that the Treasury would start selling. Through the use of forward contracts, Gould had now bought more gold than existed on the free market. Paradoxically, this was potentially a very strong position, because when the sellers had to deliver and could not get the stuff, where would they have to buy it? From Gould, of course, who would be able to dictate the price. But why, then, did it stop at 146? Was it because Grant would sell?

Fortunately, the President was coming to visit Gorbin soon, and Gorbin convinced Grant that he should sit on his hands. Encouraged by this, Gould told his old friend Fisk that he could be part of this fantastic raid – one of the greatest in history – and one that was backed by everybody from the President to the doorkeepers in Congress. Gould told Fisk that he could be in charge of the gold purchases and of spreading rumors to colleagues in the Gold Room. Fisk jumped in and started buying on his own account through forward contracts on "phantom gold" – gold that was actually not there. The sellers were selling short for future delivery, hoping that the Treasury would release some gold, which they could snap up at a lower price. Gould told Fisk that Grant wanted to see gold at 1000 dollars, a rumor which Fisk quickly passed on to the traders.

This was the time when (as John Stuart Mill would have predicted) the public joined in. Soon, you saw dentists, merchants and even farmers from all over the country buying up gold in anticipation of further price increases. The power of this new wave of buy-orders came as a shock to the professional short sellers, who started covering their contracts by buying at any price as the 146-dollar barrier was broken. But Gould was no longer buying. He knew time would eventually run out, and had in fact started to sell. Fisk knew nothing about this and kept buying on his own account what was, in fact, Gould's gold. Then it happened. Grant sent Gorbin a letter warning him that the Treasury would start selling. Gorbin immediately insisted that Gould should close his account and pay out his profit. Gould agreed to this if Gorbin would keep silent about the letter. He knew that he was on the verge of disaster. He still had his cash stock plus 35 million worth of forward contracts – to sell it would be like moving an elephant through a public restaurant without anybody noticing. And he probably only had a few days or even a few hours the next morning to do it.

His first decision was to leave Fisk behind. One elephant might just be able to sneak out unnoticed. There was no way that two could do it. So the next morning, he encouraged Fisk to keep buying, while he speeded up his own secret sales. Amazingly, the gold kept rising as the public kept buying. Steadily and at an enormous trading volume, it edged up dollar by dollar. Meanwhile, Gould sold and sold until there was nothing left to sell. But he kept on selling, building up an increasing short position in the forward contracts. A reporter from the *New York Herald* saw the drama and described it in this way:

> The revengeful war whoops of the furious Indians, the terrific yells issuing from a lunatic asylum, would not equal in intensity the cries of speculators in the Gold Room.

As the public kept buying, gold kept advancing and the atmosphere was loaded. Would it eventually top 1000 dollars? Was Grant in it or not? Would the Treasury sell? Then, at 12:07, when the price had just reached 165, the announcement arrived: the Treasury would sell.

It has been estimated that Gould made 1.5 million dollars within the next 14 minutes. During these 14 minutes, the price of gold fell from 165 to 133 dollars, and all the paper profits of the bulls were wiped out. The bears had been saved from their squeeze, and Gould had succeeded with his scheme. As a consequence, Gould became the most detested man in Wall Street, and as Fisk said of him: there was "nothing left but a heap of clothes and a pair of eyes."

## THE END OF THE BOOM

Gould had kept his interests in railroad stock. At this time, the public interest in railroad stocks was as high as ever. But the fact was that over-capacity was developing as too many rushed to gain market share (John Stuart Mill's "competitive investment"). After 1868, the annual construction of new railroad mileage had soared, and now pressure could be felt. Gould controlled the Erie Lake Railroad, which competed with Vanderbilt's New York Central Line, and Vanderbilt had just lowered his price from 125 to 100 dollars per carload. Gould decided to try to regain his market share by reducing his price to 75 dollars. Vanderbilt then moved to 50 dollars. Gould moved to 25 dollars. And then Vanderbilt moved to 1 dollar – far below his production costs. After that, Vanderbilt got all the business. In fact, he got much more business than there had ever been before, as Gould started to buy up steers in Buffalo to ship them through the New York Central Line.

This price war was symptomatic of the situation. Prosperity had lasted too long and people had invested in too many businesses that could not pay back the interest. During 1872, 89 railroads defaulted on their bonds, including Gould's Erie Lake Railroad. Out of 364 listed railroads, 260 were unable to pay any dividends. By the end of the year, more and more of the railroad stocks started sliding at the stock exchange, and the atmosphere grew more cautious. In Europe, the situation was very similar. After years of booming investment in building sites, commodities and railroad stocks, things were getting shaky and confidence began to slide.

## TOTAL COLLAPSE

Sometimes, panic starts in the most unexpected places. This time, it began in Austria, where a wave of fear suddenly came just after the opening of the Vienna World Exhibition on May 1st, 1873. Many Austrian banks were up to their ears in railroad shares and were dragged down as marginal speculators failed. Soon, the panic spread to Germany, and from there on to Belgium, Italy, Switzerland and Holland. On September 8, 1873, it reached Wall Street. On that day, the New York Warehouse and Security Co. defaulted. And then nobody could stop it:

September 13: Kenyon, Cox Bank defaulted
September 17: Pandemonium defaulted
September 18: Jay Cooke and Co. defaulted

The 19th of September started calmly, but during the afternoon, most of the railroad stocks suddenly started to fall. It was suspected that this was engineered single-handedly by Jay Gould, who was thought to have unloaded all his railroad shares beforehand. The fall immediately turned into all-out panic, in which everybody desperately struggled to find a buyer for their shares. The next morning, the doors of the stock exchange never opened, and the President rushed for an emergency meeting with his Treasury secretary and several officials and businessmen, including Commodore Vanderbilt. The problem had only one solution, and unlike the British Bullion Committee 76 years earlier, these people only needed a few hours to choose that solution:

"Increase the money supply!"

The Treasury released 13 million dollars for purchasing government bonds, and ten days later, the exchange was reopened. But the fact that the exchange reopened did not mean that the crisis was over. The panic was the beginning of a depression the magnitude of which America had never seen before. Unemployment in New York rose to 30%, then to 40%, and then 50%. The construction of new railroad mileage dropped from 5870 miles in 1872 to 4097 in 1873, and further to 2117 in 1874. In 1875, it reached the bottom with 1711 new miles added. John Stuart Mill had been right: confidence mattered, and so did speculation. A boom could take place even if stimulated by neither an increase in the money printing nor any external stimulus. It could take place if people reduced their savings, if velocity of money increased, or because of competitive investment. And a bust could appear simply as a reaction to a boom. One hundred and fifty-four years after the collapse of Law's scheme, it began to look more and more as if instability was an inherent property of the capitalist economy. Maybe there was an invisible hand to restore the balance after waves of collective greed and fear, but it was sorely needed: people were only human.

*Chapter* **6**

# Seven Pioneers

On two occasions I have been asked, "Pray, Mr Babbage, if you put into the machine wrong figures, will the right answers come out?" I am not able rightly to apprehend the kind of confusion of ideas that could provoke such a question.

*Charles Babbage*

Within a new team of students entering a university, there always seem to be one or a few who are exceptionally bright and creative. It was the same as Trinity College in Cambridge bid welcome to a new group of hopeful youngsters in 1810. One of these new students, a 19-year-old boy named Charles Babbage, fit that description very well. Bright? Yes. Creative? Oh yes!

The young man had chosen to study chemistry and mathematics, but he soon discovered that he strongly preferred the latter. He was good at math; so good, in fact, that he soon thought he understood it better than his tutors. Together with some friends, he founded the "Analytical Society," which would, among other things, promote new developments in the study of the field.

It was fascinating. Well, fascinating except when you had to calculate logarithm tables. There was only one way to do that: two men would calculate an entire table by hand, independently of each other. Then one would read out his figures, and the other check against his. One day at the university, Babbage was sitting with such a logarithm table in the Analytical Society room, when another member came to ask him what he was doing. Babbage looked up and gave a surprising answer: he was thinking of whether it was possible to make a machine that could do such calculations automatically.

## Cogwheels, Steam and Punch-cards

That moment changed his life. As soon as the idea had entered his mind, he began working on the project. Shortly after, he constructed a simple, mechanical device, which could facilitate the calculation of their tables. But while he had been working on this little machine, his mind had been wandering. Maybe mankind could go much further? Maybe you could construct machines that could solve all kinds of mathematical questions, and thereby accelerate the development of human understanding? Maybe mankind could even some day build machines that could *think*?

On June 14, 1822 he presented a paper entitled *Observations on the Application of Machinery to the Computation of Mathematical Tables*. It described an advanced mathematical machine, which would be driven by a steam engine and a system of falling weights. The idea gathered considerable interest, and work commenced the following year on the largest government-financed project in Great Britain. Babbage expected that he could have the machine finished within two to three years. That estimate turned out to be very wrong, however, because while his instrument-makers worked on the machine, Charles Babbage worked on its specifications. Whenever his team had finished a part, Babbage had improved the design, and all the cogwheels had to be dismantled and the whole thing reconstructed. This went on and on, driving everyone mad, and the project finally shipwrecked altogether as his chief toolmaker quit after ten years.

Babbage's reaction to this defeat was unusual. Instead of giving up, he now raised his ambitions even higher and began the design of a much more sophisticated machine, but this time only on paper. It would be gigantic. Driven by six steam machines, it would be programmable with punch-cards and able to perform up to one calculation per second!

## Another French Physician

When Charles Babbage embarked on this new project, a Frenchman, Clement Juglar, was only 24 years old, and still studying medicine at university. Juglar was born in Paris on October 15, 1819, the son of a doctor from Basses-Alpes and a mother from Normandie. Three years later he graduated (like Quesnay) as a doctor, but he could never concentrate entirely on this occupation; his interests were directed more towards questions of social and economic orientation, and especially the process of change in the economic environment. When he was 29, he began working with social studies, and two years later he published a number of articles in the *Journal des Economists* about the fluctuations in births, marriages and deaths in France. The articles also investigated fluctuations in prosperity in France, and this was what later became his absorbing interest.

The year 1862 became an important one for both Charles Babbage and Clement Juglar. In that year, Babbage's first, simple calculation machine was displayed at London's Science Museum, where he spent much of his time telling the audience about his "computer," which was finished on the drawing-board, but still not built. In the same year, Clement Juglar, who was then 43 years of age, published what became his conclusions regarding the courses of economic fluctuations: *Les Crises commerciales et leur retour periodique en France, en Angleterre et aux Etats Unis.* Although few took notice of this book at the beginning (maybe because of its title?), it was revolutionary.

Clement Juglar had discovered something that the classical economists had missed. Thornton had mentioned deceptive oversupply of money, and Mill had described competitive overinvestment. Overstone had focused on regular business fluctuations, but had not done much to map or explain them. Earlier writers had found many traces of inherent instability, but also inherent factors which contributed to stability. They considered monetary factors, such as money supply, interest rate and velocity of money, and real factors, including random disturbances, investment, saving, (under)consumption and (over)production. And as practical businessmen, they also remembered to include some surrealistic factors, such as public confidence, folly and panic. But remarkably, none of these giants had attempted to hammer out a coherent, unifying theory to explain business cycles. Why was that?

Because, amazingly, *they hadn't discovered them.* When you read their books and articles, you could find many references to "crises," but although Petty had used the term "cycle" in his *Treatise of Taxes and Contributions* from 1662, none had realized that this phenomenon could take place even if nothing happened to initiate it. They had all considered booms and crises to be caused by specific phenomena – by external shocks or mistakes. In some cases, as we saw with Mill, they had found phenomena which could lead from one excess to the opposite. But none of them had treated these phenomena as phases of a fundamental, wavelike movement inherent in a capitalist economy. And because they didn't see it that way, none of them had focused very much on the possibility of mapping and calculating the dynamics of a system.

Clement Juglar's new book was entirely different from the earlier literature written about crises. He realized before anyone else that the frequent crises were not simply a number of independent accidents, but a repeated, periodic manifestation of inherent instability in the economic organism. Having perceived this, he moved on to classify the different phases in this cyclic movement. He wrote of the "upgrade", the "explosion" and the "liquidation" phase. To classify these, he collected and analyzed statistical time series covering the longest possible timespans. Studying these long time periods, he believed he was able to identify an average duration of the cycle of nine to ten years. Clement Juglar expressed an understanding that the instability was inherent, when he wrote:

The only cause of depression is prosperity

Depression did not happen, he thought, because something had gone wrong. Depression came because something had gone too well. This notion was in complete contrast to the dominant "mistake" view of the day; that crises occurred because of irresponsible issuance of paper money, the presence of monopolies, abuse of customs privileges, trade barriers, failures of harvests, etc. No, crises came because of prosperity!

Juglar made two improved editions of his book and kept studying the business cycle problem throughout his life. He never contributed much more than his first book (and its later editions), and he never got much closer to an explanation of the cycles than relating them to a credit cycle, but this contribution was, in any case, quite enough for one man.

It is often the case in science that important facts and concepts are described many times without the authors really understanding the significance of what they saw. Only when somebody realizes the full meaning of the events can we really say that it has been "discovered." Before Juglar's book, many had described elements of economic instability, but they had not understood the concept of cycles. After Clement Juglar, scientists would rarely say that they studied "crises." They would study "trade cycles." As Schumpeter later would express it:

It was he who discovered the continent; several writers had discovered islands near it before.

Even shortly before he died at the age of 86, you could still find Clement Juglar bent over his piles of statistics, curious to the end. Charles Babbage was also enthusiastic to his last days. After his exhibition in 1862, he returned to his project, and visitors in his last years found him still eager to show off his workroom. Like Juglar, he understood the significance of his work, and to the end he believed that mankind would some day build his computer, and that it would eventually change the way science worked. What neither of the two thinkers could know, however, was that the machine Babbage had envisioned would eventually reveal secrets about these cycles that were almost beyond belief. However, Charles Babbage's machines would be of little use to the economists if there were no relevant equations with which to feed them. Hardware needs software, and someone had to develop coherent mathematical representations of economic behavior.

## MATHEMATICAL MODELS

Enter Leon Walras, an engineer born in Normandy, France in 1834. His father was an economist, and Leon learned a lot from him, including the view that economics is about maximizing utility. He tried to enter Ecole Polytechnique, but failed twice before making it into the lesser Ecole des Mines instead, where he soon dropped out.

That was not a promising start to an academic career, and he decided instead to live a more bohemian life with mixed jobs in literature and journalism, teaching himself more economics along the way. At one point he wrote a romantic novel, at another he worked as a clerk at a railway, then as a journalist and then as a lecturer. And then he wrote two books about philosophy. In 1870, he applied for a teaching job as the first chair of Political Economy at the University of Lausanne. The line-up of candidates can't have been very impressive, because the board voted narrowly to give this somewhat dubious character the post.

Lausanne is located on hillsides facing Lake Geneva and has a breathtaking view of the Swiss and French Alps. Walras must have liked either the place or the job (or both), because he stayed in the same place and job for 22 years, and for the first time in his life he became successful. In 1874, he wrote an article about mathematical solutions to economic problems: *Principe d'une theorie mathematique de l'echange*. Walras continued to develop his network of fellow economists, with whom he corresponded frequently. In 1889, he published the first version of his *Elements of Pure Economics*, which he kept improving in new editions over a number of years. The book started with a description of pure and applied economics – a sort of state-of-the-art résumé. Then he continued to state that economics must be described in mathematical terms, where marginal analysis could be applied. This was followed by sections that provided detailed descriptions of how mathematical principles could be used to describe and analyze one economic problem after the other. His main approach was to describe a general equilibrium, a scenario where the activities of all market participants ("agents") add up to create a stable situation. Gradually, page by page, he guided the reader towards a complete model. First he introduced a very simple scenario with just two agents exchanging goods in a barter economy. Then he added multi-party exchanges, then multi-product exchanges, then production and the markets for productive services, then saving, then capital formation, then money and finally credit. The whole construction was based on various simplifying assumptions, including that there was perfect competition, perfect mobility and perfect price flexibility. He would, under each scenario, show how an equilibrium situation could be developed, although he did mention that several alternative equilibriums were a possibility.

Walras's mathematical approach to economics was somewhat reminiscent of the way that a physicist would model the behavior of a machine. This was no coincidence; Walras was influenced enormously by Newton and by the French mathematician Pierre-Simon de Laplace. He was also very inspired by a book of static mechanics by Louis Poinsot – in fact so much so that he kept the book by his bedside for several decades.

## Mr Jevons and the Sun

While Walras worked on the methods for analyzing economics, there were still others who began looking for explanations for Juglar's cycles. William Stanley Jevons was a good example. He was born in Liverpool in 1835 and had gone to University College in London. However, his father had lost his business in the crash of 1847, and Jevons had consequently been forced to leave his studies and work instead, and it took him no less than 12 years to earn enough money to go back and complete his studies. During his career, Jevons provided a number of great contributions to the body of economic thought. In 1871, just one year before the great crash, he published his book *The Theory of Political Economy*, where he provided a valuable description of marginal analysis and provided the first description of "rational man" – an assumed person in economic constructs that would only make rational decisions. He explained how rational consumers would try to maximize their utility and would stop spending money on a given item when they thought that the marginal utility would be higher if they spent the next money on something else.

And then there was the issue with the sun. Jevons knew from first-hand experience how painful economic depressions could be, and he was probably inspired by the crash of 1873 when he started writing a series of articles (published between 1875 and 1882) about business cycles. One of his sources of inspiration was Mill's *Principles of Political Economy*. Jevons noted Mill's emphasis on public mood swings, but he thought that his assumptions were highly inadequate for explaining the recurring booms and depressions, which he found were relatively regular. Which process would explain why people get greedy and scared at regular intervals? Mill had not solved that problem at all. So Jevons had looked everywhere for some external factor in the economy that could stimulate these big fluctuations. He thought and he speculated while pouring over mountains of statistics. The first basic conclusion that he reached was that agriculture (the harvest) constituted a very important part of the economy, so it was possible that the explanation came from something that happened on the farms. But what could it be? Diseases in the crops?

The explanation that he finally proposed was that it was fluctuation in the intensity of sunshine – created by the regularly occurring "sunspots" (large fireballs on the surface of the sun that appear at regular intervals). His first article – coinciding with the great crash of 1875 – provided an attempt to show that there had been an 11.1-year cycle in the British grain harvest from 1254 to 1400, and that this corresponded very well with the cycle in sunspot activity, which astronomers at the time claimed was 11.1 years. Increased sunspot activity would create increased sunshine, which stimulated plant growth and thus led to a better-than-average harvest. Case solved!

Well, perhaps not quite. The astronomers would soon after revise their sunspot cycle length to 10.45 years, and this meant that Jevons's model got embarrassingly out of synch. So he looked at the harvest statistics again and concluded (surprise, surprise) that the actual cycle length had in fact been 10.45 years, and not, as he had stated previously, 11.1 years. So not to worry: the theory was OK.

The problems did not stop there, however. New British crop reports did not fit into his model, and he was now forced to make another adjustment. His new claim was that sunspots led to crop fluctuations in other countries, and that these fluctuations had an indirect impact on British trade and manufacturing. This meant that there was no strict, direct causality between the sunspots and the business cycles in Britain, but a strong indirect one. This indirect effect was created both because of the change in the price, quantity and production of agricultural products, but also (now that the theory was known) by the merchants' expectations about sunspots: they would discount sunspot fluctuations in their planning decisions. The mere expectation of sunspots could thereby create economic cycles even if, for whatever reason, the sunspots failed to appear at the expected time. This was, of course, a brilliant and truly innovative way to explain inconsistencies between what a theory predicted and what the data showed. Few bought it, though. There were not many of his contemporaries who truly believed that sunspots were a primary explanation of business fluctuations – or that they even were relevant (and no sane scientist believes it now).

What remains of Jevons's sunspot theory (and of many of Karl Marx's theories) are not the faulty conclusions, but the analytical approaches. Modern economists often use the term "sunspots" today, and what they refer to are not bursts of fire on the sun, but situations where phenomena that by themselves do not affect the economy, can alter common beliefs and thus indirectly affect the economy. Jevons's approach survived.

## THE QUANTITY THEORY OF MONEY

One reason that Jevons's work isn't forgotten, is that he networked a lot with other economists, and received a lot of reviews. His book *The Theory of Political Economy* was, for instance, reviewed by the famous astronomer Simon Newcomb. Astronomer? But why would an *astronomer* review a book about economics?

That's a rather strange story, and it gets stranger still when we consider that Mr Newcomb wasn't actually educated as an astronomer. Simon Newcomb was an herbalist by education. Let's take that from the start. Newcomb had never gone to school, but had been educated at home by his father instead. When he was sixteen years old, he got a job with an herbalist who called himself "doctor," but Newcomb soon realized that there was no science behind the so-called doctor's prescriptions. It was all based on loose postulates and superstition; the man was a charlatan. Newcomb finally made the decision to walk out, so he just left and literally, well, walked out and then continued for 190 kilometers (120 miles) to the port of Calais, where he persuaded a captain to take him on as seaman. And that brought him home to Salem in Massachusetts, where his father lived.

Newcomb found a job as a teacher in Salem, but used his spare time to study all sorts of scientific literature. In 1856, when he was 21 years of age, he got another job in Washington, and this brought him close to libraries, where he could read even more science, in particular about his pet subject, which was math. It was here that he one day borrowed a translation of Laplace's *Mécanique Céleste*, and realized to his frustration that he couldn't understand it. He decided to do something about that; to get a job where he could learn more. Here is what he wrote in his *Reminiscences of an Astronomer* from 1903:

**Figure 6.1** Simon Newcomb. Newcomb was an herbalist, mathematician, astronomer and economist, and he became a recognized leader in the last three of these disciplines. Reproduced by permission of The Mary Evans Picture Library.

> I date my birth into the world of sweetness and light on one frosty morning in January, 1857, when I took my seat between two well-known mathematicians, before the blazing fire in the office of the "Nautical Almanac" at Cambridge, Mass. I had come from Washington, armed with letters from Professor Henry and Mr Hildard, to seek trial as an astronomical computer. The men beside me were Professor Joseph Winlock, the superintendent, and Mr John D. Runkle, the senior assistant in the office. I talked of my unsuccessful attempt to master the "Mécanique Céleste" of Laplace without other preparation than that afforded by the most meagre text-books of elementary mathematics of that period. . . .

> I was then in my twenty-second year, but it was the first time I had ever seen any one who was familiar with the "Mécanique Céleste" . . . My own rank was scarcely up to that of a tyro; but I was a few weeks later employed on trial as computer at a salary of thirty dollars a month.

While working here he also studied at Harvard University, and this became the beginning of an impressive ascent in the academic world. Simon Newcomb became Professor of Mathematics and Astronomer at the Naval Observatory in 1862. In 1877, he became Director of the

American Nautical Almanac Office, and editor of the *American Journal of Mathematics,* founding member and first President of the American Astronomical Society and then no less than President of the American Mathematical Society.

He is, to this day, regarded as one of the founding fathers of modern astronomy, and his work became more and more brilliant and respected; so much so, in fact, that he eventually received so many American and international awards and honorary memberships that it would take two pages just to list them. He also published numerous books and articles about the positions of objects in the sky, on how to forecast their movements, about mathematical challenges behind such calculations, and much, much more. This is where our story gets strange, because about a third of his publications were not about astronomy or theoretical math at all, but about politics and economics. One of them was *Principles of Political Economy* from 1885, where he introduced a very clear distinction between flows and stocks, and illustrated the circularity of income through a drawing of different people connected by arrows, showing how they made payments to each other. However, the most important part of his book became a statement of a rather simple relationship. He called it the *equation of exchange,* but it was later reintroduced by Irving Fisher as the *Quantity Theory of Money,* which is how we know it today. Here is what it says:

$$MV = PQ$$

where

$M$ = money supply
$V$ = velocity of money
$P$ = prices of goods and services
$Q$ = quantity of goods and services

This model is not a theory to explain economic dynamics, but it is a statement of a rather central relationship that can be useful as a reference point for many theories. We shall elaborate to it numerous times during the rest of this book, but for now, at least we know where it came from.

## ATOMS OF PLEASURE

A machine will always work with a specific well-defined purpose, like making a wheel spin, or the spindle of a weaving machine move. The same applies to economic machinery: it has to work towards well-defined goals. One of Walras's contemporary authors contributed to the definitions of these goals. His name was Francis Ysidro Edgeworth. Edgeworth was born in Ireland but didn't go to school – he was taught at home. He managed subsequently to enter university and later became a lecturer at Trinity College in London. However, he was not very highly regarded there. There were two reasons for that. First, he had a highly peculiar style of writing, filled with Greek quotes and references to classical literature (his publications were in fact so difficult to read that even other professional economists could have severe difficulties digesting them and understanding what they actually meant). Secondly, he tended to be so humble that the readers often didn't recognize him for the truly original thoughts that he sometimes introduced.

Edgeworth had noted that the people participating in the economic machinery were often supposed to be "rational men" trying to maximize individual "utility." Now, the problem was how to define this utility, and how to break it into its smallest possible units. In 1881, he proposed to define it in terms of "atoms of pleasure." These would not be easy to measure, though:

> Atoms of pleasure are not easy to distinguish and discern; more continuous than sand, more discrete than liquid; as if it were nuclei of just-perceivable, embedded in circum-ambient semiconsciousness.

No wonder they found him hard to read.

## WALRAS'S SUCCESSOR

The purpose of Walras's economic machine was, you may say, to maximize the production of Edgeworth's atoms of pleasure, and Walras's ideas gained a considerable following. He was a pioneer – a person that inspired other people – so, when he retired, in 1892, it was important for the university to find a successor that would be able to follow in his footsteps and continue to inspire and lead the new movement. It chose Wilfredo Pareto, an engineer who had been born in Paris but spent most of his life in Italy. Pareto had chosen a career in the railroad industry, where he worked as engineer and later as director of two companies. It was not until 1890, when he was 42 years of age, that he began studying economics before taking up Walras's previous chair in Lausanne in 1893. Pareto worked there for seven years before he inherited a fortune and decided to retire. However, he stayed in Switzerland and kept writing about economics until his death in 1923.

Pareto's great advantage was that he was an engineer by education and that he had a long technical work experience behind him. He had, therefore, a formidable knowledge of mathematics, which he applied constantly throughout his works. His disadvantage was that he, like Edgeworth, was a terrible writer, with a style that resembled that of a highly intelligent man that is very drunk. He would often state a lot of half theories at the same time on the same page, then move on to something else, only to finish the thoughts much later in the text.

Pareto's name is used very frequently in modern times when economists refer to "Pareto optimum" or "Pareto equilibrium" as the state of an economic system where it produces the largest possible number of Edgeworth's atoms of pleasure. The methods that he and Walras developed would be used again and again as the first business cycle theories were developed.

---

### WHAT THEY ARE BEST REMEMBERED FOR

*Charles Babbage*

- Inventing computers
- Pioneering operations analysis

*Clement Juglar*

- The first to use time series, such as interest rates, prices and central bank balances, systematically and thoroughly to analyze a well-defined economic problem. This approach became standard for business cycle research and economics in general
- Describing the morphology of business cycles (their phases) in a way that was frequently used later
- The first to understand clearly that depressions were adaptations to the situations created by the preceding prosperity

*Leon Walras and Wilfredo Pareto*

- The application of math to model the economy
- General equilibrium models

*William Stanley Jevons*

- "Sunspots," the effect whereby economic/financial systems change simply because people expect them to change

*Simon Newcomb*

- The quantity theory of money, describing the relationship between money and real activity

*Francis Ysidro Edgeworth*

- The concept of atoms of pleasure

# Part II

## The First Business Cycle Theories

If economists could manage to get themselves thought of as humble, competent people on a level with dentists, that would be splendid.

*John Maynard Keynes*

# Chapter 7

# The Golden Era

I can calculate the motions of heavenly bodies, but not the madness of people.

*Isaac Newton*

It was in the year 1876, 14 years after the publication of Juglar's book and five years after Charles Babbage's death, that Ricardo's and Mill's old "Political Economy Club" held a centenary celebration of "the Foundation of Economic Science." Centenary because it was 100 years since Adam Smith had published *The Wealth of Nations*. Chairing this meeting was Mr Gladstone, with Mr Lowe on one side and the French Minister of Finance, Mr Leon Say, on the other. After the usual extravagant dinner, Mr Lowe stood up to give the first presentation. The message in his speech was that he did not feel that the future of political economy would have that much to offer:

"... at present, so far as my own humble opinion goes, I am not sanguine as to any very large or any very startling development in political economy."

He thought that improvements from sociology might contribute a bit to furthering political economy, but not much. The developments in this science had culminated:

"The controversies which we now have in political economy, although they offer a capital exercise for the local faculties, are not of the same thrilling importance as those of earlier days; the great work has been done."

So was indeed the spirit of english economic science at the time. So much had happened since *The Wealth of Nations*; so many great contributions from Thornton, Say, Ricardo, Mill, Marx, Bagehot, Jevons, Juglar, Edgeworth, Walras, Pareto and many others (not to mention Law, Cantillon and Quesnay, who came before Smith) that there couldn't be much left to say.

## Changing Words To Equations

He was wrong. The period that followed just after his speech has since been called the golden age of business cycle research, since it was here that so many important concepts were discovered. One of the young lions on the tail of the problem was Alfred Marshall, an upcoming British economist.

Marshall was 34 years of age and taught Moral Sciences at Cambridge University when Lowe's speech was made. He was a mathematician by education and had originally gone to Cambridge to teach just that. He was interested in many other things, however, and not the least in how to find a cure for poverty. But as he began to propose his own solutions to this problem, he was ridiculed by his colleagues and friends. "He had no business discussing this subject . . . ," they said, ". . . unless he had some basic training in business or political economy." So he decided, reluctantly, to study some of the basic books about economy. At first he read John Stuart Mill's *"Principles,"* and afterwards many other works, including Ricardo's. However, there was something peculiar about the way he read them. He would sit with a pencil and convert every essential concept into mathematical equations. Just for himself. Just as a way to make sure that he really understood it.

He became hooked on economics, and began a new direction in his career where he would produce theories of a quality that would put the words in Mr Lowe's speech to shame. Alfred Marshall had a tendency to delay the publication of his books because he kept searching for perfection, but they all came out in due course. The first contribution came with his book *Principles of Economics* from 1879, which included a new theory about business cycles. Here is what he wrote about prices:

> For when prices are likely to rise, people rush to borrow money and buy goods and thus help prices to rise; business is inflated and is managed recklessly and wastefully; those working on borrowed capital pay back less real capital than they borrowed, and enrich themselves at the expense of the community. When afterwards credit is shaken and prices begin to fall, everyone wants to get rid of commodities and get hold of money which is rapidly rising in value; this makes credit fall all the

faster, and the further fall makes credit shrink even more; and thus for a long time prices fall because prices have been falling.

Just as he claimed that prices can "fall because prices have been falling," he described a similar effect on the stock exchange in his *Money, Credit and Commerce* (1923):

> Some speculators have to sell goods in order to pay their debts; and by so doing they check the rise of prices. This check makes all other speculators anxious, and they rush in to sell.

Marshall was trying to find his way through the puzzle of economics and he stumbled upon many previous assumptions that just could not be right. Take, for instance, Say's Law from 1803, which, with beautiful simplicity, had stated that:

> Supply equals demand

Here was definitely a case where missing detail was important, for any businessman experiencing a recession in the 19th Century could ask: "How has Say made such a name for himself by claiming that? Because what the law stated isn't true. Whenever there is a crisis – which is bloody often – you can't sell a damned thing, and *that* is the bloody truth!" So, during recessions, the law should rather be:

> Lots of supply. But where the $*!#% is demand?

Say's Law made sense when speaking of aggregates over the very long term, but not in the short term, because clearly, supply and demand drifted away from each other during recessions.


## KNUT WICKSELL

It was actually John Stuart Mill who had first pointed out that savings rates can fluctuate, and Juglar had related his business cycles to credit cycles. How could there be a credit cycle if people immediately spent what they had just earned, as Say assumed? However, it was the Swedish economist Knut Wicksell who made the first large departure from Say.

Born in Stockholm in 1851, Knut Wicksell was the son of a wealthy businessman and real estate broker. He had lost both of his parents when reaching 15, and so he inherited enough money to study math and physics. Over the years his interests drifted towards social sciences and economics, and he decided therefore to seek a post as economics teacher at the University of Uppsala. This posed a bit of a problem, though, because economics was taught at the Law School, where all teachers needed a law degree – which took four years to get. Or at least that was the norm: Wicksell decided to get one and made it in just two years. He was bright all right, but he also had a combative personality. While he qualified at an early age for a professorship, he didn't get it until age 52, as he refused to sign the mandatory application to the King, because it included the following remark: "Your Majesty's most obedient servant." He wasn't His Majesty's bloody servant! At another time he served two months in jail for making blasphemous remarks during a lecture.

Wicksell took his inspiration from many previous thinkers, but one of his favorites was David Ricardo. He liked, in particular, the economist's pamphlet *The High Price of Bullion*, which inspired Wicksell's most important theoretical contribution: the concept of the "natural rate of interest." The core of his idea, which he described in *Interest and Prices* from 1898, was this:

- We know that low interest rates stimulate business, and that high rates inhibit it. But what is "low" and what is "high"?
- We can answer that by considering what businesses earn if they invest. Let's say, for instance, that they can make an average return of 6% on new investments. We call that the "natural rate"
- Now, let's assume that they can borrow money for 2%. We can call this the "real rate." They can, in this case, make the difference, which is 4% profit, on borrowed money and will therefore go ahead and invest
- But if the bank rate is 10%, then the businessmen stand to *lose* 4% and will consequently not invest (unless they are stupid). The economy will stagnate or contract

This concept of "real" versus "natural" rates was utterly simple, but it remains a cornerstone of many theories to this day.

## JOHN HOBSON

Now that Say's Law was open prey, it didn't take long for the next assault to occur. It came from John Atkinson Hobson, a schoolmaster and part-time lecturer in Oxford and London. He thought that *lack of demand* was the key problem in business cycles, because people saved some of their income and this was then invested in new capacity. Perhaps wage earners didn't save that much, but the rich capitalists did, and this led to overinvestment.

The first time he explained this was in his book *The Physiology of Industry* from 1889, but he continued to elaborate in various publications until 1910. He also proposed a radical solution: tax companies heavily, or nationalize them and use the proceeds to raise demand.

None of this gained him friends in business or academia. Shortly after publication of his first book in 1889, he lost both of his university teaching posts, was constantly ridiculed in the *Economic Journal* and was essentially barred from the Political Economy Club. The poor man never regained any academic post, but he did become a pioneer in so-called underconsumption theory.

## DRAINING OF FREE CAPITAL

Just five years after Hobson's first book appeared, another with a somewhat different approach arrived on the scene. This was *The Industrial Crises in England* by Ukrainian economist Mikhail Tugan-Baranovsky, and it was based on the core assumptions that:

- There could be big time lags between when money was earned and spent, and . . .
- . . . there also could be a time lag between money being saved and invested

Tugan-Baranovsky would often compare the economy to a steam machine. Every day people would save up money, which he called "free capital," and this would accumulate like the steam in the boiler. As this steam built up over time, the pressure on the piston would grow, until eventually it moved up. The same with money; savers wanted a good return, and as time passed, they would lose patience and look for a higher yield. Free capital was thus invested in "fixed capital" (machines, factories, etc.). That process would generate income and wealth throughout the economy. However, at some point, there wouldn't be much free capital left (like when steam runs out in the steam machine), and as the build-up of fixed capital leveled off, the economy would go into reverse, leaving much of the new production capacity idle.

Tugan-Baranovsky was a Marxist at heart, but while his analysis took its basis in Marxist thinking, he just couldn't agree with Marx that the capitalist economies would drift towards a final collapse. They were just cyclical, he thought, and that gained him some enemies on the left.

## TECHNOLOGICAL INNOVATION AS TRIGGER

Another contributor to "the golden age" was Arthur Spiethoff, a German professor specializing in business cycles, agreed with Tugan-Baranovsky that the economy was cyclical, but who published two books in 1902 and 1903 where he argued sensibly that Tugan-Baranovsky's model missed an explanation of *why* the conversion of free capital to fixed capital should occur in waves. Why not just smoothly?

The answer, he claimed, was the development of new technologies. Technical innovation created new business opportunities, and it was the pursuit of these that brought the previously idle money to be released. Or, to use Wicksell's terminology, new technology raised the natural interest rate above the actual rate, and this triggered the investment boom. And then, as the new businesses evolved, the whole process stopped and went into reverse, as Tugan-Baranovsky had already described.

## PROBLEMS AHEAD

When Spiethof's books appeared, the economic environment was pleasant. So pleasant, in fact, that it might appear that business cycles had ceased to exist. Things were so calm that readers of newspapers in the US seemed more interested in local scandals and the sports pages than in any major economic events. Railroad tycoon Jay Gould was getting divorced, for instance, and his wife was demanding 250 000 dollars in annual support. What a wonderful scandal! People were also interested in the financial pages, though, because the prices of their stocks had been rising rapidly for years.

And for good reasons. The US economy had been growing rapidly since 1897, interrupted only by brief soft patches. American exports had almost doubled during the ten years to 1907, as had the money supply, and total assets in financial institutions had grown from 9.1 to 21 billion. Times were very good indeed, and it was no wonder that Teddy Roosevelt had reported in his message to Congress in December 1906 that: "We still continue to enjoy a literally unprecedented prosperity." However, students of business cycles could have some reason to be worried. Remember the big crash in 1816? And in 1826? And 1837? And the one in 1847? And in 1857?

And then again in 1866? Well, it had been about ten years between each. The timing had been less even after that, but perhaps that 10-year thing still had some merit? Now, the last recession had been in 1895, when England and Continental Europe had led the way with a crisis triggered by gold and mine stocks. So perhaps time was up again?

## Tight Money

Perhaps it was, because there was a little problem with money rates. Gold production had fallen behind economic growth during the last part of the 19th century, and money was now getting tight as everyone wanted to borrow and invest. Very tight, in fact. British money rates had increased from 4 to 6% in late 1906, and American call money rates fluctuated wildly – from 3% to no less than 30. Various railroad tycoons were beginning to feel the problem now; when they had tried to roll over debts during early 1907, they found it impossible to sell longer maturity bonds and had to resort to 1–3 year maturities. James J. Hill, who controlled the Great Northern Railway Company, warned that the American economy needed a steady flow of at least one billion dollars in new liquidity to avoid "commercial paralysis" – and he didn't see that happening.

The American bull market broke on March 13, as equities fell into a huge air pocket, with many blue chips giving up more than 25% before making a very modest rebound. This rebound was deceptive, though, because the shortage of liquidity was getting steadily worse, and prices of equities and commodities fell steadily over spring and summer. A recession commenced in May. These problems were not limited to America. The Japanese stock exchange took a huge dive in late April following a series of local defaults, and there were signs of fear in Europe as French and English buyers imported increasing amounts of gold from America, while dumping their shares. In August, the city of Boston tried to float a bond issue but could only find bidders for 200 000 out of the total four million dollar issue. And then, by October 1907, everything went from bad to ugly. Two reckless gamblers, Otto Heinze and Charles Morse, had acquired control of various small banks and trust companies, and they were illegally using their funds in an attempt to engineer a short squeeze on the United Copper Company. Their plan: buy a critical amount of shares and call options to force short sellers to cover their positions by buying up shares at ever-higher prices. Such a short squeeze in a weak market isn't easy to control, though, and it failed miserably. In October, the word spread about what had happened, and nervous clients of Heinze and Morse's companies started withdrawing funds. This triggered a chain reaction spreading to other banks and trust companies.

## A SAVIOR

There were panic calls for leadership, and this was offered four days after the run had started. The man who volunteered to take charge was 70 years old and had just caught a severe cold, but he was a formidable personality, and if anyone could stop the tide, it ought to be him. It was J.P. Morgan, the leader of a huge industrial and financial empire.

The work was cut out for him. Over the next days and weeks, Morgan was confronted with one disaster after another; and all requiring swift action. Sometimes the problems were particularly urgent. On October 23, the Lincoln Trust lost 14 million dollars in deposits within a few hours, and bulletins from the Trust Company of America came in during the day. At 1 pm, its cash holdings were 1 200 000 dollars. Twenty minutes later, they had fallen to 800 000 and at 2.15, they were just 180 000 – enough for only a few minutes. Morgan found a way. The following day the president of the stock exchange ran over to Morgan's office to tell him that there would be numerous failures unless someone lent money to the brokers. Morgan called a meeting with a number of bank presidents, and as it started, he asked the representatives from the exchange how much was needed? "25 million dollars," they said. And when? "Within 15 minutes." The banks complied and released 27 million dollars within 5 minutes. Morgan had again found a way.

He continued to lend money to the weakest institutions when he could, and encouraged others to do the same. At one point, when he couldn't find the cash needed anywhere, he devised a new kind of money: "scripts," which the issuers would promise to convert to real money when they could get some. He also managed to persuade the Treasury secretary to deposit 35 million dollars of government money by various banks, who immediately forwarded them to the Trust Company, which was on the brink. And then, on top of everything, the mayor of New York City showed up in his office on October 28 to announce that the city couldn't raise money to pay its obligations. Morgan's solution was to arrange for the clearing house to accept the city's bonds by paying with "scripts." The mayor turned his books over to Morgan, who was subsequently for a while the guardian of the city of New York.

Morgan's schemes worked in the end: the financial panic ended before the end of the year, with the Dow Jones stock market index reaching its bottom on October 21, down 39% from its peak in March. However, the

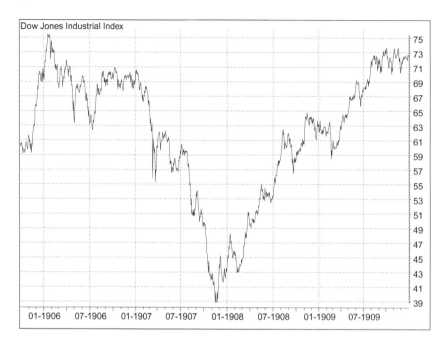

**Figure 7.1** The crash in 1907. The graph shows the performance of Dow Jones Industrials from 1906 to 1909.

recession that had started in 1907 continued into 1908, as companies couldn't find anyone to buy their products and unemployment tripled from 3 to 10%. The products were there, but demand just wasn't. People were hoarding money and neither Adam Smith's invisible hand, nor Say's Law seemed to work.

## THE ROLE OF INTEREST RATES

The American recession of 1907–8 was followed by one more in 1910–12 and again in 1913–14. There was no end in sight to business cycles, it seemed, and solutions were still sought. This was where Gustav Kassel, a Swedish professor, entered the scene. This economist wasn't the most popular figure in academia, since he had a bad habit of not crediting the people he borrowed from; his readers might, in fact, get the impression that this writer had invented just about every economic theory. It didn't help his popularity either that he entered into a long term rivalry with Knut Wicksell, who had many admirers. But Kassel did bring new thinking to the table, and he became best known for arguing that the interaction between savings, investment and interest rates could play an important role in business cycles:

- Let's say that that we are in a boom, perhaps because of new technology, as Spiethof would suggest
- Anyway, as the boom unfolds, we see Tugan-Baranovsky's "free capital" being converted to "fixed capital"
- So far, so clear. But in this phase, we see free capital being spent on investments faster than people can replace it with new free capital: savings fall behind
- And here comes the key point: the shortage of savings increases interest rates
- Higher interest rates change many business calculations. What might have looked profitable before is suddenly generating a loss because of the rising financial costs
- And so, abruptly, entrepreneurs stop investing and the economy goes into a tailspin

So, according to Kassel, *high interest rates* were often the key triggers of recessions.

### INCOME IN CAPACITY-BUILDING SECTORS

Two American economists had another take on the matter. Waddill Catchings and William Foster were both graduates from Harvard, after which Catchings had become a banker and Foster a university administrator. Catchings had been displeased with the economics lessons at Harvard, since he thought there was too much focus on the very long term and too little on short-term fluctuations. So, he dreamed of producing and supporting research into the latter. However, he just wanted to, well, get rich first.

By the time he reached 40 years of age, he was indeed quite rich, so he decided to live his dream. He quit his job and founded the Pollak Foundation for Economic Research. And then he joined forces with Foster to write several books. First came *Money*, which was published in 1923, and then *Profits* (1925) and *Business without a Buyer* (1927). Their central claim was that modern economies had a systemic tendency to drift towards underconsumption because of the following events:

- A part of an expansion is investment projects to build new machines, factories, etc. Those employed to create this new capacity are paid their salary and spend that money as long as the construction goes on
- However, once the planned new capacity has been built, these people are no longer needed and lose their jobs
- That timing is unfortunate, because the new production capacity produces a lot of new products just as the people who created them have lost their jobs. Demand can't match the new supply

They elaborated in their pamphlet *Road to Plenty*:

> To enable people to buy the product of our present facilities, we have to build new ones; and then, in order that people can buy the output of the new ones, we have to build more new ones.

So, actually, in order to avoid underconsumption, it was necessary to expand production capacity at a constantly accelerating rate, and this was obviously not realistic. So they proposed that the Federal Reserve should seek to maintain a constant annual growth in money supply of 4%, and that the government should establish a board, which should follow the economy carefully and initiate public spending and investment programs whenever the economy showed signs of underconsumption. A passive monetary policy, in other words, but an active fiscal policy.

Catchings and Foster had a good grasp of the practical realities of business (or at least Catchings did) and they expressed themselves in clear and simple ways. They were also clever at marketing their ideas: one day they offered 5000 dollars for the best negative critique of their book *Profits*. They received responses from no less than 435 people, including many from the academic community. The two authors responded that while much in what they received had merit, there was nothing in any of it that ultimately refuted their basic postulates.

## PIGOU: CYCLES DRIVEN BY PSYCHOLOGY

The business cycle theories of Hobson, Tugan-Baranovsky, Spiethof, Catchings and Foster had one thing in common: they were fairly mechanical. They didn't leave much room for irrational behavior. Mill's approach had been different, as he had emphasized human emotion. He had, for instance, spoken about how people became compelled to buy more when prices rose.

So did Arthur Cecil Pigou. Pigou was born on The Isle of Wight in 1877, the son of a retired army officer. He managed to obtain a scholarship at a prestigious public school, and after that at Cambridge University, which he entered in 1896 (aged 19). He was a talented student, and the university offered him a chair after his graduation. Pigou became a good teacher – rather brilliant, in fact – and he was highly productive. The young man published no fewer than three books during his first five years in the job. His main source of inspiration was Marshall, who held a chair in Economics at the same university, and he would often say to his students that "it is all in Marshall." However, Marshall was getting old by then and announced his retirement in 1908. This was Pigou's chance: he knew that he was still rather young and unproven, but perhaps he could take over the chair? His dreams were fulfilled: at the age of 30 he had taken over the prestigious job from the grand master!

He continued to write, and while his first three books in all honesty weren't terribly exciting, many of those that followed were. One of the best was *Industrial Fluctuations*, which came out in 1927. Here, he linked business cycles to shocks caused by real factors, as well as to psychological and autonomous economic factors. He argued that errors of optimism create subsequent errors of pessimism, and he pointed out that bankruptcies rarely destroy capital (capital equipment is merely taken over by new players when a company goes down), but that they create *fear*, and that this was the important effect. Capital changed hands in a mechanical process, but the willingness to invest in new capital was emotional and fell when people saw bankruptcies.

He did not believe fully in the notion that an invisible hand would restore a balance in a distressed economy. One reason was the way prices changed over business cycles and wreaked havoc on business plans. Another problem occurred if prices were kept too rigid when businessmen tried to maintain things as originally planned. This rigidity could prevent markets from clearing (preventing trade from taking place in a smooth manner). Pigou tried to estimate quantitatively the significant factors causing business cycles, including this price rigidity. Here is how much he thought that each factor contributed to the overall cycle:

Crop variations: one-half
Wage rigidity: one-eighth
Price rigidity: one-sixteenth

He proposed various measures that could restore balance in the markets when needed. The three most important ones were to provide better economic statistics, to stabilize prices and to pursue an active monetary policy.

One of the people that Pigou met at Cambridge University was another talented economist by the name of John Maynard Keynes. What Pigou couldn't know was that this colleague of his would later misrepresent what Pigou had advocated, then ridicule it, and at the same time use some of his best ideas. Keynes would, for instance, create the impression that Pigou suggested that salary reductions should be used as a leading remedy for depression, and that Pigou ignored the role of expectations in creating unemployment. This was in fact not true. Furthermore, Pigou had described a number of concepts that Keynes later launched in his own name. But he did it utterly brilliantly, as we shall see later.

## CAPITAL INVESTMENTS

One of the single most important discoveries in business cycle theory is the concept of *acceleration*. It appeared first in an article by the American economist John M. Clark in 1917: *Business acceleration and the law of demand* was its title. It described how investment spending could become unstable because companies that need to expand capacity would order capital equipment. This would in itself increase demand and thereby induce them to order even more capital equipment. Once the acceleration process leveled off, it would lead automatically to a slump.

Clark was great, as were Marshall, Pigou and the other economists we just met. But none of them was considered the leader of the field. No, the real guru of the age was Dennis Robertson. Robertson was born in 1890 in Lowestoft and had gone to Eton at the age of 12 and from there to Trinity College at Cambridge to study classics. He had been absolutely brilliant in these studies but had nevertheless decided to switch to economics after a while. He published his first book, *A Study of Industrial Fluctuations* in 1915 and followed up with *Money* in 1922 and *Banking Policy and the Price Level* in 1926. His first book was a major contribution to business cycle literature. One of its main suggestions was that the chief cause of economic instability was changes in the *demand for capital goods*. He described the following scenario:

- Capital investments increased because of the need for replacement or because of innovations . . .
- The new capital would then lead to increased return on investments . . .

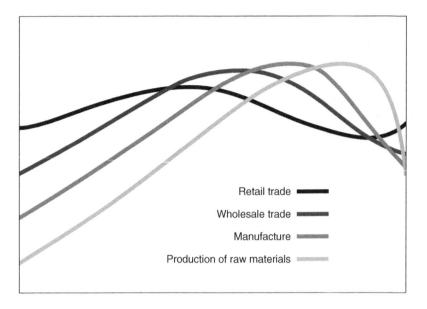

**Figure 7.2**  The acceleration principle. Due to the acceleration principle, a small amplitude in retail sales leads to larger amplitudes in wholesale, manufactured goods and raw materials.

- Meanwhile, the quantity and circulation (velocity) of money grew, leading to price rises that appeared attractive for businesses, but which couldn't last
- Interest rates rose too, but only with a lag, and thus not fast enough to give full warning to the business community
- The result would be a cumulative expansion that was much larger than the initial impulse
- The expansion stopped when interest rates caught up and prices started falling – both factors that were bad for business

To Robertson, it was typically changes in Wicksell's natural rate, caused by innovations and waves of replacement reinvestments, that led to insta-bility. He regarded the economy as basically unstable, with fluctuations that were amplified (but not caused) by changes in money supply and velocity of money. He was considered the leading authority on the subject of business cycles for half a century, and for good reasons. Capital invest-ments, real rates, prices, money supply and interest rates are still viewed as essential today.

## Overinvestment and Underconsumption

What authors such as Cantillon, Say and Wicksell described were not really what could be called "business cycle theories," because they missed a full cyclical process. But Marshall, Hobson, Tugan-Baranovsky, Spiethoff, Kassel, Catchings, Foster, Pigou, Clark and Robertson's models went much further – some went all the way. All of these ten economists from the golden age described reasons why Say's Law and Smith's invisible hand didn't work in the short term, and why this could create cyclical fluctuations, where supply fell short in the boom (perhaps leading to inflation) and demand fell short in the recession (leading to unemployment).

It is difficult to say that some of them specifically blamed the supply side and others the demand side in their diagnosis, but when it came to remedies, there were three that stood out: Hobson, Catchings and Foster. It was these three among the ten that suggested intervening on the demand side, and they have thus since been classified as belonging to the "underconsumption" school.

The other seven are then classified under the "overinvestment" school. It is interesting to note, however, that although the models of all ten economists emphasized different aspects, you could, by and large, superimpose them over each other to get a more complex system that was fairly coherent. It is, in fact, often so: when you listen to the economic debate, you may get the impression that economists disagree more than they really do.

The overinvestment and underconsumption schools were important, but they were only two of a larger number that would appear. A third one, the "monetary" school, was pioneered by a gentleman working at the very place where a lot of money comes from: the City of London and the English Treasury. Hawtrey was the name. Ralph George Hawtrey.

## Hawtrey: A Monetary View

Hawtrey joined the Treasury in 1904 and published his first book about money and the business cycle in 1913. *Good and Bad Trade*, as it was called, essentially attributed business cycles to fluctuations in *money supply*. The frequent business cycles could, according to Hawtrey, evolve in two different ways:

- *External shocks*. Some outside impulse could create a chain reaction of ripples as its effect spread from one sector to the next. However, these fluctuations would be dampened and thus disappear some time after the initial shock had ended. This is what since has been called a "real business cycle"

- *Inherent monetary instability.* Hawtrey believed that the monetary system was inherently unstable, because it was very unlikely that central bankers would manage to keep real interest rates tagged to Wicksell's obscure and ever-changing natural rate (or what Hawtrey called "profit rate") for more than brief periods

His explanation of monetary instability was largely related to the role of bank reserves. Financial regulation required any bank to have financial reserves in a given proportion to its total balance. Economic booms created confidence and increased investment activities, which meant that banks tended to lend out more aggressively. However, at a certain stage, they would reach a point where they were close to their lending ceiling. When they reached that stage, they would begin to increase interest rates so that they would attract more deposits and reduce the lending activity. This would eventually force industry to decrease stocks and production. However, it would take some time for them to adjust to the new situation, and the banks would thus continue to increase rates for some time. This meant that bank rates would drift further and further above the lower rates that would have created stability.

One of the situations that Hawtrey was most concerned about was what he called a "credit deadlock." This could occur when the reduction of interest rates didn't seem to stimulate any lending. Such a situation could arise when an excessively restrictive credit policy had killed enterprise. "You can lead the horse to the water," as they say, "but you can't make him drink." The only thing to do in such a situation was to stimulate money supply through any means.

Hawtrey was very highly regarded as a leading capacity on business cycles and monetary policy during the 1920s, but he had one problem in common with our other ten thinkers: there comes a point where you should stop spending time thinking about how things might work and just go and look at what actually seems to happen. Business cycle theory was, to be honest, a bit long on theory and short of hard facts.

---

SOME NEW IDEAS IN THE "GOLDEN ACE"

*About prices and psychology*

- Rising prices attract speculators, who drive prices further up (Marshall)

- Everyone wants to sell when prices fall (Marshall)
- Psychology and price instability play major roles (Pigou)

*About spending, savings and investment*

- Capitalists benefit most from expansions, but they also save most. Because of this saving, what is left for spending is not enough to absorb the production from the new capacity (Hobson)

*About capacity building*

- An expansion happens when free capital is converted to fixed capital (production capacity). It stops because there is no more free capital (Tugan-Baranovsky)
- The trigger for the expansion is new technological innovation, which increases profit potentials (Spiethoff)
- When a capacity building boom peaks, a lot of people who have created it are fired. This diminishes the demands that the capacity was supposed to meet (Catchings and Foster)
- The capacity-building industry orders for itself, which creates temporary spikes in demand during a period of capacity building (Clark)

*About interest rates and money*

- The economy is only in balance when the interest rates equal the average profit opportunity on new investments. If actual interest falls below that, then the economy expands. And vice versa (Wicksell)
- The drain of free capital during expansions drives interest rates up. Higher interest rates make investments less profitable than entrepreneurs had expected, so they stop investing (Kassel)
- A boom creates deceptive pricing power (which gives businesses confidence), while interest rates (which could give warning to business) are too slow to catch up (Robertson)
- Banks reach their lending limit late in the boom. This forces them to raise interest rates. Long planning periods in businesses force them to seek credit late in the cycle, and interest will thus stay too high for too long. Also, businesses may not take advantage of low rates during recessions, because they are too weak and scared (Hawtrey)

*Chapter* **8**

# The Archeologists

> For well over a century, business cycles have run an unceasing round.
> They have persisted through vast economic and social changes;
> they have withstood countless experiments in industry, agriculture,
> banking, industrial relations, and public policy; they have con-
> founded forecasters without number, belied repeated prophecies of
> a "new era of prosperity" and outlived repeated forebodings of
> "chronic depression."

> *Arthur F. Burns*

Exactly what the facts were was what interested the American economist
Wesley Mitchell the most. Mitchell studied the newly discovered business
cycle phenomenon as an archeologist would study the layers in a kitchen
mitten: he measured them, noted down every detail he could find, and
looked for clues, traces and patterns. According to his friend Schumpeter,
Mitchell read a lot and was quite familiar with the various theories about
what could drive the cycles, but his primary concern was not so much
making theories as it was of *mapping* them. "If you don't know how they
behave, . . ." he seemed to think, ". . . how can you know what there is to
explain?" In 1913, he published his first book about the subject, *Business
Cycles*. It started with a short description of the prevailing business cycle
theories. He did that, as Schumpeter later described it, with "surprising
detachment," almost as if he believed that any one of the theories might
be as good as every other. Mitchell defined business cycles in the following way:

> Business cycles are a type of fluctuation found in the aggregate economic
> activity of nations that organise their work mainly in business enter-
> prises: a cycle consists of expansions occurring about the same time in
> many economic activities, followed by similar general recessions, con-
> tractions, and revivals which merge into the expansion phase of the next

cycle; this sequence of changes is recurrent but not periodic; in duration, business cycles vary from more than one year to ten or twelve years; they are not divisible into shorter cycles of similar character with amplitudes approximating their own.

This definition contained two points of special importance. The first was that oscillations are in aggregates. Whatever drove the cycle, it seemed to influence the economy on a very broad scale. The second point was that cycles are not periodic. He repeated this important observation over and over again, fearing that people would exaggerate the regularity of the swings.

## FORECASTING TOOLS

Mitchell cofounded, in 1920, an institution for international business cycle research – the National Bureau of Economic Research, or "NBER," in New York. Here, he came to work closely with Arthur Burns, who later became Director of Research of the institute, its president and, after Mitchell's death, its chairman. Mitchell was often criticized for his "naive empiricism," but, as years passed, people gained more and more respect for his team, and eventually NBER became an internationally respected center for business cycle research (which it still is).

The scientists at NBER soon discovered that many economic and financial indicators could be grouped as "leading" the cycles, others as "coincident" with them, and still others as "lagging." A leading indicator, for instance, would tend to rise somewhat before general activity picked up – and fall somewhat before activity leveled off. These indicators stood the test of time: they remained reliable after they had been established, and they were reliable for other economies when tested there.

The Americans were not the only ones trying to map the cycles. In 1923, the German scientist Joseph Kitchin published an article with analysis of English and American data covering 31 years. Kitchin found a cycle in them, but there was something funny about it: its wavelength was different from Juglar's – very different, in fact. Kitchin found an average duration of 40 months – little over 3 years – for the cycles: less than half of what Juglar had observed. Kitchin did not discuss this difference in his presentation, but the results were important. One possible explanation was that the behavior of the economy had changed. Another was more dramatic: maybe there were several cyclical phenomena in action . . .

And this was where Simon Kuznets entered the story. If Mitchell collected many figures, Kuznets seemed to collect even more. He was a pupil of Mitchell and did much of his work under the auspices of NBER, where he published brick-sized books containing hundreds of tables and graphs covering somewhat dry subjects such as *Number of patents issued for typewriters in the United States,* or *Tonnage of Freight Moved on the Eire Canal.* It seemed that no stone was left unchanged.

One of his major works was the measurement of national income. Such availability of a figure is almost taken for granted these days, but to calculate it for the first time was something of a nightmare. Kuznets found a way, however, and without these figures, many theories developed in the following years would have been impossible to verify. But having developed a method to calculate national income, he turned to its oscillations. There, he found a cycle, and he was able to substantiate its presence with much more thorough research than Juglar or Kitchin had used. But the funny thing happened once again: Kuznets's cycle had a wavelength of neither Kitchin's 40 months, nor Juglar's 10 years. His cycle had an average duration of some 20 years. Very strange!

Or perhaps not so strange after all. The numbers of cycles one will detect in a somewhat messy time series depend on how the filters are defined. It seems that all the three economists were right, but that their cycles were dominated by different phenomena. Kitchin's was an inventory cycle, Juglar's related to Dennis Robertson's capital investments. And Kuznets? Well, shortly after he published his description of 20-year cycles, some interesting data emerged from a gentleman called Homer Hoyt. It was about property prices fluctuating in cycles that had averaged 18 years (much more about that in Chapter 23).

When the staff at the NBER investigated the different time series, they found that there had been clear Kuznets and Juglar cycles before 1885, but that shorter fluctuations had showed such large variability that they didn't really seem like cycles – more likely just reactions to random shocks. However, after 1885, their variance declined significantly, and the Kitchin cycle was born.

## GIANTS AS WELL?

Just as an ant crossing your shoes is hardly aware that it is walking on somebody else, so can human beings be part of something that they do not see because of its size. It was in 1910 that an 18-year-old student in

Russia thought he had found such a phenomenon. Nikolai Kondratieff had studied the behavior of the capitalist economy and believed he saw an oscillation in the economy of extremely low frequency – with a wavelength of more than 50 years. Nine years later, he began a scientific study of the phenomenon. In 1924, he completed an 80-page report, in which he concluded that the capitalist economy had gone through two "long waves" with an average duration of 53.3 – years and was well into the third. In 1926, he published his results in the German *Archiv fur Sozialwissenshaft*, in which he concluded:

> . . . the movements of the series which we have examined running from the end of the eighteenth century to the present time show long cycles. Although the statistical-mathematical treatment of the series selected is rather complicated, the cycles discovered cannot be regarded as the accidental result of the methods employed.

He had examined a number of time series, of which many conformed to the cycle theory, some did not, and one was counter cyclical. The first cycle had started, you might say, on the hillsides in Adam Smith's Scotland. This giant cycle was fostered by the innovations of the Industrial Revolution; by the steam engines, waterframes and power looms. The second came out of the railroad boom, which started in 1843 and ended with Jay Gould's bear-raids in 1887. The third was ignited by the construction of electrical power plants, and later reinforced by the automobile, steel, glass, road, and textile industries. It started in 1893 and was supposedly nearing its culmination when Kondratieff printed his article in 1926.

Kondratieff explained the oscillations with overinvestment in capital, which would lead to a glut, then a recession, until the invention of new technology eventually led to a new spurt of investment. However, the invention of new technology was not the sole driving force of the upswing; it was merely the trigger:

> If we are to form an idea as to the quantitative adequacy of innovation, we must bear in mind that all it should, according to our schema, be adequate for, is ignition.

The conditions for such an ignition to lead to a take-off were, he said, the following:

- A high propensity to save
- A relatively large supply of liquid loan capital at low rates

- Accumulation of these funds in the hands of powerful entrepreneurial and financial groups
- A low price level

Kondratieff's theory was received with reservations by the economists at NBER. It was, in fact, possible to explain theoretically how Clark's acceleration principle, or "self ordering" in the capital sector (that the capital sector depends on its own output to expand its production capacity), could lead to such an oscillation, but the critics were hardly being unreasonable when they claimed that two cycles and the alleged fraction of a third was very meager evidence for a theory.

## NOBEL PRIZE AND LABOR CAMP

Juglar discovered the continent and Mitchell, Burns, Kitchin, Kuznets and Kondratieff did much of the pioneer work of mapping it. Mitchell became honored and respected for his books and for the institution he built; Juglar, Kitchin, Kuznets and Kondratieff all had their cycles named after them, and three of these cycles, Juglar's, Kitchin's and Kuznets's, are today regarded as proven facts by most economists. Burns was appointed Chairman of the Board of Governors of the Federal Reserve System in 1969 and Kuznets was given the Nobel Prize in 1971.

But Kondratieff was less fortunate. He had been considered suspicious by the communists after he opposed elements of the Soviet 5-year plans. The conflict reached a critical stage when he wrote a rather unfortunate remark:

> . . . each consecutive phase is the result of the cumulative process during the preceding phase, and as long as the principles of the capitalist economy are conserved, each new cycle follows its predecessor with the same regularity with which the different phases succeed each other.

You could easily interpret this as a suggestion that capitalism would stay alive. This was in contrast to what Karl Marx had written in his *Das Kapital* from 1867–94, which, as we will recall, predicted that each new crisis would become more severe until eventually the system would collapse altogether, paving the way for a communist takeover. Nikolai Kondratieff was sent to a working camp in Siberia, where he stayed until his death. His theory was later described in the Soviet encyclopedia as follows:

> Theory of long cycles, one of the vulgar bourgeois theories of crises and economic cycles . . .

# Chapter 9

# Fisher and Babson

The first panacea for a mismanaged nation is inflation of the currency; the second is war. Both bring a temporary prosperity; both bring permanent ruin.

*Ernest Hemingway*

It was in 1898 that Irving Fisher, a promising American economist left a meeting with his doctor in a state of shock. He was only 31 years old, healthy and strong to this date, a talented mathematician educated at Yale, happily married, and at the beginning of what looked like a promising career. And now the doctor had told him that he suffered from tuberculosis, a diagnosis that was virtually identical to a death sentence. Was Irving Fisher's life going to end before it had really begun?

No! Fisher took up the battle and commenced on the only known treatment: fresh air and healthy living. He moved to Colorado, where many patients were seeking a cure for the same disease. Among these people was an interesting individual: the 22-year-old engineer Roger Ward Babson. Fisher and Babson soon realized that they had much in common, apart from tuberculosis. Both were fascinated by economics, and especially by the business cycle problem and the role of the monetary sector. They were both absorbed with the stock market and its calamities. And they were both creative characters, with an urge to advise people about all kinds of problems. It was symptomatic that they also both created an invention to facilitate the treatment of their common disease. Fisher designed a small tent for tuberculosis patients, for which he was later given a reward by the New York Medical Society. Babson's invention was an electrically heated coat and some small rubber hammers for typing with mittens on in very cold weather.

**Figure 9.1** Roger Ward Babson. "The Seer from Wellesley Hills" graduated as an engineer in 1898, but soon went into stockbroking. Courtesy of Babson College Archives.

## AN UNUSUAL OFFICE

After a while, Babson became tired of living among ill people and decided to move back to his former rental house in Wellesley Hills, Massachusetts, where he hired a secretary and set up an open-window office, where he would analyze business cycles and their consequences for the stock market. In 1909 he published his first version of a book about business cycles, *Business Barometers used in the Accumulation of Money*. It contained a thorough analysis of historical crises, and his main thesis was that excessive investment and increase of the money supply would always lead to a counter reaction. The purpose of the book was, as the title hinted, to advise stock market speculators. In this advice, he laid great emphasis on his standard ten-phase business cycle model:

1. Increasing money rates
2. Declining bond prices
3. Declining stock prices
4. Declining commodity prices
5. Declining real estate prices
6. Low money rates

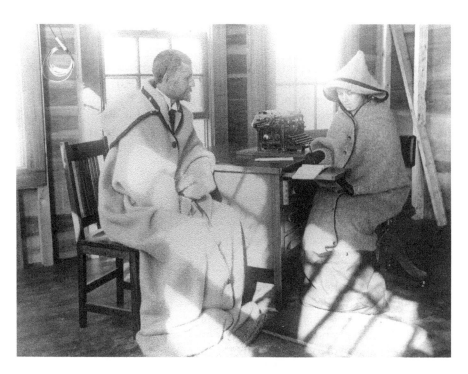

**Figure 9.2** Babson and secretary. As Babson developed tuberculosis, he set up an office with all the windows permanently open and founded his "Babson Statistical Office." In the fresh, cold air, Babson wore a coat with an electrically heated pad in the back, and his secretary, wearing mittens, used small rubber hammers to hit the typewriter keys. His company became very successful, and many stock-traders subscribed to his forecasting service. Courtesy of Babson College Archives.

7. Increasing bond prices
8. Increasing stock prices
9. Increasing commodity prices
10. Increasing real estate prices

Babson's book became an immediate best-seller, and it supported his sales of various investment newsletters. These newsletters were based on his business cycle model, the "swing-charts," which measured a number of economic indicators. His method was, in essence, quite simple: he estimated the long-term growth trend and calculated accumulated deviations around this. Every deviation in one direction would be compensated by a deviation of similar magnitude in the opposite direction. To him, business cycle analysis became a considerable source of income.

## IRVING FISHER'S EARLY WORK

Almost miraculously, Irving Fisher also recovered gradually from the disease, and he was declared completely cured in 1901. Fisher chose a more academic career than Babson. During the first years of his illness, he had still considered himself a mathematician, and it was not until the year 1911, when he was searching for a subject for a doctoral thesis, that his favorite professor, William Sumner, asked him:

"Why don't you write on mathematical economics?"

Fisher answered:

"I have never heard of such a subject."

Sumner explained the techniques Walras and Pareto had developed in Lausanne, and Fisher decided to go ahead. In 1911, the year after Babson had published his *Business Barometers*, Fisher published a book entitled *The Purchasing Power of Money*. His main theme was the destabilizing effects of inflation and fluctuations in money supply. The book contained a popularization of our astronomer and master-mathematician Simon Newcomb's equation from 1885:

$$MV = PQ$$

where we will recall that $M$ = money supply, $V$ = velocity of money, $P$ = prices of goods and $Q$ = quantity of goods. Newcomb's equation was not widely used before Fisher explained its significance (and gave it the name "The Quantity Theory of Money"). Fisher's monetary business cycle theory stated that increase in the money supply would first lead to a fall in real (inflation-adjusted) interest rates, stimulating growth in the quantity of goods produced (which is nice), and later to a rise in inflation and then in real interest rates (which is unpleasant). A large growth in the money supply would, in other words, first have positive effects, but then some nasty ones. It should be mentioned that Thornton also had hinted at these relationships.

One of the basic conceptions which preceded theories such as Fisher's was a new understanding of what banks really did. Until the end of the 19th century, most economists had tended to view banks as merely traders in money. They would receive deposits and lend to somebody else; money would simply change hands. But now the economists realized that behind the walls of these respectable institutions, something else happened; something vitally important that was largely beyond the control of governments or central banks. The banks did not only trade money; they *created* it by stimulating its velocity. Keeping this in mind, one of the key elements of Fisher's business cycle theory could be expressed largely as follows:

- The key to business cycles is bank credit, as it is the banks that create money in a modern economy
- During the beginning of a growth period, sellers see their stock of inventories diminish, so they order more
- This leads to a general increase of production, which, according to Say's Law, stimulates demand further . . .
- . . . and this means that, in spite of increased orders, inventories don't rise, so, for a time, the merchants keep ordering still more
- As producers have trouble filling this increased demand, deliveries may even be rationed, encouraging sellers to order more than they really want
- During all this time, the quantity of money expands as banks supply credit for the increased business activity. The initial effect of this expansion of money supply is a fall in the discount rate, which leads to a further rise in activity
- As some of the banks increase their lending, it increases the reserves at other banks (asset prices go up; people deposit more money), stimulating a tendency for them to increase lending too. At the same time, velocity of money accelerates as business starts to use idle reserves
- But Say's Law is not a perpetual mobile. Some of the additional income generated by increased supply is saved up. At this point, sellers will finally see their inventories up at normal levels and will reduce orders accordingly . . .
- . . . which means that now they can start paying back their debts to the bank. As they do that, money supply starts to shrink in a cumulative process which eventually leads to a slump
- As money supply shrinks, the prices of assets such as real estate, etc., but also inventories, start falling, and as the liquidation of debts can't keep up with the fall in prices, liquidation defeats itself
- This means that the collective effort of individuals to reduce their debts actually increases its burden, because the mass effect of the stampede to liquidate is swelling the purchasing power of each dollar owed

So the monetary system was unstable, as he expressed it:

The more debtors pay, the more they owe. The more the economic boat tips, the more it tends to tip.

If you would stabilize the economy (expressed as $Q$), he thought, then you should first and foremost focus on stabilizing prices ($P$):

> ... it is always economically possible to stop or prevent such a depression simply by reflating the price level up to the average level at which outstanding debts were contracted, and then maintain that level unchanged.

In 1920 he published *Stabilizing the Dollar*, and asked the publisher to insert a postcard in each copy with a request that the reader return it in case he was interested in the formation of an organization devoted to stabilization of prices and money supply. On New Year's Eve the same year, he held a dinner for 254 people (Irving Fisher had style), where he could announce that he had names of about 1000 people interested in the project. The decision to form the "Stable Money League" was subsequently made. Stabilization of prices could obviously be achieved through various methods, e.g. by making money convertible to metal (David Ricardo's philosophy), or stabilizing the quantity of money via central bank operations (Henry Thornton's philosophy). Another and less conventional method, which some of the League members preferred, was the "Compensated Dollar Plan," a system where the dollar should be revalued by 1% every time prices had risen 1%, and devalued by 1% whenever prices had fallen by 1%.

---

### HOW PRIVATE BANKS CREATE MONEY

Imagine that Fisher had inherited 100 000 dollars, which he then deposited in his local bank. (He hadn't but had married quite a rich girl). Depositing the money in the bank would surely not change his perception of how much money he had. But what would the bank do? If banking regulations required that banks kept 10% in reserve, they would rush to lend 90 000 dollars to another person, so they could collect maximum interest. Whoever borrowed this amount would surely have a purpose, and would spend the money on something – giving the money to somebody else. Now this "somebody else" would receive the money and place it in his bank – which would again lend out 90% (81 000 dollar) to a customer. And so on until the 100 000 deposited had grown to 1 000 000 dollars. In other words: when Fisher's bank received 100 000 dollars, this would enable the banking system to create 900 000 dollars of credit! And credit and money were the same, because both enabled people to spend. So money supply is largely in the hands of the private bankers, not only the central banks.

## GERMAN HYPERINFLATION

Fisher's next book came out in 1922. It was long, boring and entitled *The Making of Index Numbers*, which to his own great surprise became a best-seller. And then he left for Europe to lecture on "Business Depressions and Instability of Money" at the London School of Economics, and incidentally to study some very strange developments taking place in the German economy. A year before the First World War, four German marks were required to buy one dollar on the foreign exchange. But just before the hostilities broke out, a lot of Germans rushed to change their marks to gold, and the country had to abandon its gold standard. The war lasted far longer and was far more expensive than expected. In order to finance it, the government started issuing T-bills like never before, and all for nothing; Germany suffered a humiliating defeat in 1918 and was saddled with horrendous war reparations. The mark had fallen 50% relative to the dollar during the war, and the fall accelerated afterwards – as Thornton would have predicted. At first the fall was moderate, but then it accelerated until it eventually grew into an uncontrolled selling spree. In February 1920, the exchange rate reached 100 marks to the dollar – 25 times the pre-war rate. But it continued on and on as the money supply kept growing. To those who had saved up money, the inflation was of course a disaster. But in many ways, there was something quite nice about accelerating inflation: unemployment fell sharply, reaching less than 1% in the spring of 1922, and disappearing almost completely during the summer.

All that money seemed to breed a lot of activity, but as Fisher and his colleague, Professor Roman, found, it was activity based on a total illusion. To Fisher and Roman, everything was very cheap in Germany thanks to the low price of the mark vis-à-vis dollars, but to the Germans, everything seemed incredibly expensive. The two professors asked two female shop owners about the high prices, their answer was the blockade by the allies, wage increases enforced by the unions, freight rates and inefficient government. But when Fisher asked them if it could be because the government was simply printing too much money, the idea had seemed alien to the women. He concluded that the Germans thought of commodities and the American gold dollar as rising, while the mark was all the time the same mark. He called this absurd tendency to have faith in your own currency irrespective of its quantity "the Money Illusion."

## WHY INDEED . . .

The mark continued its free fall, however, and in the spring of 1923, a parliamentary committee was asked to investigate why the exchange rate had fallen from 18 000 marks to 30 000 during the first month of the year. When the committee held its first meeting in the middle of June, the problem had to be rephrased, however. Now it was why the exchange rate had fallen to 152 000 marks. In July, the question had changed again:

> Why is it that the exchange rate has changed from 18 000 to 1 000 000 marks for a dollar during little over six months?

Could it possibly be, by any chance, because the government was financing only 3% of its expenditure through taxes, etc., and 97% through issuing T-bills?

It was during 1923 that the price of eggs reached a level 500 million times as high as when the war stopped in 1918. It was also in that year that it became common for employees to demand salary payments twice daily. When they were paid, a truck would often come to the factory loaded with bills. The cashier would climb to the top of the pile, read out the employees' names, and throw down bundles of bills to each as he responded. The employees would then rush out to buy anything they could think of – like a newspaper for 200 000 000 000 marks, or a cup of coffee for . . . well, did it really matter? At this stage it wasn't fun any more. Unemployment came back, and there were riots in the streets. Fisher's nasty effect was showing its ugly face. He left Europe and went home to continue his work, and also to write a book about world peace.

He was prospering during these years, as he began to receive a large income from an index machine he had invented, and because his shares in the Remington Rand Corporation soared. As his personal wealth reached several million dollars, he bought a chauffeur-driven Lincoln in 1925, a luxury rather unusual for a university professor.

Fisher decided to return to Europe in 1928, partly because he wanted to meet Benito Mussolini, to whom he wanted to give some advice. At this time, Fisher was known as the most famous American economist, and also for his frequent advice to stock traders.

## A STRANGE MEETING

Mussolini wasn't a pretty man. He was bald, with a fattish face and two front teeth far apart. But he radiated an aggressive energy that would impress many visitors. And if this wasn't enough to generate respect, then it might help to consider that the wall carpet behind him was generally assumed to cover a row of soldiers armed with machine-guns. During the day of Fisher's appointment, Mussolini had received several delegations. There had been a large group of students, a team of athletes and about 100 very young cadets. But shortly after 5:30 pm, it was Professor Fisher who entered the room. Mussolini opened the conversation with the following question:

"Is this Professor Fisher?"

Fisher answered:

"Yes, is this Mr Mussolini?"

Mussolini was apparently baffled by this question, so his next sentence became total nonsense:

"Yes. Do you not speak English?"

After this odd exchange of words, Fisher started to lead the conversation on track, however:

"You are one of the few great men in the world who are interested in the subject of inflation and deflation, unstable money and stabilization."

"Ah! Stabilization! And you have made a special study of this?"

"Yes, for twenty years. I wrote you in April for this appointment. Meanwhile you have already done one thing I wanted to suggest – stop your deflation. I think that was wise. I am glad you have stopped. But there are other suggestions I would like to make . . ."

Fisher gave various recommendations for the Italian economy and delivered a written analysis of the country's situation. That Mussolini some years later should choose to declare war against Fisher's country must have seemed completely grotesque to Fisher, if he could have known it.

Shortly after this strange meeting, Fisher embarked on a boat heading for New York. As he returned, he found his secretary on the dock, who told him that a brief slump in the stock market had required her to use the full hundred thousand dollars in her agent's account to reduce bank loans. This was the very first warning of events that would later change Irving Fisher's life . . .

# Chapter 10

# Keynes and the Austrians

> A monetary system is like some internal organ: it should not be
> allowed to take up very much of one's thoughts when it goes right,
> but it needs a great deal of attention when it goes wrong.
>
> *D.H. Robertson*

There is a difference between making a mistake and repeating it. The
Austrian economist, Ludwig von Mises could understand why the Duke
of Orleans had made mistakes, but it was a wonder to him why people
never learned anything from the past. When there had been so many
recessions, why didn't governments or central bankers identify once and
for all the basic errors and prevent them from happening again? Actually,
he had his own explanation: politicians and bankers were simply led to
temptation.

## INVISIBLE INFLATION

Von Mises's explanation of the recurrence of the cycles was that politicians and central bankers tended to cut interest rates below Wicksell's
"natural rate" during periods of recovery, where the banks had ample
liquidity and wanted to expand their own business. This meant that time
after time they allowed the development of overinvestment, which eventually led to credit squeeze and then to crisis.

Von Mises believed that Wicksell had missed an important point,
however. Von Mises thought that injection of liquidity into the economy
would first lead to inflation in the *capital industry*, where the initial expansion took place, while consumer prices might still fall. Later on the process
could reverse, so that prices of *consumer goods* would rise while those of

capital goods would fall. So it was quite possible that real rates could be below natural rates without this causing generally visible inflation before it was too late to react. He thought, in words, that Wicksell's and Fisher's theories were too simple.

During the 1920s, von Mises felt that exactly this phenomenon was taking place. While Irving Fisher said the expansion of the 1920s was sustainable because it entailed no consumer price inflation, von Mises said the economy would break down because of the dramatic credit expansion – or credit inflation. The left side of Newcomb's equation had gone berserk and was due for a correction due to inherent instability in the monetary system. When the correction came, it would hurt the right side. Or, as he put it:

> There is no means of avoiding the final collapse of a boom brought about by credit expansion. The alternative is only whether the crisis should come sooner as the result of a voluntary abandonment of further credit expansion or later as a final and total catastrophe of the currency involved.

Every Wednesday afternoon from 1924, he met with the economist Fritz Machup and walked with him past the great Austrian bank, Kreditanstalt in Vienna. And every time they passed the bank, he gave the same remark:

> "That will be a big smash."

## THE TREASURY VIEW

England had, during these years, a continuing debate about whether governments should stimulate the economy during recessions or not. The opponents, who seemed to be in the majority, adhered to the so-called "Treasury View." One example of this was a White Paper published by the English government in 1929, which stated:

> Apart from its financial reactions, a big programme of State aided public works has a disturbing effect upon the general industrial position. If it is a long programme with continuity of work promised to the personnel, it draws off labour which would otherwise find employment, though perhaps with less regularity, in normal industry without being able to secure replacement.

So, according to this view, government spending wouldn't help. But this answer was obviously weak if there was high unemployment; there had to be more to the matter. One suggestion was given in a pamphlet released by the Liberal Party in the same year as the above-mentioned government paper. Its title was *Can Lloyd George do it?* The document was part of a program proposing an increase in government spending to combat unemployment. According to the pamphlet, the consequence would be reduced unemployment:

> The fact that many working people who are now unemployed would be receiving wages instead of unemployment pay would mean an increase in effective purchasing power which would give a general stimulus to trade, moreover, the greater trade activity would make for further trade activity; for the forces of prosperity, like those of trade depression, work with a cumulative effect.

The pamphlet went on to supply an answer to the standard objections from those holding the Treasury View:

> The savings which Mr Lloyd George's schemes will employ will be diverted, not from financing other capital equipment, but (1) partly from financing unemployment. (2) A further part will come from savings which now run to waste through lack of adequate credit. (3) Something will be provided by the very prosperity which the new policy will foster. (4) And the balance will be found by a reduction in foreign lending.

It stated, in other words, that fiscal spending could be self-financing to a high degree, and could stimulate much more than the initial effect. The spending of an additional pound could be not only an effective cure, but also partly self-financing.


## CHAMPAGNE AND MONEY


This pamphlet had two authors. One was Hubert Henderson; the other was the well-known economist, John Maynard Keynes. Keynes believed that the capitalist economy contained some inherent instability – a view that had become generally accepted within the vast amount of new business cycle literature. He also thought that the economy was prone to falling into permanent unemployment equilibrium, and *this* view was unusual.

When the pamphlet was published, Keynes was 46 years old and an eager participant in the debates of the day. He had been educated at Eton and Cambridge, worked in the India Office and later as a journalist, a lecturer, the manager of an insurance company and as senior Treasury official of Great Britain. He had advised the government on numerous occasions, had participated in the negotiations with defeated Germany after the First World War, and counted President Roosevelt and Winston Churchill as friends. When he was four years old, he had wondered about the meaning of interest, and when he was six, he speculated about how his brain worked. When in preparatory school, he had hired a "slave" who carried his books for him, in return for Keynes helping with the guy's homework. Then on to Eton, and then Cambridge, where he soon started to have regular breakfasts with Marshall, the famous economist. Then came his civil service examination, where he graduated as number two among all the students. The best marks he achieved in this exam were in economics, and later he explained why:

"I evidently knew more about the subject than my examiners."

He was a connoisseur of music, a friend of Pablo Picasso and a collector of modern art. He founded his own theater with an attached restaurant, where he showed great interest in planning the menus. He was on the board of several large institutions. Like Adam Smith before him, Keynes was a master of the spoken word. Like Law, he loved to play cards and roulette. Like Thornton, he had many good friends he could trust. He was married to a Russian ballerina, who was sweet, pretty and funny ("I dislike being in the country in August, because my legs get bitten by barristers," she once said). And if all this wasn't enough, he also drank lots of champagne.

And then of course there was the stock market. Like Cantillon, John Maynard Keynes was an eager investor in equities, currencies and commodities – an activity which contributed to his understanding of economic instability. He was known for making his investment decisions in the morning while still in bed, but if his research was somewhat laid-back, this can hardly be said of his actual dispositions: they were aggressive and daring. His pet market was currencies, where he believed his experience at the Treasury would secure him a competitive advantage.

This, however, didn't always see him through. In April 1920, two years before Irving Fisher went to study the hyperinflation in Germany, Keynes had already smelled an opportunity and sold the currency short. It was indeed in a down-trend when he sold it, but as it counter-reacted in a brief rally, he lost 13 125 pounds for himself and 8498 for his fellow investors. When he received a margin call for 7000 pounds from his broker, he was

**Figure 10.1** John Maynard Keynes. With an exceptional lack of modesty, Keynes was not reluctant to describe himself as the greatest living economist. Before publishing his *General Theory*, he wrote that he believed his book would "revolutionize" within ten years "the way the world thinks about economic ideas." And so in fact it did. He was a superb integrator and promoter of ideas, and he managed to change the consensus opinion that market economies always would be self-correcting. Reproduced by permission of Getty Images.

unable to pay; only two loans secured him from bankruptcy. But that experience did not discourage him. In 1924, he was appointed first bursar of Kings College, where he persuaded the board to open an investment fund, which he managed.

## DIFFERENT OPINIONS

While Keynes's views gained popularity, so did the Austrian school, which gradually found more adherents as students from Vienna University grew up and got important jobs. One of these was Felix Somary, who had studied under von Mises. As a student, Somary had been especially interested in business cycle theories, and in 1901 he had won a prize for a paper on Juglar's theories and economic crises before becoming an investment banker in Zurich. On September 10, 1926 he gave a speech at the University of Vienna. It was a very strange experience for some of his audience, because although the economy was booming and everything appeared as rosy as ever, Felix Somary predicted that the boom would end "with the bankruptcy of governments and the destruction of banks." In 1927 he met Keynes, who asked Somary what he was recommending his customers to do. Somary answered:

"To maintain the best possible protection against the coming world crisis and to avoid the markets."

But Keynes was very bullish and responded:

"We will not have any more crashes in our time."

Then he asked Somary about several specific stocks, and added:

"I find the markets very interesting, and the prices low. So where should a crisis come from?"

"From the difference between expectations and reality. I have never before seen such clouds approaching on the horizon."

But the stock market kept climbing. In the year 1928, Keynes wasn't very happy with his own investment performance, however. Whereas the English stock index had yielded 7.9%, his fund was down 3.4%. Obviously it would be most welcome if he could perform better during the following year. And many things indicated that he might. First, there was the fact that Wall Street, the world's leading stock market, was locked in a firm bull market trend, as stocks had risen almost constantly since 1924. Secondly, the economy had been just as impressive. Partially thanks to the archeologists at the NBER, Keynes had some pretty good statistical tables to consult. Table 10.1 shows some of the key numbers.

Over seven years, industrial production had risen 40%, consumption of durables 56%, and of non-durable consumer goods 17%. Inflation had been minimal, and prices had even *fallen* during the last few years. John Ford was putting Say's Law into practice by paying the workers partially with their own output, and the stockbrokers in New York saw too that money was always allocated to the strongest and the fittest. Indeed, stock trading had never been so popular before. During the preceding years, tickers, quotation boards and brokerage services had been installed on

**Table 10.1** American key figures, 1922–28; 1922 = 100.

| Year | Industrial production | Durable consumer goods | Non-durable consumer goods | Consumer price index |
|------|------|------|------|------|
| 1922 | 100 | 100 | 100 | 100 |
| 1923 | 120 | 146 | 116 | 103 |
| 1924 | 113 | 130 | 102 | 100 |
| 1925 | 127 | 176 | 113 | 104 |
| 1926 | 133 | 143 | 116 | 104 |
| 1927 | 133 | 143 | 117 | 98 |
| 1928 | 140 | 156 | 117 | 99 |

ocean liners, and radio programs had begun broadcasting stock prices at intervals throughout the day. In one factory, stock prices were posted on a blackboard from hour to hour to please workers. And one prospering market operator was supposed to have complained, with some exaggeration of course, that to keep a good cook he had to install a ticker in the pantry, that his valet refused to come on duty before the market closed, and that the street cleaners in Wall Street would pick up only the financial papers. In fact, as stocks kept rising and rising, stock trading was now considered so easy that it was almost impossible to lose. A popular joke was about a gentleman who called the manager of a brokerage house and asked:

"Does William Jones have an account here?"

"What right do you have to ask?"

"I am attorney and guardian for William Jones. He is in an insane asylum."

"His account shows 180 000 USD profit."

So, jokes apart, if people had ever doubted the virtues of a capitalist economy, this, in most observers view, was the time to give in. You could treat the system rudely like the Germans after the First World War, or like the French during and after the Sun King, and it would fail. But if you played it by its own rules, like the Americans did, it worked wonderfully. With one pillar in Detroit and the other in Wall Street, the house of capitalism seemed to be standing firmer than ever before. So Keynes was bullish on the stock market, just like Irving Fisher. There could be no doubt about the soundness of the economy.

## THE AUSTRIAN SCHOOL

The "Austrian school" of economics had tended to oppose almost any government interference, including any attempts to fine-tune the aggregate economy. Von Mises and his pupil Friedrich von Hayek were among the leading exponents of this philosophy. Von Hayek elaborated on von Mises's theories in a number of books and articles. To him, the root of the problem was that the financial sector reacted to an increase in the demand for money by producing more credit, rather than keeping money supply constant and increasing its price (interest rates). Some of his main conclusions were:

- The seeds of instability may be that interest rates fall below the natural level, thus stimulating an unsustainable boom . . .
- . . . or that new business opportunities raise the natural level, whereas actual rates stay the same
- Money supply will often increase rapidly during booms without creating any initial inflation, but this will come as the boom stops accelerating
- Furthermore, if interest rates are too low, then you will not have sufficient savings to finance investments

In other words: central bankers could erroneously allow money supply to grow far too much during a boom, because there were not any immediate warning signs. They would thereby allow savings to fall behind and would also create the conditions for a later increase in inflation (actually, Thornton had reached the same conclusion in 1802).

Another point in Austrian business cycle theory proposed by von Hayek was that low rates would encourage many "grand schemes," or lead to what modern economists call "a deepening of the capital structure." Eventually, interest rates went up, these schemes would become unprofitable and would be abandoned at great cost. During the late 1920s, von Hayek became convinced that this process was unfolding again, and that a crash was inevitable.

Almost everybody seemed to agree. Almost everybody, except "the Seer from Wellesley," Roger Babson, who for some time had warned his customers of an impending crash, and of course the ever-skeptical Austrians. One of these, our friend Felix Somary, had, in 1928, spoken to a group of economists and warned them of the large disparity between interest rates and the very low earnings yields from equities, which he called "an unmistakable symptom of a crash." He later described his surprise to see that none of the economists present, although they represented "at least a dozen theories," believed in his prediction. In the February issue of the economic journal of the Austrian Institute of Economic Research, Friedrich von Mises joined in with a new forecast of an imminent crisis in the USA.

Nobody would listen to either of them, but as Somary was on his way through France to spend his holiday in Spain in late August, he received an urgent call from Dr von Mautner in Vienna, who sought advice on behalf on Baron Luis Rothschild. The problem was that Bodenkreditanstalt, Austria's largest financial institution, was in serious trouble, and that the Austrian government insisted that Kreditanstalt should merge with it to save it from bankruptcy. Von Mautner asked what Somary would advise them to do.

"It will be the safest way to the ruin of Kreditanstalt."

"That is what I believe, but the government insists on the merger; if we pass, then they will not do anything to help Kreditanstalt, when we should need assistance."

"Let the problem of Bodenkreditanstalt be left with the government; you cannot help, when that assistance can cost your own existence, and definitively not when you are stumbling yourself."

During the summer of 1929, Kreditanstalt offered von Mises a very well-paid job, which made his girlfriend (and future wife) ecstatic. But, much to her surprise, he didn't take the bait. When she asked him why not, he answered:

"A great crash is coming, and I don't want my name in any way connected with it."

Both von Mises and Somary thought that something wasn't right. It wasn't right at all . . .

# Chapter 11

# The Great Depression

I expect to see the market a good deal higher than it is today, within
a few months.

*Irving Fisher*

If things go wrong, don't go with them.

*Roger Ward Babson*

Jesse Livermore lived on the top floor of the Heckscher Building on Fifth
Avenue. Visitors coming to see him would meet a doorman, who would
categorically deny the existence of his office, unless you could prove that
you had an appointment. In that case you'd be taken by elevator to the
18th floor, where an oversized Irish bodyguard would check you before
allowing you in. Once inside, you would find a select team of some 20
clerks and 30 statisticians, who assisted Livermore in gathering and interpreting market intelligence from all over the world. Livermore used this
information exclusively to trade his own money – a fortune which had
grown from 3 dollars and 12 cents to 30 *million* dollars over 38 years.
During the summer of 1929, the assistants had informed Livermore that
while the much-followed Dow Jones Industrial Average (which was based
on a few large stocks) was still performing well, 614 out of a selection of
1002 stocks, which the staff monitored, had actually fallen since the beginning of the year. Livermore saw this "lack of breath" as a warning sign.
Should he prepare for a bear-raid? He was looking for further clues.

## DECISIONS, DECISIONS . . .

Such a clue arrived during the afternoon of September 4th. One of his
informants said that a "high official" at the Bank of England had told

associates during lunch that day that "the American bubble had burst," and that Montagu Norman of the same bank was considering raising interest rates before the end of the month. Livermore stayed at the office until midnight, trying to figure out what was going to happen. Then he went home, slept a few hours, and was back even before his staff showed up next morning. That morning, he called everybody he could think of to discuss the situation.

At 8 am., a contact in Boston reminded him that the speaker at the forthcoming annual National Business Congress was Irving Fisher's friend Roger Ward Babson. Livermore knew what that meant. According to Babson's "swing-charts", the boom since the early 20s had created significant deviations from the long-term growth trend. It was widely known that Babson was concerned about this, but also that he was worried about rising interest rates. Decisions at the Federal Reserve bank of New York had, until recently, been dominated by Benjamin Strong, who had argued strongly against tightening monetary policy to reduce stock market gains, since he thought it would cause unnecessary damage to the economy. However, he had died from tuberculosis in 1928, and control had passed to others who wanted to deflate the stock market. They had initially just been threatening stockbrokers that made loans to margin speculators, but as that didn't work, they had started raising rates in 1928, even though inflation was slightly negative and the economy just recovering from a small slow-down. In March 1929, the money rates had risen first to 14%, and later, on the 26th, to 20%. Just as the 20% rate had been posted on the electric announcement board, a fuse had blown out, and everybody had laughed. Although stock prices had rebounded, Babson saw this interest rate spike as another clear warning sign.

Livermore was sure that Babson would talk about these concerns in his speech. Not that he thought much of Babson's analytical skills, but that mattered less. His concern was what would be the people's *reaction* to Babson's words. Livermore asked a secretary to bring the file on Babson, looked it over and put it aside. Then he called for the newspapers. He read his newspapers in a different way than almost everybody else – he had developed a feel for journalists' psychologies. Instinctively, he knew when the journalists got tired of sticking to the same attitudes. Once they did, they could suddenly swing around and take their readers with them. Livermore felt that they were ready for just such a turn: there was a lack of news and people had gotten enough economic success stories. The press was likely to cover Babson, and people were likely to listen. Livermore went short 300000 dollars of stock.

He was right. Even before the conference, a tense atmosphere developed as reporters called Babson for a summary or print of the speech; he refused to give it. This convinced the editors that the speech could be important, so the *Herald Tribune* called Irving Fisher to ensure that he would be available for a commentary. At noon, on September 5th, Associated Press sent out the news flash:

Economist predicts 60- to 80-point stock market crash.

It got extensive coverage on the radio and evening newspapers. The *Herald Tribune* called Fisher, who denied that a crash would be coming. Babson's speech and Fisher's comments were displayed on the same page in the next day's paper. Meanwhile, Livermore called his brokers to increase his short positions.

## THE MELTDOWN

This was the beginning of the great crash of 1929. Despite a bullish statement by Fisher on October 15th ("I expect to see the stock market a good deal higher than it is today, within a few months"), it kept falling. On October 21st, Jesse Livermore became furious, as he read a headline in *The New York Times*:

J.L. Livermore reported to be heading group hammering high-priced securities.

He was shorting stocks all right, but almost everything else in the article was wrong. However, instead of attacking the newspaper, he decided to get the best out of the situation. He called one of *The Times*'s editors and told him that he was going to hold a press conference to "set the record straight." What he didn't tell the editor was that nobody else was invited to the conference. At 10:00, the journalist was shown in to his office, and as he sat down, he started scribbling his observations:

Sphinxlike, imperturbable and rigid . . . he reached for the telephone resting on a ledge to his left, and carefully covering the mouthpiece with his delicate fingers, began to whisper market orders to an unidentified ally, somewhere deep in the financial district.

Only after his telephone conversation ended did Livermore acknowledge the presence of the reporter, giving him a friendly smile. The journalist asked if Livermore could confirm that he was leading a bear consortium, and Livermore handed him a written statement, where he denied this allegation. Then the reporter asked him why stocks were declining, and Livermore answered that stocks for a long time had been "selling at ridiculously high prices." The journalist reminded him that Irving Fisher had claimed that stocks were cheap. Livermore's answer to this came promptly as he slammed forward in his chair:

> "What can a professor know about speculation or stock markets? Did he ever trade on margin? Does he have a single cent in any of these bubbles he talks are cheap? Beware of inside information – all inside information. How can he possibly rely on information coming from a classroom? I tell you the market never stands still. It acts like an ocean. There are waves of accumulation and distribution."

He was, of course, unfair to Irving Fisher, who was, in fact, too exposed in the market for his own good. But on October 24th, panic exploded and the market started a nosedive never before seen in America. One broker employee described the days like this:

> "The telegraph operators handling our out-of-town business went without sleep for 30 and 35 hours, time and again. Trays with sandwiches and coffee were passed around every two hours. None of the clerks went home at all during the worst. My brother didn't sleep for 27 hours. He had been working 18 hours a day for weeks, and he was only one of hundreds of clerks. Girls at the adding machines and typewriters fainted at their work. In one odd-lot house 34 keeled over in one afternoon from sheer exhaustion. In another, 19 had to be sent home . . ."

An observer in one of the boardrooms wrote:

> I saw them sold out, dozens of them, scores of them. I watched their faces when the customers' men gave them the news. I saw men's hair literally turn white. I saw a woman faint dead away; they carried her out cold. I heard a middler-aged doctor say: There goes my son's education.

During the 1920s, stock manipulations organized by investment pools were very frequent, and the most famous participant in these pools was Livermore. With a particular taste for bear-raids, he did well during the 1929 crash, and at the start of 1931, the total of his fortune was approximately 30 million dollars. But he lost his grip, possibly because he discovered that his wife, who was an alcoholic, was having an affair with a prohibition agent. In March 1934, he filed for bankruptcy.

The crash was a reality, and it soon spread to the European markets. The English stock market ended down 6.6% for the year, and Keynes's fund netted a meager 0.8% in 1929. As regards Irving Fisher, he lost

**Figure 11.1** *New York Times* front page, October 25, 1929. It is characteristic of the media coverage of the crash that optimism prevailed almost all the way down. Previously published in Business Cycles: From John Law to the Internet Crash, Second Edition, by Lars Tvede, Routledge, London, 2001.

around 10 million dollars, or all the money he had made on his filing machine and his stock market investments.

## HAS ANYBODY SEEN THE INVISIBLE HAND?

The stock market crash of 1929 was just a beginning. After a brief revival in the spring of 1930, the market started falling again and went on in a vicious spiral until, in 1933, it had lost 85% of its value. This was the time when people started joking that whoever bought a share of Goldman Sachs would receive a complementary gun. Or that when you ordered a hotel room in a high rise, the clerk would ask if it was "for sleeping or jumping?" Down with the stock market went the economy. During these three years, the entire capitalist marketplace seemed to be falling apart.

**Figure 11.2**   Jesse Livermore. During the 1920s, stock manipulations organized by investment pools were very frequent, and the most famous participant in these pools was Livermore. With a particular taste for bear-raids, he did well during the 1929 crash, and at the start of 1931, the total of his fortune was approximately 30 million dollars. But he lost his grip, possibly because he discovered that his wife, who was an alcoholic, was having an affair with a prohibition agent. In March 1934, he filed for bankruptcy.

Industrial production fell not by 5%, not even by 10%, but by a third. Consumer purchases of durable goods fell by almost 75%. Residential building construction was down 95%. The total amounts paid in salaries fell 40% and wages 60%. It was just horrible.

At the beginning of the contraction, many families tried to keep their assets, but as the situation worsened, they had to start selling whatever they could – at whatever price they could get. One example was the sales in November 1934 following the bankruptcy of the Chester H. Johnson Gallery. During this sale, Picasso's *Supper Party* was sold for 400 dollars and a Juan Gris for 17 dollars and fifty cents. The best expression of the severity of the collapse, however, was not that people sold their assets at incredible prices, but the fact that the purchase of non-durables (like food) dropped to *half*.

Many blamed the banks because of their increasing reluctance to lend out money. Public officials urged the bankers to ease their credit policy, for example Atlee Pomerene, who, in November 1932, gave the following message to the reluctant bankers:

> "... the bank that is 75 per cent liquid or more and refuses to make loans when proper security is offered, under present circumstances, is a parasite on the community."

But no matter what people said, the bankers wouldn't do their special trick; now that the world really needed it, they wouldn't create any money. 85 000 businesses had gone under and nine million savings accounts had been lost already. Soon the press started referring to "banksters," and Clifford Reeves went even further, when he wrote in the magazine *American Mercury*:

> The title of banker, formerly regarded as a mark of esteem in the United States, is now almost a term of opprobrium . . . and we may even see the day when to be called the son-of-a-banker will be regarded as justifiable grounds for the commission of assault and mayhem.

As money supply imploded, and the Federal Reserve did nothing to prevent banks from failing, businesses defaulted by the day, and many people were freezing or starving. By 1932, unemployment had increased from 1.5 million to 13 million, or about 25% of the workforce. By 1933, the national income had fallen from 87 billion (in 1929) to 39 billion – bringing it down to the level where it had been 20 years before. Along the Hudson Riverfront, squatters were building cardboard and tin-roofed huts to protect themselves against rain and cold. Could this really be the end of capitalism? Many thought so. It was well known that Karl Marx had predicted that recessions in capitalist countries would become gradually worse and worse until the system eventually collapsed altogether.

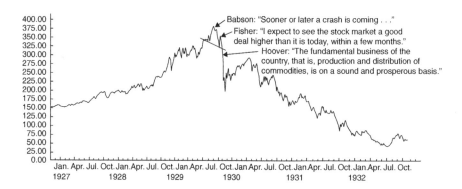

**Figure 11.3** The Great Crash 1929–1932. When Roger Ward Babson warned of an impending stock market crash on September 5, 1929, most people laughed at him. But the crash did come, and it was even worse than Babson had predicted. The market dropped by almost 85% over three years. The illustration shows the timing of comments by Babson, Fisher and President Hoover. Source: Tvede, 2002.

## KEYNES STRIKES BACK

John Maynard Keynes was not one of them. He had been blindsided by the depression as his conversations with Felix Somary clearly illustrated, but now that it was there he needed to understand why. He thought there was a technical mistake in the way politicians had run an otherwise efficient system; a mistake that could be corrected. But where was it? He began peeling layer upon layer off economic theory to find where the wrong assumptions might be, and he battled with the problem for a number of years. Meanwhile, he was also busy as a teacher, as a member of the Macmillan Committee of Finance and Industry, and writing about numerous other subjects. In 1936, a number of documents written by Isaac Newton were put up for auction, and Keynes bought many of these with his brother in what must have been one of the best bargains in history (the whole auction fetched only GBP 9030). He studied the documents carefully and used them as the basis for a paper about Newton. But he was also busy with managing Christ's College funds. During 1930, the fund lost 32%, and in 1931 25%. But then it got into gear, earning 45% in 1933, and 35% in 1934. But while Keynes's fund was very healthy in that year, the economy was definitely not, and people were now beginning to get desperate. Would this crisis never stop? When would Adam Smith's "invisible hand" come and restore order? What was wrong with the system? The depression had now lasted four years, and the figures spoke for themselves, as shown in Table 11.1.

Although Keynes did not yet have a complete theory, he wanted to convey his message. Many theorists of the time had ridiculed him before, but now they were *forced* to listen! He managed to get a meeting with President Roosevelt in which he tried to convince him. The meeting was far from successful, however; afterwards, both of them doubted the sanity of the other. So Keynes went back home to write and study, and to manage

**Table 11.1** American key figures, 1928–33; 1922 = 100.

| Year | Industrial production | Durable consumer goods | Non-durable consumer goods | Consumer price index | Money supply (M2) |
|------|------|------|------|------|------|
| 1928 | 140 | 156 | 117 | 99 | 144 |
| 1929 | 153 | 185 | 119 | 98 | 145 |
| 1930 | 127 | 143 | 97 | 91 | 143 |
| 1931 | 100 | 86 | 78 | 80 | 137 |
| 1932 | 80 | 47 | 56 | 73 | 113 |
| 1933 | 100 | 50 | 60 | 73 | 101 |

his job and his fund, which was now consistently successful – in 1935, it had a return of 33%, and in 1936, 44%.

## THE SOLUTION

Keynes's book came out in 1936, and he believed that he had found the problems. *The General Theory of Employment, Interest and Money* contained 400 pages, which were written in an elegant and entertaining prose, of which he was a master. It was rather difficult to understand, however, partly because it was so different, and partly because it was sometimes a bit, well, blurred. But it came at a time when the capitalist economy was apparently falling apart and when nobody (but the Austrians) seemed to have an answer.

The book gained fame mainly for three reasons. One was that it introduced a number of new methods for analyzing the economy. The second was that it contained a frontal attack on the conventional wisdom that recessions would be corrected automatically. It was here that Keynes believed classical economists made their most important mistake. The third reason for its fame was that it recommended a shift of political priority from price stabilization towards direct stabilization of employment and aggregate income through active use of the state budget. The central theme of the book can be summarized in this way:

- If you add up the expenditure for investment and for consumption in a country, then you get an aggregate called "national income." If productivity rises faster than this average income, then you get unemployment
- The consumption part of national income follows investment. If investment goes up, consumption goes up, since the investment process involves work and thus salaries. There is an element of Say's Law here
- The relationship is not completely simple, though. The money committed to an investment will keep circulating from hand to hand, where each receiver saves a fraction and passes on the rest until it's all saved up. This magnification of an additional pound invested is called "the multiplier." So the relationship between investment and consumption is determined by the size of this multiplier
- The system is out of balance if people save more than society invests. If, say, they save 20% of their income, then their income has to be five

times as big as investment. There is, in other words, a relationship between income, saving and investment which may or may not be in balance
- Assume now that investment has dropped below the savings that people make with their present income. In that case, income will start to drop as it is dragged down by the multiplier effect
- As consumers' income drops in this way, they find themselves unable to save the fraction they did before. This means that savings fall until they match the reduced level of investment
- In other words: society falls into an unemployment equilibrium . . .
- . . . which can last for many years due to the durability of existing production equipment (capital) and to the cumulative effect, when companies try to lower their inventory stocks

Almost any book written after the publication of *The General Theory* was distinctively different from earlier literature. To the policymakers, the most important aspect of the book was that of flexible fiscal policy. In classical economics, thrift had always been regarded as a virtue, but what Keynes suggested was the use of public expenditure as an active stabilizer, as a tool, a fiscal pendent to the monetary tool which Thornton had devised 134 years before. However, he did not go unchallenged. Any classical economist would immediately object to this theory, and a discussion could perhaps sound like this:

Classical economist:

"The concluding part of the argument is completely wrong. If investment goes down, then there will be three phenomena that put an end to the recession."

Keynes:

"I am all ears."

Classical economist:

"The first is that interest rates fall because too many people save and too few invest. Lower interest rates encourage new investment and make saving less attractive. That is one way to get the wheels spinning again."

Keynes:

"Yes, you may be right."

Classical economist:

"So you agree?? Well, then I'll carry on. The second stabilizing effect is that wages fall during recessions, and that makes new business ventures more profitable. This will also stimulate new investment."

Keynes:

"You may be right again."

Classical economist:

"Thirdly, the fall in prices of real estate, consumer goods, capital goods, etc., means that the real purchasing power of the money stock increases. This will eventually persuade everybody to start buying again."

Keynes:

"I may even agree to this too. There have been many short recessions that ended quickly without government intervention. This has to be explained, and perhaps you just did. But what do you suggest as a role for government?"

Classical economist:

"Simply to ensure financial stability by maintaining a balanced budget so that confidence is maintained until the correction arrives, which it always will."

Keynes:

"Now this is where you have to be careful, because the economic dynamics can become different from what you expect once a recession has gotten really bad."

Classical economist:

"Perhaps the revival is just a matter of longer time?"

Keynes:

"A very long time, then, and in the long term we are all dead. No, let me explain the first problem I see – it's about savings. You expect that savings will go up during a recession. Yes, they may, but just look at the American situation after the crash in '29. Could companies save? No, because while they made a total net profit after tax and dividends of 2.6 billion dollars in 1929, they generated a *loss* of 6 billion in '32. And 85 000 of them had gone bust. You can't save from a loss or if you are bankrupt. Could consumers save, then? No, they couldn't, because their aggregate income had just been cut in half. Numbers show that the average consumer saved absolutely nothing in '32 and '33. Nothing at all! I suppose they actually *wanted* to save because they were scared of the future, but they just could not find that extra cash. Could renters save? Well, apart from the disturbing fact that prices of their stocks fell 85%, they also had to endure a fall in dividends of 57% from 1929 to 1932."

Classical economist (now sounding grumpy):

"So you think savings can fall instead of rising, if things are really bad? And what is your other key point?"

Keynes:

"It relates to your argument that if the economy goes down a bit, then it may be that businessmen see the availability of idle cash and labor as an opportunity to invest. My comment here is that when the situation is as bad as after the crash in '29, their reaction becomes different. It becomes quite the opposite, in fact. Potential investors are in shock. Animal spirits take over – they are scared stiff and extrapolate the trend. They don't try to buy at the bottom because everything blew right through where they first thought the bottom would be. And it blew right through the levels where all your stabilizing factors might have worked. So the business community has what I would call liquidity preference, because they think the marginal efficiency of capital has fallen. And the numbers show that. Business expansion activities fell 94% from 1929 to 1932. And please note: the combination of falling savings and rising fear presses interest rates *up*, not down, in times of uncertainty."

Classical economist:

"Not true. Interest rates fell from 1929 to 1933, and this was one of our key points. The Fed cut discount rates from 6% just after the crash to 5% on November 1, 1929, to 1.5% in mid 1931. Meanwhile, average rates for 5-year utility bonds fell from 10.1% in 1929 to 9.3% in '30."

Keynes:

"And these bond yields fell further to 8.9 in '31, but then rose to 10% in '32 and 11% in 1933. But guess what: consumer prices fell around 25% during the same period. That made the *real* commercial interest rates, corrected for inflation, high and rising, not low and falling. Which made sense since no one could save. So the economy entered into a liquidity trap a new, terrible, but stable, equilibrium. And mind you, it *is* an equilibrium. Forget about Adam Smith's invisible hand, because once the economy gets into this deep, black hole, it is unfortunately quite stable."

---

### THE MOST IMPORTANT ANALYTICAL INNOVATIONS IN *THE GENERAL THEORY*

Four analytical concepts in *The General Theory* were especially important:

- The "propensity to consume" and "propensity to save," which were dependent on the income level
- The "multiplier"
- The point that human investment decisions are influenced by "liquidity preference" combined with "animal spirits" (as Keynes called it), and uncertainty
- The suggestion that the economy could run into a "liquidity trap," where interest rates would not fall below a given level, no matter how much money was injected, because people were scared and bearish on bonds

---

## HOLES IN THE GROUND

Keynes had one great advantage in the debate: the economy had collapsed, and people didn't know why. If Adam Smith and his followers were so smart, why was America no longer rich? Keynes's prescription for a cure was similar to what Hobson, Foster and Catchings had proposed before: additional government spending to fill the investment gap. This could be done in more or less meaningful ways. More meaningful measures could be to counter a downswing through:

- Tax cuts
- Increased transfer payments
- Increased or accelerated public investment and maintenance expenditure

Keynes noted, moreover, that his philosophy would work even if the government projects were completely silly. The government could fill bottles with money, bury them, and sell companies the right to dig them out. Because of the multiplier effect, this would lead to an aggregate effect on employment, which was much larger than the initial effect.

Keynes's book had a tremendous impact. He stressed short-term management of the economy, a view which was in sharp contrast to the laissez faire concept. Equally important was his overall method of analyzing aggregates in an operational and verifiable way. His theory was such that you could test many of its theorems and quantify its parameters. Take, for instance, the marginal propensity to consume. Using American data computed by Kuznets, he calculated this to be around 60–70%. Or take the multiplier: using Kuznets's data again, you could fix it at around 2.5.

Keynes never expected that people should read his book as an economic Bible – even as he did the proof-reading, he found that it could be much improved. Nor did he think that his ideas should be used uncritically. He was convinced that he was a great economist, but not that he had found final wisdom. Once, when he had spent an evening in discussion with a group of economists in Washington, he told his friend, Austin Robinson, that: "I found myself the only non-Keynesian present." He believed that a thinker should not postpone publication eternally like Alfred Marshall had done. Better publish interim, so that other people could absorb your thoughts and elaborate. If this was what he wanted, he had no reason to complain. Few academic books have ever been a subject of so much discussion and so much research. The scientists treated it as a pack of sledge-dogs would raw meat, and much of what Marshall, Pigou, Robertson and Hawtrey had published on business cycles seemed soon to be almost forgotten.

# Chapter 12

# Lover, Horseman, Economist

I published a few other studies on points of theory and my second big (in size) book, which seems to enjoy the most widespread obscurity, though I myself thought some of the results it aimed at explaining new and not entirely void of importance.

*Joseph Schumpeter*

It was in the fall of 1935, when the depression had lasted for five years, that the Canadian graduate student Robert B. Bryce arrived in America from London. With him on the boat, he carried manuscripts and notes from Keynes's lectures in Cambridge. Even though Keynes's book had not been formally released, most economists knew at least something about its contents. One day, a "Keynes Seminar" was held in Winthrop House, in which Bryce could explain the new ideas. Now they had a chance to ask young Bryce what exactly this Mr Keynes was trying to say. But although people were generally enthusiastic about Keynes, at least one man present didn't like what he heard. He didn't like it at all, in fact.

## A MAN OF AMBITION

This man was not just a nobody. Not even an anybody. Once he had set three goals for his life: to become the best lover in Vienna, the best horseman in Europe, and the best economist in the world. He might have failed in his first goal, and he surely had in his second. But he tended to think that he had succeeded in the third, which meant that Keynes wasn't the best. To Schumpeter, Keynes was wrong; wrong in the conclusions he drew, wrong in his methodology, and wrong in his very attitude to the science he was practising. How could normally intelligent people fall for this stuff?

Joseph Alois Schumpeter was born in Vienna in the same year as Keynes. As a child he went to school in Graz, where he did well, and was allowed to continue in a demanding school, the "Maria Theresa Academy of Knights," where he soon realized that his formidable memory and his ability to concentrate gave him an important advantage over many fellow students. In 1901, Joseph Schumpeter entered the faculty of Law in Vienna, and on February 16, 1906, only one week after his 23rd birthday, he received his law degree.

He was the kind of person who appeared to be relaxed, but who in reality worked like a beast. Often he would sit at the coffee houses in Vienna and talk for hours as if he had nothing else to do; but when he came home, he would read half the night, eager to know everything about the subject that had caught his interest. That subject was economics.

In his analysis of business cycles and of the future of capitalism, Schumpeter emphasized in particular the role of the entrepreneur. It was the entrepreneur who, more than any other factor, was responsible for each revival after a recession. Like Karl Marx, Schumpeter foresaw the eventual fall of capitalism, but for an entirely different reason. Businesses and the state would grow larger and larger, and as this happened, the entrepreneurs would disappear, and renewal in society with them.

Joseph Schumpeter's first job was in Egypt, where he was responsible for rationalization of a sugar refining factory. He did that with great success, and was able to observe how technological innovation led to increased profitability – an impression which was probably important in shaping his later theories. When he came home from his daily work, he would continue on another project. He had decided to write a book about economics, which should be nothing less than the German language match to English classics.

Written over just a year and a half, the book, which contained 657 pages, was published in 1908. Schumpeter was now 25 years of age and decided to quit business to pursue an academic career. He returned to Vienna and started preparations to earn the right to teach political economics at university level. In June 1909, at the age of 26, he received the "venia legendi," with the title of "privatdozent." At that time, he had already published 22 book reviews and 9 journal articles in addition to his book. He was more than ready for the academic world.

But maybe the academic world wasn't quite ready for him. People found the young Schumpeter irritating and offensive. For one thing, he dressed up like a Count. Another thing was the way he spoke in public.

**Figure 12.1** Joseph Schumpeter. In his analysis of business cycles and of the future of capitalism, Schumpeter emphasized in particular the role of the entrepreneur. It was the entrepreneur who, more than any other factor, was responsible for each revival after a recession. Like Karl Marx, Schumpeter foresaw the eventual fall of capitalism, but for an entirely different reason. Businesses and the state would grow larger and larger, and as this happened, the entrepreneurs would disappear, and renewal in society with them. Reproduced by permission of Corbis.

Like an experienced old professor, he always spoke without manuscript, typically with a gracious smile and often with an arrogant attitude. So when the young, hopeful man got his first job, he was sent to the place usually preferred for troublesome old professors: the remote Czernowitz.

## THE CZERNOWITZ YEARS

Schumpeter left Vienna in September 1909, and soon after his arrival in Czernowitz, the dean of the Faculty held the first meeting of the teaching session with the professors. They all arrived wearing dark woolen suits and high collars, and sat down to wait for the meeting to be called to order. But one chair was empty: that of the young, new professor from Vienna. Finally, the door opened and Joseph Schumpeter entered, wearing not a dark suit, but boots, jodhpurs and hunting jacket. He was late because the meeting was too close to his daily ride, he explained – was it possible that the dean could make the next meetings a little later, so he could get time to change? They didn't send him back, and eventually he gained many friends (and girlfriends) in Czernowitz. He stayed for two years, and none of his colleagues ever forgot him. Which other young professor had ever insisted on eating in white tie and tails while being in his own, humble place? Once, Schumpeter became very upset at the university librarian, who wouldn't allow his students to borrow books about political economics. They ended up in a shouting match until the librarian finally challenged him to a duel with swords. Schumpeter accepted, and they had their seconds arrange for the contest. Schumpeter was well trained in sword-fighting, and after a short fight, he nicked the librarian's shoulder. The seconds immediately intervened, and the fight was over: Schumpeter apologized for the whole affair, the librarian apologized as well, and after that the students were allowed to borrow books about political economy.

## CLUSTERS OF INNOVATION

The Czernowitz years were not only fun and games, however; Joseph Schumpeter was writing his second book, *The Theory of Economic Development*. It was published when he was 29 years old, after he returned to Vienna. It contained original theories, which built on Spiethoff's concept of new technology as a trigger of booms, but Schumpeter elaborated Spiethoff's ideas by emphasizing the behavior of entrepreneurs. In the capitalist economy, he claimed, innovation arrives in clusters, and these clusters explain the business cycles. And innovation is not the same as technological discovery. It is the process where people convert these discoveries in to business. Many thought this sounded unlikely: "Why should innovation arrive in clusters? Why not in a steady stream?" Because, he claimed, the conditions of slumps facilitate innovation:

> One favorable circumstance, which always facilitates and partly explains a boom, must be particularly remembered, namely the state of affairs created by every period of depression. As is well known, there are generally masses of unemployed, accumulated stocks of raw materials, machines, buildings, and so forth offered below cost of production, and there is as a rule an abnormally low rate of interest.

Such a situation was ideal for entrepreneurs, who merely pieced these factors of production together in new and more profitable ways, which opened new markets. So, during hard times, there would be more innovation that would lead not only to local prosperity, but to a general boom. One reason for this was that innovation typically happened in new companies:

> . . . it is not the owner of stage-coaches who builds railways.

> . . . the vast majority of new combinations will not grow out of the old firms or immediately take their place, but appear side by side, and compete, with them.

This meant that innovation would not only change the nature of activity, but increase its total level. A second reason why innovation created business cycles was that once the entrepreneur had broken the new path, more and more would follow:

> . . . the successful appearance of an entrepreneur is followed by the appearance not simply of some others, but of ever greater numbers, though progressively less qualified.

Thirdly, the development of new industries meant increased demand for capital, raw materials, services and new by-products, and thus a general spread of derived demand to other industries. Eventually, this would lead to overinvestment and distress as the prime effect of the innovation dried out and old companies were forced out by increased costs and competition.

## CREATIVE DESTRUCTION

In *The Theory of Economic Development*, Joseph Schumpeter used a term that would become famous. He talked about "creative destruction" when describing processes whereby old structures are destroyed to free production resources for new and more efficient structures. What happened during these phases in the business cycle was that entrepreneurs with new and more productive ideas used credit to build up their businesses. Once they were able to take their new products to the market, they would obviously compete against suppliers of older products. The result was that the more old-fashioned producers were forced out so that factory halls, office space and people that were previously employed in the old structures became available for the entrepreneurs. The economy could not grow very fast or at all if this destructive process didn't take place.

One day he met with Felix Somary and the economist Max Weber at Café Landmann in Vienna, and soon they came to discuss socialism. Schumpeter was strongly opposed to socialism, as he believed that such a system would have very few innovations and would suppress its people. He said that the debate over socialism would now cease to be a paper discussion, as there would be a real experiment to observe in Russia. Weber agreed, but worried that the Russian experiment would lead to incredible human suffering and would end in a catastrophe. "That may very well be . . .," answered Schumpeter, "but it will be a nice laboratory for us." Weber was shocked over this cynical attitude and a discussion followed, which became louder and louder until the other guests stopped talking and started staring at the combatants instead. Finally, Max Weber ran out of the cafe, and Schumpeter laughed to Somary and said "How can you argue so hard in a coffee house?"

## ROUGH TIMES

In 1919, a new socialist cabinet was formed in Austria, and the social democrats' leader, Dr Otto Mayer, was looking for a state Secretary of Finance. Apparently unaware that Schumpeter nourished strong sympathies for the laissez faire philosophy, he suggested him for the post. Schumpeter accepted and immediately after proclaimed his new policy. He would:

- Reduce money supply through a one-time capital levy
- Adopt a fixed exchange rate policy
- Establish an independent central bank
- Put emphasis on indirect taxation
- Promote free trade

He rented a suite at the Vienna Waldorf Hotel and a countryside castle with a stable of horses – to get ready for the battle of his life. But the battle could not be won; the rest of the government had completely different views to Schumpeter, and one of their first steps was to establish a commission to nationalize a number of industries. Schumpeter successfully prevented many of these nationalizations, but after only six months he was forced out of government. They had discovered that he was anything but socialist.

After this disappointment, he went into private business. It started when some conservative MPs struck a deal according to which Schumpeter was given a banking concession. He now made an alliance with the Biedermann bank, which was a private bank in need of a concession to go public. The bank had the money, and as Schumpeter had the concession, he became partner – with an attractive salary as well as a large credit-line. Eager to make it big in a hurry, he rushed to invest in various industries, and after a few years, he seemed to be very well off. But in 1924, Austria had been hit by recession and almost every investment he had made turned sour. Before the year was through, he had lost his job, was deeply indebted, and was left feeling that he had wasted a lot of time. After some university years in Bonn, in 1927 he accepted an offer to teach at Harvard, and borrowed most of the money needed for the boat ticket. Then, seven years later, he found himself sitting in Winthrop House listening to this young Canadian student telling about the supposedly "ingenious" theories of Mr Keynes.

Schumpeter felt that Keynes underestimated the inherent stability of capitalism, and that he was wrong in letting too high savings take the blame for recessions – it was these very savings which permitted entrepreneurs to innovate and create new growth, Schumpeter thought. And further, Keynes was wrong in his very attitude to economic science. Schumpeter believed scientific economists should stick to analysis only – and leave policy matters to politicians. In *The General Theory*, Keynes not only gave recommendations, but it seemed to Schumpeter that he had decided upon these first and then developed a theory which could justify them afterwards.

## THE UNIFYING THEORY

Now we know why Schumpeter didn't think much of Keynes and why he was so irritated when attending the "Keynes Seminar" with Bryce in 1935. When the event took place, Schumpeter was himself in the process of writing a book about the instability problem; a kind of "Grand Unifying Theory" of business cycles. He had embarked, in 1933, on this "Krisenwerk," as he called it in his diaries, and had believed it could be finished by 1935. But as the work progressed, it swelled, and when rumors of Keynes's book stole the spotlight in 1935, Schumpeter wasn't even half finished (he was beginning to tell his friends that it had turned him into a "galley slave"). In fact he had to continue his work for several more years until it was finally published in 1939 – at a time when any non-Keynesian theory was considered almost irrelevant.

The 1095-page book (in two volumes) was impressive. The first 219 pages dealt with pure theory. First, he discussed behavior according to the equilibrium theory, and then he introduced his entrepreneurs, who were responsible for innovation – much like he had described in his *Theory of Economic Development*. Clusters of innovation were responsible for the "first wave" – the initial business cycle movement. The next step was to introduce "the secondary wave." He wrote:

> There is no need to emphasize how great a mass of fact now enters our picture. Indeed, the phenomena of this secondary wave may be and generally are qualitatively more important than those of the primary wave. Covering as they do a much wider surface, they are also much easier to observe; in fact they are what strikes the eye first, while it may be difficult, especially if the innovations are individually small, to find the torch responsible for conflagration.

So the secondary wave amplified the initial impulse so much as to almost hide it from the eye. This amplification was created by the multitude of phenomena described by other writers, such as debt deflation, forced liquidations, group-think, etc. After the first impulse had arrived, less entrepreneurial people believed that they could benefit from the growth created by the entrepreneurs – a belief which was deceptively self-fulfilling in the short term. In the longer term, however, everything gained during the secondary wave would be wiped out, and only the benefits created by the first wave would remain. So the first wave was "evolution," or structural, while the second was tremors around this evolutionary growth path. But the timing of those tremors dictated when innovations would surface: the downswing in the secondary wave created the conditions necessary for the entrepreneurs. Because of the secondary wave, the primary evolution occurred in steps.

## SIMULTANEOUS CYCLES

His third step was to introduce several, simultaneous cycles:

> There is no reason why the cyclical process of evolution should give rise to just one wave-like movement. On the contrary there are many reasons to expect that it will set into motion an indefinite number of wave-like fluctuations which will roll on simultaneously and interfere with one another in the process.

He had believed from the outset in a single-cycle hypothesis, but as he analyzed the problem still closer, he realized that there had to be several cycles in action, as innovations had very different propagation patterns. In reality, there could be an indefinite number of simultaneous oscillations, but he chose to simplify this scenario by assuming the presence of three dominant cycles: Kondratieff's, Juglar's and Kitchin's – all of these with very irregular durations (Figure 12.2).

From page 220, the book contained a thorough analysis of business cycles through history. He dated capitalism from the 12th or 13th century, when mankind had introduced the first credit instruments, but he concentrated his analysis on the most recent 300 years – including John Law, whom he regarded as an entrepreneur who created his own credit. This analysis also suggested a theory to explain occasional deep depressions:

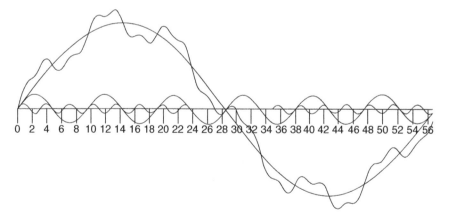

**Figure 12.2** Schumpeter's three-cycle schema. Schumpeter believed that there were many simultaneous oscillations playing out, some of them strong and others weak. He thought that congruence of troughs in several of these phenomena could lead to depressions. Previously published in Business Cycles: From John Law to the Internet Crash, Second Edition, by Lars Tvede, Routledge, London, 2001.

... it is clear that the coincidence at any time of corresponding phases of all three cycles will always produce phenomena of unusual intensity, especially if the phases that coincide are those of prosperity and depression. The three deepest and longest "depressions" within the époque covered by our material – 1825–1830, 1873–1878, and 1929–1934 – all display that characteristic.

We have already investigated these episodes. 1825–30 was our story with President Jackson and Philip Hone's diary. The 1873–79 depression was the railroad crash just after Jay Gould's gold raid. And 1929–34 was the so-called "Great Depression". So this is how Schumpeter saw them; as coincidence of downswings in Kondratieff, Juglar and Kitchin cycles. But the fact that the Great Depression in particular lasted for so long needed an additional explanation: why didn't the Juglar cycle pull the economy back up in 1935 like it had in 1879?

His explanation for this was the accumulated effect of anti-business policies. First, there was a rise in direct taxation of the highest brackets. Schumpeter believed that this was generally accepted as an intermediate measure "as a sacrifice to be made in a national emergency," but later it was regarded as a permanent deterrent against initiative. Secondly, the government imposed a tax on undistributed corporate income, which stimulated an immediate distribution of corporate income as dividends, but which Schumpeter believed had "a paralyzing influence on enterprise and investment in general." He believed that companies were much more willing to invest reserves, which they were now impelled to distribute instead:

> One of the causes of the efficiency of private business is that, unlike the politician or public officer, it has to pay for its mistakes. But the consequences of having to do so are very different according to whether it risks owned or borrowed "funds," or whether a loss will only reduce surpluses or directly impinge upon original capital.

And later:

> All this, it is true, vanishes from the economist's mind as soon as he buries himself in the mechanics of aggregative theory.

A third reason for the failed revival was, according to Schumpeter, that minimum wages were forced up, making it more difficult for industry to "repair its damaged financial structure." A fourth reason was competition from government industries, and a fifth reason was new anti-monopoly policies. Schumpeter believed that all such anti-business measures "obviously tended to reinforce each other." As he expressed it:

It is surely not too much to ask economists to realize that behavior in human societies differs from behavior in animal societies or in physical systems, in that it not simply reacts to "disturbances," but to interpretive and anticipative – correct or false – diagnosis of them.

He believed that the sum of all the anti-business measures had a disastrous psychological effect on business. Not only were businessmen objectively threatened, but they felt threatened. Later he continued:

> . . . it is only necessary to reflect that any major change in the relations between the individual and the state, including any major shift in favor of the latter of the shares in total private revenue earned, involves changes in the fundamental habits of mind, the attitudes to life, and the valuations at least of those who are immediately concerned.

As Schumpeter attributed the pivotal role in revival to entrepreneurs – and not to consumer spending – it is quite obvious why he didn't think raising salaries was a wise thing during a depression. But what about the increased government spending which was the potential positive effect created by increased taxation? You could sense a clear address to Keynes (who was only mentioned twice and in seven footnotes in the entire book) when he wrote:

> . . . the writer entertains no doubt that slump will give way to recovery as the new spending program within the 4 million deficit budgeted for 1938 unfolds during the fall of 1938, but also that tapering off will again be attended by the symptoms of – according to the way in which it is effected – recession or depression. This should make us both envious and thankful: envious because fellow economists will be able to enjoy so delightful a verification of their views, thankful because in other fields – medicine, for instance – people do not reason like that, or else we should all be morphinists by now.

Even as the book was published, Schumpeter knew that he was too late. The whole world had turned towards Keynes, and the name of the game had become fiscal stabilization measures. During the first 18 months in print, Schumpeter's book sold only 1075 copies. Just two American professors used it as a textbook, and only for one year. The academic community was not interested in Schumpeter's micro-economy.

**THE MOST CITED MACROECONOMISTS ON MONETARY ISSUES
AND BUSINESS CYCLES, 1920–39**

The success of economists is sometimes measured by how often they are cited by other scientists. Patric Deutscher constructed the figures in Table 12.1 below by scanning all articles classified under the headings "Aggregative and Monetary Theory and Cycles . . ." and "Money, Credit and Banking" in the Index of Economic Journals. The table illustrates the clear dominance of Keynes, which was steadily increasing during the period (in the years 1920–30, Keynes ranged 10th with Fisher and Mitchell as the most frequently quoted). Joseph Schumpeter ranked 17th to 18th for the period illustrated.

Table 12.1 The most cited macroeconomists on monetary issues and business cycles, 1920–39. Source: Deutscher, 1990.

| Rank | Name | Number of citations |
| --- | --- | --- |
| 1 | J.M. Keynes | 200 |
| 2 | D.H. Robertson | 104 |
| 3 | I. Fisher | 73 |
| 4 | A.C. Pigou | 72 |
| 5 | R.G. Hawtrey | 66 |
| 6 | F. von Hayek | 58 |
| 7 | A. Marshall | 43 |
| 8 | W.C. Mitchell | 42 |
| 9 | G. Cassel | 40 |
| 10 | J. Hicks | 35 |
| 11 | R. Harrod | 35 |
| 12 | G. Haberlar | 34 |
| 13 | A. Hansen | 32 |
| 14 | K. Wicksell | 31 |
| 15 | J.M. Clark | 25 |
| 16 | W.S. Jevons | 23 |
| 17 | C. Snyder | 22 |
| 18 | J. Schumpeter | 22 |
| 19 | J. Robinson | 20 |
| 20 | S. Kuznets | 19 |

# Chapter 13

# The Problem with Money

Money isn't everything but it sure keeps you in touch with your children.

*J. Paul Getty*

Hyman Minsky was born in America in 1919, the son of two devoted socialists. He grew up with his parents, went to school, and followed the family tradition of joining the socialist party. Then he joined the University of Chicago, where he received a BSc degree in mathematics. However, he soon realized that pure mathematics shouldn't be his professional focus; he was much more interested in society and economics. In 1942, he enrolled in the Littauer School of Administration at Harvard, but had to leave after just one semester to join the army. In late 1945, he was sent overseas; first to Newport in England and then to Paris, Frankfurt and finally Berlin. Minsky's stay in Berlin provided him inspiration that would influence his research later on. He was assigned to work in the Reports and Planning Brigade of the Manpower Division under a man named David Saposs. Saposs was a labor economist with a doctorate from Wisconsin, and he was a leading member of the anti-communist left. Many of the people who worked for him shared his political views, and so did Minsky. Minsky claimed later that his experiences working with Saposs led him to conclude that abstract models were helpful in developing thoughts and analysis, but that they were not the final goal. The final goal was to deduct real conclusions with a basis in real situations and events. He thought, like Joseph Schumpeter, that this could only be done if you had an understanding of the prevailing institutions and the relevant historical framework.

Minsky returned to the States after the war, and there he decided to study at Harvard rather than Chicago. However, after he had been there for some time, he started wondering about some elements in the teaching curricula. One was the way that his teacher Alvin Hansen (the leading disciple of Keynes) covered fiscal policy. Minsky found that Alvin Hansen used a very orthodox Keynesian program when addressing the rules of conventional and counter-cyclical fiscal policy. Furthermore, the way Hansen interpreted Keynes was, Minsky thought, rather mechanistic. Hansen didn't address uncertainty, which Minsky had understood was a vital element of Keynes's thinking, and the professor was virtually ignoring money and financial markets.

Minsky studied at Harvard until 1949 before receiving an appointment at Brown University, where he stayed from 1949 to 1955 and wrote his doctoral thesis. Alvin Hansen expected that Minsky would work with him, but Minsky had at that time met Joseph Schumpeter and decided to work with him instead. The subject that he would explore was the relationship between market structure, banking, the determinants of aggregate demand and business cycles. Minsky's approach to economics continued to develop further and further towards the attitude that Saposs had first inspired: economics had to be practical and realistic. Very theoretical constructions without roots in the actual realities were of little value.

Minsky was a good writer and he published rather a lot. His first really important article was *Central Banking and Money Market Changes* from 1957. He introduced here a distinction between *two concepts of liquidity*:

- The liquidity that central banks could control by dealing with it directly. This was bonds and money markets
- Cash flows that drove other asset markets such as shares and real estate

He argued further that you could distinguish between *two price levels*:

- The prices of current output, such as food, cars and holidays, which were widely dependent on labor costs
- The prices of capital and financial assets, such as stocks, bonds and art, which incorporated uncertainty and depended on yields. Since yields represented future cash flow, the valuations depended on income that was expected over time

Minsky would always use Keynes as his main theoretical reference, and one of his literary milestones was his book *John Maynard Keynes*, which he published in 1975. However, he disagreed a lot with the way that most economists interpreted Keynes, and also to some degree with what Keynes himself seemed to have meant.

## INHERENT FINANCIAL INSTABILITY

Minsky assumed, like Keynes (and unlike the neoclassicists), that capitalism had significant, inherent instability. He observed that it mainly was private investment that drove the economy, and that these investments fluctuated much more than other components of the economy, since they depended on investors' subjective evaluations of the future. Keynes had considered this aspect when he wrote about investors' short-term focus ("in the long run, we are all dead"), their "animal spirits" and their tendency to hold on to cash during recessions and depressions ("liquidity preference"), but Minsky found that Keynes's followers largely ignored these aspects. The financial sector was a main source of instability in a capitalist economy, he said, since this particular sector was motivated by many other factors than merely technology and market interest rates, and these motivations could lead to instability. He saw himself as an expositor of "financial Keynesianism," and he talked about a "Wall Street View" and "Money-Manager Capitalism," to give a name to the approach that emphasized the problems created by the financial sector. The processes he described were common:

- Expansionary public policy created the basis for private investment booms driven by debts an increase in federal debt would, for instance, add to private stocks of low-risk financial assets and decrease the risk-exposure of private balance sheets . . .
- . . . and this led to booms and overinvestments
- The government would eventually intervene to avoid the potential resulting crash . . .
- . . . and this intervention meant that the financial sector didn't suffer the full consequences of their previous irresponsible credit expansion

These recurrent cycles of irresponsible financial behavior followed by government bailouts created a more and more fragile financial sector, he claimed. Decisions about investments were taken in boardrooms, he said, and one of the main factors that was often considered there was the general conditions for financing, rather than the basic soundness of the projects. Increases in asset prices during a boom were an important factor here, since assets could be used as collateral for loans. This created nonlinearity that could create considerable instability: increasing asset prices contributed to the creation of money (for instance when financial assets were used as collateral for loans). And all of this could happen while everybody (the "agents") was acting rationally to optimize their own gain; they might even be forced to follow the prevailing trend simply to survive. He claimed that each phase of the business cycle created changes in the financial environment that led to the next phase.

Minsky's "Wall Street Paradigm" was very different from the mainstream "Barter Paradigm" that was used by most economists (ignoring the financial sector). He declared war on the neoclassical approach, mainly by making three unorthodox statements:

- Persistent employment cannot be explained by market rigidity alone. Assume that salaries actually did fall during a recession, as the neoclassicists would expect. The result would be that prices would fall as well, and companies would consequently postpone investments. Furthermore, they would be squeezed by the increasing cost of debt service (Fisher's debt deflation theory)
- The wide fluctuations in financial markets are relevant. Neoclassicists ignore the financial sector, basically assuming that it is efficient. But it isn't. Central banks can control the prices of some bonds and of interest rates, but they have no direct control over the prices of any other investment asset
- Unemployment does not come from market rigidities. It comes from uncertainty about the future among business executives; an uncertainty that is reflected by fluctuations in investments

Inefficiencies in the financial sector could consequently be a key culprit for major economic disasters like the depression of the 1930s.

## CHARLES KINDLEBERGER

Minsky had an ally in Charles Kindleberger, a man who worked in the Federal Reserve Bank in New York during the late 1930s, and had experienced there how complex a task it is to reignite a paralyzed economy. Kindleberger would later on leave the bank to work in the State department, where he was involved in the Marshall Plan after World War II. In 1948, when he was 38 years of age, he decided to leave government altogether and instead join the world of academia to specialize in crashes and panics. His approach was largely historical. He read through piles of material about crises throughout history to identify common elements, and he published his results in a series of books, in which he showed numerous examples of situations where financial markets clearly had been completely irrational, and where manias had been followed by deep depressions. He characterized the typical phases around a financial mania as:

- Speculation
- Financial distress
- Crisis
- Panic
- Crash

One of Kindleberger's books, *The World in Depression, 1929–1939* from 1986, provided an analysis of the terrible events that he had experienced personally. He stated here that collapse in money supply could not explain the depression, since money supply fell more slowly than prices. This meant that the real purchasing power of money actually went *up* from 1929 to 1931. Secondly, he couldn't accept any theory that blamed the stock market crash and its negative wealth effect for the economic collapse – the collapse in production began before the stock market crashed. The one book that Kindleberger became most famous for was *Manias, Panics and Crashes* from 1978. This classic was wonderfully old-fashioned, in as much as he didn't include a single mathematical equation. Here is what he wrote in the 2000 edition:

> A colleague has offered to provide a mathematical model to decorate the work. It might be useful to some readers, but not to me. Catastrophe mathematics, dealing with such events as falling off a height, is a new branch of the discipline, I am told, which has yet to demonstrate its rigor or usefulness. I had better wait. . . . It seems to me to bog the argument down, as well as to involve an inordinate amount of work with greater costs than benefits.

### FRIEDMAN AND THE UNIVERSITY OF CHICAGO

Another scientist focusing on monetary factors as key sources of instability was Milton Friedman. He came from a poor Brooklyn family which had emigrated to the United States from part of Austria–Hungary. Friedman graduated from high school at the age of 15, went to Rutgers University just after his 16th birthday, and supported himself afterwards. As a college student, he decided to study math to become an actuary, but when he saw the effects of the Great Depression, he became interested in economics. So, when he received offers of two scholarships, he chose to study economics at the University of Chicago. One of his mentors there was Simon Kuznets, who would later supply the facts and figures for many of Friedman's analyses.

During World War II, Friedman worked in various state departments, where he developed a long-term skepticism about economic forecasts and about the efficiency of government intervention in the economy, and also a belief that the economy should be as free as possible. He stated, for instance, that:

> The most important single central fact about a free market is that no exchange takes place unless both parties benefit.

In 1948 he joined NBER, where his task was to continue monetary research after Mitchell. Gradually, Friedman became known as the theorist among the staff at the Bureau. Then, in 1976, he received the Nobel Prize because he had been the leading figure in one of the most important developments in economic thinking of his century: the monetarist revolution.

---

### THE GREAT INTEGRATOR–PROMOTERS OF ECONOMICS

Many economists develop important theories without becoming famous for them. Others have the talent for integrating, rephrasing, interpreting and promoting ideas. They are the "integrator-promoters," and it is them who have the largest impact on society and who gain most fame. It is probably fair to say that Fisher, Keynes, Samuelson and Friedman were the four greatest such economic integrator–promoters of the 20th century. All of these four superstars developed new and original theories, but they were equally adept at giving new meaning to existing theories and creating an impact through speeches, publications, interviews, magazine columns, etc. and by meeting with senior politicians. Friedman even had his own TV program.

---

The idea of fixing monetary growth rate had actually been orthodox at the University of Chicago since the 40s, but over the years, Friedman had become still more convinced of how the business cycle problem should be handled: *society should manage the business cycle problem simply and only by ensuring a constant growth of money stock.* While proponents of active interventionism were getting in trouble with their ever more complicated simulation models, Friedman did like Irving Fisher had done; he dug out Newcomb's old quantity equation of money:

$$MV = PQ$$

We will recall that the left side of this equation was *Money* multiplied by *Velocity* of money. The right side was *Price* of goods multiplied by *Quantity* of goods. Friedman's first point was that it was incredibly difficult to manage the economy through the use of active counter-cyclical measures. Once you realized that the economy was diving, it would take too long before fiscal measures would take effect. And when such measures finally worked, it was quite likely that the upswing had already started, so that instability was increased. Besides, there were clear indications that government borrowing to finance additional spending crowded out private borrowing (the old "Treasury View"). The point was that inherent instability could be found in both sides of the equation. The left side ($MV$) was unstable because of inherent self-reinforcement caused by, for example, the initial drop in interest rates during monetary expansions, competition in the bank sector, etc. The right side ($PQ$) was unstable because of inventory effects (Metzler), the accelerator (Clark), overinvestment (Mill), clusters of innovation (Schumpeter), etc. And together they became even more unstable because of positive feedback between monetary and real events (Minsky). But in any equation you could, of course, stabilize the whole if you stabilized just one side. And the left side – the monetary part – was much easier to stabilize than the right side.

Friedman's postulate was backed by a growing bulk of research indicating that a strong correlation between money supply and business cycles did exist – with the former leading the latter. In 1963, he published *A Monetary History of the United States 1867–1960*, written with Anna J. Schwartz. Their research showed that *over the long term, money growth was wholly reflected in inflation, but not in growth:*

$$MV = \mathbf{P}Q$$

So much so, it seemed that they declared and often repeated that inflation was "a purely monetary phenomenon." But the short term was different. Over the short term, monetary fluctuations were responsible for business cycles:

$$MV = P\mathbf{Q}$$

**Figure 13.1**   Milton Friedman. One of the great economic thinkers of the 20th century, Milton Friedman launched a major school of thought rooted partly in Austrian economics. Reproduced by permission of Corbis.

Every severe business contraction in the United States since 1867 had been preceded by a large monetary contraction. On average, monetary growth preceded economic peaks by about half a year, and economic troughs by about a quarter of a year. The Great Depression in the 1930s had been accompanied by a large contraction in the money supply – a contraction which the Federal Reserve at any point could have halted – but never did. After the crash in 1929, American interest levels had fallen to very low levels, but money supply had fallen by a third anyway – something that most observers at the time had not been aware of. The Federal Reserve had generally assumed that raising interest rates during an expansion and lowering them during a recession was enough to sta-bilize the economy. But according to Friedman, acceleration in the growth of money stock spurs spending, but once this spending has picked up, people become less cautious and start reducing their monetary reserves. Brokers at the stock exchange soon realize that this will lead to growing inflation, and so they mark down bond prices. This means that money supply could keep expanding even as interest rates on bonds were rising. Rising interest rates were, in other words, no guarantee that excessive money growth was being checked. And the opposite could also happen:

interest rates and money supply could fall together. To solve this problem, you had to shift from the "I-regime" (management through interest rates) to the "M-regime" (management through money supply). Managing money supply would include, but not be limited to, manipulating interest rates.

---

STABILIZING A SYSTEM

Simon Newcomb's equation, $MV = PQ$ can be used as a framework to describe the essentials of various proposals to solve the business cycle problem. Some examples of proposed solutions are highlighted in Table 13.1.

**Table 13.1** Proposed solution to stabilizing parts of Newcomb's equation and hence solving the business cycle problem.

| Stabilize what? | Simplified description | Early proponent |
|---|---|---|
| $PQ$ | Use central bank intervention tools ($MV$) to stabilize aggregate output | Henry Thornton |
| $P$ | Adopt gold standard to ensure stable prices | David Ricardo |
| $P$ | Re- or devaluate currency to stabilize inflation | Irving Fisher |
| $Q$ | Use fiscal policy to increase or reduce aggregate output | John Maynard Keynes |
| $MV$ | Use central bank management tools to ensure a stable, moderate growth in effective money supply; ignore fluctuations in aggregate output | Milton Friedman |

---

THE CRITIQUE OF THE PHILLIPS CURVE

The New Zealand-born economist Alban William Phillips (who spent most of his life in Britain) had, in 1958, published a paper (*The relationship between unemployment and the rate of change of money wages in the UK 1861–1957*), where he described how unemployment had been lowest in periods with more inflation. Irving Fisher had actually also mentioned

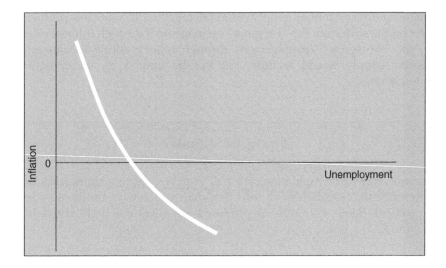

**Figure 13.2**    The Phillips curve. This graph illustrates the Phillips curve as it was originally described. Friedman believed it was, in fact, vertical. Today, most economists subscribe to the "accelerationalist" hypothesis, which assumes that an accelerating inflation reduces unemployment, but only until the growth in inflation eventually stops. Then you get inflation and unemployment. Previously published in Business Cycles: From John Law to the Internet Crash, Second Edition, by Lars Tvede, Routledge, London, 2001.

this, and our Duke of Orleans had experienced it first hand as his free use of the printing press led to a (temporary) wave of prosperity. Two top economists, Paul Samuelson and Robert Solow, picked up on the theme and contributed to making this relationship part of mainstream thinking. It was given the name the "Phillips curve" (even though it might have been called the Fisher curve) and became, for a time, part of mainstream thinking (Figure 13.2).

Friedman was critical of this theory. He did accept that there could be a relationship between unemployment and inflation within the timeframe of the Kitchin cycle, but it was short term only:

• Society has a natural unemployment level, which is dependent on structural characteristics of the labor and commodity markets, market imperfections, the cost of gathering information about job vacancies and labor availability, the cost of mobility, etc. When people have adjusted completely to any given inflation rate, then the unemployment rate will drift towards this structural level

- The only way to force unemployment below this rate is to make money supply rise faster than anticipated inflation. This process will create inflation after a lag, however
- Since people learn from what they see, anticipated inflation will trail after real inflation. Because of this, you have to force money supply further and further up if you want to maintain it above anticipated inflation. As a consequence, you end up with ever-accelerating inflation if you insist on maintaining unemployment below the natural rate . . .
- . . . until the economy collapses in hyperinflation or until (more likely) someone finally decides to pull the brakes. In both cases, you end up with huge unemployment as aggregate demand starts falling, while anticipated inflation is very high

So, according to this "acceleration" view, using inflation to create work was like peeing in your pants: at first it would feel warm, but would soon turn very cold. The Phillips curve was only a short-run phenomenon, just as had been demonstrated in France during the Mississippi bubble and in Germany after World War I.

## RATIONAL EXPECTATIONS

During the early 1970s, the capitalist economies went into a very serious recession, partly triggered by the oil crisis. Several governments reacted (against some of the monetarists' advice) by increasing money supply to stimulate growth, but this time it didn't work at all. The result was not growth and low unemployment; it was inflation and continued unemployment.

This called for an explanation, and the most widely accepted theory was supplied by Robert E. Lucas, another economist from the University of Chicago. Lucas's explanation was simple. Assume it is widely published that money supply is going to accelerate. Government officials take the opportunity to announce that it is therefore safe for businesses to invest and employ more people, as new growth in output will follow the increase in money supply:

$$MV = PQ$$

People are smart, however. They have seen it all before and know that eventually the growth in money supply will lead to inflation. So companies raise their prices immediately, and unions respond by demanding higher salaries. So, alas, all you get is rising inflation, but no growth:

$$MV = PQ$$

The suggestion that people will adapt to government stimuli in a way that may make them self-defeating was termed the theory of "rational expectations." The events during the 1970s fitted much better with Friedman's and Lucas's models than with models assuming a long-term Phillips curve trade-off.

---

### THE POLITICAL BUSINESS CYCLE

W. Nordhaus and E.R. Tufte both proposed a theory of a so-called "political business cycle." Nordhaus presented the idea in his article *The Political Business Cycle* from 1975, and Tufte followed with a book called *Political Control of the Economy* from 1978. Both authors suggested that politicians regularly would stimulate the economy up to an election so that they would be more likely to be re-elected. This meant that you could expect politically stimulated booms before elections followed by recessions after.

---

# Part III

## A Hidden World

The atomic hypothesis that has worked so splendidly in physics breaks down. We are faced at every turn with problems of organic unity, of discreteness, of discontinuity – the whole is not equal to the sum of the parts, comparisons of quantity fail us, small changes produce large effects, the assumption of homogeneous continuum is not satisfied.

*John Maynard Keynes*

# Chapter 14

# The Simulators

Mathematicians are a species of Frenchman: if you say something to them, they translate into their own language and presto! It is something entirely different.

*Johann Wolfgang von Goethe*

It is every economist's worst nightmare to publish a new epoch-making theory at exactly the same time as somebody else. However, this was exactly what happened to Henry Schultz, Jan Tinbergen and Umberto Ricci. In 1930, these three economists each published his own description of a theorem that was later named "The Cobweb Theorem." All three published their theorems in German, and two of them, Tinbergen and Ricci, even published them in the same issue of the same magazine!

## COBWEBS

Their idea was rather simple. Imagine a number of farmers who have to decide what proportion of their land should be dedicated to the production of potatoes. If the price of potatoes is very high one year, then everybody will rush to plant more potatoes. But the next year, when they all bring a mountain of potatoes to the market, oversupply depresses the price. Disappointed, they skip most of their potato production – only to see that the consequent lack of supply in the following year forces the price back up. And so on; they keep trying to adjust, but never get it right.

It is quite clear that the cobweb assumption could add more than a twist to Adam Smith's invisible hand hypothesis. Adam Smith assumed

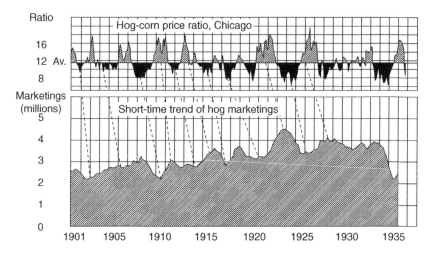

**Figure 14.1**  The Cobweb Theorem. This graph illustrates how the number of hogs brought to the market always lags after increases in the hog–corn price ratio. It appears that the poor farmers are tricked repeatedly by letting present conditions decide future supply. Source: Ezekiel, 1938. Previously published in Business Cycles: From John Law to the Internet Crash, Second Edition, by Lars Tvede, Routledge, London, 2001.

correctly that businessmen would quickly identify attractive niches in the market and fill them to gain profits. But just two factors can make the whole system begin to oscillate: one is the *time lag* between investment and production, and the other is *incomplete information* about what the competition is planning to do. And both assumptions seem quite realistic, don't they?

The cobweb was described as a phenomenon in the commodities market. But if you think of it, it was really very similar to John Stuart Mill's thesis from 1826 about the general economy. An "economic cobweb" can occur if too many competitors, dissatisfied with price levels, simultaneously decide to cut their production. Or if many companies, attracted by an unexpectedly high price, say in a new market, decide to invest in production equipment for this market. This mistake is called "competitive illusion" (Mill called it competitive overinvestment), and it can obviously lead to overproduction. After the introduction of the cobweb concept, it could be said that a local cobweb phenomenon in a significant sector might pull the entire economy with it; crowd psychology gluing people and industries together, trapped in one giant web. It is even possible that central banks can struggle with it as they try to get the money supply right, as the Austrian economists suggested.

## NORWEGIAN SWELLS

The important aspect of The Cobweb Theorem was not really the assumption of insufficient knowledge – after all, such an assumption is quite trivial and penetrates almost any business cycle theory. (If everybody knew everything, speculators would soon eliminate cycles by arbitrage). The important aspect was that of time lags. The theorem showed that even some very simple time lags in a very simple system could lead to significant fluctuations. But cobwebs were not the only examples of such inherent instability with very simple explanations. Another example was the so-called "Sciffbaucycles." In 1938, the Norwegian professor Johan Einarsen published an article, *Reinvestment Cycles and their Manifestation in the Norwegian Shipping Industry*. In this classic, he described a phenomenon that he had discovered in the Norwegian ship-building industry: after a boom in ship construction, well-defined "echoes" seemed to occur in the construction level at certain intervals (Figure 14.2). His choice of the Norwegian industry for investigation was deliberate: first of all, it was well described statistically; second, it was the world's third largest fleet; and third, Norway had lost about half its ships during World War I, and after that the reconstruction of most of the fleet had taken place over just two years, 1920 and 1921. His curves showed:

> a distinct five-year cycle with peaks in the years 1884, 1890, 1895, 1899, 1906, 1912, 1916, 1920, 1925 and 1929.

It seemed reasonable to assume that these echoes were due to either repair or sale – in both cases, the time interval depended on the average length of time it took for critical wear and tear to take place. To distinguish these events, he investigated which ships were bought by somebody who had just sold other ships beforehand. He called this category of investment "replacement." Among replacements he found a clear pattern, which peaked at nine and again 19–20 years from initial purchase – the same cycle length as Juglar and Kuznets cycles. The five-year cycle could, in other words, be generated by overlapping replacement echoes. So here you had a lag between investment and reinvestment, which was quite different from the cobweb phenomenon, but which could also lead to systematic fluctuations. Just like the cobweb phenomenon, such a lag could constitute at least a partial explanation of the turning points of business cycles. Einarsen wrote:

> It seems to me that the theory of pure reinvestment cycles will give a satisfactory explanation of how this turning-point takes place, and how it takes place quite automatically.

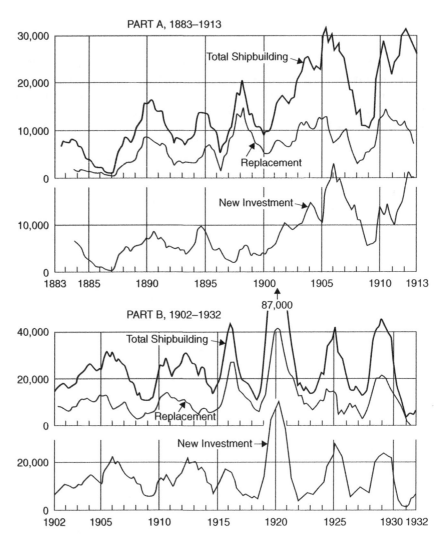

**Figure 14.2**   The echo phenomenon in Norwegian ship-building. The graphs illustrate total ship building, replacement and new investment for Norwegian ship-owners. The upper graphs cover the years 1883–1913; the lower ones cover 1902–1932. There seems to be a clear five-year cycle in replacement construction. Source: Einarsen, 1938. Previously published in Business Cycles: From John Law to the Internet Crash, Second Edition, by Lars Tvede, Routledge, London, 2001.

The cobweb and echo theorems were proposed during a decade where the methodology of business cycle research started to shift. Before, most authors had put the emphasis on a Mitchell-style "exhaustion" explanation of the turning point; that the economy was subject to self-reinforcing trends, which continued until stopped by some exhaustion mechanisms. The upper turning point was explained by lack of capital (monetary theory), lack of saving (underinvestment), lack of production resources or demand (overinvestment), etc. The lower turning point was largely seen as the opposite phenomenon; that it had become so easy and profitable to invest and innovate that people had come out of their holes for that reason. Now, more and more inherent processes, which could contribute to turning points, were being described, and how all these processes could work was best demonstrated with small, mathematical simulations. Leon Walras, Wilfredo Pareto, Alfred Marshall, Irving Fisher, and many others had already integrated mathematics in economics, but now almost any economist used mathematical simulations – at least from time to time. They were paving the way for "econometrics."

## THE NIGHT TRAIN

Integrated, econometric simulation is an idea that is often associated with Dutchman Jan Tinbergen, one of the three authors behind The Cobweb Theorem, and with Ragnar Frisch. What you do, when you model the economy in Tinbergen's and Frisch's "econometric" way, is that you first try to describe the governing rules of the economy. Instead of using words, you describe each rule as an equation, like Alfred Marshall had done to enhance his own understanding. Such an equation can be an "identity," in which you simply define the building blocks of a variable – as, for instance, your definition of "gross national product." Or it can be a quantitative relationship like, say, the relationship between gross national product (GNP) and consumption. An equation for GNP could look like this:

$$GNP = C + I + G + X - M$$

where

$C$ = personal consumption
$I$ = private investment
$G$ = government purchases
$X$ = exports
$M$ = imports

In this equation, GNP is an identity. When you have defined such an equation, the next step is to estimate parameter values. Let us say that you think you can forecast the following values from the information you have:

Private investment (*I*)     = 1000
Government purchases (*G*) = 1200
Exports (*X*)              =  800

When you come to income and imports, you find it a bit trickier, because they are, most of all, depending on GNP – which is exactly what you wanted to estimate. So you define the relationship between each of these two and GNP. And that relationship is estimated simply by calculating what it has been on average for as many years back as you can, or as you find relevant. Let us say that you study Kuznets's and Mitchell's old figures (for the USA) and find the following historical correlations:

Consumption is 70% of GNP  or *C*  = GNP * 0.70
Imports are 15% of GNP       or *M* = GNP * 0.15

Given these two relationships, you have in fact a total of three equations. To solve the problem, you simply have to merge them and insert the parameter values. Now it looks like this:

GNP = GNP * 0.7 + 1000 + 1200 + 800 – GNP * 0.15

which means that

GNP = 3000 + 0.55GNP

so that

GNP = 6666.7

Voila! But in reality, of course, it is much more complicated than that. To begin with, the number of important, initial equations of an economy is large, and some of them have exponents, square roots, and what not. Anyhow, when you have all these, you start a step-by-step integration until you have a single, large equation left. This elimination process is called the "night train analysis," because you often find correlations under way which have never seen the light of day before, but which must be true, if the rest is true. When you play with math, it might start spitting new stuff out. Sometimes new stuff that is so good that you can use it as a basis for a new theory.

Anyway, the next step is to make the model dynamic. This is done by modifying the construction into differential equations, which relate leading, coincident and lagging elements of future conditions to each other. And the last step is to test the models against statistical data to try to find a pattern. This is where Ragnar Frisch, one of the two pioneers of economic simulation, really excelled.

## THE STICK AND THE ROCKING HORSE

Ragnar Frisch was born in Oslo in 1895, the son of the gold- and silver-smith, Anton Frisch, and his wife Ragna. Frisch had originally planned to follow in his father's footsteps, and started as an apprentice in the work-shop of the famous Oslo firm, David Andersen. However, his mother soon got a strong feeling that the job would not be satisfactory for his inquisi-tive mind, so she insisted that he should study at a university. He became an economist, studied math afterwards, and began subsequently to inte-grate the two disciplines along the lines of Walras and Pareto. He pro-posed to call the combined discipline "econometrics."

In 1930, he agreed with Schumpeter and Fisher to create a forum for this econometrics, and "The Econometric Society" was born. One of their first problems was to find funding for it, but they found a surprising solu-tion. There was a stockbroker who wanted to understand the underlying nature of economic markets better. This was Alfred Cowles, who was not only a stockbroker, but also the second biggest shareholder in the Tribune Company. He had, for a number of years, published a newsletter where he provided stock market forecasts, but one day in 1931 he did something highly unusual: he wrote to his subscribers that he would close down the service because he didn't think that forecasts worked! Nor did he think that anyone else could do much better; he had studied the track records of other newsletters and found them all to be poor. So he decided instead to con-tribute to the development of economic science. Struggling with the com-plexity of his market models, he one day picked up the phone to call Harold Davis, a mathematician working at the University of Indiana and asked him an unusual question: would Davis be able to create a mathematical model that described the behavior of a system with 24 different variables?

Davis responded that it wasn't clear to him why anyone would have a need for such a model, but yes, in principle, he might be able to help. They decided to meet, and the meeting went very well. The outcome of their talks was that Cowles, who was well off, offered to sponsor the Econometric Society. Furthermore, he proposed to sponsor publication of a magazine that the society had considered publishing, and also to set up a commission, called "the Cowles Commission," which would support the econometric work and arrange various scientific discussion events. The publication he sponsored, which would be called *Econometrica*, would have Ragnar Frisch as its editor.

The first issue of *Econometrica* was printed in 1933. Frisch wrote the introductory editorial, where he stated that the main purpose of the magazine was to combine abstract theory with observation, so that theory didn't lose touch with reality. The focus of the publication would be general economic theory, he claimed, as well as business cycle theory, statistical theory and statistical information. Frisch had, meanwhile, become very interested in the fundamental causes of the business cycle problem, and he had, like many economists before him, spent hours poring over diagrams that illustrated past business fluctuations. One of the things that he observed was that most diagrams illustrating actual business cycles seemed to display some, albeit limited, degree of regularity. Not so regular that you could predict them by the calendar, but more regular than a purely random phenomenon. So business cycles didn't appear to be pure noise; they were independent "things" – phenomena that required their own explanation. The problem that he struggled with was why they displayed this relative regularity. Could it be because they simply had inherent dynamics that created recurring cycles, or did the economy receive external shocks at regular intervals (as proposed in Jevons's dubious "sunspot" theories)? He didn't believe much in either explanation. But how could you then explain the relative regularity? He played with various models until he finally believed that he had the answer. So, one day in 1933, he sat down and began writing an article.

## IMPULSE AND PROPAGATION

Its name was *Propagation Problems and Impulse Problems in Dynamic Economies*, and it has become one of the real classics in business cycle theory. This was not because it stated something very complicated or abstract (it didn't), but because it was the first to state very clearly how a series of random shocks could stimulate economic fluctuations that seemingly had some regularity. In other words: how the economy could generate order out of chaos. He invited his readers to think about what happens when you hit a rocking horse randomly with a stick. The movement of the stick is fast and swift. However, the subsequent movement of the horse is completely different. It is cyclical and continues over a long period of time. He then continued to provide a few simple mathematical models with economic variables to illustrate how economic shocks ("impulse") would create cycles ("propagation"). Frisch demonstrated often to his students how this worked. He would show them how you could add a series of completely random shocks to his model. The result was that it generated cyclical movements that were very different and much more structured than the shocks that caused them. The most interesting observation here was that:

- The *amplitude* of the cyclical fluctuations depended strongly on the shocks . . .
- . . . but the *duration* of each cycle was much closer related to the inherent propagation mechanism

Frisch disagreed with almost any other economist at the time on one issue: he believed that the economy in itself was stable: the rocking horse would only rock if there were external impulses to provoke it. No hits with the stick would mean no cycles, but there would, in reality, always be lots of hits with the stick; lots of external shocks, and the rocking horse would consequently rock all the time in a cyclical, but complex, pattern.

## SLIDE RULE AND SQUARED PAPER

To Ragnar Frisch and Jan Tinbergen, the mathematical modeling methods held a number of clear promises:

- They would uncover whether existing theories were complete
- They would force economists to state theories with absolute clarity
- They would provide a good way to locate differences of mind between theorists
- They would make it possible to test any theory

One of the things Jan Tinbergen used his methodology for was to model the business cycle. If he had used Walras's original methods, he would have needed an enormous number of equations (his colleague Pareto once estimated that Walras would use 70 699 equations to calculate what happened when 100 people traded 700 different commodities). Tinbergen had the advantage that a number of macroeconomic relationships had already been established with fair certainty; not the least by Keynes. This limited the necessary amount of equations dramatically.

His first attempt was on the economy of his own country. Equipped with a slide rule and squared paper, he set out to develop a mathematical simulation model for the Dutch economy. He knew that the task would be far from easy. First of all, to use the Wicksellian period analysis, he needed a deep understanding of the dynamic relationships. If, for example, consumption was dependent on income, was it then dependent on *past* income, the *present* or the *anticipated future* income? Second, he couldn't just use any mess of equations, even if they were all correct and relevant. The number of variables would have to be identical to the number of equations, so that he could isolate any one variable and test its simulated run against reality. But the greatest challenge was in the essence of the holistic thought: if he made just one significant error some place – just a single one – then the whole construction might give a completely wrong result. It was like putting the science itself on the exam table. Did the economists understand or did they not understand all major aspects of the economic system? Econometrics would show.

## A Project for the League of Nations

To posterity, it is clear that they did not. But his results, presented in 1936, were a scientific milestone nevertheless. The system consisted of 24 equations, out of which eight were identities. When you inserted your estimated parameter values, you could estimate the behavior of the entire system. This was of interest to the League of Nations, where a long-term research project to find solutions to the business cycle problem had been initiated six years earlier. They had picked two Dutch economists for the task. Von Haberler was asked to examine and evaluate all existing business cycle theories, which he did in his book *Prosperity and Depression*, dated 1937. Afterwards, Tinbergen would test them statistically to see whether they conformed with reality. Tinbergen grouped the phenomena together and tested the hypothesis surrounding each group. In 1939, he published his results in two articles. He concluded, among other things, that fluctuations in profits were by far the most important explanation of aggregate investment fluctuations in most sectors.

John Maynard Keynes was asked to make a review of Tinbergen's first article. He was reluctant to write it, but once he did, it became one of the most quoted reviews in the history of science. Here is an extract:

Prof. Tinbergen is obviously anxious not to claim too much. If only he is allowed to carry on, he is quite ready and happy at the end of it to go a long way towards admitting, with an engaging modesty, that the results probably have no value. The worst of him is that he is much more interested in getting on with the job than in spending time in deciding whether the job is worth getting on with. He so clearly prefers the mazes of arithmetic to the mazes of logic, that I must ask him to forgive the criticisms of one whose tastes in statistical theory have been, beginning many years ago, the other way around.

He criticized the methods for a number of weaknesses; for instance, that you had to know every important parameter, that spurious oscillations could be hidden in the real structure, and that his assumptions about linearity could be unrealistic. In essence, he claimed that Tinbergen's models could only explain cycles if he assumed that they were pushed by other, exogenous cycles. To explain inherent turning points, he would need to introduce nonlinear correlations. Keynes concluded:

I have a feeling that Prof. Tinbergen may agree with much of my comment, but that his reaction will be to engage another ten computers and drown his sorrows in arithmetic.

Which was exactly what he did. He engaged a number of computers (the meaning of "computers" at the time was people doing calculations by hand), and in 1939 he published a business cycle model for the United States to analyze fluctuations in the period 1919–1932. This time, he had taken a clue from Minsky and Kindleberger and added a financial sector, with equations describing the behavior of bonds, shares, money rates and money supply. The model, which had 48 equations (twice the number in the Dutch model), tended to swing in a 4.8-year cycle, but only when continuously excited. Left alone, it would soon fall to rest. That, of course, seemed rather unsatisfactory if one wanted to explain, for instance, the Great Depression.

Keynes did not fall to rest. When Tinbergen had published a reply to him in 1940, Keynes's comment was polite towards Tinbergen, but not towards econometrics:

There is no one, therefore, so far as human qualities go, whom it would be safer to trust with black magic.

Keynes's basic education in economics had not been very extensive. His four years at Cambridge had mainly been dedicated to mathematics and outside interests, and it is likely that he was more influenced by his experiences in business and money management than by the prevailing academic schools. These experiences led him to the conclusion that reality was much too complex to be modeled correctly in a macroeconomic system of equations. A very important hint of this complication appeared in an article the same year that Tinbergen published his model of the American economy. The author of that article was a 24-year-old graduate from Harvard.

## Two Principles Combined

It was one of the older professors at Harvard, Alvin Hansen, who, in 1939, had come to think about an important question. Hansen had become America's leading Keynesian and was eager to integrate Keynesian thought with earlier, classical concepts. So he asked one of his brightest students, Paul Samuelson, if he could somehow develop an integration between the "Keynesian" multiplier and the "classic" acceleration principle, which had been pioneered by Clark, but also incorporated in the theories of, among others, Spiethoff, Robertson, Mitchell, Aftalion, Pigou and Harrod.

What intrigued Alvin Hansen and his student was the fact that the accelerator and the multiplier were two, in principle, simple concepts, but no one had investigated what would happen if they were combined. Would the resultant dynamics, for instance, exhibit dampened cycles? Or accelerating growth? Or something entirely different? And would it fit at all with observed reality? Because if not, then you had real trouble! The young Samuelson started by creating a simple table combining the two effects in a model economy. He gave it the following rules:

- Government expenditure was fixed at "1.00" every year
- Consumption was always half the national income in the preceding year (at that time, economists had discovered that "propensity to consume" was rather influenced by past income)
- Investment was always half the increase in consumption between the past and the present year (which fitted with Keynes's assumptions of investors using the rear mirror rather than the binoculars). This relationship between consumption growth and investment can be termed "the accelerator relation"
- Total income was the sum of government expenditure, consumption and investment

**Table 14.1** Combining the multiplier with the accelerator. These are the numbers in Samuelson's calculation. The negative numbers for investments in periods 6, 7 and 8 should be interpreted as marginal effect, implying that an additional government spending of 1.00 per year would mean that investment in years 6–8 would be *lower* than if the government had not tried to stimulate!

| Period | Government | Consumption expenditure | Investment | National income |
|--------|-----------|------------------------|------------|-----------------|
| 1 | 1.00 | 0.0000000 | 0.0000000 | 1.000000 |
| 2 | 1.00 | 0.5000000 | 0.5000000 | 2.000000 |
| 3 | 1.00 | 1.0000000 | 0.5000000 | 2.500000 |
| 4 | 1.00 | 1.2500000 | 0.2500000 | 2.500000 |
| 5 | 1.00 | 1.2500000 | 0.0000000 | 2.250000 |
| 6 | 1.00 | 1.1250000 | −0.1250000* | 2.000000 |
| 7 | 1.00 | 1.0000000 | −0.1250000 | 1.875000 |
| 8 | 1.00 | 0.9375000 | −0.0625000 | 1.875000 |
| 9 | 1.00 | 0.9375000 | 0.0000000 | 1.937500 |
| 10 | 1.00 | 0.9687500 | 0.0312500 | 2.000000 |
| 11 | 1.00 | 1.0000000 | 0.0312500 | 2.031250 |
| 12 | 1.00 | 1.0156250 | 0.0156250 | 2.031250 |
| 13 | 1.00 | 1.0156250 | 0.0000000 | 2.015625 |
| 14 | 1.00 | 1.0078125 | 0.0078125 | 2.000000 |

Table 14.1 shows what happened in this simple model.

It illustrates a time journey in an economy with fixed parameters (a propensity to consume of 0.5; an acceleration relation of 1.0). It shows that the national income – given Samuelson's rules – can experience dampened cycles if subject to permanent fiscal stimulation (dampened cycles eventually fall to rest, in contrast to the behavior of cobweb systems). The basic reason for these fluctuations is that Samuelson inserted lags in the equation; he made investment and consumption dependent on the past, not on the present.

But Samuelson didn't stop there. He conducted a series of re-runs in which he experimented with the values of his parameters, that is, with marginal propensity to consume and the investment relation. This is called a "factor analysis," and Figure 14.3 shows what he found.

So the young graduate student had now found an answer to his professor's question. The answer was that, depending on the actual values of the two parameters, the income in this model society could exhibit:

• Stability
• Dampened cycles
• Explosive cycles or
• Extreme growth

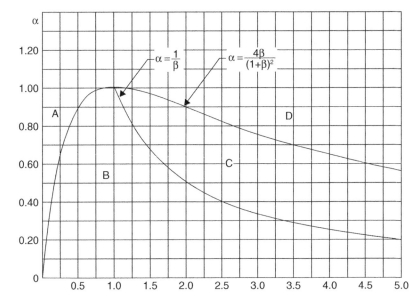

**Figure 14.3** Factor analysis for Samuelson's simulation of the accelerator and the multiplier. The horizontal axis represents values of the acceleration relation, and the vertical represents the propensity to consume. The graphs illustrate the boundaries between factor combinations with different behavior. Region "A" represents combinations leading to stability, region "B" is combinations leading to dampened cycles, region "C" is explosive cycles, and region "D" combinations that lead to extreme growth. Source: Samuelson, 1939. Previously published in Business Cycles: From John Law to the Internet Crash, Second Edition, by Lars Tvede, Routledge, London, 2001.

## THE NEOCLASSICAL SYNTHESIS

Samuelson's article was one of the works that stimulated the beginning of what would later be called "the neoclassical synthesis." This was a new line of thought that developed during the 20th century, and which made four basic, simplifying assumptions:

- All people (or so-called "agents") are consistently rational
- The best way to model economic action is to model how individual agents behave to maximize their own gain, and then aggregate the sum of this individual behavior to create macro-models

- Free market mechanisms provide the best solution to achieving economic coordination
- Free markets are generally inherently stable

The neoclassical models were mainly inspired by classical models. It was about rational individuals (Adam Smith's self-interest) optimizing their atoms of pleasure (Edgeworth) to create a system that found its own balance (Adam Smith's invisible hand). The economy was modeled from individuals up: the sum of individual behavior created an aggregate behavior (Walras and Pareto).

It had several scientific and practical advantages. A clear strength was the fact that it was based on an elegant modeling approach. Any model that is based on simulations of how its smallest entities behave has the potential to be more correct and more flexible than a model that makes gross assumptions on the macro level, as Keynes and Friedman did. Secondly, the systems found their own equilibrium. You could change any parameter in the models, and they would then find a new equilibrium after a transition period. This meant that you could derive a clear answer to any question, like "what effect will it have if we raise taxes by 3%?" The flip side was that the assumptions had to be really simple in order to make the models workable: it was, for instance, basically assumed that people were rational and that markets were efficient – something that Keynes had disagreed with. The neoclassical synthesis evolved over the years until it, according to Paul Samuelson (1955), was "accepted in its broad outlines by all but about 5% of the extreme left and the extreme right among writers."

---

### ARROW, DEBREU AND THE NEOCLASSICAL TRADITION

The neoclassical tradition reached a milestone when Nobel laureates Kenneth Arrow and Gerard Debreu in 1954 published a famous article entitled *Existence of an Equilibrium for a Competitive Economy*. This article provided something that almost looked like a proof of the existence of Adam Smith's invisible hand. However, many economists would later question the realism of this assumption, and Arrow would even join their ranks.

---

The fact that neoclassical theorists assumed that markets were rational and efficient did not mean that they pretended that business cycles didn't exist. It would be absolutely coherent to assume that markets are efficient and people rational and at the same time observe business cycles if these were caused by series of external shocks, like Ragnar Frisch's "stick." The basic assumption was that shocks that were external to the marketplace itself caused the fluctuations. But the neoclassicists explained these fluctuations with factors that were not inherent to the way a free market economy works.

## MONETARY OR REAL FACTORS?

The neoclassicists assumed initially, like Marshall, Wicksell and von Hayek, that monetary changes were largely responsible for business cycles (however, this doesn't make von Hayek a neoclassicist, since he didn't believe in rational agents and efficient markets). The early neoclassicists, who focused on monetary explanations for business cycles, took two directions:

- *Assuming relative price confusion.* Increased money supply raised all prices. However, individual producers assumed mistakenly that they had a particular price benefit (a relative price increase), whereas the actual reality is that all prices are rising
- *Assuming "permanent – transitory" confusion.* People do not understand changes in money supply and therefore do not know whether price increases are temporary or transitory

However, the focus of the neoclassical school turned gradually more and more towards "real" factors (meaning anything that wasn't monetary).

### "EQUILIBRIUM" AND BUSINESS CYCLES IN A NEOCLASSICAL CONTEXT

The neoclassical approach to business cycles comprised an original source of fluctuations and a propagation mechanism, which may amplify and transmit initial fluctuations to the rest of the economy. The term "equilibrium" in these theories referred to the propagation mechanism, while "monetary" or "real" referred mainly to the supposed sources of the fluctuations.

## Real Business Cycle Theories

The concept of real business cycles was not new. Jevons had, for instance, proposed it with his failed "sunspot" business cycle theories, and Spiethoff and Schumpeter with their waves of innovation.

The basic assumption of the neoclassical real business cycle school was that the main causes of business cycles were shocks caused, for instance, by new technical innovations, changing habits, wars, political changes, or nature (the main focus was on supply shocks – changes in the output of something). These models were not assuming that the economy would respond proportionally to everything that hit it – or when it got hit. The assumption was that there were inherent propagation mechanisms that converted the effects of the external shocks into more regular, recurrent movements of contractions and expansions. However, the theoretical approach had a new and odd angle: it stated that *the economy always was in equilibrium, even when it fluctuated widely!*

The explanation was simple: markets were efficient and they would always seek equilibrium. What happened was that the economy from time to time received a shock, and it would each time move through a step of transitory phases, all of which represented the best equilibrium possible at the time. The movement was smooth and "cyclical" simply because there was a natural, balanced propagation mechanism that played out as a response to the shock. You could call a real business cycle a "floating Walrasian equilibrium." The attraction of this approach was that you could preserve the neoclassical equilibrium models and their foundation in microeconomics and yet explain business cycles.

The first significant attempt to describe modern real business cycle theory appeared in an article in *Econometrica* in November 1982. The article was written by Finn Kydland, a professor from Carnegie-Mellon University in Pittsburgh and Edward Prescott, who was an adviser in the Research Department of the Federal Bank of Minneapolis and Professor of Economics at the University of Minnesota. The title of the article was "Time to Build and Aggregate Fluctuations." This article described the so-called real business cycle model – the stick and rocking horse model previously introduced by Ragnar Frisch, whereby business cycles were caused by external shocks, and where the cyclical movements were created by the inherent propagation mechanisms as the effects of the shocks rippled through the economic systems.

## FLAPPING IN THE WIND

Real business cycle models were nice from a theoretical/modeling point of view, but they generated an unusual amount of critical articles. A typical example came when Prescott presented an article about real business cycle theories ("Theory Ahead of Business Cycle Measurement") at a conference in 1986. One of the responses was an article ("Some Skeptical Observations on Real Business Cycle Theory") by Larry Summers, the Harvard professor who would, in 1999, be appointed Secretary of Finance of The United States – possibly the most powerful economic position in the world. Summers's response expressed a rather unfavorable view on real business cycle theories:

> These theories deny propositions thought self-evident by many academic macroeconomists and by all those involved in forecasting and controlling the economy on a day-to-day basis. They assert that monetary policies have no effect on real activity, that fiscal policies influence only through their incentive effects, and that economic fluctuations are caused entirely by supply rather than demand shocks.

And he continued:

> If these theories are correct, they imply that the macroeconomics developed in the wake of the Keynesian revolution is well confined to the ashbin of history. And they suggest that most of the work of contemporary macroeconomists is worth little more than that of pursuing astrological science.

Summers argued that the parameters in Prescott's model were not right:

> Prescott's growth model is not an inconceivable representation of reality. But to claim that its parameters are securely tied down by growth and micro observations seems to me a gross overstatement. The image of a big loose tent flapping in the wind comes to mind.

Other than concluding that the parameters were wrong (and that the whole thing reminded of a loose tent flapping in the wind), he concluded that it was difficult to identify the external shocks that should cause the actual business cycles people had experienced. Every growth era and every crash or recession should have an external cause, but they were very often nowhere to see. What seemed, in most cases, to be a much more obvious explanation was internal nonlinearity. He explained how real business cycle theorists could go wrong:

- Proponents of real business cycles would measure technical innovation through average productivity statistics . . .
- . . . but studies based on interviews with companies showed that productivity typically fell during downswings not because of an external shock, but because companies chose to keep their employees in order to have them stand by for better times

Another element in real business cycle theories that Summers couldn't accept was that they claimed to be "tested" even though they did not involve price data. Price data would reveal whether it was supply or demand shocks that were taking place, but without them you wouldn't know. Finally, he saw the assumption of efficient markets clearing (as the neoclassical approach suggested) during a depression as very unrealistic:

Read any account of life during the Great Depression in the United States. Firms had output they wanted to sell. Workers wanted to exchange their labor for it. But the exchanges simply did not take place. To say the situation was Pareto optimal given the technological decline that took place between 1929 and 1933 is simply absurd, even though total factor productivity did fall. What happened was a failure in the exchange mechanism.

Summers's alternative explanation was that there was convincing evidence suggesting mechanisms that often lead to breakdowns of the exchange mechanism and credit markets.

Proponents of the real business cycle approach claimed that its key strength was that it provided a microeconomics foundation to business cycle research, and that this foundation was coherent with mainstream neoclassical economics. However, opponents like Larry Summers claimed essentially that the abstractions and simplifications that they had to make in order to fit the models were so many and so gross that the result had very little relationship to reality. What they had done was to remove anything that could create inherent instability from their models – any of the positive feedback loops, etc. that were popping up everywhere when you studied real events. They ignored most of the factors that created most of the fluctuations.

## THE PROBLEM WITH EQUILIBRIUM

Samuelson had combined just two simple phenomena and showed how complicated their joint behavior could be. But the point was that the business cycle theories proposed so far contained descriptions of at least five different, nonlinear categories of feedback phenomena:

- *Positive feedback loops.* Vicious circles, in which a given event stimulated another, which, in turn, stimulated the first. Examples are early theories of momentum trading (Mill, Marshall), and self-ordering (As in Clark's accelerator and Metzler's inventory cycles, which we will study closer in Chapter 15)
- *Echoes.* Clusters of investment in durable capital goods (like ships) or consumer goods (like cars). Einarsen's ship-building cycles were such echoes
- *Cascade reactions.* Chain reactions with a built-in amplifier effect. This was typical in "mass-psychology" theories, which we shall examine later. It was also evident when Schumpeter said that secondary effects of clusters of innovation were far stronger than the primary stimulus
- *Lags.* Phenomena in which an action or event appearing "now" had an effect that surfaced later in time. Cobwebs (Tinbergen, Ricci) and accelerators (Clark) were examples of such phenomena, as were many underconsumption and overinvestment theories (Hobson, Tugan-Baranovsky, Spiethoff, Catchings, Foster, Kassel, Robertson, Hawtrey, Fisher, Keynes, von Mises, von Hayek)
- *Disinhibitors.* Phenomena in which potential negative feedback processes were temporarily blocked by positive feedback processes. There were elements of these in psychological theories about momentum trading (Mill, Marshall, Pigou), as well as in self-ordering (Clark, Metzler)

## The Feedback Concept

Nonlinear feedback illustrated complicated statistical dependency between past and present. The many feedback phenomena that the economists had described over time came in two kinds, "positive" and "negative." *Positive feedback* phenomena pushed the system away from the smooth trend movement. *Negative feedback* phenomena, on the other hand, pulled the economy back towards the smooth trend. Adam Smith's invisible hand was a negative feedback concept, and so were any explicit explanations of business cycles' turning points.

But the problem was the mere abundance of feedback phenomena that had been discovered: there was something frightening about the rapidly rising number of theories and rules which seemed plausible. Given the complexity of the combined dynamics, how could anybody ever be able to develop a clear picture of the overall behavior – let alone be able to forecast it? Had the selection process in capitalism created a system so complicated that nobody would be able to figure it out? Just imagine if loops fitted into chain reactions, some of which were amplified to form cascades, all of which were subject to echoes, and the whole damned thing equipped with a multitude of lags and disinhibitors! Damn!

It became increasingly clear that to understand business cycles, it was not enough to pile more and more mathematical rules for the economy on top of each other. Someone would need to look through the fog and find the essence. As Samuelson's simulations had indicated, there could be a very strange world hidden behind the neat logics of the simulators – a world which was about to surface. But in the year the two articles by Tinbergen and Samuelson were published, the Second World War broke out. More and more of the competent scientists would now be asked to switch from whatever they had been doing to military research.

---

### MACROECONOMIC MODELS

Lawrence Klein was one of the first to introduce the term "macroeconomics" in his article "Macroeconomics and the Theory of Rational Behavior" from 1946. Klein introduced the team approach to macroeconomic model building, whereby large groups of scientists worked together to create large aggregate simulation models with several hundred or several thousand equations. Large-scale econometric models normally contain at least 100 equations that represent different aspects of macroeconomic behavior, with additional equations that represent definitions, external inputs and constraints. They exist in all shapes and forms, but the typical modern model is nonlinear and complex, and it will typically combine elements from neo-Keynesian models (assuming market inefficiencies) with elements from neoclassical models (assuming market efficiency). Some of the best-known commercial models for business cycle research are Data Resources, Inc (the DRI Model), Lehman Brothers ("Sinai-Boston Model"), Chase Econometrics, Wharton Econometric Forecasting and Associates ("The Wharton Model"), and Lawrence Meyer and Associates (The LHM&A Model). The best-known public models include the NBER model, and project LINK, which combines a number of local models to create an international super-model. The LINK project expanded so that, as early as in 1987, it included over 20000 equations, representing 79 macroeconomic models.

# Chapter 15

# Brains of Steel

Then it took the next seven years after that to convince them that they hadn't all thought of it first.

*Jay Forrester*

The war was raging, and the students at the Moore School, Philadelphia, were talking. There was a room that had been sealed off, and something strange was going on in there. Every day you could see the same scientists and technicians, with special clearance, walk in and out of the former classroom. What were they doing there?

## BABBAGE'S MACHINE

They were creating history. Those who were allowed inside for the first time would see something entirely unexpected; something completely different from anything mankind had ever built before. It was big. It was strange. It was even kind of macho.

It was a man-made computing device, like the one Charles Babbage had dreamed about 80 years before. The reason that it was being built now was that it was desperately needed. Remember the logarithm tables that Babbage and his friends had been struggling with? Well, now the army needed something like that, and a lot of it, and very fast. One of their problems was the calculation of alternative trajectories of grenade shells fired from artillery. This required repeats of complex calculations again and again in order to simulate the paths. Now the army might need new tables desperately, as the Allied forces' firing tables were off in Northern Africa, because the ground there was softer than in Maryland.

At first they had considered calling it "Electronic Numerical Integrator," but then they had added two more words: "... and Computer". "ENIAC," as it was abbreviated, was supposed to be the first artificial brain, a multi-purpose ultra high-speed computer based on, not steam power, cogwheels and falling weights, of course, but on something much faster and much smaller: electronics. The first initiative to construct the machine had been taken by John V. Mauchly, head of the Physics Department at Ursinus College near Philadelphia. In 1940, he had written to one of his students that he hoped to be able to build an electronic computing device, which would have all the answers as fast as the buttons could be depressed. Few people had believed that it could be done, but one of his students, J. Presper Eckert, immediately understood the vision and gave support to the idea. On April 9, 1943, the project was officially approved, and fifty people were assigned to the task under the leadership of Mauchly and Eckert.

The machine they had to build was, in some ways, different from what Babbage had envisaged. It wasn't controlled by its own internal memory, but instead by plug boards, by which the machine was physically connected to determine how the problems were to be solved. It was also supposed to be orders of magnitude faster.

One day in April 1944, the men called in two women working on a differential analyzer to show them a breakthrough on ENIAC. They set up two accumulators with 500 tubes each, and as Mauchly pressed a button, the fifth neon bulb in the first accumulator lit up. At virtually the same time, the number "5" appeared to the fourth place on the second accumulator. The two women were shocked. Was this a "breakthrough"? Had this large team of scientists worked so hard to achieve so little – to be able to transfer a figure from one unit to another? But then the two men explained. The "5" appearing at the fourth place in the second unit meant "5000". The two units had multiplied five by 1000. The machine had demonstrated that it could perform a multiplication in 0.0024 seconds! That was 4000 times faster than the machine Babbage had dreamed of building.

Two months later, one of the engineers working on ENIAC, Herman Goldstein, spotted John von Neumann, a short, heavy-set man, while he was waiting at a railroad platform for a train to Philadelphia. Neumann was considered the world's greatest living mathematician by many. Indeed, his intelligence was beyond dispute. He could recite books which he had read years before, ad verbatim. He could often, within a few minutes, solve mathematical problems in his head that other mathematicians spent hours or days with. Goldstein indicated to Neumann that he

**Figure 15.1**  The ENIAC. This computer weighed thirty tons and generated so much heat that it had to be cooled by a special air force cooling system. It had over 19 000 vacuum tubes, around 1500 relays and several hundred thousand resistors, capacitors and inductors. Reproduced by permission of Corbis.

was working on the construction of an electronic computer, and soon after, Neumann decided to contribute to the ENIAC project.

The fact that the world's most famous mathematician had decided to give support to the project convinced many decision-makers that the electronic computer could have much more potential than they had formerly expected. In December 1945, the team had finally assembled the whole machine. Dominating the room completely, it was 80 feet long, eight feet wide and three feet deep. It had 40 panels, 4000 knobs and 4000 red neon tubes to show the functions of various parts inside it. These parts included 10 000 capacitors, 6000 switches and 17 468 vacuum tubes. It was later said (although this is perhaps not true) that when they turned this giant machine on for the first time, the lights dimmed in the city of Philadelphia.

Once the ENIAC had been built, it didn't take long before work commenced on a more sophisticated computer, the EDVAC, which had approximately 4000 vacuum tubes and 10000 crystal diodes when completed.

## PROJECT WHIRLWIND

It was at about the same time that von Neumann and Eckert received a 27-year-old visitor, Jay Forrester, from Massachusetts Institute of Technology, M.I.T. Jay Forrester was a graduate in electrical engineering, and he came because he had a great task in front of him: he had been asked to build a real time flight-simulation computer. It had been decided that this flight simulator would be digital, so Forrester was now visiting all projects that were doing something with digital computing to gather information. In January 1946, his project was approved under the popular name "Whirlwind." It became the largest computer program of the late 1940s and early 1950s, with 175 employees. When the central frame was erected in 1948, it occupied $230\,m^2$ (2500 square feet). Among the improvements were faster speed and less downtime (only a few hours per day). Forrester's Whirlwind program became a major success, and the technology was later used for a sophisticated air defense system.

In 1956, Jay Forrester was approached by the president of M.I.T., however, who asked if he would be interested in coming back to M.I.T. to work at the Sloan School of Management. Forrester agreed, as he saw a very interesting potential for the new computers, which had implications in a number of sciences: their enormous capacity permitted vast experimental simulations. You could use the computers to test an equation by checking whether the results looked reasonable, and then maybe modify the parameters a bit before trying again. He called this new discipline "Systems Dynamics."

## METZLER AND INVENTORY CYCLES

Forrester was interested in business cycles, and soon he and his staff began working on a model of inventory cycles. The most basic principle of inventory cycles can be described as follows:

**Figure 15.2** The Whirlwind computer. Jay Forrester designed and supervised work on the Whirlwind I computer, at M.I.T., which may be described as the world's first reliable high-speed computer. The photo shows Jay Forrester (far left, standing) and Norman Taylor (far left, pointing) inspecting completed circuitry. Picture used with the permission of The MITRE Corporation, Copyright © The MITRE Corporation. All Rights Reserved.

*Scene one, the premises of a car manufacturing company*: The economy is growing and the boss, Mr Smith, is consequently increasing his inventories in expectation of growing sales. However, after a while he concludes that they are large enough, so he reduces his next orders for inventories.

*Scene two (car parts supplier)*: The boss in the car parts facility, Mr Jones, is waiting for calls from Mr Smith with new orders, but the last order he receives is smaller than usual.

*Scene three (university lecture hall)*: Economic guru, Mr Keynes, explains to his students that if consumption falls in one sector, then the effect will be amplified through the multiplier effect.

*Scene four, Mr Smith's office*: The economy slows down because of the multiplier effect, so Mr Smith is suddenly concerned about the size of his inventories. He decides not to order any inventories at all for a while.

*Scene five, Mr Jones's office*: Mr Jones is waiting for the next call with inventory orders from Mr Smith, but the phone is just silent. So Mr Jones has to lay off some people, and decides to take a critical look at *his* inventories. Better bring them down a bit . . .

A fair amount of literature about inventory cycles existed at the time that Forrester and his team began to look at them, including 'The Nature and Stability of Inventory Cycles' by Lloyd Metzler, which had appeared in the *Review of Economics and Statistics* in 1941. Metzler's inventory models had a lot of similarities to the accelerator/multiplier models that Samuelson had described in 1939. Metzler's models showed that inventory fluctuation might result in a range of alternative parameter regimes:

- Damped monotonic
- Constant monotonic
- Explosive monotonic
- Explosive oscillations
- Constant oscillations
- Damped oscillations

### MODELING THE INVENTORY CYCLE

Forrester had held discussions with people at General Electric, who were troubled by the fact that their factories would be working three shifts, seven days a week in one year, and a few years later would be half shut down. He then made a hand simulation of the problem as he saw it, which was then converted into a board game for refrigerator manufacturing.

Forrester's board game would later take on its own life, as other people converted it into a board game centered on beer, where players used an electronic play-board, which illustrated four sectors in the world of beer:

- Brewery
- Distributor
- Wholesaler
- Retailer

Sessions would typically involve three to eight teams of four players, where each participant was responsible for one of the four sectors. It was a very simple inventory management task, and one would think it was a piece of cake to manage.

## WILD OSCILLATIONS

It wasn't. The game was initially only played by students at M.I.T., but later it spread to other universities in other countries, and was played by thousands of people, from high school students to chief executive officers of large companies. The experience was always the same: human behavior created instability. Many years later, Sterman of Sloan School of Management, M.I.T., published the results from 48 games played over four years. The 192 participants had been business executives as well as undergraduate (MBA) and PhD students at M.I.T. In every game, he had let consumer demand be identical, and extremely simple: four cases per week the first four weeks, then eight cases per week the last 36 weeks. There was instability and oscillation in all 48 trials. Between weeks 20 and 25, there was an average backlog at the brewery of 35 cases – more than nine times the increase in weekly consumption! Second, there was a clear amplification of instability, as the initial disturbance of four cases per week in consumer demand was amplified through the chain. On average, the initial increase had been amplified 700% when reaching the brewery. So, instead of stabilizing a system exposed to external shocks, the subjects ended up amplifying the disturbances. This is illustrated in Figure 15.3.

After such early simulations, Jay Forrester and his team started building a dynamic multi-sector computer model of the United States economy. The model was based on some core principles:

- Decision making in each sector was not based on mainstream theory of optimum economic equilibrium, but based on actual human behavior widely observed (not unlike in the beer game). Special attention was given to reservoirs/buffers such as inventories, goods in process, employee pools, bank balances and order backlogs
- A number of nonlinear relationships known from reality were incorporated

The team investigated at first the production sector alone, where they kept capital fixed, so that production could only vary through various inputs of labor.

In the next steps they expanded the model by (realistically) allowing fluctuations in goods and capital, which resulted in additional fluctuations similar to Kuznets and Kondratieff cycles.

Jay Forrester thought the conclusions could have radical implications for the understanding of business cycles. First, they indicated that the

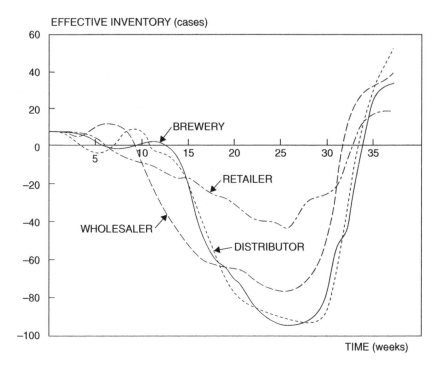

EFFECTIVE INVENTORY (cases)

TIME (weeks)

**Figure 15.3** Effective inventory in actual performance of the beer game. It can be seen that effective inventory in three of the sectors became very negative (large backlog) for a long period after the small demand shock, culminating in two sectors at levels corresponding to more than ten weeks' demand. After 32 weeks, it finally caught up – only to become much too large. Picture used with the permission of The MITRE Corporation. Copyright © The MITRE Corporation. All Rights Reserved.

Phillips curve could be wrong. Before the 1970s, the Phillips curve concept had been widely accepted. This curve expressed a simple trade-off between unemployment and inflation. If you wanted low unemployment, you had to accept a fairly high inflation. (In the United States, for instance, as late as in 1970, the major econometric models indicated that you could reach a low unemployment level by accepting inflation of 4%). But what Jay Forrester's simulations showed was that the economy could indeed be dominated by several business oscillations, as Schumpeter had suggested in 1939. If so, then there might not be any such simple relationship between inflation and unemployment, he claimed. Instead, it could very well be that the economy could have both, or neither, of the two evils, depending on the mode of all three cycles:

Potentially, three different and largely uncoupled dynamic modes may exist. First could be the business cycle that yields a cyclic variation in both wage change and unemployment and gives rise to the Phillips curve relationship. Second could be the Kondratieff cycle that may be producing its own, larger increase in unemployment. Third could be the usual relationship between money supply and prices that is producing inflation. If these different modes are sufficiently separate, then money supply affects inflation without reaching the problem of unemployment.

Forrester suggested that economists were at a risk of misinterpreting current events if they were not aware of these potential independent cyclical phenomena. If his assumption was correct, then the econometricians might be missing some vital points in their endeavors to make forecasting systems for the economies.

---

### THREE ECONOMISTS' CRITIQUE OF THE PHILLIPS CURVE THEORY

The Phillips curve describes a trade-off between inflation and unemployment. The relationship was first mentioned rather casually by Fisher, and then described statistically by Phillips. It became a mainstream theory when Solow and Samuelson co-wrote an article about it in 1960 (*Analytical Aspects of Anti-Inflation Policy*). Some of the most important objections against this theory were given by Jay Forrester, Milton Friedman and Robert Lucas. A simplified version of their critique is given below.

- *Jay Forrester*: fluctuations in wages and employment are both results of business cycle dynamics, so inflation is not an independent driver of employment. Increasing money supply can increase inflation, but with little effect on employment
- *Milton Friedman*: experience shows that inflation does not reduce unemployment. Growth in the inflation rate does reduce it, but continuous growth in the inflation rate is obviously neither sustainable, nor desirable
- *Robert Lucas*: people tend to have rational expectations. If you attempt to stimulate the economy by injecting money, then people will anticipate inflation. Businesses will raise prices and unions will demand higher wages to compensate. The result will be "stagflation," which is increased inflation but no additional growth

The relationship is deceptive, as we saw as early as with the paper-money-induced Mississippi bubble in 1720. This became widely recognized during the late 1970s, where there was high inflation and unemployment simultaneously, and knowing the critique of fine-tuning policy, central bankers in the USA, England, Japan and Switzerland finally adopted monetarist policies by targeting annual growth ranges for monetary expansion from that time (the Japanese policy failed miserably in the 1990s, however).

# Chapter 16

# Fat Tails and All That

Everyone knows what a curve is, until he has studied enough mathematics to become confused through the countless number of possible exceptions.

*Felix Klein*

The Whirlwind computer project was still very young, and Jay Forrester had not yet begun his studies of economic instability, when a small paper entitled "Long Term Storage Capacity of Reservoirs" was published in April 1951 by the American Society of Civil Engineers. The author of the paper was H.E. Hurst, a hydrologist who had worked on the Nile River Dam Project since 1907. Judged by its title, it should have little relationship with the business cycle models that Forrester later developed, but actually it had. Hurst's primary object was to propose a method for dimensioning water reservoirs, or dams. And what happened in water reservoir systems had interesting similarities with the problems encountered when you had economic reservoirs – like the inventories in Forrester's game.

Hurst's problem wasn't simple. The most important part was to forecast the natural fluctuations in the discharge levels from each river and lake involved. Obviously, there were many statistical problems, including rainfall, runoff and discharges of tributaries, etc. Hurst had descriptions of the discharges since 1904, but how could he be sure that this limited period was representative for the future? What if the dams were flooded?

## THE FAT TAIL PROBLEM

Most people with a basic knowledge of statistics would probably start out with a simple approach to this problem:

Natural phenomena are usually subject to a Gaussian distribution pattern – a so called bell-curve distribution. Such must also be the discharge levels, and with more than 40 years of observation, you can easily calculate the average and the standard deviation. Fill that into your Gaussian distribution equation, and you can calculate the likelihood that the fluctuations will exceed any critical level.

Neat and simple. But Hurst knew that there was a problem, since many natural phenomena tend to have "fat tails," and a higher than expected top, when compared to a Gaussian distribution. This meant that they had a tendency towards extreme outcomes.

Hurst believed that natural systems often had three characteristics. First of all, they contained *positive feedback*, in the sense that any initial random event tended to be "self-amplifying." That explained the drift towards extreme events. Secondly, there was an element of *chance*. And third, there were some *"circuit breakers"* that could interrupt trends. He developed a simple card game that exhibited behavior like that, and the outcome of this game had fat tails. After this, he decided to create a mathematical system to test systems for that behavior, which he called "re-scaled range." He used three basic variables and one constant:

*N*, the number of observations of, for example, days, years or whatever

*R*, the distance ("range") between highest and lowest value recorded during *N*

*S*, the "standard deviation"; the average distance from each single observation to the average of all observations

*a*, a constant, an individual figure which is characteristic for any natural case you investigate

Then he introduced the following relationship:

$$R/S = (a \times N)^H$$

It was the "*H*" in the equation that would reveal the feedback in the system. A normal, Gaussian distribution would have an "*H*" value of 0.5. A system with infinite *negative* feedback would have $H = 0$ and one with infinite *positive* feedback would have an *H* value of 1. Hurst used his system to test the behavior of numerous systems in nature, and found many with *H* values higher than 0.5. Many, in other words, that had strong, positive feedback processes, and therefore fat tails.

## BENOIT MANDELBROT

One other scientist obsessed with fat tails was Benoit Mandelbrot. While Hurst was enjoying his sundowners in Egypt, perhaps overlooking the dusty streets of Cairo, Mandelbrot might be on his way to IBM's high-tech research center in Yorktown Heights, USA. Mandelbrot was dabbling with mathematical problems of all sorts, and had come across exactly the same phenomenon as Hurst: he found fat tails in the most surprising places. One example was on the blackboard in Hendrik Houthakker's office at Harvard. Mandelbrot was invited to give a lecture there in 1960, and as he entered Houthakker's room, he saw on the blackboard a bell-shaped drawing with two fat tails. Houthakker explained what the drawing illustrated: it was the statistical distribution of price changes for cotton.

In a way, cotton was ideal for statistical tests, because the daily price data was both correct and available from far back in history. When Mandelbrot left after his speech, he carried with him a box with Houthakker's cotton data on computer cards. Afterwards, he sent to the Department of Agriculture for more data, covering price movements back to 1900. Analyzing these, he found fat-tail distributions regardless of whether he was looking at daily or monthly data.

## PHARAOHS AND BUSINESS CYCLES

Mandelbrot distinguished between two dynamic properties:

- The "Noah effect" or "infinite variance syndrome," where the small movements were interrupted by violent, discontinuous jumps due to disturbances
- The "Joseph effect" or "H-spectrum syndrome," which was the inherent tendency of prices to move in trends, as described by Hurst

The price movements he saw in cotton had to be a reflection of both; partly chance and partly necessity. The Noah effect took place when the economic system was pushed around by exogenous, unpredictable events. The Joseph effect occurred when you had, in Mandelbrot's words, "a very low decay of statistical dependence." The Joseph effect meant that during sustained periods of time, every observation was statistically dependent on a number of preceding observations, just like in Hurst's strange game of cards. In choosing a name for this dynamic property, Mandelbrot also let the Bible inspire him:

> The term "Joseph effect" is, of course inspired by the Biblical story of the seven fat and seven lean years (Genesis 6:11–12). The Pharaoh must have known well that yearly the Nile discharges stay up and then down for variable and often long periods of time, so they exhibit strong long run dependence and a semblance of business cycles, but with either visible or hidden sinusoidal components.

## COMPUTER MUDDLE

Mandelbrot was not the only scientist exploring nonlinear behavior. At M.I.T., the American meteorologist Edward Lorenz had programmed his radio-tube computer to simulate weather forecasts. The computer, a "Royal Macbee," did one of the things that computers are very good at: it made chain calculations. First, you fed into it the data describing the weather on a given day, for example wind speeds, atmospheric pressures, temperatures and humidity. Given this, the Macbee would calculate the weather for the next day, which it would again use as in-data for the third day, and so on. In about one minute, the Macbee could simulate the development of 24 hours.

One day in 1961, five years after Jay Forrester had started his system dynamics studies at the same institution, Lorenz looked at a simulation that he regretted having broken off too early. He decided to continue it, but with a small overlap period to check that it was indeed a continuation of what was already calculated. So he took the data printout and copied carefully the values for a given day into the computer. Then he put it to work, and went down the hall to get himself a cup of coffee. When he came back after an hour, he found something which was rather odd: in the "overlap" period of the two calculations, they did in fact not overlap as they should have. Everything in the system was completely predetermined: the in-data and the equation were entirely controlled by him, and they were entirely identical in the two runs. But the simulations diverged, in the beginning a little, and later a lot. What could be wrong?

The problem was the size of the print paper. The figures on this paper had only three decimals, as there wasn't space for more. He had copied figures with three decimals into the program, although the program in fact operated with six figures. So the difference in the overlap calculation was due to differences starting in the fourth decimals of the initial data. The more he thought about this, the more incredible it appeared: Apparently, you couldn't make a long-term weather forecast unless you knew, say, temperatures, with four or more decimals. It was not enough to know if the temperature in a given place on "day one" was 21.563 degrees, or if it was, in fact, 21.563975 degrees. To have such figures for all the variables, covering the whole globe, was utterly impossible. With little regard to publicity, Lorenz published his observations in *The Journal of Atmospheric Sciences*, under the title "Deterministic Non-periodic Flow".

If anybody read the article, they didn't make much fuss about it. During the following ten years, it was quoted less than ten times by other authors. But then, in 1972, a scientist at the Institute for Physical Science and Technology at the University of Maryland came across it – and was delighted. He started copying it and giving it to anybody who cared. One day, he gave it to James Yorke, a mathematician working at the same institute. Yorke understood the importance of the message, that long-term unpredictability could be a property inherent in a nonlinear system. In 1975, he published his own article about the subject. It appeared in the popular *American Mathematical Monthly* with a title that no one could ignore: "Period Three Implies Chaos."

That last word in the title became the expression which people would afterwards use to cover deterministic, yet complicated and unpredictable, phenomena. "Deterministic Chaos" would often be described as systems with behavior that when tested by standard statistical methods appeared random, but which were, in fact, deterministic – and thus not random at all. The article became widely read and quoted.

### DON'T BLAME THE METEOROLOGISTS

It is clear that Lorenz had learned from Yorke when he published a paper in 1979 with the title: "Predictability: Does the Flap of a Butterfly's Wings in Brazil Set Off a Tornado in Texas?" If readership is a success criterion, this article worked. The chaos concept was catching on, and scientists started doing research about it everywhere. The flap-in-Brazil paper explained that a butterfly in Brazil could determine whether there would be a tornado someplace else six months later. Even if the meteorologists seized power in the world and, determined to make weather forecasting the primary objective of mankind, covered the entire surface of the earth with small weather stations one foot apart and up in the air to the outer extreme of the atmosphere – even then they would never be able to make long-term weather forecasts. Even if all these billions of weather stations continuously sent all their data to a giant central computer, equipped with perfect mathematical simulation software, even then it wouldn't work. Because it just might happen that a butterfly flew between two of these measurement stations, releasing a small gust of wind that they couldn't record with sufficient precision – and that the unrecorded effect of that movement of the air would amplify through positive feedback and decide whether that tornado would come or not. By now, Lorenz's point was clear: feedback systems could be very "sensitive to initial conditions" – a property that would later be called "the butterfly effect."

## SOMETHING FISHY

Feedback systems are notorious not only in economics and climatology, but also ecology. When Robert May developed a mathematical program for simulation of fish populations in 1971, he came across a peculiar phenomenon. His equation was designed to calculate how large a fish population would grow under various assumptions. When he had entered the chosen values for the variables into the computer, the model would simulate the ecologic behavior until the size of the population gradually settled down to some fixed level. If he changed a parameter, it would settle down on a new equilibrium level.

One of his variables was fertility – the ability to lay eggs, so to speak. If the fertility was very low, the population would obviously die out. At higher fertility levels, it would reach a different equilibrium. But the peculiar thing was this: if he entered a very high fertility level, then the simulation never found equilibrium; the population kept fluctuating endlessly and without any apparent pattern. The string of mathematical feedback that created this chaotic behavior looked like this:

$$X(n + 1) = r * X(n) * (1 - X(n))$$

What this equation expresses is very simple. The left hand side of it simply means "the next value of X." And this next value of X is what we find on the right side: it is a constant, "r," multiplied by the present value of X, multiplied by one minus the present value of X. This little (and very simple) piece of feedback mechanics created equilibrium at low parameter values, but chaos at high values of "r." This was interesting not only for the fun of it, but indeed because such equations were quite common in simulations of many kinds of dynamic system – including economics. Like a small gene in a giant DNA molecule, such an algorithm could lie hidden in a giant simulation equation. And you would never notice the effect unless you made a multitude of factor analyses of the system dynamics with your computer. So, as Charles Babbage had foreseen, the computer was really revolutionizing science.

### BUTTERFLY EFFECTS AND FEIGENBAUM CASCADES

Many of the first thinkers in economics were not really economists. Quesnay and Juglar were doctors, for instance, Say, Walras and Pareto engineers, and Newcomb a mathematician and astronomer. Chaos theory was now triggering a new invasion of the discipline by outsiders. Suddenly, you found physicists and math experts from around the world making economic simulations. This happened in Copenhagen as well, where a team lead by Erik Mosekilde started to play with improved versions of Forrester's business cycle model. They wanted to investigate whether it was likely or not that cycle synchronization could lead to major depressions, as Schumpeter and Forrester had suggested. Consider this: if there were several, cyclical phenomena, then you couldn't just consider the total output to be the sum of the individual oscillatory movements, as illustrated in Schumpeter's drawing from 1935. The likely outcome was much more complicated, because each cyclic phenomenon would *interact* and interfere with the others. They decided to test this hypothesis by subjecting a Kondratieff model to Kitchin's and Kuznets's oscillations, respectively. Figure 16.1 shows how their Kondratieff model behaved.

Their Kondratieff model turned out to have an average cycle length of 47 years, and the three curves on the graph illustrate capacity, production and orders, where orders turn first, then production and finally capacity. The model shows a system that is inherently unstable because of self-ordering in the capital sector (ordering of capital for production of capital, but with a time lag).

The researchers would now proceed to create a model to simulate the Kuznets cycle, and this turned out to have a cycle length of 22.2 years. Now what would happen to the Kondratieff if their Kuznets was imposed on it? They tried, and found that the Kondratieff automatically would stretch its length by around 40% to synchronize with three Kuznets cycles for each of its own (Figure 16.2).

They also created a simulation of a Kitchin cycle, which turned out to have an inherent cycle length of 4.6 years on their computer. They tried now to impose this on their Kondratieff model, and found that it

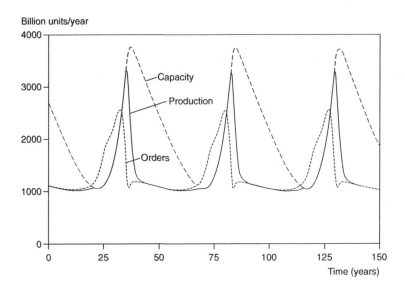

**Figure 16.1** A Kondratieff cycle simulation. This is a simulation of the Kondratieff cycle based on a modified version of The System Dynamics National Model from the Sloan School of Management. Source: Mosekilde, Larsen, Sterman and Thomsen, 1992. Reproduced by permission of Erik Mosekilde.

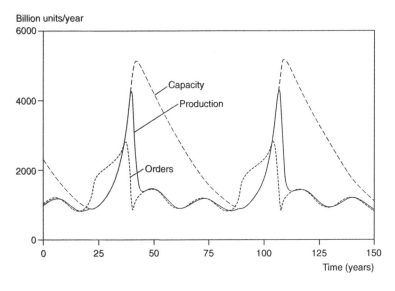

**Figure 16.2** Simulation of automatic synchronization between Kondratieff and Kuznets cycles. This simulation was conducted by subjecting the Kondratieff model mentioned in Figure 16.1 with an external sinusoidal oscillation given a period of 22.2 years, corresponding roughly to a typical Kuznets cycle. Source: Mosekilde, Larsen, Sterman and Thomsen, 1992. Reproduced by permission of Erik Mosekilde.

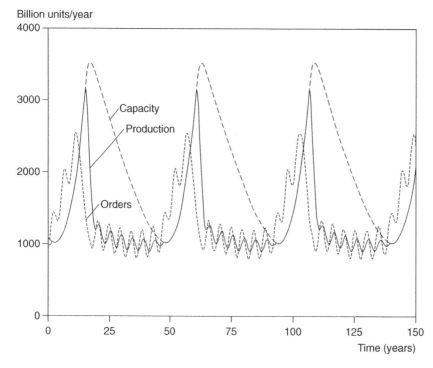

Billion units/year

**Fig. 16.3** Simulation of automatic synchronization between Kondratieff and Kitchin cycles. Source: Mosekilde, Larsen, Sterman and Thomsen, 1992. Reproduced by permission of Erik Mosekilde.

automatically developed synchronization with ten Kitchins for each Kondratieff. This remained intact as long as they kept the inherent Kitchin cycle length between 4.47 and 4.7 years. However, beyond that interval of Kitchin cycle lengths, the synchronization became more complicated. The synchronization process also proved sensitive to amplitude of oscillations. Figure 16.3 illustrates their synchronization when they kept the Kitchin cycle at 4.6 years.

Our next illustration from their experiments (Figure 16.4) looks completely different from any economic simulations made before the introduction of chaos theory (and perhaps could be used in psychology tests – to this author it looks like a giraffe surrounded by sails). What this graph actually illustrates is a so-called "phase space." The scientists again took their Kondratieff model and superimposed another cycle with a given combination of amplitude and duration each time. And then they did this again and again until they had covered a huge range of amplitudes and

Forcing amplitude

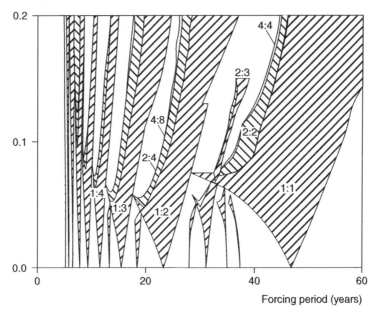

Forcing period (years)

**Figure 16.4**   Phase space of Kondratieff synchronization with external cycles. The graph illustrates how the Kondratieff responded when other cycles of different durations and amplitudes were superimposed. Source: Mosekilde, Larsen, Sterman and Thomsen, 1992. Reproduced by permission of Erik Mosekilde.

durations. The graph shows these durations on the horizontal scale (going from 0 to 60 years) and the amplitudes on the vertical scale. Every spot on this graph is the result of a complete simulation, and shaded areas show combinations where the Kondratieff would synchronize with the external cycles; the white areas are combinations that were chaotic. The ratio written by each shaded space is the number of external cycles that would play out within each Kondratieff.

Let's now look at the final graph, Figure 16.5, which is the strangest of them all. It shows the result of numerous calculations, where the superimposed, external cycle in each case had a duration of 19.6 years, but where its amplitude (horizontal scale) was changed a bit in each calculation. The vertical scale here is the maximum value found for capital formation. The graph shows how it evolves from a single solution to two, four, eight, etc., and finally chaos.

KS Capital$_{max}$

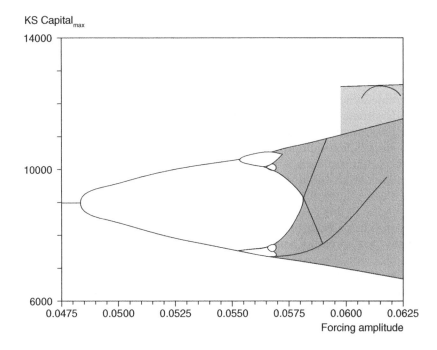

Forcing amplitude

**Figure 16.5** Feigenbaum cascade in cycle synchronization. Source: Mosekilde, Larsen, Sterman and Thomsen, 1992. Reproduced by permission of Erik Mosekilde.

## THE MAIN IMPLICATIONS OF CHAOS

Chaos theory has taught us how nonlinear systems can behave. It has also inspired the development of new tools in science, engineering, software writing, etc. The most important features characteristic of such systems are these:

- *Extreme sensitivity to initial conditions* (Edward Lorenz's butterfly effect). This means a distinct barrier against long-term prediction
- *Self-similarity* (Mandelbrot's fat tails in different scales). There can be a tendency for patterns to look similar in different scales, but they will not copy themselves forever into endless fractal dust, as in the "pure" equations
- *Multiple attractors* in some parameter intervals (the bifurcations in Say's Feigenbaum Tree). A system may easily have several stable solutions at

a given time, and random shocks may push them from one stable position to another

The work of chaos theorists gives us a basic understanding of the nature of some economic and financial systems, which makes it easier for us to determine which groups of practical forecasting tools can have validity in various situations. System dynamics, in particular, is important to the other basic mathematical approaches in economics, which are statistics, econometrics, neural networks and artificial networks. Let's imagine, for instance, that someone is using a given econometric long term forecasting model. We could now test its behavior over a policy space with tools from chaos theory and perhaps find that it produces chaos. Our conclusion would, in this case, be that the model either was grossly incorrect, or that it was impossible to forecast the system. Or it could perhaps show us that the system could be forecast within some boundaries only. System dynamics would give us a better feel for what we were dealing with.

Such implications of chaos were some of the incredible things that Samuelson had no means of predicting (due to the lack of electronic computers) when he opened the lid to the world of nonlinear dynamics in 1939. Nor could he see what happened in people's minds when they engaged in wild speculation frenzies. But that is what we will study in the next chapter.

---

### USING COMPUTERS FOR ECONOMIC ANALYSIS

To gain a good understanding of the economy, a combination of analysis tools must be applied. The list below gives a brief and very simplified overview of the most important quantitative analysis tools:

| Method | What you typically do | Examples of what you typically achieve |
|---|---|---|
| Statistics | Use statistical standard equations to describe how statistical data ("observations") are correlated. The statistician tests the actual data | • Classify statistical behavior<br>• Measure parameter values, such as "mean," "standard deviation," "$H$-exponent," etc. |

| Method | What you typically do | Examples of what you typically achieve |
| --- | --- | --- |
| | against any of these statistical templates | • Provide indications of the nature of the governing rules of the system<br>• Detect, classify and measure correlations in the behavior of different time series |
| Econometrics | Describe the economy with a system of simultaneous equations (typically very large). You will then insert present parameter values and calculate how the economy should evolve in the future. This is a chain calculation, where the output from one calculation (one time period) becomes input for the next | • Forecast the economy<br>• Simulate what will happen if given changes occur (i.e. higher taxes, lower interest rates, etc.)<br>• Test the validity of economic theories<br>• Detect, classify and measure repetitive patterns in given time series<br>• Measure economic correlations<br>• Discover new economic correlations |
| System dynamics | Describe the economy, or parts of it, with a set of equations. You investigate how this plays out as a result of different policies. You repeat these calculations again and again, each time modifying policies slightly, until a "phase space" or "policy space" of parameter values is mapped. | • Understand how the dynamic behavior of a system may change, depending on policies<br>• Identify policy intervals that give the best behaved systems |

| Method | What you typically do | Examples of what you typically achieve |
| --- | --- | --- |
| | Expressions of dynamic properties are measured throughout the policy space | |
| Neural networks | Feed a number of financial/economic time series into a software program. These programs will then test continuously for statistical correlations and, as they find them, create an econometric forecasting model | • Forecast the economy<br>• Forecast financial markets<br>• Reveal the patterns<br>• Continuously produce forecasts/ recommendations |
| Artificial intelligence | Observe (partly through on-site interviews) how successful human experts forecast economic and/or financial events. Their decision process is then expressed as equations. As real data are fed into these equations, they start generating forecasts and activity recommendations | • Forecast the economy<br>• Forecast financial markets<br>• Develop theories |

# Chapter 17

# Monkey See, Monkey Do

The only normal people are the ones you don't know very well.

*Alfred Adler*

Doubt! To those who trade on the stock exchange, there is no worse feeling than that of *doubt*. This state of mind does not normally evolve as a consequence of a single event; it is rather because several incidents don't quite fit into your world view. As each of these incidents occurs, a small seed of doubt is sown in your subconscious, and as days pass it grows, until, without any ready explanation, you reach the point of mental riot. Suddenly you feel that you have been walking on the thinnest ice that may break at any moment. Almost panicky, you conclude that you must reverse your actions instantly. It was exactly that feeling that many stock-traders experienced on Saturday, October 17th, 1987.

### THE SEEDS OF DOUBT

Larger portfolio managers and speculators in the world were probably quite aware of the existence of the typical business cycle sequence that Roger Babson had described in 1911:

Industry, as a whole, generally follows several months behind stock prices.

One of Babson's conclusions had been, as many traders knew, that it could be easier to forecast economic movements through studies of the stock market than to forecast the stock market through economic studies.

They would also know that stock markets now were official leading indicators. But bonds had turned out to be even better. As even Henry Thornton had observed in 1802, interest rates tended to rise as the upswing matured. In a paper published by the National Bureau of Economic Research in 1966, *Changes in the Cyclical Behaviour of Interest Rates*, Phillip Cagan concluded for the interest rates:

> ... The evidence therefore supports the following generalizations: (1) Interest rates maintain a sequence, with the active open-market rates usually turning first and the rates of negotiated and inactive markets usually turning last. (2) All long rates used to, but no longer, lag far behind short rates ...

As Cagan mentioned, the lag between short and long rates seemed to have narrowed by 1966, but before the global equity boom started in 1982, the sequence was again perfectly classical. Another financial characteristic of business cycles was that of credit quality. In 1955, the business cycle specialist Geoffrey Moore had given a speech for the American Finance Association, in which he described financial conditions that could precede a depression:

- A rapid increase in the volume of credit and debt
- A rapid, speculative increase in the prices of investment goods such as real estate, common stocks and commodity inventories
- Vigorous competition among lenders for new business
- Relaxation of credit terms and lending standards
- Reduction of the risk premiums sought or obtained by lenders

During such conditions, he had explained, the quality of new credit would worsen progressively. To the best traders it was no secret that a lot of these signals for a reversal were present now. First of all, there had been a rapid credit expansion during the preceding years, which had now turned, however. As the dealers could read in newsletters from *The Bank Credit Analyst* and other analysts, the financial liquidity had been falling since the beginning of the year. Secondly, American interest rates had started to rise in August, 1986. That in itself had been okay, because everyone knew that money rates could rise for a year or more before the stock market was damaged. But now the trend had been going on for 14 months and, during the summer, it accelerated.

The next development had been in Treasury bonds. They had been able to stay firm for a long time after the money rates had started rising. Eventually, however, T-bonds had been dragged down, as they almost always were. That was in April, 1987, and when they fell, they fell dramatically.

## BULLISH CONSENSUS

Another warning was the market sentiment. Every dealer worth his salt knew that the time to sell was when everybody else seemed most bullish. The problem was to find out exactly when this point was reached. Now it looked more and more as if it actually happened in August. That was the month when *Business Week* published a 25-page *Mid-year Investment Outlook* full of positive stock market comments. It was also the month when "Hadady Bullish Indicator" had rung the alarm. This weekly indicator, produced by a Californian research company, contained a weighted index of the published investment recommendations for more than a hundred leading American banks, brokers and investment advisors. The rule of thumb in Hadady's indicator was, simply stated, that you should sell if more than 70% of the advisors recommended to buy. That figure had been reached in August, just the day before the market peaked. Since then, prices had been falling gradually.

The last detail was by far the worst, however: on Friday, October 16, Dow Jones Industrials had fallen by an enormous volume – no less than 108.35 points, the worst nominal fall ever. As most traders knew, David Ricardo's old rule about cutting losses and letting profits run wasn't silly. Now, many investors had substantial losses – was it time to bail out? Peter Lynch, the famous manager of the mighty Fidelity Magellan Fund, had left the USA the day before the disastrous Friday. Now, as he was playing on the Irish Killarney golf course, he was worrying whether he should really be on holiday at all. His putting was just disastrous, and when the game was over, he couldn't remember his score – his mind was elsewhere. Peter Lynch was afraid his shareholders would lose money. A lot of money. So were many others. Dealers met in local bars all over the world to discuss the latest events. Why had Dow Jones fallen so far? It was scary. It had fallen after a sustained bull market, stimulated by an enormous credit expansion. Sentiment had peaked, and interest rates were rising steadily. And it was only five days until the 58th anniversary of the 1929 crash. In 1929, the initial fall had also been under heavy trading volume – an unpleasant resemblance. And oops! 58 years, you said? Wasn't there something about a "Kondratieff cycle"? Better have another beer!

## STORMY MONDAY

Monday October 19th didn't start well at all. In Tokyo, the index dropped by a modest 2.5%, but in Hong Kong it fell 11%, after which trading was suspended. When the European markets opened, London and Zurich dropped 11%, Frankfurt 7% and Paris 6%.

Jean-Luc Lepine, the director of Banque Demachy, went to a business dinner at one of Paris's elegant restaurants that night. When the meal started, he knew the Dow Jones had already collapsed; it had beaten Friday's record and was down by an incredible 180 points. But by the time dessert arrived, the Dow Jones was now down 300 points. As he was preparing to leave the restaurant, somebody told him it was down by 500, which Lepine thought was a joke. Measured in percentages, such a fall would be worse than ever seen before, despite presidential assassinations, riots, the Great Depression, Vietnam, Korea and two World Wars. This time there was nothing, absolutely nothing, to explain such a collapse, or even the terrible drop of the Friday before this weekend. But it was happening. People were selling in panic for no clear reason.

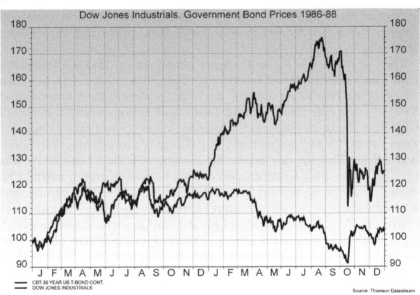

**Figure 17.1** Market rotation up to the crash in 1987. The graph shows indexation of CBT 30-year bonds and Dow Jones Industrials. The two markets tracked each other rather closely until early 1987, when bonds began to fall while equities rose. The crash of October '87 closed much of the gap. Previously published in Business Cycles: From John Law to the Internet Crash, Second Edition, by Lars Tvede, Routledge, London, 2001.

Actually it wasn't only people that wanted to sell. About 25% of the sales orders were generated by the silent army of computers. But the rest of the sellers were human, and one of them was George Soros. Expecting a crash in Japan, Soros had shorted Japanese stocks while remaining long on Wall Street. Now, he was heading for shelter, and in what an American trader described as "the worst sales he had ever seen," the Quantum Fund started offering S&P futures contracts in lots of a thousand through Shearson. The brokerage house asked 230 to begin with, but as the other traders circled around his lots like vultures, the price plummeted to between 195 and 210. As soon as his orders had been cleared, the prices started to recover, however, and they closed at 244.50. It was later estimated that the Quantum Fund had sold its contracts at a discount to the underlying shares of 250 million USD. At the same time, Soros had sold individual shares at prices that were sometimes the lowest of the day.

The Dow Jones Index ended the day 506 points down. It had lost 23% of its value in seven hours, and was down some 40% since its peak in August. Peter Lynch's Magellan Fund had lost two billion dollars. The American break had taken the whole world with it, wiping out paper values around the globe of 2.4 trillion dollars in one single, terrifying blow.

And then it was all over. The crash stopped after just two days, and when dealers reported to work on Wednesday October 21st, the markets were calm again. And then they resumed their bull market, climbing steadily from day to day until most of them hit all-time highs within two years.

So what was that all about? Robert Shiller, one of the leading specialists in irrational financial markets wanted to know, so he sent out 2000

**Table 17.1** The ten largest one-day declines in the Dow Jones Industrial Average. Black Monday takes the price with a large margin, which is interesting since nothing interesting happened up to and during this fall, except, of course, the fall itself.

| Rank | Date | Close | Net change | % Change |
| --- | --- | --- | --- | --- |
| 1 | 10/19/1987 | 1738.74 | −508.00 | −22.61 |
| 2 | 10/28/1929 | 260.64 | −38.33 | −12.82 |
| 3 | 10/29/1929 | 230.07 | −30.57 | −11.73 |
| 4 | 11/06/1929 | 232.13 | −25.55 | −9.92 |
| 5 | 12/18/1899 | 58.27 | −5.57 | −8.72 |
| 6 | 08/12/1932 | 63.11 | −5.79 | −8.40 |
| 7 | 03/14/1907 | 76.23 | −6.89 | −8.29 |
| 8 | 10/26/1987 | 1793.93 | −156.83 | −8.04 |
| 9 | 07/21/1933 | 88.71 | −7.55 | −7.84 |
| 10 | 10/18/1937 | 125.73 | −10.57 | −7.75 |

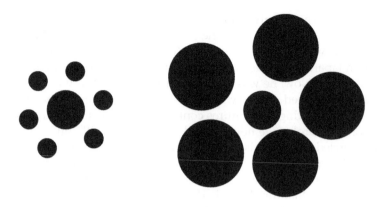

**Figure 17.2**   Which central circle is bigger? Or are they the same size?

questionnaires to private investors and 1000 to institutional investors. He received a total of 889 responses. They were interesting. Very few could cite any economic or political news that had compelled them to sell. No, they sold because markets were falling! It also emerged that many had thought that markets were overvalued, even at the time when they bought before the crash, and that some 10% had used a defined "stop-loss policy." Around a third had been affected specifically by the market penetration of technical trend indicators. All of this seemed to suggest, of course, that people collectively can appear rather irrational. So the big question is this: is it normal for an individual person to think in irrational ways?

## GETTING THE PICTURE

Take a good look at Figure 17.2, and then answer the following question: How do the two circles in the center of each group compare? Is the one to the right smaller than the one to the left? Or the same size? Or is it bigger?

You are a completely normal and sane person if you think it is smaller. But it *is* the same size. Perhaps you have sometimes wondered why the sun and the moon seem so much bigger when they stand just over the horizon, as if they were closer. They aren't, but we think they look that way. We think anything on the horizon is bigger than the same thing in the sky.

**Figure 17.3** Are these lines parallel?

Let's try another one. Take a look at the lines in Figure 17.3. Are they parallel or not?

Again, you are normal if you think they aren't parallel. But they are. Here is a third one: take a look at the four lines in Figure 17.4 and decide which of lines "A", "B" and "C" is the same height as the "test line."

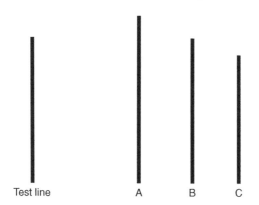

Test line         A     B     C

**Figure 17.4** Which line has the same height as the "test line"?

You may expect this to be a real trick question like the others, but your intuitive answer in this case is actually correct: "B" is the same height as the test line. Tests have shown that 99% of all people agree with that. So what's the point of that question? Well, in 1965, the psychology professor Solomon Asch devised a test where he took a group into a room and asked each of them this question. He would then mix some of his own cooperators into each group and instruct these to give the wrong answer "A." Here are the results of how the people that were not his cooperators answered under different circumstances:

- No one has answered before: 1% give the wrong answer "A" or "C"
- One person has given the wrong answer before: 3% will answer "A"
- Two people have given the wrong answer before: 13% will agree that "A" is the right answer
- Three or more have given the wrong answer before: 33% will equally conclude that "A" is the right answer

This is a striking example of group-think, which is a typical phenomenon in social psychology. It shows that people are not always rational. Does that mean anything? Should it change our view on the role of investments and speculation in business cycles and asset price movements, for instance?

Economists have had many different views. Neoclassical economics builds on Adam Smith's notion of efficient markets, and may conclude that while the individual isn't always smart, the average of all individuals is. Milton Friedman went very far in that direction when he claimed that speculation can't be destabilizing, since successful speculators buy low and sell high, which stabilizes a market. And the unsuccessful ones who do the opposite? Well, they will lose their money and leave the game quickly.

However, there was a rather good alternative view: a limited number of skilled investors may buy low and sell high, whereas a much larger number of unskilled investors, who change over time, do the opposite. This concept is not entirely new. We saw in Chapter 14 that John Stuart Mill in 1826 divided market players into "professional gamblers" and "rash speculators." The first category, he thought, would have a basic understanding of the forces behind demand and supply, whereas the latter would simply trace price movements; a behavior which amplified fluctuations. He also emphasized a psychological aspect of competitive over-investment, which happened, he wrote, because of a "universal propensity of mankind . . . to overestimate the changes in their own favor."

## EARLY EMPHASIS ON PSYCHOLOGY

Mill was not the only early writer to emphasize psychology. Pigou, for instance, went very far when he made this statement:

the varying expectations of businessmen . . . and nothing else, constitute
the immediate causes or antecedent of industrial fluctuations.

There was a tendency, he argued, that people would extrapolate recent
trends into the future and thereby create self-reinforcing herd behavior.
One of the reasons was that information and insight was difficult to
obtain, he thought, so many or most would just jump on the bandwagon
and imitate what they thought experts were doing – like the 33% in
Solomon Asch's experiment.

Marshall wrote about psychology as well, when he suggested that
rising prices could attract buyers. And then there was Keynes, of course,
with his frequently cited reference to "animal spirits." His best piece,
however, was his now famous beauty contest metaphor, where he compared the stock market with some US newspaper competitions, where
competitors should choose the picture they thought most would prefer
among 100 female portraits.

> Professional investment may be likened to those newspaper competi-
> tions in which the competitors have to pick out the six prettiest faces
> from a hundred photographs, the prize being awarded to the competi-
> tor whose choice most nearly corresponds to the average preferences of
> the competitors as a whole; so that each competitor has to pick, not the
> faces which he himself finds the prettiest, but those which he thinks like-
> liest to catch the fancy of the other competitors, all of whom are looking
> at the problem from the same point of view. It is not a case of choosing
> those which, to the best of one's judgment, are really the prettiest, nor
> even those which average opinion genuinely thinks the prettiest. We
> have reached the third degree when we devote our intelligences to
> anticipating what average opinion expects the average opinion to be.
> And there are some, I believe, who practice the fourth, fifth and higher
> degrees.

Charles Kindleberger and Hyman Minsky also allocated a significant
role to psychology. Kindleberger, for instance, wrote in *Manias, Panics and
Crashes* that:

> Manias and crashes, I contend, are associated on occasion with general
> irrationality or mob psychology.

Many other economists mentioned psychology in their business cycle
theories, but often in very vague terms.

## 16 WAYS TO BE IRRATIONAL

The change came when more and more psychologists and economists made specific laboratory experiments to uncover how many people could be irrational. Some of the leaders in this research area were Amos Tversky, Daniel Kahneman, Robert Shiller, Richard H. Thaler and Meir Statman. These and other scientists have, over the years, uncovered a number of specific common errors that can contribute to explanations of economic and financial instability because they create a herd mentality. Here are 16 of the most striking examples:

- *Representativeness effect.* We tend to think that trends we observe are likely to continue
- *False consensus effect.* We generally overestimate the number of other people that share our attitudes
- *Regret theory.* We try to avoid actions that confirm that we have made mistakes
- *Anchoring/framing.* Our decisions are influenced by input that seems to suggest the correct answer
- *Assimilation error.* We misinterpret information that we receive so that it seems to confirm what we have done
- *Selective exposure.* We try to expose ourselves only to information that seems to confirm our behavior and attitudes
- *Mental compartments.* We divide phenomena into different compartments and try to optimize each compartment rather than the whole
- *Selective perception.* We misinterpret information in a way that seems to confirm our behavior and attitudes
- *Overconfident behavior.* We overestimate our ability to make correct decisions
- *Hindsight bias.* We overestimate the likeliness that we would have been able to predict the outcome of a past series of events
- *Confirmatory bias.* Our conclusions are unduly biased by what we want to believe
- *Adaptive attitudes.* We develop the same attitudes as people we associate with
- *Social comparison.* We use the behavior of others as a source of information about a subject that we find difficult to understand
- *Cognitive dissonance.* We try to avoid evidence which shows that our assumptions have been wrong, or we distort it, and we try to avoid action that highlights the dissonance

- *Ego-defensive attitudes.* We adapt our attitudes so that they seem to confirm the decision we have made
- *Prospect theory.* We have an irrational tendency to be more willing to gamble with losses than with profits. This means that we stick longer with losing positions than with winning positions

Another important change to the role of psychology is the massive application of so-called "technical analysis" in financial markets. This amounts to computer models that forecast markets on the basis of psychological phenomena. These may spot major turning points at an early point, but can also induce their users to follow trends.

These and other phenomena can be added up to explain why investment trends may take on their own life and eventually overshoot any fundamentally justified level. These investments may be in new industries, listed equities, bonds, property, commodities or even art. Let's take an equity bull market as an example of how this may play out.

## THE PSYCHOLOGY OF TRENDS

Let's consider a situation where a stock market has been rising for some time, and where we reach the point where people get emotional about it. Charles Kindleberger is often quoted for his remark: "There is nothing so disturbing to one's well-being and judgment as to see a friend get rich." This would, in scientific terms, amount to hindsight bias and regret theory. As markets rise, we believe (erroneously) that we actually knew that they would go up before it happened. We will thus feel a strong regret and will try to correct our perceived error by buying on the first little setback in the price (Figure 17.5).

**Figure 17.5**  Positive feedback loops based on the hindsight effect and regret. Previously published in The Psychology of Finance, by Lars Tvede, John Wiley & Sons, 1999, with permission.

**Figure 17.6** Positive feedback loops based on chart-based buy recommendations from technical analysts. Previously published in The Psychology of Finance, by Lars Tvede, John Wiley & Sons, 1999, with permission.

The rising prices will soon catch the interests of technical analysts, who will issue chart-based buy recommendations (Figure 17.6).

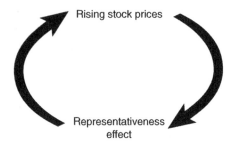

**Figure 17.7** Positive feedback loops based on the representativeness effect. Previously published in The Psychology of Finance, by Lars Tvede, John Wiley & Sons, 1999, with permission.

As prices rise further, the representative effect will start to take hold in our minds (Figure 17.7). This is the effect whereby we naturally think that a recent trend is representative for what we will see in the future. We will thus be more inclined to buy more.

After the bull market has progressed even further, there are more and more investors that have made significant profits. While frequently taking profits on individual investments, many will tend to reinvest the whole in the same bull market. Social psychologists call this "playing with house money" after a phenomenon known from casinos. Many people that have won a lot of money during a gambling evening will keep gambling until it is lost again, because they don't feel that it is real money they play with – it is "house money." They separate their recent gain from the rest of their wealth, keeping it in a mental compartment for gambling (Figure 17.8).

**Figure 17.8**   Positive feedback loops based on people's tendency to feel that they "play with house money." Previously published in The Psychology of Finance, by Lars Tvede, John Wiley & Sons, 1999, with permission.

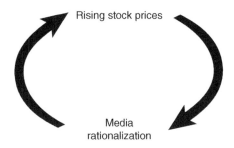

**Figure 17.9**   Positive feedback loops based on media rationalizations. Previously published in The Psychology of Finance, by Lars Tvede, John Wiley & Sons, 1999, with permission.

All of this will, of course, not escape the attention of the press, which mainly is preoccupied with reporting the mood of the moment, thus seemingly rationalizing the bull market (Figure 17.9). This is backed by reports from financial analysts, which (under heavy group pressure) provide far more buy recommendations than sell recommendations. Adaptive attitudes, cognitive dissonance, assimilation error, selective exposure, selective perception, confirmatory bias and social comparison may all be in effect here.

As a bull market extends into a financial bubble, there may be more and more warning signs appearing. However, a false consensus effect will leave many with the erroneous impression that there are more people agreeing with their bullish assessment than is in fact the case (Figure 17.10).

The final phases of a financial bubble are those where many of the skilled investors will go short. But it is difficult to pick the exact timing of the turning point, and short sellers may be forced to buy back their

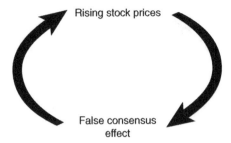

**Figure 17.10**   Positive feedback loops based on the false consensus effect. Previously published in The Psychology of Finance, by Lars Tvede, John Wiley & Sons, 1999, with permission.

**Figure 17.11**   Positive feedback loops based on stop-loss buy orders from people that have sold short too early. Previously published in The Psychology of Finance, by Lars Tvede, John Wiley & Sons, 1999, with permission.

positions as markets often continue to rise beyond the expected level (Figure 17.11). This then creates a final blow-off – a dramatic acceleration in the price rises – just before the final peak is reached.

## ADDING IT UP: THE EMOTIONAL ACCELERATOR

While all of these phenomena have been scientifically tested in laboratory experiments and are very real and embarrassingly widespread, it is not easy to fit them into specific macroeconomic models. What technical analysts have done instead is to model the overall results – and not without success. However, for the purpose of the next sections, perhaps it would be reasonable to bundle them all up and give them a simple name. The sum of all the psychological phenomena leading to irrational momentum trading may be called an "emotional accelerator" (Figure 17.12).

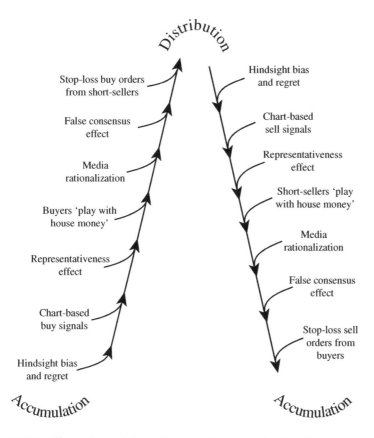

**Figure 17.12** Illustration of the entire emotional accelerator. Previously published in The Psychology of Finance, by Lars Tvede, John Wiley & Sons, 1999, with permission.

The term "accelerator" seems relevant here, as it has been used (by Clark and others) to describe phenomena (in Clark's case in capital investment) whereby the growth of output triggers new demand for the same output. Clark's capital investment accelerator is triggered by the *change* in output and not its level. The psychological phenomenon described above has a similar effect, in as much as it is the *change* in financial prices that induces people to buy or sell, which again reinforces the trend. There are a few critical aspects of the emotional accelerator that should be borne in mind:

- It is, as mentioned, mostly triggered by *financial price movements*. It is mainly the feedback between publicized prices and personal emotions that tie individual attitudes to collective feedback processes. However, other factors, such as the role of media, are involved too
- Early investors enter the game because they understand value. Late investors enter the game when they have seen a significant price movement that catches their attention. The emotional accelerator will thus kick in like a turbo charger, but only when a trend has already run for some time
- It works both ways
- It involves cascade reactions, where several factors kick in to reinforce the trend
- It is subject to occasional, abrupt amplifications

The two last aspects call for some elaboration. Our emotional accelerator does work both ways, but not all is the same on the way up and down. Bear markets in asset prices tend to be associated with far lower trading volumes than bull markets, which can be explained with ego-defensive attitudes, prospect theory, mental compartments and cognitive dissonance. (There can also be a purely rational reason for this, though, as sales of a leveraged asset, such as a house, may unmask insolvency). Furthermore, turning points at troughs tend to be more sudden than peaks.

## ATTENTION, UNEASINESS AND ANXIETY

Then there is the aspect of abrupt amplification. This happens mostly when markets fall and evolve from a controlled downward drift to an outright panic. But why do panics evolve?

The explanation can be found in the phenomena called "attitudes." These are nature's inventions to simplify things for us. We may, for instance, have heard of many reasons why shares should go up, and many why they should go down instead. Our attitude is what we have concluded, and it is emotionally tied to what we think, do and feel. They are useful as psychological crash helmets that make us calm, well adjusted and socially adapted, freeing us from constant backbreaking speculation on all kinds of different problems.

Now, imagine that financial markets make a big surprise movement against us. Let's say that we have been bullish on shares and then they suddenly fall like rocks. Perhaps we take this in stride, and perhaps it doesn't change much in our attitudes (since attitudes by nature are stable), but it does change our *attention*. Attention is partly determined by social experiences. Many studies have shown that our attention is determined largely by what other people around us pay attention to. If the stock market falls, then it will at least tell us that other people are paying attention to risk factors rather than to bullish arguments. So, seeing the market fall, we start paying more attention to such factors ourselves, and this creates the beginning of a *cognitive dissonance*. Somehow, we begin to feel that this market might actually have good reasons for selling, so we don't feel so good any more, and as the market falls further, that uneasiness begins to evolve into *anxiety*.

This is a natural and often necessary reaction in cases of danger. Most animals can feel anxiety, for instance (flies seem to be exemptions), and it has helped them to survive. It can involve restlessness, difficulty with concentration, fatigue, muscle tension, sleep disturbances or even going blank. It puts us in a state of mind (and body) where we become very susceptible to outright *panic attacks*. Panic has its own symptoms, such as palpitations, sweating, trembling, etc., but what is most important is that it is a distinct state of mind, where we suddenly *can change our attitudes very abruptly*, and this could explain why market movements suddenly can become discontinuous.

The object of speculation in a bubble can be vintage Ferraris or impressionist paintings, and this wouldn't rattle the world economy the least bit. However, it's another matter if it is real estate or equities that get caught up in the fewer. These are large markets, and the impact of bubbles in them can become substantial, as in the famous Dot Com Bubble from the year 2000.

*Chapter* **18**

# Dot Bomb

If at first you don't succeed try, try again. Then quit. There's no use
being a damn fool about it.

*W.C. Fields*

We do not know how many computers Charles Babbage thought the
world would need when he described his first one in 1822, but Thomas
Watson, the Chairman of IBM, made himself instantly quotable in 1943
by suggesting a specific number:

"I think there is a world market for maybe five computers."

Five? That was a bit on the low side, but perhaps he hadn't imagined
how small they might become later on. Here is a prediction from *Popular
Mechanics* in 1949:

Where a calculator on the ENIAC is equipped with 18 000 vacuum tubes
and weighs 40 tons, computers in the future may have only 1000 vacuum
tubes and perhaps weigh 1–1½ tons.

However, Watson was at least more optimistic than the editor of business books at Prentice Hall, who made this statement in 1957:

I have traveled the length and breadth of this country and talked with
the best people, and I can assure you that data processing is a fad that
won't last the year.

Data processing lasted the full year and then started growing rapidly.
And then came silicon, and then PCs, fiber optics, LANs, PDAs, mobile

phones and jelly beans (the tiny computer chips that are embedded in many products). And then the Internet. All of this converged to change the computer business from a single 30-ton machine in Philadelphia to a serious business and then a revolution, and finally, during the 1990s, the largest peace-time capital investment explosion the world had ever seen. The number of Internet users grew from 50 million in 1996 to more than 400 million in 2000. And jelly beans? There were around 6 *billion* in operation by 2000. Two exponential phenomena were key to the events:

- *Moore's Law*, which stipulated that chip capacity would double every 18 months, while its price fell by half
- *Gilder's Law*, which said that the total bandwidth of telecommunications would triple every 12 months

A third key factor behind the events during the 1990s was the increasing adoption of so-called "open standards" in high-tech markets. Open standards meant convergence, and this again meant that applications were able to run on larger and larger numbers of different systems provided by different vendors. So open standards created economies of scale and benefits for the end-users.

The fourth driver of this capital spending boom was a new, global trend towards deregulation of telecommunications markets, which led to the formation of many start-up telcos and a rush among new and old operators to fend off the upstarts with innovative and competitive services. The Internet turned out to be one of the main instruments in this battle, which drew down prices. The combination of core innovations (leading to new applications), open standards (leading to technical convergence) and deregulation (leading to falling prices) enabled the exponential growth in the number of Internet users and in revenues. This revenue again stimulated the frantic development of new core technologies and new applications – positive feedback loops created sustained growth.

## NETWORK EFFECTS

These positive feedback processes were not the only factors in play. One of the changes that created sustained growth was a phenomenon called the "network effect." This term described the situation where the value for a given user of being connected to a given network rose in exponential proportion to the number of other people connected to the same network. The Internet created a very powerful network effect, since the value of being connected rose – at least within some parameter intervals – in exponential proportion to the number of users. A network with one million users had a value to each user that was far higher than the combined value of two separate networks that had half a million users each. This phenomenon was called Metcalfe's Law. The result was that Internet data traffic doubled every 3–4 months.

## INCREASING RETURNS

Another interesting phenomenon in the so-called "digital economy" was the possibility of increasing return. Conventional economic theory assumed that corporations had decreasing returns on investment (lower return on each new dollar that they invested). However, companies that supplied digital output, such as software and Internet services, could experience a different return structure; they might find that their return on each new dollar invested was actually *larger* than the return on the previous dollar invested in the same concept. The main reasons were:

- The network effect (Metcalfe's Law)
- Minimal marginal costs of replicating their software or accepting additional network users
- The possibility for large players to become de facto standard providers

So, supply stimulated more supply (increasing return) and demand stimulated demand (network effect) – a hypercharged variation of Say's Law. And there was even more to it. We have seen that most neoclassical economic models assumed that people had perfect information, and that money, goods, services and people could flow freely. Everyone knew that this wasn't really true, but they also knew that every new innovation in communication and transportation technology brought the economy one bit further towards those assumptions. The canals, the railroads, the cars, the telegraph and the telephone had each brought the economies closer to being truly effective. Each of those innovations had made it easier for people to exchange money and to move money, goods, services and people to the places where they could be most efficiently used. The Internet was, in this connection, a giant step forwards towards free and efficient markets:

- The Internet created transparent markets, which intensified price competition

- The Internet enhanced productivity by enabling disintermediation of middlemen, stimulating collaborative work approaches and accelerating the exchange of software (and thereby its own continued development)
- The Internet enabled e-commerce, whereby you could buy virtually anything from anywhere and have it shipped to wherever you were
- The Internet made it possible to find jobs anywhere
- The Internet made it possible to trade assets and transfer money from a desk-top to any company anywhere

All of this meant productivity gains and low inflation, and low inflation meant low interest rates, which, combined with growing earnings, meant substantially higher equity prices. This, combined with a demographic boom of middle-aged people saving for their pensions, meant access to an abundance of capital available for new Internet projects, which again fed the boom. There was no lack of positive feedback loops in this capital investment boom.

## BUBBLE BATH

The boom was massive, and with any massive boom come the bubbles. New Internet companies were founded every day, and it seemed, at least for a time, that no one investing in Internet upstarts could possibly lose. Either the companies succeeded to the point of making it to an IPO (initial public offering) – in which case, the venture capitalists could sell out based on billion-dollar market capitalizations; or the company didn't really make it, in which case you could always sell it for a few hundred million dollars to someone who needed the people and the infrastructure. There was virtually no way to lose, at least not if you had a broad portfolio of investment!

The transition from a great bull market to outright bubble was difficult to pinpoint, but many professionals in the business saw the initial public offering of Theglobe.com as the transition point. When this company went public in November 1998, the shares were offered at nine dollars apiece. However, they soared to no less than 97 dollars during the first trading day, and settled at USD 63.50 a share, a gain of more than 600% in a single day. This was rather remarkable, since the company during the nine months prior to its IPO had booked total revenues of just USD $2.7 million. It had no proprietary technology, no patents and was not a leading website by any measure. And yet, the market valued it at around one billion dollars on that magic day. As ZDNet asked Bill Bass, an analyst at Forrester Research Inc. to give a comment, he responded:

> "I cease to be amazed at what happens with Internet stocks. I'm 'amazed' fatigued."

Bill Bass was not the only analyst to be alarmed. One of the best articulated warnings of the state of the market was given in the book *The Internet Bubble: Inside the Overvalued World of High-Tech Stocks – And What You Need to Know to Avoid the Coming Shakeout*. The authors of the book, Anthony and Michael Perkins, had identified an index of Internet companies that they tracked, and they wrote an article in *San Jose Mercury News* in February 2000, where they summarized some of their concerns:

> The 315 Internet companies we (the authors of *The Internet Bubble*) track would have to grow at a compounded annual rate of 96 percent over the next five years to justify their current stock market valuation. This is almost twice the historical growth rate of Microsoft (53 percent). The total market capitalization of these companies is more than $1.2 trillion, but based on only $29 billion in revenue in 1999.

Valuations had gone up and up, until the point where the market cap of Yahoo! exceeded the combined valuations of Boeing, Caterpillar and Philip Morris, despite the fact that these companies had 339 times as much revenue and 159 times the earnings.

## MELTDOWN

The Internet/technology crash began during the spring of 2000. It was global – hammering high-tech and computer, telecommunication and Internet stocks from Paris to Bombay, Tokyo and the US exchanges. While indexes fell dramatically, the behavior of individual shares was even wilder. In Japan, Softbank and Hikari Tsushin fell so quickly that they hit downward trading limits almost daily when the panic reached its crescendo. Numerous shares fell more than 95% from their peaks. And, by the way, you could buy the shares in Theglobe.com for around one dollar apiece by August 2000. It was, by then, almost 90% down from its initial offering price less than two years before, and close to 99% down from its peak.

The Dot Com bubble contained many ingredients of standard business cycle theory. First, it was a *capital spending cycle* peaking ten years after the previous one (Juglar). It was triggered by new *technological innovation* (Spiethoff) and *clusters of innovation* (Schumpeter), which gave it a flavor of being a *real business cycle* (Kydland, Prescott). Hardware and software companies were themselves great users of hardware and software, so there were strong elements of *self-ordering* (Clark). This also took the form of sunspots (Jevons), as the conviction that the market would be huge in no time made it grow even faster. The *inventory cycle* was also present, as companies hoarded parts in order to be able to fulfill demand (Metzler). The scramble for market share created *deceptive pricing power*, leading to a severe case of *overinvestment* (Mill). Let's quote again what John Stuart Mill wrote in his paper *Currency and Commercial Distress* from 1826:

> Everyone calculating upon being before all his competitors provides himself with as large a stock as he thinks that the market will take off; not reflecting that others, like himself, are adding to the supply, not calculating upon the fall of price which must take place as soon as this increasing quantity is brought to the market. This deficiency is soon changed into an excess.

Monetary conditions played a role too, as *interest rates were too slow to catch up* (Robertson), as returns on financial investments ran (for a time) far ahead of interest rates, *leaving natural rates far higher than real rates* (Wicksell). It's difficult to separate overinvestment from *underconsumption*, but we can see the latter too. A huge amount of paper wealth was generated, but among a relatively small number of entrepreneurs and investors. Most of this wealth was saved or invested, and not spent on final products, so demand couldn't keep up with supply (Hobson).

The boom led, in its final stages, to severe *bottlenecks* and *capital shortage*, in particular as employees demanded ever higher compensation packages (Schumpeter) and *suppliers of funding reached their limits* (Tugan-Baranovsky, Hawtrey). Furthermore, the *drain of free capital drove interest rates up* at the late stages, which made investments less profitable and capital more scarce (Kassel). Once the trend finally turned, most of the factors above turned into reverse. Furthermore, a lot of the people who had created the new business were fired and/or saw their paper wealth vanish, leading *to a decline in demand at the time when production capacity had just peaked* (Catchings and Foster).

And then there were financial markets. Rising stock prices attracted *speculators*, who drove prices further and further up as the effect of the

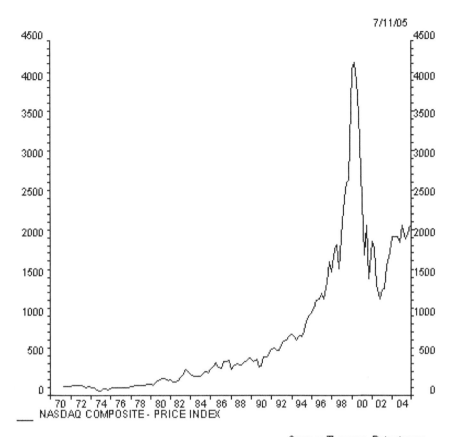

7/11/05

**Figure 18.1** NASDAQ 1970–2005. This index rose around 1000% in the 10 years from 1990 to 2000 before making a spectacular collapse. Reproduced by permission of Datastream.

emotional accelerator played out (Marshall, Pigou). There were clearly plenty of *animal spirits* (Keynes), and rising asset prices created increased *collateral value*, and thus *acceleration in velocity of money* (von Mises, von Hayek, Schumpeter, Minsky, Kindleberger). Rising asset prices also stimulated the *collateral effect*, where high asset values generated more business, which again was good for asset prices (Bernanke, Gertler and Gilchrist); see Chapter 22. There was clearly also a strong case of *emotional accelerators*, as the trend was feeding on itself (Tversky, Kahneman, Shiller, Thaler, Statman).

What the Dot Com bubble illustrated most of all was that the rational world that neoclassicists modeled on their computers, and that the Internet was supposed to enhance, did not always work as efficiently as one perhaps would think. It was a reminder to academics that, as Albert Einstein once expressed it:

"Everything should be made as simple as possible, but not simpler."

# Part IV

## The Essence

*Chapter* **19**

# The State of the Art

As far as the laws of mathematics refer to reality they are not certain;
and as far as they are certain they do not refer to reality.

*Albert Einstein*

The Boston area is generally considered a very nice place to live. Located
not too far north of New York, it has a beautiful bay, fine beaches, green
surroundings, a well-kept old city center and a lively nightlife. It is also
known for having the largest concentration of academic institutions on
Earth (which would explain the nightlife). Three of these, Cambridge,
Harvard and M.I.T., emerged after WWII as centers for a new approach
to business cycle theory.

## FROM SCHOOL TO SCHOOL

Their new approach followed almost 300 years of debate; a discussion that
seemed to have gone full circle. It had all started with the assumption that
every economic crisis was caused by specific shocks or policy errors, and
then (after Juglar) by the idea that they instead constituted an inherent
part of how the economy worked. We have seen how economists developed explanations involving numerous factors, such factors as innovation, imbalances in overall savings and investments, disproportionate
investments in some sectors, inventory build-up and liquidation, changes
in business cost structures, deceptive pricing power, debt deflation and
inherent monetary instability. These were later classified into categories
such as "underconsumption," "oversaving," "monetary" and "debt deflation" schools, but many are hard to fit in, since they explain a cyclical

phenomenon where different factors in different sectors trigger a cycle of events. At the end of the day, it was a chicken-and-egg situation, where there was no ultimate trigger.

The first economists generally had assumed that there wasn't too much to do about it, and that the economies in any case would return to growth if left alone during crises. Some went further. It wasn't only pointless to intervene, they thought, no, it was essential – maintain a balanced budget and keep inflation low, they claimed. Keep up appearances and you would see confidence, investment and spending return soon enough. Others went further still. Some of the Austrians tended to believe that cycles were not only unavoidable and self-correcting, but they were even *useful*. Schumpeter, for instance, believed that business cycles were a key driver of creative destruction and economic growth and renewal. He would, therefore, in the middle of the Great Depression of the 1930s, enter his classroom at Harvard with the words:

> "Gentlemen, you are worried about the depression. You should not be.
> For capitalism, a depression is a good cold douche."

It was, however, this very depression that convinced many that the economy could, under some conditions, become trapped in equilibrium with stagnation and high unemployment. This approach, which became known as Keynesianism, focused on inherent instability created by fluctuations in profits, investment, credit and other variables. Keynesianism not only described how markets could fail, but also how governments could intervene to bring it out of unemployment equilibrium.

Keynes's approach dominated completely during the 1950s, as it was central to the curriculum at Cambridge, Massachusetts, as well as at Harvard and M.I.T. and numerous other places. One of the most influential advocates was Samuelson from M.I.T. (the man who had made the multiplier/accelerator simulation under the guidance of Alvin Hansen in 1939), whose best-selling book *Economics* from 1948 became mandatory reading for thousands of students across the globe – it sold, in fact, several million copies. Samuelson was not only a leading textbook writer, scientist and teacher – he even became advisor to President Kennedy and received the Nobel Prize together with Robert Solow.

## CROSS-CURRENTS

Samuelson's fame had grown even further as the magazine *Newsweek* had the brilliant idea of letting him and his main opponent, Milton Friedman, write duelling columns where they could argue for their conflicting views – Friedman of course representing monetarism as the next hot school in the arena. Interestingly, it was Friedman who seemed the overall winner of this battle, as events during the 1970s indicated that the assumption of an inflation/unemployment trade-off was misguided. Friedman's camp had been further reinforced when Lucas (one of Samuelson's former students) published his famous book about rational expectations, in which fiscal stimulus could lead quickly to inflation rather than growth. After this, it wasn't just a Samuelson/Friedman battle, but rather a battle of Samuelson/Solow against Friedman/Lucas.

---

### RATIONAL EXPECTATIONS IN BUSINESS CYCLE SIMULATIONS

Robert E. Lucas proposed, in his book *Studies in Business Cycle Theory* from 1981, that the expectations used in models should be rational. This assumption of rationality and equilibrium is really an extension of the core principles proposed by Adam Smith. One of the reasons that so many economists have endorsed it is that it makes theoretical modeling very easy. Economic models assuming that all is rational tend to have stable equilibria. Such models are today known as "neo-classical economics" (it was Karl Marx who introduced the term "classical" to describe Adam Smith and his immediate successors).

Almost all modern business cycle models contain equations that include expectations. The concept of rational expectations is introduced by letting the theoretical "agents" have the same expectations about the future as the expectations of the model itself.

---

The battle was not clear-cut, though. While Samuelson continued to offer typical Keynesian explanations to macroeconomic phenomena, he would also teach his students the use of mathematical microeconomic models featuring the rational behavior that Lucas advocated. And Lucas himself had not claimed that people in reality were completely rational or that government should do absolutely nothing. He agreed with the other camp that government actually should play at least a limited role. This was the beginning of an era in which more economists accepted some views from Keynes as well as from Friedman, where Keynesianism gradually became redefined as "New Keynesian Economics" and where monetarism evolved into "New Monetary Economics."

## New Monetary Economics

The New Monetary Economics approach was more focused on new development on the micro-level. The scientists would, for instance, study new monetary innovations that would change the effective money supply or velocity of money. Many of these changes might not show up in the official money supply statistics, but could be important anyway. The other main school, New Keynesian Economics, evolved during the 1970s and emphasized a number of problems:

- That competition could be imperfect because of monopolies, regulations, etc.
- That wages sometimes could be fixed at levels that were too high to enable full employment (because of unions)
- That markets could be too thin to clear
- That markets at times didn't clear because of irrational fear or greed ("animal spirits")
- That market behavior (mainly in financial markets) could become irrational because of sunspots
- That some sectors of the economy (in particular in high tech industries) could have increasing returns on investment, which would inhibit competition

## New Keynesian Economics

New Keynesian Economics was grounded in Lucas's rational expectations models, derived from individual utility and profit maximization, not from aggregates. It was, in other words, based on microeconomic assumptions, and its models assumed that an economy that was below full employment could be brought to full employment through several channels:

- Inherent market dynamics would drive down salaries to a level where more companies would employ more people and where prices of produced goods would fall, which would enable people to buy more units (a typical classical assumption)
- Intervention, either through public expenditure or through monetary expansion, would create full employment

The New Keynesian Economics did not claim that one of these outcomes always was more efficient than the other; it all depended on the flexibility of the labor markets in the given situation. However, the change in Keynesianism, as well as in monetarism, became symptomatic for a new main distinction in analytical approaches. Keynes and Friedman had mainly examined the economy "top-down," but Lucas, the New Keynesian Economics school and the New Monetary Economics had taken more of a bottom-up approach.

## THE MACRO VERSUS MICRO BATTLE

Top-down means macro. The macroeconomists tried to focus on the large things that really mattered while ignoring much else. The approach was based on assumptions about overall phenomena. The other camp was the so-called "microeconomists," who focused on how individuals behaved and then aggregated this behavior into larger-scale models. This camp was called "neoclassical." Many of the neoclassical microeconomists used a special language where many sentences started with the words: "Let . . .". These sentences typically would introduce a list of simplifications that could be rather unrealistic, if not outrageous. They might, for instance, include a statement that there was perfect competition, that everyone had perfect knowledge and that there was perfect labor mobility, a market for any desire and no changes in tastes or technology.

The difference between the two analytical camps was not only in the choice of methodologies. It was also in the focus: the macroeconomists typically would focus on malfunctions, whereas the neoclassicists described how the economy found its balance. This difference in focus was not because one camp consisted of pessimists and the other of optimists. It evolved because of an issue that was inherent to the analytical approaches:

- The macroeconomists used models that didn't necessarily assume any inherent equilibrium
- The microeconomists, on the other hand, used general equilibrium models (which assumed rational expectations and inherent equilibrium). These models were often much more elegant and flexible than the macroeconomists' models. However, the necessary underlying assumptions would be so limiting that the final result of the models could have little practical relevance

The two camps didn't remain separated, however. More and more economists from one camp started to pick good elements from the other. More and more traditional macroeconomists would, for instance, change their style so that they still focused on inaccuracies in the economy, but began to use microeconomic modeling to simulate it. And the micro-economists would start to accept that human beings are not entirely rational, and they would start to build positive feedback into their models to create less stable, but more realistic, results.

## A SPECTER OF THEORIES

The economists at the leading academic institutions in Boston (and other places) had witnessed the continuous change in focus from one school to the next and then the next, and they had seen how supporters of some schools had adapted some of the best analytical approaches from competing camps. They had also witnessed how the range of reasonably credible business cycle models had continued to grow and grow.

What they were facing by the new millennium was a landscape where business cycle models could be divided according to four main dimensions:

- *Cycles:* endogenous models assuming that the instability was caused by nonlinearity in the economic system
- *Ripples:* exogenous models assuming the instability came from external shocks
- *Predictable:* deterministic models assuming that economic behavior was relatively predictable and orderly
- *Chaotic:* stochastic models assuming that the behavior was relatively complex and unpredictable

All of the models had drifted towards a few common assumptions:

- Focus more on aggregate supply, its determinants and effects
- Assume that markets are fully competitive and that markets tend to clear
- Assume rational expectations

There had also for a while been a shift of focus from internal instability to external shocks. There had been several reasons for this. One was simply mathematical convenience: modeling inherent instability meant use of nonlinear functions, while models based on external shocks could be linear, which meant that it was easier to work with. Another reason was a growing belief that the capitalist economy had come closer to a structure where it had a stable balance.

**Table 19.1** Overview of different approaches to business cycle modeling.

| | "Cycles" (Endogenous models assuming that the instability in the economic system is caused by nonlinearity) | "Ripples" (Exogenous models assuming that instability comes from external shocks) |
|---|---|---|
| "Predictable" (Deterministic models assuming that economic behavior is relatively predictable) | *Predictable cycles* These models describe economic systems with inherent nonlinearity that creates fluctuations. Some models produce regular fluctuations, (which is unrealistic), others produce chaotic movements, and some are somewhere in the middle. Most classical and neoclassical models would fall into this category. | *Predictable ripples* This group of models assume that the economy receives external shocks with a somewhat predictable pattern, and that these shocks are responsible for business cycles. Jevons's sunspot theory, which postulated that regular changes in an external factor (sunspots) could drive the economy, was the first model in this category. Political cycles might also belong here. |
| "Chaotic" (Stochastic models assuming that economic behavior is relatively complex and unpredictable) | *Unpredictable cycles* This group includes models that assume rational expectations and equilibrium. However, they assume that there is more than one possible equilibrium, and that it could be difficult or impossible to predict which of its several potential equilibria the economy will find. Furthermore, the models assume that the move from one equilibrium to another could be triggered by a random event. Such events could trigger changes in general (rational) expectations and thus become self-fulfilling (like Jevons's sunspots). These theories tend to focus on financial instability as a major cause of business cycles. | *Unpredictable ripples* Models focusing on external shocks and unpredictability dominated in the 1980s. They assume an intrinsically stable equilibrium (neoclassical approach) and that the business cycles will only occur if the economy is continuously exposed to external shocks (the "rocking-horse-and-stick" view). These "real business cycle" models typically suggest dynamic behavior, where the amplitude of fluctuations is determined mainly by the size and frequency of the shocks, and where the length and sequence of cyclical events is determined by the inherent nature of the propagation mechanism. The shocks can either be random or serially correlated (like war, manias, habits, technology, policy changes), but they will not be regular or in any way predictable. |

However, each of the categories of models had their advantages and disadvantages. The *endogenous, deterministic* models (predictable cycles) were attractive, because they could generate undamped cyclical solutions, asymmetries, irreversibility and discontinuities – which meant that they generated something that looked like the real world. Furthermore, they could be based on relatively realistic assumptions about permanent structures in the economy. However, the problem with this category of models was that they often produced behavior that could only be predicted in the relatively short term. Butterfly effects would obscure the longer-term behavior.

The *stochastic, endogenous* models (unpredictable cycles) had some of the same advantages and disadvantages. They described some of the phenomena that Keynes had seen when he talked about the economy falling into traps. Ormerod referred to these models in his *The Death of Economics* from 1994:

> The realization that there might be many craters so deep that, once having got into them at once, our imaginary player can never get out, has been of great concern to economic theorists in the past decade or so. The implication of such a situation is that there is not just one but many possible solutions to the equations which describe a competitive economy. In other words, there is not just one equilibrium in the economy, but many equilibria.

And later:

> If there is a unique solution to the equations which describe a competitive economy, large changes can be analyzed within this framework, since the economy by definition always ends up at the unique equilibrium position. But with many solutions it is possible to make statements only about the consequences of small changes in the locality of any particular solution. Otherwise the economy might not slide back into its original crater, but be shifted to a position in the field which goes into a different crater altogether.

The *deterministic, exogenous models* (predictable ripples) were the most problematic of them all. There were virtually no economists that believed that this category of models described anything but very marginal phenomena.

And finally, the *stochastic, exogenous* models (unpredictable ripples) were elegant, since they managed to maintain equilibrium. However, they were not widely accepted since they did not appear very realistic (it should be mentioned, though, that few, if any, proponents of real business cycle models actually claimed that technology shocks accounted for all fluctuations. Prescott, for instance, claimed that they accounted for "more than half the fluctuations in the post-war period, with a best point estimate near 75 percent").

## PREMATURE DEATH

People have always made fun of economists, but they were now themselves beginning to express more and more frustration. One problem was that models were remote from reality. It was, for instance, well known that Sir John Hicks, who had received his Nobel Prize for his work in general equilibrium theory, had later on largely abandoned the concept, simply because he didn't find it realistic. Many, if not most, of the authors that had contributed during the post World War II era, had mainly been concerned with the theoretical possibilities rather than with what actually causes business cycles. There had generally been much too little regard for how the pieces fit each other and how they matched events in the real world – if indeed they matched at all. Each model had often dealt with a few phenomena that were treated in isolation, which made it impossible to assess whether they were realistic or not. It could seem like a jungle, but behind all this discussion there was, in fact, more agreement than an outsider might think. Almost any economist would agree that business cycles existed despite all the complexity, and that there was some system to the way they worked. We shall, in the next chapter, take a little imaginary journey to see two reasons why that was so.

# Chapter 20

# Three Questions

> I can stand brute force, but brute reason is quite unbearable. There is something unfair about its use. It is hitting below the intellect.
>
> *Oscar Wilde*

Imagine this: some years from now, Adam Smith calls a conference in the afterworld. The understanding of business cycles has evolved so much since his own time on Earth, he thinks, that it would be fascinating to gather the best economists of all time to discuss it over a working lunch.

The room is full of economists, and as he stands up to open the meeting, they all start clapping. Then, the applause gets stronger and stronger until everyone joins in a rhythmic clapping, amplified by stamping feet. Adam Smith! This man is very popular.

"Errr, thank you very much," says Adam Smith as he starts fumbling with a pile of written notes,

> "Gentlemen, I have called you to this conference for two reasons. The first is that you are some of the best thinkers that ever were in economics. You are the heroes. The second is that all of us have dealt with the question of economic instability. The purpose of this conference is to get an answer to two questions that I think are basic, and then to get an overview of what we think business cycles really amount to in praxis."

Then he turns around and writes something on the whiteboard:

*Isn't the business cycle problem really an unmanageable hairball.*

"A hairball?" whispers one German economist to another, "That would explain why my books got so long!" " – and so incomprehensible!" answers the other. Smith studies his notes again.

"I want to introduce you to what I will now call the hairball problem. Mill and Marshall suggested that rising prices would make people buy more, not less. These are examples of positive feedback loops. Einarsen's ship-building cycles are echoes. Schumpeter's "swarms" of entrepreneurs are cascades. Keynes's liquidity trap involves disinhibitors. And almost all of your theories involve lags. Take the accelerator, for instance. *And they involve so many sectors, so many phenomena, that honestly; it can look a bit like an unmanageable hairball.* How may anyone who is not an extreme expert in the matter make sense of it? So, here comes my first question. Can anyone in this room find a way to explain business cycles to a common man on the street? And here I don't mean describe them. I mean *explain* them."

Silence. "Come on," says Smith, "someone must be able to explain it in a simple, intuitive way." Silence again. But then a man stands up and says:

"Sometimes I have thought of business cycles as similar to resonance. I was an engineer before I became an economist and so I know resonance in trains. These have lots of moving parts, and they tend to shake. Same with cars, by the way. I think business cycles are quite similar to the resonance problems that can drive a train or car designer crazy."

"Interesting approach," says Smith, "carry on."

"Well, I can elaborate a bit on the similarities. There are three ways to reduce resonance in cars, for instance. The first is to *remove the primary source of instability*. If, for instance, a windshield creates it, then change its design until the problem disappears. In economics, this would be similar to removing a positive feedback process such as automatic wage indexation. The second measure against resonance is to *produce counter waves*. I think this is what Keynes and the other underconsumption theorists proposed. And the third is to install *shock absorbers* around the sources of oscillations, for instance over the wheels and around the engine. Unemployment payment would fall in that category. And also the monetarists' principle of stabilizing money supply. When performed successfully, monetary measures stabilize the right side of Newcomb's quantity equation simply by fixing the growth rate on the left side."

Adam Smith stands up again

"Thank you, that was not bad at all. Every man on the street should be familiar with resonance, even if they may not know the actual expression for it. So now we move on to my next question."

He turns to the whiteboard and writes:

*Why do all the economic phenomena in business cycles create a few, distinctive waves?*

Our economy is surely a lot more complex than any single machine. Imagine that we glued all the millions of machines in the modern world together – from the smallest electric toothbrush, to the cars, the trains and the jet engines – into one, huge humming ball. Isn't that what the economy is? There are millions of people making decisions about money all the time, millions of products and services, hundreds of sectors and thousands of subsectors. Should each of these not create their own resonance with their own frequency? So how can we get to this huge, slow overall resonance that we are, in fact, observing?

"May I?" asks one delegate. Smith nods.

"Thanks. Can you all remember when we were clapping after the morning session? At first, everyone clapped independently, with their own, fast rhythm. However, think about this: after a while, we transitioned from fast, incoherent clapping to a slower, synchronized rhythm. There was no one conducting us, but we did this anyway. This phenomenon is called mode-locking. Mode-locking happens when a number of initially uncorrelated processes lock spontaneously into each other's rhythm to create a strong, aggregate movement. An example: if you hang two mechanical clocks side by side on a wall, they will often synchronize because of the small mechanical impulses that travel through the wall. Given a vast multitude of processes in the economy, which can contribute to instability, you would end up with something very similar to random noise if it were not for this powerful phenomenon. It is because of mode-locking that a boom can spread from one sector to many, as supply creates demand, activity creates money, and money creates supply."

"But there is more than one cycle . . .?" says Smith.

"Yes, because cyclical processes can adapt themselves somewhat to a mode-locking process, but only within limits. So, if you have some occurrences that tend towards very slow frequency oscillations and others that are faster, then you get several clusters of phenomena creating several simultaneous cycles. Slow-moving clusters will often be related to business activities with large commercial friction, where planning, financing, etc. takes years."

"This, I think, was a very good summary and explanation," answers Smith. "It also sets the scene for what we want to do next. We want to, errrr, eat lunch. But listen now, I want you all to sit together during this break and discuss a joint presentation of how you think business cycles play out in praxis."

He turns yet again to the whiteboard and writes:

*What are the most important practical symptoms of business cycles?*

Lunch is generally enjoyed, and there is much discussion about business cycles and many other subjects. There are, however, also some rather heated discussions at some of the tables. Adam Smith rises again as coffee has been served. "Now for the formal part of this little lunch gathering," he says. "May I ask for a spokesman?"

"I am," says one, "and I will get straight to the point and pick up where we left it before lunch. We were discussing clusters of activity that create cycles. Well, we think there are three such major clusters." "And these are . . .?" asks Smith.

The first is *inventories*. These bear the main responsibility for the so-called Kitchin cycle, which our honored colleague described as lasting 3–5 years. We now think the best assumption is that it averages about 4.5 years. The second big cluster is *capital spending*. This seems to bear the main responsibility for the so-called Juglar cycle, which averages some nine years. And the third big cluster is *property*, which bears prime responsibility for what is normally called the Kuznets cycle, lasting roughly 18 years on average. By property we mean both property prices and building construction.

Our second observation is about co-movement of the three cycles. Because of the mode-locking, there is a tendency for turning points of the different cycles to coincide when possible. They can, for instance, lock into a pattern where every second Kitchin trough coincides with a Juglar trough and every fourth also with a Kuznets trough. These episodes can be serious and lead to depressions and Keynes's liquidity trap, unless central banks and/or governments intervene in a timely and proportionate manner. This may have happened in 1825–30, 1873–78, 1929–38, 1974–75 and 1990–91.

Our final observation is about the reliability of all that I have just stated. The duration of the Kitchin cycle is 4.5 years. The others can vary quite a bit more, and none of them can really be called "periodic" by its strict definition, even though their duration should depend largely on the propagation mechanism, which shouldn't change much over time.

"What about the Kondratieff cycle?" asks Smith.

The group raised several issues about it. First, what our Russian colleague measured in his otherwise brilliant studies was primarily inflation and not necessarily overall business activity.

Secondly, we think one would need some ten observations – lasting more than 500 years – before the math experts in this room would agree that we have a statistically reliable sample of the phenomenon. That moment will be reached somewhere past year 2300.

Furthermore, the cycle didn't seem to behave as expected after the mid 1970s. The 1990s should have been a very weak period according to the model, but it featured, in fact, the so-called "Goldilocks" economy. This was interrupted in 2000–2002, but then came a huge surge forwards driven by emerging markets. Not at all what the theory predicted.

However, our most important critique was that we can't see any solid theory to support it. The group agreed that the phenomena that should explain the first Kondratieff cycles in fact seemed to be isolated technological innovations, such as the development of steam machines and spinning mills, computers and the Internet, or political changes, such as the expelling of the Gang of Four in China, the fall of the Berlin Wall, etc. It is very difficult to see such events being caused by some cyclical phenomenon. Consider, for instance, which cyclical phenomenon should lead Tim Berners-Lee to invent the Internet protocol. Such phenomena seem rather to be independent external shocks."

"So no Kondratieff cycle?" says Smith.

"No, most of us think not. But there are other forces in play. All expansions can lose steam for a few months for no clear reason, and contractions can also halt for a short while before resuming. These phenomena are often called "soft" or "strong" patches. We think these small oscillations are either reactions to external shocks or cyclical behavior in smaller clusters of phenomena that are not fully understood."

Adam Smith rises from his chair again

"I thank all of you. I am sure that each of you will take away your own conclusions, but for me there is one element that stands out. I think mankind has come very far towards understanding the business cycle problem, but we have also realized that while the best experts will have reasonable suggestions to where their economies are heading in a cyclical context, they can never be absolutely sure. So the task of dealing with this phenomenon will always challenge, whether you are a business manager, a financial investor, an entrepreneur or a finance minister."

"Or a central banker," shouts one from the crowd with a grin.

"Oh yes," answers Smith, "central bankers indeed. Their task is perhaps the hardest."

# Chapter 21

# The Five Main Drivers of Cycles

Errors using inadequate data are much less than those using no data at all.

*Charles Babbage*

We have already seen that most early economists had practical experience. Law, Cantillon, Thornton, Ricardo, Hawtrey and Catchings were bankers, Say and Pareto industrialists, Newcomb an astronomer, Mill an employee of the East India Company, Quesnay and Juglar doctors, Schumpeter manager in an Egyptian refinery and finance minister, and Keynes, well, *that* list is just too long. While these thinkers were focused on understanding the real world, many later scientists have often seemed more obsessed with mathematical beauty. The result has been an abundance of partial theories, and often too little focus on the context of these theories. Wassily Leontief complained, for instance, that over 50% of the articles in *American Economic Review* during the 1970s comprised mathematical models with no data.

## THE MONEY-MAKING MACHINE

The problem with data is, of course, that unlike a mathematical equation, they tend to be difficult to nail down beyond any criticism. However, we shall now try to look at a few. Let's make a little thought experiment and think of the global economy as an economic machine. Not a machine like the sleek watch on your wrist; not even like the smoothly humming engine in your car. No, think of a big, shaky, noisy thing; of something like what Charles Babbage's giant steam computer would have looked

**Table 21.1**   The five main elements in economies causing business cycles.

| Monetary cycle drivers | Economic cycle drivers |
|---|---|
| • Interest payments | • Asset prices<br>• Building construction<br>• Capital spending<br>• Inventories |

like – a huge machine from Charles Dickens's time with pistons, cogwheels and levers that pull weights up and down while steam fills the room. Now imagine that the floors tremble when this machine is running, because there are five massive pistons going up and down with different speeds. Occasionally, they even happen to reach their low point simultaneously, and this gives a bump big enough to leave cracks in the floor and an uneasy feeling in your stomach.

If this machine really *should* symbolize an economy, then we would be able to give each of those pistons a name. We would know from our exploration of business cycle theory that their names could be "Money," "Assets," "Building Construction," "Capital Spending" and "Inventories." We would call the first of them "Monetary" and the other four "Economic," and we would see the former as providing steam to the economy and the latter as converting this to real activity (Table 21.1).

But what are we talking about in real money? How much does each of these phenomena contribute to business cycles in reality? That is actually a rather difficult question; first because each of these elements interferes with the behavior of the others, and secondly because we have to venture into the considerable fog of economic statistics to seek an answer. We will nevertheless do so in this chapter, while bearing in mind that every single number we will dig up has been disputed for very credible reasons by very wise people. We should also be aware that it's difficult to separate the roles of our five entities clearly, which all goes to say that what follows isn't by any means precise. However, what it *should* be able to do is to give us a very basic sense of proportions, and this is really all we need for our purposes.

So let's get on with it. First we need to pick a sample year that was reasonably normal. We will here use the year 2004 (although 1994, for instance, would have been just as fine). Year 2004 was neither at the peak of a bubble, nor at the trough of despair and depression. It was a rather middle-of-the-road year, and should therefore suit our purposes quite well.

So here comes our first number: The World Bank has estimated that the sum of all haircuts, car productions and everything else we did in 2004 added up to 41 trillion dollars, when using the so-called "Atlas" method. That's a GDP of 41 000 000 000 000 dollars, and it is a measure made at the right side of Newcomb's equation,

$$MV = PQ$$

Such a big number doesn't mean a thing to anyone, but we need it for perspective as we move on, starting with asset prices.

## INTEREST PAYMENTS

Interest payments is an important symptom of monetary conditions, but it is one of the most difficult statistics to find in aggregate numbers; we have to take them one country at a time, look at national income tables and then add them up from personal, corporate and government sectors. They actually vary a lot from country to country, depending on the state of government finances, public exuberance, credit culture and institutions, as well as applicable interest rates, but the average seems to be around 3.6–5% of GDP. An increase in interest payments will lead to an increase in interest income as well, so we cannot mechanically estimate what changes in interest rates will mean to a closed economy. The effect is, rather, to increase saving and thus decrease spending and investments, which of course slows down the economy.

So that was our first number, and we can now move on to our second critical driver, which is asset prices.

Assets can be divided into those with *fixed* prices, such as cash and bank accounts, and those with *variable* prices, such as property and equity. It's the variable part we are interested in here, and it's the gross amount, not the net amount after deduction of debts. UBS estimated that the value of residential real estate in developed countries was around 70 trillion dollars in 2004. We make that 60–80 trillion and add that residential real estate in developing countries (which is not well documented) perhaps was worth some 15–20 trillion. Add to that the value of global investable commercial real estate of 5 trillion and closely held private property of 10–20 trillion.

There were various estimates of the size of equity markets, but almost all came in at around the number given in the *IMF Global Financial Stability Report 2005*, which puts the number for 2004 at 37 trillion dollars,

**Table 21.2**   Estimate of global variable-price assets in 2004, in trillion dollars.

|  | Trillion dollars; 2004 |
|---|---|
| Residential property, OECD | 60–80 |
| Residential property, emerging markets | 15–25 |
| Commercial property | 15–25 |
| = Total property | 90–130 |
| Bonds | 45–55 |
| Equities | 35–40 |
| Gold | 1.6–2.0 |
| Collectibles | 0.3–0.6 |
| Total, all variable-price assets | 172–228 |
| –estimated double-counting of assets owned by listed companies | –2–8 |
| Total gross variable-price assets excluding double-counting | 170–220 |

which we will make 35–40 trillion. The same report estimated that bond markets were valued at 58 trillion in 2004, versus 52 trillion the year before. Merrill Lynch's report *Size and Structure of the World Bond Market: 2004* estimated that the bond markets were worth about $45 trillion by the end of 2003, a number that was largely confirmed in McKinsey Global Institute's *$118 Trillion and Counting: Taking Stock of the World's Capital Markets*, which put it just two trillion lower, but again for the end of 2003. We will just assume that bond markets were worth 45–55 trillion in 2004. Some of the bonds are financing the property, but this is OK for us, as we are looking for gross variable price assets, not net. However, there is surely a bit of double counting when listed companies own bonds, equity in other listed companies and, in particular, property. Let's remove 2–5 trillion on that account, and we get to the round estimate of 170–220 trillion in assets.

There were other assets, though: the total stock of above-ground gold was around 1.6–2.0 trillion, and we can also add collector items, etc. How we reach these numbers is described in Chapters 24 and 25. Table 21.2 shows what we end up with for our sample year.

The sum of the asset value numbers in Table 21.2 should lead us to the conclusion that global gross variable-price asset values come in at the high side of *400–500% of GDP*. It should be noted here that the numbers in this example are from 2004, and asset prices would constitute a somewhat lower fraction of GDP if we had picked a period with high inflation instead, and it would have been higher if we had chosen a bubble episode (it was certainly much higher for the Japanese economy at the start of 1990).

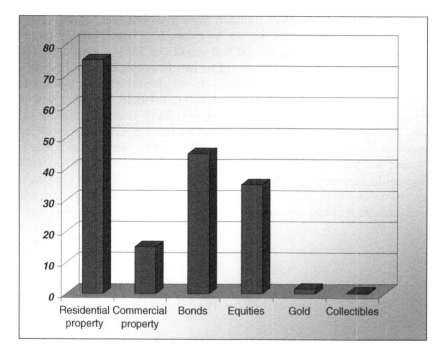

**Figure 21.1** Approximate distribution of different gross variable-price asset classes in modern economies, % of total.

It is important to take note of how much of global gross variable-price wealth is based on property. Real estate typically accounts for approximately *half of all variable-price wealth.*

Asset prices tend to fall before GDP and to continue falling for a while after GDP has turned down (we will examine this much closer in Part V). So what do asset price movements do to economic growth? They have several different impacts, but the most important is the so-called "wealth effect," which is the phenomenon whereby people spend more as they see their wealth increase, and vice versa. How big is that effect?

A lot can be (and has been) said about how wealth effects work over time, depending on population segments and asset categories. The question is complex, and it is even quite possible that it's neither linear nor symmetric in bull and bear markets, but what we need for now is just a simple rough guess of the order of magnitude, and the consensus number is that the wealth effect is 4% *of changes to aggregate asset values.*

Let's play a bit with that. Imagine a booming global economy, where asset prices break out of their normal valuation range (400–500% of GDP) and rise briefly to *six* times GDP. Then they turn and fall by a third; a drop equal to 200% of GDP. What would that loss do to spending? Well, if we accept the 4% wealth effect number, then it would mean that we lose 200% * 4% = *8%* real growth in GDP. An example of how that might work: instead of four years with annual real growth of 2%, we would get four years with no growth at all. It could be much worse, though. Just think about the Great Depression, where assets fell around 80%. Or Japan after 1990. The wealth effects of those asset declines should take time to work off, and they did. A calculation example: if asset prices have risen to a very bubbly 700% of GDP and then fall to 200% of GDP, then we have removed the equivalent of 500% of GDP in asset values. Multiply that by 4% and we get . . . no, that can't be true . . . yes, it is: we lose *20%* of GDP. That could play out, for instance if our 2% annual real growth is replaced with two years with 2% *negative* growth followed by around six years with zero growth. It could also simply mean *ten years with zero growth.*

---

### ESTIMATING THE WEALTH EFFECT

The tables below summarize the results of various studies of the wealth effect.

Table 21.3   Estimates of the wealth effect.

| Name of study | Main conclusion regarding wealth effect in % of asset price movements |
| --- | --- |
| Modigliani, F. and Tarantelli, E. The consumption function in a developing country and the Italian experience, *American Economic Review*, **65**, 1975. | 4–8%, with an average of 6% |
| Mayer, C. and Simons, K. International Evidence on the determinants of saving, *Journal of American Real Estate and Urban Economics*, **22**(2), 1994. | Around 4.2% |
| Rossi, N. and Visco, I. National Savings and Social Security in Italy, *Recierce Economiche*, **49**, 1995. | 3–3.5% |
| Brayton, F. and Tinsley, P. *A Guide to FRB/US*, Board of Governors of the Federal Reserve System, Finance and Economics Discussion papers #1996–42, 1996. | Around 4% |
| Ogawe, K. An Econometric Analysis of Japanese Households Behavior, *Financial Review*, **25**, 1992. | Around 4% |

**Table 21.3**   *Continued*

| Name of study | Main conclusion regarding wealth effect in % of asset price movements |
|---|---|
| Caporale, G. and Williams, G. *Revisiting Forward Looking Consumption and Financial Liberalization in the United Kingdom*, London Business School, Discussion Papers, #20, 1997. | 3–5% |
| Ludvigson, S. and Steindel, C. How important is the stock market effect on consumption?, *Economic Policy Review*, Federal Reserve Bank of New York, **5**, 1999 | Around 3% |
| Desnoyers, Y. *L'effet de la richesse sur la consummation aux Etats-Unis*, Banque du Canada, Document de Travail #2001–14, 2001. | Around 5.8% |
| Mehra. The Wealth Effects in Empirical Life Cycle Aggregates Consumption Equations, *Federal Reserve Bank of Richmond Quarterly Review*, **87**, 2001. | Around 3% |
| Juster, F.T., Lupton, J.P. Smith, J.P. and Stafford, F. *The Decline in Household Saving and the Wealth Effect*, Board of Governors of the Federal Reserve System, 2004. | Average wealth effect is 3%, but it is as high as 19% for directly held equities |

**Table 21.4**   The ten worst calendar years for Dow Jones Industrials. The wealth effect of stock market falls can be considerable when falls are in the magnitude listed here.

| Ranking | Year | Close | % Change |
|---|---|---|---|
| 1 | 1931 | 77.90 | −52.67 |
| 2 | 1907 | 58.75 | −37.73 |
| 3 | 1930 | 164.58 | −33.77 |
| 4 | 1920 | 71.95 | −32.90 |
| 5 | 1937 | 120.85 | −32.82 |
| 6 | 1914 | 54.58 | −30.72 |
| 7 | 1974 | 616.24 | −27.57 |
| 8 | 1903 | 49.11 | −23.61 |
| 9 | 1932 | 59.93 | −23.07 |
| 10 | 1917 | 74.38 | −21.71 |

## BUILDING CONSTRUCTION

There exists a term in economics called "gross fixed capital formation," and this includes

- Construction capital formation
- Housing
- Machinery and equipment capital formation
- Other construction

This total is around a fifth of most developed economies, and a part of it is construction of commercial and residential buildings. The global housing construction market (residential buildings) accounted in 2004 for approximately 9% of GDP and 12% in Europe (it should be noted that about half of construction activity in mature markets tends to be for refitting). The percentage was far lower in China (3–4%), but growing much faster there (property markets comprise a larger proportion of GDP in rich countries than in poor countries). So there we have it: approximately 9% of the global economy is spent on housing construction and probably another 2–3% on commercial property construction, taking the whole to somewhere around *11% of GDP* – we could call that 10%, if it is easier to remember. Around 5–6% of the total workforce is normally involved in this sector, but many more are involved indirectly, including those working with mining and refining of the related commodities (cement, steel, lumber, copper, etc.).

About one fifth of property construction activity is often public and rather stable, but the rest is highly cyclical. A drop in property construction by a third would cut over 3% from GDP, which doesn't sound huge, but we shall bear in mind that it surely would be associated with a drop in property prices, which would remove another significant chunk due to the wealth effect.

## CAPITAL SPENDING

Our fourth large driver of cycles is what we call *capital spending*, which is investment in machinery and equipment, but not buildings. Combined private and public capital spending constitute some *10% of GDP* in most economies (although far higher in rapidly growing emerging markets). Some of this is public and thus rather stable, but most is private.

Capital spending is often associated with some new core innovations, as Spiethoff and Schumpeter emphasized, and every large wave of capital spending had some distinct sector leaderships. Previous booms were led by spinning machines, steam engines, steel ships, railroads, electricity, automobiles, aircraft, chemicals and many other sectors, and each of them had their bubbles and crashes. We will all recall the wild spending boom in information technology, telecommunications and the Internet during the late 1990s, and we can't completely erase from our memories how abruptly that stopped after March 2000. Capital spending cycles are obviously amplified by competitive overinvestments, as well as by the accelerator phenomenon, whereby industry orders goods from itself in order to expand its capacity.

How important is it? Let's say that capital spending is 10% of GDP, and that it drops by a third because of a significant recession. That would be around 3% of GDP. It should also be associated with a loss of equity wealth. If equities in a normal year are around 90% of GDP (they were 37 trillion in 2004, as compared to a GDP of 41 trillion), then let's say they have risen to 130% at the peak and then fallen to 60% as the capital spending cycle turned down. That would be a drop in asset values equal to 70% of GDP. That 70% multiplied by 4% wealth effect would remove *2.8% of GDP*, which is bad, but not nearly as bad as a similar percentage drop in property wealth.


## INVENTORIES


The last big swing factor in our economies is *inventories*. Forrester's inventory simulation or Mosekilde and Sterman's beer game illustrated how inventories could fluctuate more than final demand – much, much more, in fact. Inventories typically constitute some 6% of GDP and 3% of GDP growth during expansions, but it fluctuates a lot around these numbers. One reason for this volatility is that inventories contain a disproportional amount of durable goods, such as TVs, DVD players, refrigerators, air conditioners and cars, which people stop buying when they are concerned about the future. Close to a third of inventories in many countries consist of cars and car parts (which are also durable, especially if they are German). There is not much beer and milk in inventories, since this flows very quickly from manufacturer to consumer. Nor is there any inventory of services such as haircuts and dentist visits, which represent the least cyclical parts of the economy.

So how bad are inventory cycles? Well, here is an example: if inventory ordering drops by a third, then we will see a loss of around *2% of GDP*. It's unpleasant, but clearly not awful, and it's usually not amplified by any meaningful negative wealth effect. Rather on the contrary. While asset prices may fall at the beginning of an isolated inventory correction, they will often reverse course quickly as interest rates fall.

---

**SIZE MATTERS**

The following orders of magnitude are typical for an average economy in an average year:

|  | *% of GDP* |
|---|---|
| *Financial drivers* | |
| Asset values | ~400–500 |
| Wealth effect in proportion to asset price changes | ~4 |
| Interest payments | ~5 |
| *Economic drivers* | |
| Building construction | ~10 |
| Capital spending (machinery and equipment) | ~10 |
| Inventories | ~6 |

---

## CYCLES ARE DIFFERENT

Much research on business cycles describes them as if they were all alike. There are many examinations of how asset prices fluctuate "over the business cycle," for instance, but there are big differences between how things pan out if a specific cycle is dominated by a movement in property, in capital spending, or in inventories (or any combination of those), and if it is associated with a sharp rise in short, as well as long, interest rates or not, if it involves significant wealth loss, and finally if it leads to banking crises and currency crises.

Let's continue this little exercise with a table, in which we imagine a disaster stagflation scenario (simultaneous inflation and stagnation) involving collapses in property as well as capital spending cycles. The numbers we will use are not based on any scientific study, and thick books could be written about why they might be wrong. However, they *should* give a rough idea of the numbers we have to play with in the real world. Let's say that this episode came after a huge boom, and that debt levels had become high, that the central bank had hiked interest rates because of rising inflation, and that bond rates had gone up for the same reason and because of capital shortage, so that total interest payments had risen from the normal 5% to a horrendous 9% of GDP, taking out 4% per year for the first two years of contraction (we assume here that the payments ultimately would be to foreign lenders and the central bank, so that they all left the system). And let's say that building construction and spending on machinery and equipment each fell by a third, as there was overcapacity, and a banking crisis amplified the problems. We can also add that asset prices made a fall equal to 150% of GDP. Then we could finally top it up by adding that companies got scared and stopped ordering inventories for a while, and that this removed another 2% of GDP (it should be noted that inventories might nevertheless rise during the beginning of the contraction). What would those numbers add up to? Table 21.5 shows that the total loss would be 15%.

This is how depressions happen, and the 15% in our imaginary example would probably be removed from trend GDP over a number of years.

But how do depressions then stop? Well, some of the contraction runs its course by itself, as the Austrian economists would emphasize, but it would certainly help a lot if inflation falls and central bankers feel free to reduce interest rates dramatically (especially if bond yields go down too). They will normally be able to do that quickly if there is no currency crisis, and if inflation falls with the contraction, as it normally would, then this might reduce interest payments from 9% to perhaps just 3 or 4% of GDP. Furthermore, such a reduction would trigger rising asset prices and thus reverse the wealth effect. It would also stimulate new residential construction, and, after a longer lag, spending on corporate building construction as well as machinery and equipment. The most likely sequence of events leading our imagined terminally ill economy out of its funk would consequently be this:

**Table 21.5**   Imagined disaster scenario in stagflation environment.

| Business cycle driver | What happens? | Aggregate effect on GDP |
| --- | --- | --- |
| Total variable-price asset values | Fall by 1.5 times GDP | −6% |
| Building construction | Falls by a third | −4% |
| Capital spending | Falls by a third | −3% |
| Inventory ordering | Falls by a third | −2% |
| = Total GDP loss | | −15% |

1. Drop in interest rates → drop in interest payments
2. Drop in interest rates → rising asset prices = reversal of wealth effect
3. Drop in interest rates → revival of residential building construction
4. Inventories reach, after a time lag, more conservative levels → inventory cycle turns up
5. Employment rises → increased consumer spending
6. Corporate profits rise and capacity gets stretched → renewed corporate fixed investment

### STABLE SECTORS

The last important aspect of our broad numbers game is that our economies do have sectors that are rather stable or even stabilizing. Most consumption is of services and non-durable goods ("consumer stables") – at least in developed economies. This means newspapers, drugs, grocery, beer, haircuts, office cleaning, visits to the doctor and dentist and

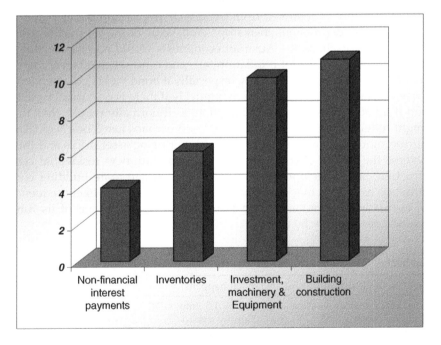

**Figure 21.2** Typical approximate proportions of major swing factors in modern economies, % of GDP.

other stuff that doesn't change much over business cycles. Around 85% of private and public consumption in most countries falls within these categories, and this is a stabilizing factor. Even more so is the public sector, which accounts for between some 20 and 55% of GDP, with most developed countries keeping it around 40%. This sector is, if anything, slightly counter-cyclical, since social spending is increased during recession, and tax revenues increase during booms. However, consumption of consumer discretionary items is more cyclical and will respond to changes in monetary conditions in particular, and also to changes in employment and employment outlook, which again follows the main cyclical drivers.

So the public sector is slightly counter-cyclical, and consumption of non-durable goods is huge and rather stable. Then there is consumer spending on durables and housing, but that is rarely the primary cause of cycles; it's part of the transmission mechanisms for the main cycle drivers.

So what's left? Commodities? Well, their demand, supply and prices *do* change a lot, but they only account for approximately 1 trillion out of a 41 trillion economy (2004), which is some 2.5%. Commodities were once central to the performance of almost any economy in the world, but not any more. Their movements can cause lots of tumult in Brazil or Russia, of course, and fluctuations in oil prices can still make a dent in Germany, Japan or the United States, but not nearly as much as they used to.

# Chapter 22

# The Ten Challenges of Central Banking

> The fact that our economical models at The Fed, the best in the world, have been wrong for fourteen straight quarters, does not mean they will not be right in the fifteenth quarter.
>
> *Alan Greenspan*

It is February 17, 2000, the economy is booming and NASDAQ is testing its all-time high. Alan Greenspan has just delivered his presentation at one of the standard congressional hearings, and it is now time for questions. The word is passed to a Republican Congressman, Ron Paul, who is concerned about an issue. He has seen statistics of growth in the category of money supply called M3, and it seems that this has expanded much faster than the economy as a whole since 1992. So why has the Fed allowed that to happen, he wants to know. Greenspan's answer is a bit disturbing:

> "... We have a problem trying to define exactly what money is ... the current definition of money is not sufficient to give us a good means for controlling the money supply ..."

A bit puzzled, Mr Paul responds:

> "Well, if you can't define money, how can you control the monetary system?"

Alan Greenspan's answer:

> "That's the problem ..."

Defining money *is* a problem. But it is not the only one that central bankers have, when they try to steer monetary policy in a volatile world. There are, in fact, at least ten major challenges involved in this job. You have to choose a certain strategic approach to the problem, for starters. That's one challenge. Then there are the questions of defining and measuring the "*M*," "*V*", "*Q*" and "*P*" in Newcomb's famous equation. That's four more challenges. Four additional tasks are to be able to halt critical declines in velocity of money, to tackle asset bubbles, to avoid over-stimulation and to deal with foreign exchange rates. And finally, there is the challenge of maintaining credibility in the market. Central banking in a cyclical world isn't easy, and we shall now see why.

## CHALLENGE # 1: CHOOSING A STRATEGIC APPROACH

Irrespective of which flavor central bankers prefer, they will need to pull their strings. Here are the three basic tools that central bankers use very often:

- *Change discount rates.* A reduction of interest rates will, for instance, stimulate more lending and less saving throughout society, as Henry Thornton observed in 1802
- *Buy or sell government bonds from commercial banks.* These transactions are credited/debited to commercial banks' accounts with the central bank. This modifies their excess reserves, and thus their ability to lend
- *Increase or decrease commercial banks' reserve requirements.* Increasing these means preventing commercial banks from lending out more relative to their reserves, and vice versa

So central banks interact with commercial banks, and these will then interact with consumers and companies (Figure 22.1). A good reason why central banks use commercial banks as intermediary to consumers and companies is that commercial banks possess considerable information about their clients, so that they can better distinguish between good and bad projects.

Whatever the central bank does is supposed to get amplified through the system. The immediate effects of central bank activity are felt through changes in the quantity and price of money (interest rates). However, this is followed by a derived effect, which is called the "financial accelerator," whereby companies increase their profits if they borrow cheap money. Use of new low-interest rate loans makes them more profitable and

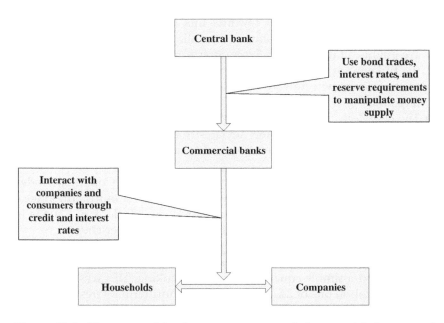

**Figure 22.1** How central banks manage money. It is essential that central banks interact entirely through commercial banks, and they are thus dependent on the health of these banks.

valuable, thus they seem more creditworthy, and so the banks offer them even more loans. Another, secondary, effect is that monetary stimulus often leads to falling currency, which stimulates exports and thus domestic growth.

The key question for central banks is, of course, *when* to add or remove money from the system, and *how much*? This is where central bankers have somewhat different styles. The economy is like a machine with a huge number of moving parts, and each monetary style will emphasize different moving parts. We can divide these styles into "flavors":

- The *Austrian flavor* means keeping money supply as stable as possible while not trying to micromanage the economy. This approach, which means stabilizing "MV" in Newcomb's equation, was particularly popular in the 1980s (as a reaction against inflation problems in the 1970s) and in Japan during the 1990s. Friedman was a great advocate, but modified his view somewhat over the years
- The *Swedish flavor* means identifying the "natural rate" (average returns on business investments, as described by Knut Wicksell), and

manipulating actual rates towards this natural rate. This approach became gradually more common after the 1980s

- We might call it an *English flavor* (after Keynes) to focus on identifying the full employment growth rate, or speed limit, of the economy, and try to steer growth towards that level – no more, no less. This means targeting "*Q*"
- The *New Zealand flavor* is to publish a specific inflation target ("*P*") and intervene whenever inflation deviates from this level. Started in New Zealand in 1989, this approach spread to more than 20 countries within the next 15 years
- The *Canadian flavor* is to use a so-called Monetary Conditions Index (MCI) as benchmark. This index, which is based on short-term interest rates as well as exchange rates, was introduced by Bank of Canada in the early 1990s and has since become popular in other countries
- A recent approach, which we may call the *American flavor*, was introduced by Professor John Taylor from Stanford University in 1993, when he devised a simple equation for central banking. This was based on a target inflation rate of 2% and a "neutral" short-term interest rate of 4%. The mechanics of his equation were such that the actual interest rate should be determined partly by how inflation deviated from the target of 2%, and partly by how economic growth deviated from its long-term speed limit. Excessive inflation or growth would lead to increasing interest rates, and vice versa. This is now called the "Taylor Rule," and is often used as a reference point for discussions of central banking policies
- And finally, there is the *Zimbabwean flavor*, which is to produce as much money as possible

There are, in reality, not many (if any at all) doctrinaire central bankers left, and most will now combine models with different flavors (except the Zimbabwean) plus significant human judgment to reach their decisions. However, nothing in central banking is easy. Take, for instance, the Austrian flavor, where you try to stabilize *MV*. The first problem here is simply to define "*M*," as Greenspan mentioned at his hearing in February 2000. Let's dig a bit deeper into that problem.

### CHALLENGE # 2: DEFINING MONEY, "*M*"

How do you define money? Well, any encyclopedia would suggest that money is a unit of account, a store of value and a medium of exchange.

That's clear, and there have been numerous examples of such money: copper bracelets, amber, cylinders cut from coral, furs, dried fish, grain, sugar, tobacco, playing cards, nails, rice, or even slaves. The Greeks used silver as their currency, and the Romans introduced gold coins after conquering the Etruscans. Modern money is divided into the following subcomponents:

- *M0*, which is coins and notes. It is, in other words, cash
- *M1* is money that is readily available for making a payment. It is cash (M0), plus checking accounts and travelers' checks
- *M2* is M1 plus other, fairly liquid stores of value: savings accounts, money market accounts, small certificates of deposit, money market mutual funds, overnight Eurodollars and overnight repurchase agreements
- *M3* is M2 plus somewhat less liquid forms of savings: large certificates of deposit, institutional money market accounts, and fixed-term deposits, fixed-term repurchase agreements, etc.
- *M4* is M3 plus private sector holdings of building society shares and deposits and sterling certificates of deposit
- *M5* is M4 plus holdings by the private sector (excluding building societies) of money market instruments (bank bills, Treasury bills, local authority deposits) certificates of tax deposit and National Savings instruments (excluding certificates, save-as-you-earn schemes and other long-term deposits)

M0, M1 and M2 are often called "narrow money," whereas M3, M4 and M5 are "broad money." Another and more recent classification is *MZM*, or Money of Zero Maturity, which measures the supply of financial assets that its owner can spend without giving any prior notification to a bank. MZM is equal to M2 without any of its time deposits (since they would require bank notification), but with the addition of money market funds from M3. It is, in other words, a measure of really liquid money, or money that is likely to have high velocity. All of this is fairly clear. But read now what Friedrich von Hayek wrote in his article *Denationalization of Money: An Analysis of the Theory and Practice of Concurrent Currencies* from 1976:

> Money does not have to be legal tender created by governments. Like law, language and morals, it can emerge spontaneously.

Emerge spontaneously? Well, we have already seen how J.P. Morgan devised "scripts" as emergency money during the crisis of 1907. The digital age has brought new examples: electronic telephone cards, cyber loyalty schemes, event smart cards, prepaid smart cards and frequent flyer miles. The latter may, for instance, be valid tender for purchase of wine, hotel stays, cameras, airline tickets and car rentals. It smells like money, but was never issued by a central bank. The central bankers' big complication is not frequent flier miles, though; it is variable-priced assets. These are not issued by central banks, but they can, in many ways, act as if they were money. So that is our third challenge.

## CHALLENGE # 3: TACKLING ASSET BUBBLES

On January 27, 2005 the American Real Estate Roundtable held a meeting in Washington, D.C., where one of the speakers, Roger W. Ferguson, Jr, a member of the Board of Governors of the Federal Reserve Board, made a very interesting presentation about asset prices and business cycles. Some of the graphs from Ferguson's presentation are shown in Figures 22.2, 22.3 and 22.4 and they show how asset prices tend to turn at around the time of the inflection point in growth, where the output gap is at its lowest (or a bit after), and well ahead of recessions. This shows, as Roger Ward Babson had pointed out in 1911, that asset prices are barometers, which discount future events. However, their behavior can also amplify business cycles. Ferguson concluded:

> "Recessions are almost always accompanied by asset-price declines. But such declines sometimes appear to be the *source* of adverse surprises, and asset-price busts may subsequently have disproportionately adverse consequences. Falling asset prices create a negative wealth effect and restrain consumption. By making collateral less valuable, they also increase the risk of lending to businesses and thereby worsen the lending terms faced by borrowers. When asset prices fall substantially, lenders may also find themselves holding substantial amounts of nonperforming loans that are backed by what may have become, in some cases, worthless collateral. For this reason, recessions that are preceded by asset-price booms and busts may also be associated with problems in the banking industry. In such episodes, the ensuing loss of intermediation may serve as an additional force acting to prolong and deepen what might otherwise have been a milder recession."

Another study of the matter appeared in Chapter two of *IMF's World Economic Outlook 2003*. This study drew on equity price indices covering mostly the period from 1959 to 2002 for 19 industrial countries, and housing prices mainly beginning around 1970 and covering 14 countries (both indices deflated by the CPI). The authors made a clear distinction

(a)

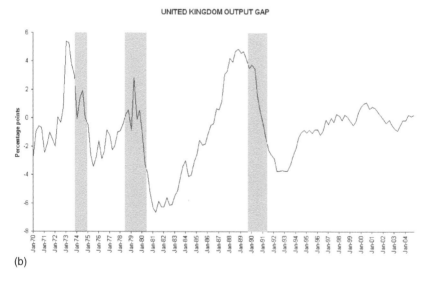

(b)

**Figure 22.2** Aggregate asset prices and economic activity in the United Kingdom, 1970–2003. The shaded areas indicate periods with recessions. (a) shows aggregate asset prices and (b) shows the output gap. Which means whether economic growth is above or below it's long-term sustainable level. It is striking how asset prices turn down at the time or slightly after the output gap peaks, and that asset prices in each case fall well ahead of recessions. Source: Ferguson, 2005, Bank of International Settlements, National Data.

(a)

(b)

**Figure 22.3**   Aggregate asset prices and economic activity in the USA 1970–2003. The shaded areas indicate periods with recessions. (a) shows aggregate asset prices and (b) shows the output gap. Asset prices are here, as in the UK, turning down well before recessions. Source: Ferguson, 2005, Bank of International Settlements, National Data.

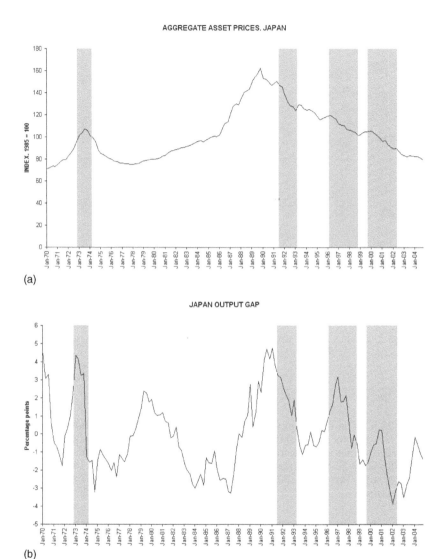

**Figure 22.4** Aggregate asset prices and economic activity in Japan, 1970–2003. The shaded areas indicate periods with recessions. (a) shows aggregate asset prices and (b) shows the output gap. The graphs show how the period with massively rising asset prices had no recessions, whereas the subsequent decline was associated with an exceptional cluster of recessions. Source: Ferguson, 2005, Bank of International Settlements, National Data.

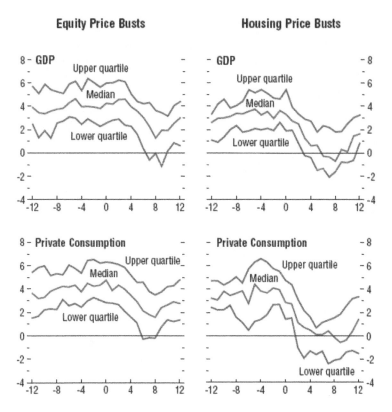

**Figure 22.5**   The fallout in GDP from equity and house price busts, respectively. The graphs show that house price busts typically are associated with the worst declines in economic aggregates. The vertical scale in this figure and in Figures 22.6–22.8 are quarters before and after culmination in bust. Source: Helbling and Terrones, 2003. Reproduced by permission of International Money Fund.

between the effects of busts in equity markets and in property markets. The first interesting conclusion from the study is that the overall fallout associated with housing price busts was much more severe than the calamities in cases of equity market busts. This is shown in Figure 22.5.

The authors then went on to investigate what happened to two of our main business cycle drivers – capital spending ("private spending in machinery and equipment") and private construction spending. Again, the results showed that the fallout was far greater in cases of house price busts, as can be seen in Figure 22.6.

They also investigated what happened to credit and money supply, and the conclusion was, yet again, that the greatest contractions (by far) came with house price busts. This is shown in Figure 22.7.

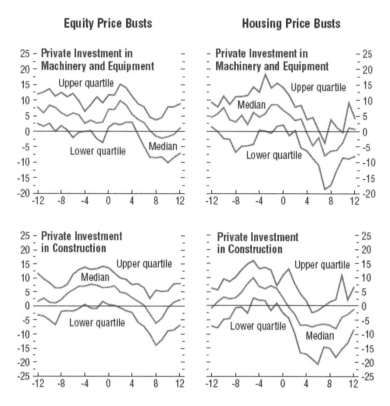

**Figure 22.6** The fallout in capital spending and building construction from equity and house price busts, respectively. Both of the variables decline much more during house price busts than during equity cycle busts. Source: Helbling, and Terrones, 2003. Reproduced by permission of International Money Fund.

And finally, they asked themselves what the cross-correlation between house price and equity market performance was. The result, which is shown in Figure 22.8, was that house price busts led to far bigger falls in equity markets than vice versa.

Our final graph from this study (Figure 22.9) shows how banks' provisions for loans had changed during periods of bust in house prices and equity prices ("provisions of loans" means that banks write off loans that they fear can't be repaid). The conclusion was very clear: busts in equity prices were not associated with any crisis in banking at all (on average), whereas house price busts lead to significant increases in provision of loans (this is given in Figure 22.7 money supply). So the overall conclusion from this was that house price busts have far more severe implications than equity price busts.

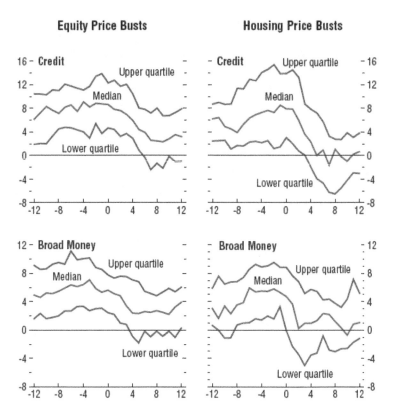

**Figure 22.7** The fallout in credit and money supply from equity and house price busts, respectively. The graphs show that both of these monetary indicators fall more when house prices collapse than when equity markets go through busts. Source: Helbling and Terrones, 2003. Reproduced by permission of International Money Fund.

We have already seen that asset markets normally amount to around 400–500% of GDP, that the wealth effect is around 4%, and that it therefore can have significant impact when asset prices move rapidly. And they often do: the combined market capitalization on NASDAQ fell, for instance, 2.2 trillion dollars from March 1st, 2000 until one year later; a loss equivalent to 45000 dollars per American household. That's a lot. Now, let's bear that in mind and then take yet another look at our old workhorse, Simon Newcomb's equation:

$$MV = PQ$$

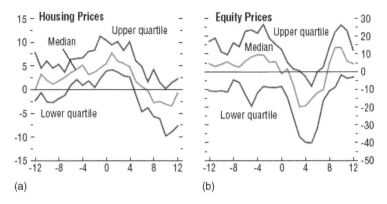

**Figure 22.8** The cross-correlation between busts in house prices and in equity prices. (a) shows what happens to housing prices when equity prices go through a bust. They will typically decline modestly after around six quarters, but the upper quartile showed no declines at all; just deceleration. The opposite correlation is shown in (b), where it can be seen that equities declined strongly and rather quickly after each house price bust. Source: Helbling and Terrones, 2003. Reproduced by permission of International Money Fund.

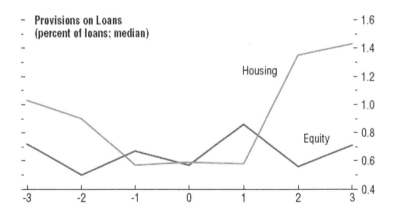

**Figure 22.9** Bank provision on bad loans during busts in house prices and in equity prices. The vertical scale here is years before and after culmination of the bust. The graph shows that collapses in equity prices typically involve very limited increases in bad loan provisions after one year, and then return to normality in the second quarter. Collapses in house prices, on the other hand, are associated with much larger provisions, starting in the second year. Source: Helbling and Terrones, 2003. Reproduced by permission of International Money Fund.

The process of creating an asset such as a house or a gemstone forms a part of "$Q$" in this equation; such an activity is a *flow*. However, the finished house or gemstone will subsequently become an *asset* that could be *sold* or used as *collateral*, and it will then remind a bit of "$M$." One might even argue for introducing additional definitions of money including these assets. Perhaps we could imagine "M13" defined as "M12 plus commercial real estate," and "M14" as "M13 plus fine art," etc. It is evident, for instance, that an increase in the value of existing property increases building construction activity, or the "$PQ$" of construction. We should, at the very least, consider that assets to some extent work as "$M$," and that their rise therefore effectively can boost "$MV$." One can argue, of course, that as long as assets aren't used in direct barter, they will always require real money for their transactions. This may be, but as they are perceived as wealth, they will, at the very least, tend to speed up the velocity of money. It actually seems as if investment bankers Goldman Sachs were thinking along those lines as they devised their "Financial Conditions Index," which includes not only short-term interest rates and corporate bond yields, but also the dollar's trade-weighted index and the stock market capitalization relative to GDP. Goldman Sachs included, in other words, asset prices in the measure of monetary stimulus.

Another complication is that if "$MV$" rises, then it doesn't only affect the "$P$" of consumer prices. It could also affect the "$P$" of asset prices. It could be, for instance, that fierce commercial competition and supply shocks make consumer price inflation almost impossible, so that central banks can stimulate considerably without raising consumer price inflation. We could recall Say's Law that stated that supply equals demand. The situation in an *asset inflation* environment is that supply of consumer goods outpaces its demand, whereas demand for assets outpaces its supply.

This is what happened when the North American markets opened in the 18th century, and when China, India, etc. opened from around 1990. Such an environment can stimulate increasing trading volume and prices in assets. This can then lead to a process whereby rising asset prices increase collateral values, which, in turn, lead to increased lending and thus velocity of money. It's quite nice when it happens, but it does tend to become circular:

- An inherently de-inflationary environment forces central banks to stimulate (to avoid deflation)
- This monetary stimulus leads to asset inflation
- Owners of assets perceive them as a sort of money and use them as collateral . . .

- . . . which means additional monetary stimulus . . .
- . . . leading to more asset inflation

Economists have known about the risks of asset inflation for a long time, of course. It was a cornerstone of Austrian economics, and Hamilton Bolton, the founder of the private research institute *Bank Credit Analyst*, in 1967 published a book entitled *Money and Investment Profits*, where he wrote:

> At any time, part of the money supply is store of value and part is medium of exchange, and these two parts are probably changing in relationship to each other. But the medium of exchange part is also, at any time, splintered into the part going into real new output and the part going into other real transactions – second-hand cars, or Corot paintings, or, for that matter, common stocks and bonds.

The decline of Japan after 1990 was associated with a decline in the assets that Bolton spoke about. Japanese industrial land prices fell 22% during 1991 to 2001; while commercial land prices declined 54% and residential land prices 41% (average golf club membership prices dropped a whopping 90%). The combined declines in Japanese asset prices from 1991 to 2001 were over twice the GDP, as total wealth of individuals was cut by half. The real growth rate of Japan's GDP from 1992 to 2002 averaged a petty 1.1% and was down to just 0.1% during 1998–2002. This even as the state consistently borrowed heavily to provide stimulus. The low growth rates were accompanied by persistent deflation, leading to classical debt deflation and a liquidity trap.

The Japanese central bank expanded money supply rapidly during the 1980s because the traditional measure of inflation (CPI) grew very slowly; they were stabilizing traditional "$P$," but not "$MV$," as Austrian economists (and Milton Friedman) would have proposed instead. Nor did they stabilize the "$P$" of assets.

So could that mistake have been avoided? Should central banks try to manage asset prices? Let's call in the experts. Here is a statement from Ludwig von Mises:

> Expansion of credit does lead to a boom at first, it is true, but sooner or later this boom is bound to crash and bring about a new depression. Only apparent and temporary relief can be won by tricks of banking and currency. In the long run they must land the nation in profounder catastrophe. For the damage such methods inflict on national well-being is all the heavier, the longer people have managed to deceive themselves with the illusion of prosperity which the continuous creation of credit has conjured up.

This quote is from 1934 (*Socialism*), so how about some more recent assessments? Here is Alan Greenspan, the director of the US Federal Reserve from 1987 to 2006 commenting on the Dot Com Bubble at a symposium in Wyoming in 2002:

> "Such data suggest that nothing short of a sharp increase in short-term rates that engenders a significant economic retrenchment is sufficient to check a nascent bubble. The notion that a well-timed incremental tightening could have been calibrated to prevent the late 1990s bubble is almost surely an illusion."

Another expert is US Federal Reserve Chairman Bernard Bernanke, who (before his appointment) made a series of speeches and articles discussing the problems after the Japanese meltdown and the Internet crash. He would often divide the approaches to emerging asset bubbles into three classes: "do nothing," "lean against the wind," or "aggressive bubble popping." Bernanke agreed with many others that asset bubbles could be hugely destabilizing, and that they often led to a disproportionate and ineffective flow of money into the bubbly sectors. When it came to his three alternative approaches to them, though, he dismissed aggressive bubble popping entirely. Why? Let's think of Newcomb's equation yet again: $MV = PQ$. A central bank targeting a stable consumer price ($P$) would actually also implicitly manage $Q$, he said, because $P$ will only behave when $Q$ is close to its speed limit. This would mean that while asset bubbles could boost $Q$, this would be incorporated in what the Fed was targeting, and thus indirectly accounted for.

Bernanke had another argument against aggressive bubble popping: the central bank's instruments were far too blunt. He stated, as did Greenspan, that attempts to pop a bubble in parts of the economy could inflict huge and unintended damage to other sectors. And there were more arguments against aggressive bubble popping: it often would be difficult to determine if, in fact, there was a bubble or not when people claimed so. A rather striking example: Alan Greenspan made a speech in December 1996, where he hinted that the stock market might be in a state of "irrational exuberance." This caused considerable consternation. Where might he have gotten that from? Perhaps from the two respected economists, Robert Shiller and John Campbell of Yale University, who had just made a presentation about this subject to the Fed. Rather alarmingly, these two experts had concluded that equity markets with the Standard & Poors Index trading at around 750 were priced at no less than three times their fair value (which should be approximately 250). That would be an absolutely massive overvaluation (if it was true). Equities kept rising strongly for another three years, though, and when the great crash came in 2000–2002, it never took the index lower than 800, which was still over three times what the economists had assumed fair five years earlier.

Having said this, though, it shouldn't be too hard for any competent economist to see that Japanese real estate was overvalued when its combined value reached 150% of all property in the rest of the world combined, or that Internet shares were more than a tad overpriced when their market capitalizations reached 500 times their revenue. But then again, if we put ourselves in the shoes of Japanese bankers in the late 1980s, we will discover that they not only struggled with containing an asset bubble, but also with the risk of deflation and a stubbornly rising currency, so anything they did to deflate asset markets could increase their two other problems. However, not popping it led to disaster: when the economy went into deep freeze, it seemed that attempts to push money back into the system just didn't work. Why? Because velocity of money had slowed to a crawl, and this brings us to the fourth of the great challenges.

### CHALLENGE # 4: MEASURING VELOCITY OF MONEY, $V$

Some parts of the money supply flow quickly from hand to hand, while others seem stickier. We have already seen that MZM defines money that tends to be fast, and M1 has a high velocity too – especially the physical money within it. The money market funds within M2 are pretty quick too, but the other M2-specific elements may be slower. M3 contains elements that are slower still. Just think of the fixed-term deposits. How quickly will money change hands if it has been deposited in a bank on a fixed term?

So how do central bankers calculate velocity of money? Using Newcomb's equation, of course, plus basic math. "$MV$ equals $PQ$", they say so:

$$V = PQ/M$$

Velocity of money is, in other words, the number of times the stock of money turns over per period in order to finance the expenditure on nominal GDP. It's GDP divided by the amount of money.

Let's suppose that there is a recession and that our bankers have increased the money stock $M$ to stimulate new growth – but it isn't working! What will they do? They will first check if overall velocity has been declining, and then study the relative performance of narrow and broad money. This will show them where their money is going. If velocity really *is* falling, then they will probably see that the amount of broad money outperforms narrow money.

Consider now a situation where velocity of money actually *does* fall, thus offsetting attempts to stimulate. Money gets stuck somewhere in the chain, but where? The first suspects are consumers. Perhaps money may get sticky when it reaches the consumer's hands because people are scared and are building up precautionary cash reserves – spare money for difficult times. This may even be held in physical cash if they think banks may default. Some typical symptoms of concerned consumers are falling velocity of physical money, rapidly increasing money market funds and low/falling business/consumer confidence.

That brings us to the commercial banks. A bank expects that people pay back their debts in due course, but banks face problems during recessions, because those are times where only *solid* clients return cash; the weaker ones can't. This means that the banks end up with declining business volume and increasing average credit risk – a double squeeze. This can lead to Keynes's "liquidity trap": commercial banks' balance sheets become so damaged that they dare not, or cannot, pass on any of the central bank's money (according to the so-called Basel Accord, which has more than 100 countries as signatory, banks are only allowed to lend out as long as they meet specified capital requirements).

Banking crisis escalate when financial institutions begin to default. Each time a bank goes under, it causes losses and pain among taxpayers, shareholders, depositors and creditors. Furthermore, banks will, over time, develop valuable information about the creditworthiness of their clients (or lack of it), and this knowledge is largely lost if they default. This means that many creditworthy clients of bankrupt banks will have problems refinancing their loans with other institutions that don't know them. Furthermore, the mere *threat* of banking failures can mean that banks lose confidence in each other, thus inhibiting the free flow of money. Two of the most common symptoms of Keynes's liquidity trap are that share prices of banks sink, while bond prices go up, and that measures of sticky money (M3 or M4) outpace measures of fast money (M1 and MZM). This happened in the world depression in the 1930s and in Japan in the 1990s, where the number of regional banks that could meet a required 8% capital ratio fell from 50 in March 1990 to only four in September that year.

Another reason for stickiness could be that Irving Fisher's "debt deflation" is at play: asset prices are falling, so balance sheets are deteriorating, thus leading to a vicious cycle of distress sales and debt repayment, which slows down velocity. The symptoms of debt deflation include high debt levels, high debt servicing costs, and, of course, rapidly falling asset prices. It can be amplified if there is a currency crisis at a time where many companies have borrowed heavily abroad. Japan in the 1990s, emerging Asia in 1997–98, and the aftermath of the Dot Com crash in 2000 are examples.

What difference does it make if a recession deteriorates to the point where there is a banking crisis? A study made in 2001 by Hoggarth, Reis and Saporta showed that the total output losses following a banking crisis averaged *6–8% of GDP*, but rose to *10% of GDP* if this came with a currency crisis as well. These numbers show what society as a whole would lose, but the three economists also studied the costs of intervention, lost taxes, etc. for governments, and found that this was *12% of GDP* in developed countries and *18% of GDP* in emerging economies, averaging 16% for all countries. The costs depended strongly on whether there was a currency crisis, though. Whereas they were *4.5% of GDP* for banking crises, they rose to a whopping *23% of GDP* for dual crises (the government's losses can exceed aggregate loss for society, since much of the government's costs relate to redistribution of money). These costs are gigantic, so it's obviously nice if they can be avoided. The question is how? That's our fifth challenge.

## CHALLENGE # 5: HALTING CRITICAL DECLINES IN VELOCITY

Central bankers will, in most cases, tackle a critical slowdown in velocity by continuing with traditional stimulus in the expectation that it will, in fact, work, if given enough time. There can be situations, though, where they get into *real* trouble, and this is our fifth great challenge of central banking. Real trouble is when a central bank has reduced interest rates to zero, but realizes that even that hasn't provided enough stimulus. Or if the commercial banks can't sell as many government bonds to the central bank as it is asking for. This is where central bankers may consider unconventional remedies, as shown in Table 22.1.

Japan suffered from all the three symptoms of falling velocity and sticky money during the 1990s: people were hoarding money, bank balance sheets were too fragile to enable new credit creation and asset prices were declining rapidly, but the central bank nevertheless reacted at a snail's pace and failed to use many of the unconventional strategies that could have resolved their problems faster.

However, we should not forget that while there are spectacular examples, where central banks have failed to stimulate enough, there are many more where they have stimulated *too much*. One issue here is to

**Table 22.1** Extraordinary measures to reverse declines in volatility.

|  | Build-up of precautionary cash reserves | Debt deflation | Liquidity trap |
| --- | --- | --- | --- |
| Specific symptoms | • Falling velocity of physical money<br>• Rapidly increasing money market funds<br>• Low/falling business/consumer confidence | • High corporate/consumer debt levels<br>• High debt servicing costs relative to cash flow/disposable income<br>• Falling property prices<br>• Falling equity prices | • Rise in M3/M1 and M3/MZM ratios<br>• Fall in bank equity prices relative to government bond prices |
| Unconventional central bank remedies | • Issue/increase guarantees for customers' bank deposits | • Buy equities<br>• Buy real estate<br>• Buy longer dated bonds<br>• Buy mortgage-backed bonds<br>• Buy corporate bonds<br>• Intervene in currency markets to create devaluation of currency<br>• Publish inflation target numbers | • Offer fixed-term loans with low or zero interest to private banks, allowing the banks to use a range of asset classes as collateral<br>• Commit to keeping overnight rates at zero for a prolonged period of time<br>• Announce specific targets for long-term interest rates and commit to supporting bond prices with unlimited purchases |

make accurate forecasts of future economic growth. This is the central banker's challenge # 6.

## CHALLENGE # 6: FORECASTING GROWTH, *Q*

We will recall that the core of our so-called "English" flavor of central banking was to steer growth towards its natural speed limit. However, you can only steer if you can forecast. This is what leading indicators are for, and different organizations use such indicators in different ways. However, we can study the ones used by the US Conference Board for the

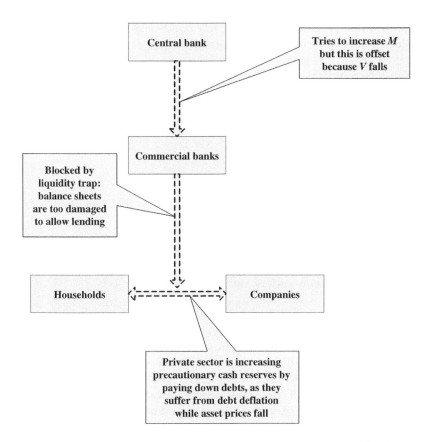

**Figure 22.10** Breakdown in the monetary flow process. Central banks may be "pushing on a string" if commercial banks are unable or unwilling to create new credit. Such a situation is most likely to follow a severe property price bust.

American economy as our example. The first indicator within the Conference Board's index is the phenomenon that really starts it all; it is the expansion of money supply, which is considered a prime mover:

• Money supply, M2

All the other indicators within the index are mainly moving as a result of what happens to money supply. Two of them are what we call financial indicators:

- Interest rate spread, 10-year Treasury bonds less federal funds
- Stock prices, 500 common stocks (S&P 500)

These two indicators are very good, partly because financial markets make great efforts to predict and discount the future, and partly because equity investors use interest rates to discount future earnings, and interest rates are leaders. There is also another leading indicator that builds on expectations:

- Index of consumer expectations

The next three tell us about economic activity that has already been decided, but which will take some time to play out:

- Building permits, new private housing units ("housing starts")
- Manufacturers' new orders, consumer goods and materials
- Manufacturers' new orders, non-defense capital goods

One of these three, building permits, is the best economic (as opposed to financial) predictor of economic revivals. This is so because residential housing construction is such a big business, and because consumers drive the beginning of virtually every upswing. Next on the Conference Board's list are two expressions of how companies respond when they see the first signs of life: they don't hire more people, but they *do* ask those already onboard to work more. And they run into a bit of an order backlog, which leads to slower deliveries:

- Average weekly hours, manufacturing
- Vendor performance, slower deliveries diffusion index

The final indicator in the leading index is about unemployment, which falls as activity picks up:

- Average weekly initial claims for unemployment insurance

Composite leading indicators tend to lead with 6–8 months before economic peaks and 2–4 months before troughs. This, at least, is what you find when you study long-term historical graphs comparing the indicators with GDP. However, using leading indicators in praxis is not as easy as it may appear from a historical graph. One problem is that most of the data is somewhat delayed when published, and that you need to observe a change in the trend over several months before you can feel sure that it means anything. So there we have it: if the lead at a trough comes out at two months, and the data is released with almost two months' delay, then it gets hairy.

In the late 1980s, Geoffrey H. Moore (the economist from NBER who later founded ECRI, the Economic Cycle Research Institute) introduced two proposals to enhance forecasts. One was to segregate some co-called "long leaders" from the rest. These were indicators that had a particularly long lead ahead of the economy. He found four of these:

- Real money supply
- Bond prices
- New building permits
- Ratio of prices to unit labor costs

Having studied these for the period 1948 to 1989, he found that a composite index of these indicators had turned, on average, 14 months before economic peaks and eight months before troughs. That was far better than the Department of Commerce composite index (which was somewhat different then than it is now). A composite index of the leading indicators that are not "long" have turned an average of eight months before tops and just two months before bottoms. Moore's other proposal was to focus on "promptly available indicators." These leading indicators were not better than the rest, but they were released with an average of three weeks' less delay.

It is possible to go further still. It has turned out that it gives a better signal to look at leading indicators divided by lagging indicators than just leaders in isolation. The Conference Board uses seven such indicators. The first are about loans and money:

- Ratio of consumer credit outstanding to personal income
- Value of outstanding commercial and industrial loans
- Average prime rate charged by banks

These show that people are getting extended and money tight. The next are about rising costs:

- Change in the consumer price index for services from the previous month
- Change in labor cost per unit of labor output

Then there is one relating to alarming build-up of inventories:

- Ratio of manufacturing and trade inventories to sales made

And finally one relating to employment:

- Inverted average length of employment

It is a particularly strong signal for the economy if the leading indicators rise while these lagging indicators (which signal bottlenecks and exhaustion) fall.

The last approach to enhancing the forecasts of $Q$ in Newcomb's equation is to use specific subleaders. ECRI publishes a Leading Construction Index (for real estate), as well as numerous indices for aggregate economic activity, specific sectors, trade and inflation.

How do decision makers forecast economic activity in reality? There are many ways, but a lot do like ISI, a famous Wall Street company that uses a number of small, simple equations that are easy to understand. The managers at ISI study the prediction of each of these mini models, compare them to each other, read the news and create diffusion indices of American and international economic data releases which they classify as either positive or negative. And then they sit down and form their own opinion, which is, by the end of the day, intuitive (but it isn't published by the end of the day. They update it twice a day to all their clients!).

## CHALLENGE # 7: AVOIDING OVERSTIMULATION

If central bankers claim to aim for "2% inflation" (or another level), then it's in all likelihood CPI (the Consumer Price Index) to which they refer. CPI is a fairly good indicator of the prices consumers have to pay, even though it is slow to compensate for changes in spending habits and hopeless in compensating for changes in quality. It's still the best there is.

Inflation has been a recurring pest to societies. Early examples were seen when a flood of silver from the New World caused devastating inflation in 16th and 17th century Spain, and when massive discoveries of gold in California, Australia and South Africa caused inflation problems in the 19th and early 20th centuries. We will also recall how the Duke of Orleans created inflation in 18th century France by printing too much money (to John Law's horror), but more extreme examples of such incompetence were seen in Germany, 1922 (5000%), Chile, 1973 (600%), Bolivia, 1985 (12000%), Argentina, 1989 (3100%), Peru, 1990 (7500%), Brazil, 1993

(2100%), Ukraine, 1993 (5000%) and Zimbabwe, 2003 (600%). Hyperinflation has normally happened in countries where governments used their
central banks (which were not independent) to spend far more than their
economy allowed for. Much has been said about the menace of inflation
over the years. Let's quote John Maynard Keynes, for instance:

> By a continuing process of inflation, government can confiscate, secretly
> and unobserved, an important part of the wealth of their citizens. By this
> method they not only confiscate, but they confiscate arbitrarily, and,
> while the process impoverishes many, it actually enriches some. The
> sight of this arbitrary rearrangement of riches strikes not only at secu-
> rity, but at confidence in the equity (or fairness) of the existing distribu-
> tion of wealth.
> As the inflation proceeds and the real value of the currency fluctuates
> wildly from month to month, all permanent relations between debtors
> and creditors, which form the ultimate foundation of capitalism, become
> so utterly disordered as to be almost meaningless; and the process of
> wealth-getting degenerates into a gamble and a lottery.

And here is Ludwig von Mises:

> Government is the only institution that can take a valuable commodity
> like paper, and make it worthless by applying ink.

And Friedrich von Hayek:

> I do not think it is an exaggeration to say history is largely a history of
> inflation, usually inflations engineered by governments for the gain of
> governments.

Paul Volcker, the central banker that really broke the inflation after the
1970s, expressed it this way:

> Inflation is thought of as a cruel, and maybe the cruelest, tax, because it
> hits in a many-sectored way, in an unplanned way, and it hits the people
> on a fixed income hardest.

However, of all the memorable statements on inflation, the one that
always needs to be borne in mind is this one by Milton Friedman:

> Inflation is always and everywhere a monetary phenomenon. To control
> inflation, you need to control the money supply.

His was an absolutely central observation, of course. The logic of
Newcomb's equation dictates that inflation always must be associated

with continued, excessive growth in money supply (it could, in theory, be associated with continued declines in $Q$, but not in praxis).

There is a fairly recent example of overstimulation which evolved into a major, global menace: the great inflation of the 1970s. This episode, which ranks among the greatest, collective central banking errors of its century, led to inflation rates reaching over 25% in Britain by the mid seventies, and some 20% in Japan, 15% in France, and 10% in the United States. How could such a massive blunder take place in countries that most of the world's best economists called home?

It was probably due to a combination of problems. One was that many politicians and economists thought that you could obtain a permanent reduction in unemployment by accepting a somewhat increased inflation rate, as the Fisher curve had seemed to indicate. The second was that they overestimated their economies' non-inflationary speed limit. And finally, there were many that didn't make the connection between money supply and inflation in the first place. They blamed rising oil prices, bad weather, food shortages, greedy companies, unfair unions, etc., and some of them concluded that price and wage controls were the way to fight it; not monetary tightening.

Milton Friedman was upset about all this, of course. Yes, he said, rising oil or food prices do give an immediate inflationary impulse, but that will mean that people have less to spend on other prices, and inflation will thus taper off again unless there is too much money around. In 1968 he made a presidential address to the American Economic Association, where he tried to explain that the Phillips curve trade-off between unemployment and inflation only worked in the short term. He continued to work on this theory and tried to estimate how long it would take before a monetary expansion finished stimulating economic growth (and thus reduced unemployment) and how long it took before it led to inflation. In 1992 he put a number on the time lag from monetary expansion to peak effect on inflation: the average was 20 months for M1 and 23 months for M2.

$$MV \rightarrow Q \rightarrow P$$

It is this sequence of events that makes excessive money creation so compelling to some. The first effects of monetary stimulus are positive (rising $Q$) and it is only later that the negative effects of excessive stimulation surface (rising P).

## CHALLENGE # 8: FORECASTING INFLATION

Are there any ways to forecast inflation other than looking at money supply and statistics of average time lags? There are indeed. Many institutions (including numerous investment banks) have developed systems of leading inflation indicators. A pioneer here is (again) Geoffrey Moore, who developed two of these systems in the 1980s – one for the *Journal of Commerce* and the other for his Center for International Business Cycle Research at Columbia University. The former was based on spot prices for 16 widely used industrial materials (cotton, polyester, burlap, print cloth, steel scrap, zinc, copper scrap, aluminum, tin, hides, rubber, tallow, plywood, red oak, benzene, crude petroleum). If the prices of these go up, then consumer prices should follow, he claimed. Moore's other index contained seven elements, where the first three were related to bottlenecks:

- Percentage of working-age population that is employed
- Growth of the *Journal of Commerce* industrial materials spot index (as mentioned above)
- Growth rate in aggregate debt (business, consumer and federal government)

The theory behind these three indicators was that bottlenecks in labor, commodities or capital would lead to rising prices. The next three were related to observations of price increases that would gradually work through the system to reach the consumer:

- Growth rate of an index of import prices
- Dun & Bradstreet survey of business expectations with regards to selling prices
- National Association of Purchase Managers' (NAPM) price diffusion

The final was about suppliers, indicating whether they were short on capacity and therefore likely to raise prices:

- NAPM vendor performance

Another pioneer was Michael Niemira from PaineWebber, who used the following inflation indicators:

- Vendor performance
- The ratio of employment to population

- NAPM price survey
- Federal Reserve's trade weighted dollar index

ECRI, the Economic Cycles Research Institute, which was also founded by Geoffrey Moore, has developed the "Future Inflation Gauge" based on:

- NAPM vendor performance
- Import prices
- Industrial material prices
- Real estate loans
- Total debt
- Civilian employment rate
- Insured unemployment rate
- Yield spread

The NAPM Vendor Performance Index has since become one of the most closely followed indicators for central banks and their watchers. The US experience has been that NAPM Index values above 55 tended to be good indicators that the Fed would tighten. Conversely, easing cycles have rarely been brought to an end until the Fed saw NAPM drop below 50 or 45.

A fourth leading inflation index, the "Morosani Index," produced by Cyrus J. Lawrence Inc., was based on capacity utilization compared to the trade-weighted level of the dollar. Yet other indicators that have been used include gold, M1 and the CRB commodity index, which consists of corn, oats, soybeans, soybean meal, wheat, soybean oil, cocoa, coffee, sugar, cotton, orange juice, lumber, pork bellies, hogs, live cattle, copper, gold, silver, platinum, crude oil and heating oil.

In 1999, two economists at NBER, James Stock and Mark Watson, published a study of how different leading inflation indicators worked. Their research included no less than 190 economic indicators for the US economy, covering the 28-year time-span from 1959 to 1997. They raised a simple question: Could any of these indicators beat unemployment as an inflation indicator?

An obvious candidate as forecasting tool would be money supply, they thought, but their research couldn't find a very clear correlation: it didn't beat unemployment as an indicator. So how about interest rates? Nope, not very good. Commodity prices, then? Sounds obvious, since that was what Moore's *Journal of Commerce* Index was based on, but it didn't work either. Another study had actually found that there was some correlation between prices of commodities, gold and oil and CPI, but it wasn't what you would expect: rising prices of raw materials tended to be followed by . . . *falling* CPI. This matches Friedman's observation that as prices of some items go up, it is normal that prices of others go down, if money supply is constant. It may also simply reflect the fact that commodity prices are lagging indicators of the business cycle, so, whereas inflation also comes in late, there is not much reason to believe that it comes later than commodity prices. Anyway, back to Stock and Watson: did they find any forecasting tool for CPI that worked better than unemployment? Yes, they did: the best way to forecast CPI was to use an aggregate, weighted index of all their *activity indicators*, including industrial production, real personal income, trade sales, non-farm payrolls, capacity utilization and housing starts. Activity is $Q$, and this worked as a forecasting tool for CPI, or $P$.

This is interesting, because it shows the sequence of events that Friedman and even Thornton had argued for: a monetary stimulus, $MV$, will, on average, have its maximum impact on economic activity $Q$ first and on inflation $P$ after. It is now generally believed that the impact of monetary stimulus on output comes after six to nine months, and the impact on inflation after 12 to 18 months. Both lags are very variable, though, which is why the lag time from $MV$ to $P$ is very hard to predict, whereas the lag from $Q$ to $P$ is shorter and thus less variable.

We now have dealt with problems of defining and forecasting $M$, $V$, $Q$ and $P$, and with complications such as asset inflation, banking crises, debt deflation, crashes and hyperinflation. So what other challenges can a central banker possibly have? Well, there is the issue of foreign exchange. To understand why this may be a problem, we shall turn back the clock and visit a central banker whose job suddenly became rather difficult.

## CHALLENGE # 9: TACKLING FOREIGN EXCHANGE RATES

Norman Stewart Hughson Lamont was 48 years old when he became his country's leading central banker in 1990. "Chancellor of the Exchequer" was the title; ministerial head of the British central bank. Such a job required a strong background, which he most definitely had. Coming from a distinguished family, Norman Lamont had studied at Cambridge before working in the City, where his positions included Director of Rothschild Asset Management. He had also joined Parliament and held various positions in the Departments of Energy, Industry and Defence.

Lamont's new job as head of a central bank had its rewards, but it also involved large responsibilities and sometimes large problems. Perhaps even *very* large problems. By September 1992 he had, in fact, a problem that was rather huge. It was mainly about a Hungarian speculator called Soros.

George Soros had been born in Hungary in 1930, the son of a Jewish lawyer. His father had obtained false identity papers for him during World War II, and the family had to spend some of the war hiding in the attics and concealed stone cellars of various homes. He survived though, and moved to London when he was 17. Dirt poor, but hopeful, he financed his studies by painting houses, picking apples, or working as a railway porter, lifeguard, or assistant in a manikin fabricating workshop. His weekly budget was initially £4 a day, and he kept a record of all his spending in his diary.

He graduated in 1956 from London School of Economics, but struggled to get by, partly as a waiter in the elegant Quaglino's restaurant, where he sometimes ate the leftovers from rich people's meals, and partly by selling ladies' bags and jewelry in Blackpool – a blue collar holiday resort. He wasn't having a very good time, and if anybody had told him then that he would one day challenge the powers of the British Chancellor of the Exchequer, well, he surely wouldn't believe it (nor would the man he would eventually face off with, since Lamont was only a 14-year-old schoolboy by then).

George Soros decided to become a philosopher and worked on a draft of a treatise, but in the end he could not make sense of it, and decided to drop the whole thing. His career was all misery, until one day, he had the idea to write to all stock brokerage houses in the City to apply for a job. He was offered a position with Singer & Friedlander as arbitrage trader in stocks. Later, he received an offer to work in New York with F.M. Mayer as a stock market analyst. After this job, he worked in several other stock-broking companies until, in 1969, he founded the Quantum Fund with a partner. He was now 39 years old, and things were beginning to work out.

Quantum Fund was one of the world's first hedge funds, and a very successful one. An investment of 100 dollars in his fund at its foundation in 1969 would have grown to no less than 16 487 by 1985.

Soros and his lieutenant, Stanley Druckenmiller, became interested in the British pound over the summer of 1992. The currency had joined the European Exchange Rate Mechanism (ERM) in October 1990 (before Lamont's appointment) with a central rate of 2.95 Deutschmarks to the pound, and it could fluctuate in a 6% band. Joining this mechanism hadn't been Lamont's idea, and letting it happen just before a serious recession wasn't smart anyway. The UK's inflation was three times as high as Germany's, and the British economy was in a severe recession by 1992. Soros and Druckenmiller thought that the UK would have to devalue. Druckenmiller suggested that they should bet 3–4 billion dollars against it, but Soros didn't agree on the amount. This would be like shooting fish in a barrel, so why not make a really big bet? Really big! Like, eeer, 15 billion dollars?

They started by selling short seven billion dollars. As a part of their strategy, they also bought British stock and French and German bonds – markets that were likely to benefit from a devaluation of the pound. On Tuesday September 15, 1992, the currency started falling rapidly, and although the Bank of England responded by buying 3 billion pounds to support the exchange rate, the market ended the day very weak. During the evening, Mr Lamont had a dinner with the American ambassador, but, perhaps a bit impolitely, he tried every ten minutes to reach the officials in the Bundesbank, hoping to convince them to cut German money rates. When he finally got them on the line, however, they wouldn't help. After the dinner he met with officials from the Bank of England to make a game-plan for the next day. They agreed to start with intervention from early in the morning, perhaps followed by an increase in interest rates later.

The next morning at 7:30, the traders of the Bank of England started as agreed, by buying up USD 2 billion worth of pounds. One hour later, Mr Lamont called the Bank of England and John Major (Prime Minister at that time) to discuss the situation. At 10:30, Lamont called Mr Major again to suggest an increase in interest rates of 2%. Major agreed, but the pound kept falling anyway. Although the Bank of England ended up spending 15 billion pounds during the day, the battle was clearly lost. It was 7:00 am. New York time when Stanley Druckenmiller called George Soros to break the news:

"George, you've just made 958 million dollars!"

Within the following ten months, Spain devalued three times, Portugal twice and Ireland once.

This story illustrates that it isn't entirely impossible to make close to a billion dollars in a day, of course, but it is also a brilliant illustration of a problem that Milton Friedman had called a "Trilemma;" that it is impossible to achieve more than any two of the following three objectives at the same time:

- Control of exchange rates
- Control of the price level
- Freedom from exchange controls

This brings us to Robert Lucas and his theories of rational expectations, because whatever central banks want to achieve, their success is more likely if people *think* they will succeed. And that is our last, major challenge for central bankers.

## CHALLENGE # 10: MAINTAINING CREDIBILITY

The theory of rational expectations is now often incorporated into the econometric models used by central banks, so that they assume, for instance, that people expect the same future inflation as the econometric model (through iterations) calculates. Rational expectations, in the eyes of a central banker, would be that things evolve, well . . . , as they think they should. They can try to mobilize (or "anchor," as economists say) such expectations by announcing, for instance, inflation targets or fixed exchange bands. The balancing act is to announce policies and targets that can be achieved with reasonable certainty, however.

Management of expectations may work, but it may also deteriorate into games of mirrors, which brings us close to game theory and a lot of very complex math. Especially so, perhaps, if the public includes people like George Soros, who are determined and bright, but not always in agreement with central bankers. However, the central banker does at least have one advantage in this battle: while no market player can know what the central bank will do, the bankers know quite a bit about the other side. They know about public interest rate expectations, because there are highly liquid financial contracts tracking the expected future of long and short-term interest rates. They can also study the market's longer term interest rate structure and use this as a basis for estimating what real interest rates might be. Furthermore, because they know what people expect, they are also familiar with how the market reacts to surprises. A surprise change of money rates of 25 basis points (0.25%) will, for instance, typically give an instant change in the stock index of some 1% – at least in the US. Such knowledge is gathered through what economists call "event studies."

This is where their advantages end, though, because their intellectual challenge is considerable, and their largest problem may simply be to make up their mind. A financial speculator can abandon any of his market positions at any time and often in no time. Central bankers don't have that privilege. First, in order to appear credible when managing expectations, they may never seem indecisive – once they choose a policy direction, they have to stick with it for a while. Secondly, they will typically want to give people time to adjust to policy changes. If they raise rates, for instance, they prefer to do it over a long time in small increments, so that market participants have time to adjust their behavior in good order.

## CASH, CREDIT AND CREDIBILITY

Perhaps we should end the discussion of central banking and business cycles by imagining an honest job advertisement for a head of a central bank:

### CENTRAL BANKER WANTED

You will be expected to use cash, credit and credibility to stabilize economic growth and inflation in our economy. You will understand that these variables will fluctuate as a result of three different cyclical phenomena involving inventory, capital spending and real estate, as well as numerous other cyclical and structural variables, and that while these phenomena are distinct, they are also interacting in somewhat chaotic patterns.

You will be provided with a vast flow of information, which may, however, be rather dated once you get it and subject to meaningful revisions after you get it. You will nevertheless use this input as a basis for your decisions, which will have immediate impact on foreign exchange, money, bond and stock markets, delayed impact on aggregate output and even further delayed impact on inflation.

You will be aware that policy impact on inflation takes place at a time window which may be beyond a realistic forecast horizon, and that you will not be able to control whether such inflation plays out in prices of consumer goods or investment assets. You will know, however, that if asset inflation indeed does take off, then it can lead to significant fluctuations in future output and inflation, and thus interfere with your task.

Finally, you will accept that whenever you change your stated policy, you have to stick to this for a sustained period of time in order to show that you are fully in command of all the tasks set out above.

Applicants who have a problem with negative press need not apply. Salary and pension subject to negotiation.

# Part V

## Business Cycles and Asset Prices

All nations with a capitalist mode of production are seized periodically by a feverish attempt to make money without the mediation of the process of production.

*Karl Marx*

# Chapter 23

# The Mother of All Cycles: Property

> Historically, stocks have not represented as big an asset class as homes. I think they're passing homes. I think it makes sense that they pass homes. I think the idea that homes are a great investment doesn't make sense to me, because everybody can make homes.
>
> *Jim Cramer*

The year is 1932, and we are at the Property Auditor's Office in Chicago. It's the Great Depression and unemployment is massive, so the clerks in this institution appreciate the relative safety of their jobs. Every day has its small tasks, such as keeping proper records of all real estate transactions in this great city. The staff are also serving a sort of library function; people are allowed to come here and request documentation for up to five real estate transactions at a time.

A young girl who works as a clerk at the office has noticed that there is a nice fellow who uses this service a lot; he just keeps coming back to ask for more and more of these files. It seems, in fact, like this man actually intends to read *each and every* file they ever produced! His name is Homer Hoyt.

## A THOROUGH INVESTIGATION

This curious gentleman is 37 years of age and reads more into real estate files than most. Having received a law degree at the age of 23, he now works as a Chicago real estate broker and consultant – and he is very smart. Now he wants to become more than just a player in this market; he wants to be a leading expert. Homer Hoyt has decided to write the world's first truly comprehensive study of cyclical fluctuations in property values, which he will use as a platform for a PhD in economics, and subsequently for a book, if he can find a publisher.

It works out as planned; Hoyt receives his PhD in 1933 and gets his thesis published in book form the same year. A superb investigative study spanning 519 pages, with 206 illustrations and tables, Hoyt's *One Hundred Years of Land Values in Chicago* contains detailed descriptions of every phase of Chicago's expansion from its very beginning as "a hamlet of a dozen log huts in 1830," as he calls it, into a sprawling city by 1933. The first parts of the book – up to page 279 – are pure description of what happened during these 103 years. It is not until page 368 that he gets to the core of the matter: the quest for cyclical fluctuations in land prices. So what does he find?

- First, that there does indeed seem to be a phenomenon you could call "property cycles"
- That these cycles are very slow
- That while they are slow, they are also huge and can get very ugly when turning down
- That property cycles do not necessarily coincide with cycles in commodities and equities – it looks like investors often alternate between the three markets
- That the biggest money in real estate is made from purchases during busts, but that you would be surprised by who it is that makes these killings – it's often not the experts

These are his main conclusions. Let's study each of them a bit closer.

## HOYT'S REAL ESTATE CYCLE

After examining not only the statistics during his 103-year period, but also all the commercial, political and demographic events surrounding them, Hoyt decides to describe his real estate cycle as consisting of 20 phases. Here they are:

1. Gross rents begin to rise rapidly.
2. Net rents rise even more rapidly.
3. As a result of the rents rise, selling prices of existing buildings advance sharply.
4. It pays to erect new buildings.
5. The volume of new construction rises.
6. The volume of building is stimulated by easy credit.
7. "Shoestring" financing swells the number of new structures.
8. The new buildings absorb vacant land.
9. Optimistic population forecasts during the boom.
10. The vision of new cities in cornfields: the method of subdividers.

11. Lavish expenditure for public improvements.
12. All the real estate at full tide: the peak.
13. The reverse movement begins: the lull.
14. Foreclosures increase.
15. The stock market debacle and the onset of the depression in general business.
16. The process of attrition.
17. The banks reverse their boom policy on real estate loans.
18. The period of stagnation and foreclosures.
19. The wreckage is cleared away.
20. Ready for another boom, which does not come automatically.

Hoyt finds that this dramatic sequence of events had repeated itself five to six times during the 103 years of investigation.

## MOVING WITH A SNAIL'S PACE

Hoyt's 20-phase cycle is slow. It takes a number of years from the pick up in demand for real estate until the market responds. Land must be zoned, then subdivided, then sold. Then it may just lie idle for a very long time. Once plans are actually made for construction, they must be submitted for approval and perhaps go through several modifications before permission is obtained. This means another number of years before all this new real estate is finished and appears on the market. When it finally does, there may be oversupply. Then comes the crisis, and it takes many years before the wreckage is cleared out. Here are the timings that Hoyt found: Chicago land values peaked in 1836, 1856, 1869, 1891 and 1925, which meant intervals of 20, 13, 22 and 34 years, respectively.

These cycles are shown in Figure 23.1. What is clearly visible in this graph is a peak in construction activity in 1912, where land prices didn't move much. If we count this as another real estate peak, then the intervals become 20, 13, 22, 21 and 13 years, meaning an average of 18 years. That's a snail's pace, at least when we compare it to the 4.5-year Kitchin cycle or the 9-year Juglar. However, this has to be put in context. Studies of cycle duration in any time series can lead to different results depending on filter definitions. The Bank of International Settlement, for instance, has analyzed property cycles with a fine filter and shown cycles with average duration similar to the inventory cycle, but many of these short property cycles have minimal amplitude. Most visual inspections of property prices will reveal a difference between very minor fluctuations and very large cycles averaging approximately 18 years. Property markets can breeze over many shorter cycles in the general economy without correcting much if at all.

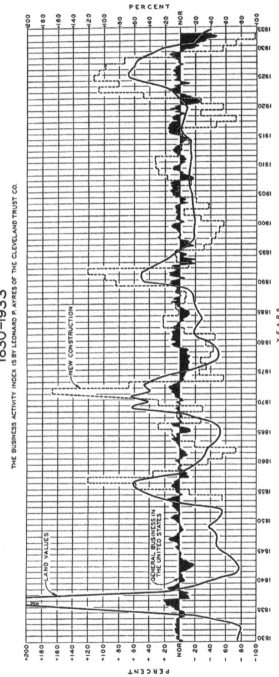

Figure 23.1   Land prices in Chicago, 1830–1933.

## VERY LARGE AMPLITUDE

Hoyt's 18–20 year property cycle is slow, but it has huge amplitude. Hoyt illustrated this by comparing it with other variables: whereas general business activity (GDP) was never, over his 103 years, more than 16% above its trend, and bank clearings (credit) never overshot more than 28%, he found that real estate sales peaked at 131% above normal, new construction 167% above its trend line, and subdivision of plots no less than 540% above trend: The real estate cycle had been equally radical at downturns, where new construction could fall by no less than 98% and subdivision of plots by 100% – subdivision could simply cease to take place. This is, by any measure, huge cycle amplitude.

The economic impact of real estate cycles is also massive, he found, because the decline phase, where a bubble is unwound, can take a very long time. Hoyt found that the shortest period where real estate activity was below trend was no less than ten years, and the longest lasted as much as 26 years. This "cleaning up the wreckage" process is, in other words, a huge and long-lasting drag on the economy. Furthermore, whilst tops in property cycles are not very strongly tied to peaks in stocks and commodities, the crises in real estate coincided with a general malaise in every case over the 103 years. One reason is that real estate tends to equal approximately 2–3 times annual GDP, so when it hurts, well, it really hurts. Many subsequent research papers have confirmed this finding. Numerous other studies have shown links between property crises and general financial crises.

## ASSET ALLOCATION ALTERNATION

Figure 23.1 shows the relationship between commodities, property values and equities, and Hoyt observes that they tend to alternate rather than coincide. This may be explained partially by wars, he concludes, as a war in progress pushes up demand for commodities, the return of soldiers means demand for real estate and the subsequent economic revival creates demand for consumer goods, which benefits stock prices.

## THE ART OF BOTTOM-FISHING

Hoyt suggests that most investors/speculators specialize in commodities or real estate or equities. He concludes that the big money obviously is made by buying very cheaply during a crisis, but also that it is often not real estate specialists that succeed in doing just that, since they may be caught up in the downturn themselves, and thus be highly illiquid, when properties get really cheap. It is consequently often people from other sectors who are liquid enough to pick up land and real estate when opportunity knocks. He finds that some of the best, cyclical property deals in Chicago during the 103 years were made by John Jacob Astor, a fur trader, Marshall Field (wholesale and retail trade) and Potter Palmer (trade and hotel business). None of these were real estate experts, but they were all liquid at the bottom of a property crisis – and took advantage of it.

## MORE STUDIES

Homer Hoyt's book became an instant classic in economic literature. He joined the Federal Housing Administration the year after he had published his book, and was visiting Professor of Land Economics at the Massachusetts Institute of Technology and Columbia University from 1944–46. He was also co-author of *Principles of Real Estate* (with Arthur Weimer); another classic that was published in 1939. Later on, he returned to the commercial side of real estate and made a decent fortune there. In 1979 he donated a significant property in Florida to an institute which today bears his name (the Homer Hoyt Institute). And how about family? Well, since he had to go so often to the Property Auditor's Office to borrow real estate records, he married the nice clerk that had seen him passing by so many times.

Homer Hoyt's description of property cycles was exceptional for his time, and while he probably underestimated the roles of unemployment, wealth, liquidity and interest rates, it is hard to find much in his book today that is really wrong. However, *One Hundred Years of Land Values in Chicago* was only a beginning of our understanding of property cycles – many other works have followed. It took, for instance, just another two years after Hoyt's book before Arthur Burns (of NBER and later Chairman of the Board of Governors of the Federal Reserve System) published detailed descriptions of real estate cycles in his excellent *Long Cycles in Residential Construction*, and Clarence Long of Princeton University followed soon after with the article *Long Cycles in the Building Industry* from 1939 and *Building Cycles and the Theory of Investment* from 1940.

However, many of the early studies were limited by lack of nationwide or international statistical data, and it is not until the 1990s that a clear picture of international property cycles and their behavior over a very long time could be painted. But before we turn to this research, we should just quickly size up the object of inquiry: what *is* property?

## CLASSIFYING PROPERTY MARKETS

There is private and public property. About 20–25% of property construction activity is often public and rather stable, but the rest displays the cyclical fluctuations that Hoyt observed. Property markets comprise a larger proportion of GDP in rich countries than in poor countries, which means that they represent a disproportional part of the growth as national income increases. We have already seen that property values typically amount to around 2–3 times GDP, but may move beyond these boundaries. We have also seen that property construction averages a bit over 10% of our economies.

Most real estate research focuses on four categories of build property: residential, retail, office and industrial. These account for the bulk of the market, where approximately 75% is residential. The remaining 25% is hotel and convention, construction land, parking and agricultural land.

Most property is closely held, but some is traded through liquid vehicles and thus called "quoted." The price movements in closely held real estate transactions can be followed through local statistics, whereas activity in public real estate funds can be tracked through indices such as GPR 250, which tracks 250 liquid, listed property companies. This index represents less than 10% of the overall quoted real estate market, but is representative of the whole. NCREIF Farmland Index tracks US farmland. Owners of farmland will typically rent it out for a steady income, which tends to increase with inflation. Approximately one-third of the US quoted farmland land is forest, which is tracked by the NCREIF Timberland Index. So these are some of the ways to track property market prices. But how about the value of property? The key terms here are:

- *NOI* (net operating income), which is total operating income minus operating costs. Operating income may include rents, parking fees, laundry/vending fees, etc. Operating costs are repairs, insurance, administration costs, utilities, property taxes, etc. (These costs do *not* include financing costs, capital expenditure, income taxes and amortization of loans)
- *Capex* (capital expenditure), which is the cost of making improvements (but not maintenance)
- *Debt service*, which is interest and repayments on financing (such as mortgages)
- *Net cash* (net cash flow), which stands for NOI minus capex and debt service expenditure
- *CAP rates* (capitalization rates) are the expected rates of return calculated as annual NOI divided by purchase price of the property (making this a similar benchmark to P/E for equities). It is, in other words, the

cash flow before financing costs, income tax and improvements in percentage of purchase price. Expected value of a property can be estimated by dividing its NOI by prevailing cap rates for its category

- *DCR* (debt coverage ratio). This is NOI divided by debt servicing costs (interest plus repayments on principal). Most lenders will want this ratio to be at least 11.1 to 1.3, so that the owner can service debt and has spare cash flow for maintenance, etc.

CAP rates tend to be 1–1.5% (100–150 basis points) higher than long-term interest rates. An example: a property is bought for USD 10 million and generates 0.6 million in net cash flow. So CAP rates are 6%. This could be reasonable if financing costs are approximately 4.5% – the investor would then have a margin of 1.5% to pay for improvements and income tax, but would also have the hope that inflation or prosperity would increase income and selling value of the property over time. An investor may accept lower CAP rates at the time when the property is bought, if he thinks NOI will rise over time. However, since CAP rates are compared to interest rates, they should trend upwards if interest rates go up, which – all else equal – means that the market prices of property should fall, if interest rates rise.

---

### REAL ESTATE INVESTMENT VEHICLES

There are three major vehicles for trading real estate:

- *Direct ownership.* This provides the potential to change the asset, but may also involve considerable work
- *Open-ended real estate funds.* These funds allow their investors to trade at net asset value, which is based on appraisals. This ensures a fair value, but will also force the funds to maintain a liquidity reserve so that they can handle redemptions
- *Real Estate Investment Trusts* (REITs). These are closed structures like normal equities, which means that they can be traded but not redeemed. Since they are a vehicle for another investment class, they tend to be tax exempt at the corporate level, as long as they commit to paying out most of their earnings (typically 85–100%) in dividends

REITs provide the most convenient tools of these three. It is, for instance, easy to short REITs if a bubble in real estate has developed.

---

The situation for owner-occupied residential real estate is somewhat different, as there is no income, and thus no NOI. The substitute is what economists call "reservation value," which is bad English for the lowest price you will sell at, which should equal the number of Edgeworth's atoms of pleasure the property can provide after running costs (thus the term "reserve" in auction markets for the seller's minimum price). The actual reality seems to be that private households buy pretty much as much real estate as they can finance whenever they have confidence in the future. Furthermore, as the average quality of houses rises and as the fraction of income needed for bare necessities falls with increased prosperity, there will be a trend towards spending an increasing part of income on property as real incomes rise. However, there are (as Hoyt observed) many episodes where these basic valuation studies indicate that property has become wildly expensive or dirt cheap. Let's see why this can happen.

### PROPERTY CYCLES IN REALITY

We can approach the matter by relating to Simon Newcomb's now very familiar law $MV = PQ$ (or Money times Velocity of money equals Prices of goods and services times Quantity produced). Figure 23.2 shows the elements of Newcomb's equation on its left side, and lists some of its most visible economic effects on the right – we view it like this because we want to elaborate this approach later on.

Bearing these phenomena in mind, we can now imagine that we are at the beginning of an expansion: $MV$ has increased, consumer spending has picked up, central banks have reduced interest rates and bond rates have followed too. Many consumers have decided to take advantage of this cheaper financing to build or buy new homes. Housing starts picked up approximately six months before GDP turned up (we will recall that housing starts are the best economic of the leading indicators – only beaten by some of the financial leaders).

This is the background, and now comes the first rotation in property markets. Prices of apartments, single-family houses, retail and hotels start to rise. People return to full-service hotels, which have been rather empty during the recession, and gross rents start to climb. Net rents rise even faster, as costs are outpaced by income, and mortgages are often fixed for years anyway. (An example: Hoyt found that while office rents increased 90% from 1918 to 1926, costs only increased 31%, which meant that real estate profits rose no less than 300%). However, professional developers hesitate to start new construction as development costs have gone up, so they try to meet rising demand by renovating existing buildings.

The interest in office rentals picks up approximately one year after the return of demand in residential property. This phase will also encourage

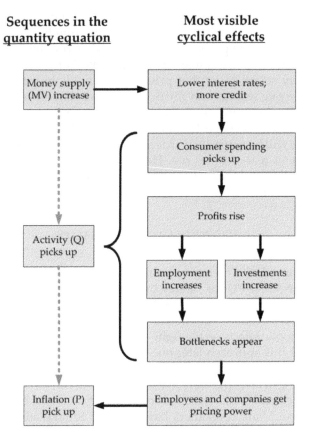

**Sequences in the quantity equation**

**Most visible cyclical effects**

Money supply (MV) increase

Lower interest rates; more credit

Consumer spending picks up

Profits rise

Activity (Q) picks up

Employment increases

Investments increase

Bottlenecks appear

Inflation (P) pick up

Employees and companies get pricing power

**Figure 23.2**   The quantity equation and a sequence of its most visible effects.

white collar business (particularly in the service sector) to look for good office space while prices are still reasonable. "Good" means downtown, so downtown offices get filled up first, leading to rising prices here. Interest rates typically are falling during this phase, which reduces mortgage costs and therefore enhances affordability. Consumers will often begin to over-commit at this stage, as they tend to underestimate the true costs of buying at higher prices when inflation and interest rates are falling. Interest rates are, after all, low because inflation is expected to be low. Low interest rates make initial mortgages low, but real mortgages (corrected for inflation) will not fall as quickly as if inflation was high. They are thus cannibalizing more on future income than they may realize.

## CRUISING ALTITUDE AND SPECULATION

We are now approaching the middle of the expansion, where the economy grows steadily, prosperity spreads and production capacity gets tight. Land prices are beginning to advance strongly as existing real estate inventory is sold out. This is a forewarning of a construction boom, which will be encouraged by sound business models and easy access to cheap financing. Access to financing is enhanced partly by the perception that investing is now more safe and profitable, and partly because the existing real estate can be used as collateral for more investments – in real estate. Car sales are brisk at this stage, and parking spaces do well.

The expansion is eventually getting a bit long in the tooth, but while consumers have drawn down a fair amount of their savings, they are still spending. Industry, meanwhile, is struggling to keep up with demand, so it starts to build new capacity, which gives the economy a late boost. Capacity building means that prices of industrial properties (R&D flex and industrial warehouses), as well as industrial land, rise smartly. Residential land leads the revival in land prices. Office seekers are now forced to look outside the main centers, so suburban office spaces thrive, and land for office building picks up. Inflation may have begun to rise during this phase, and hotels and parking lots enjoy (unlike other income-based real estate sectors) the ability to raise prices continuously. Consumers are doing great and many can afford to move from apartments to single family homes, which causes the latter to outpace the former. There are many subdivisions of plots now, and some are buying for speculative purposes. Financing is getting easier still, and many developers can start projects using very little money of their own.

Meanwhile, the new building activity absorbs vacant land, which leads to windfall profits for land owners, and land speculation takes off as more people want to buy ahead of future demand. This is the beginning of a speculative fever, where real estate promoters publish wildly optimistic forecasts for future growth rates using the most optimistic academic research (more conservative scholarly projections are ignored). They are also creating marketing material showing future settlements on bare land. This is pushed through aggressive sales methods.

The boom attracts the interest of local authorities, which wish to support the growth by re-zoning more land and constructing new supporting infrastructure. This gives buyers of subdivided plots more confidence that further development is imminent, but it also makes the land useless for farming should these expected urbanizations fail to materialize.

## OVER THE EDGE

We pass the top now. Consumers are maxed out, industrial capacity building has peaked, and the mere cost of rentals and construction begins to hurt the business community. The demand for real estate levels off as replacement sales outpace new demand. Rents decelerate, vacancy rates increase and property prices go into decline, even as construction activity continues to expand, perhaps one year after GDP has peaked.

The first serious casualty is land, which goes straight into a deep freeze: no one is buying any more. Bricks-and-mortar markets follow soon after. No real estate performs well in this phase, but some sectors are nevertheless more stable than others. The best relative performers here are limited-service hotels (as people abandon their full-service competitors) and retail, because while people can't buy houses and cars any more, they are still OK with smaller stuff. This means that power centers and 1st tier regional malls do reasonably well.

The worst threat of this phase is deflation, which is particularly bad for variable-price sectors like hotels and parking lots, which may have fixed mortgage costs but are forced to reduce prices. Some of the more dubious owners of heavily mortgaged property may now seek to swap these amongst each other for above-market prices, in order to book baseless paper profits to calm down their nervous lenders. Others take comfort in their long-term financing and leases, which they think will shield them from the general malaise and rapid movements in the stock market (and they would, if the slump was brief, but property crashes can take a very long time).

## FINAL COLLAPSE

Distress! Times are really bad now, and the decline in real estate markets reinforces the broader, economic contraction, since building construction (which is falling very rapidly) tends to average around a quarter of total investments and around 10% of GDP in average economies – and since wealth is falling too.

Property owners are now slowly beginning to feel the full consequence of the contraction, as more and more of their rental contracts expire and either aren't renewed, or can only be renewed at lower prices. Financial distress begins to appear, and insolvency, increased mortgage delinquency, foreclosures and defaults abound as property is moved to the hands of receivers, who slash rent rates drastically, which forces yet more property owners into fierce competition and distress. It is, in particular, less desirable properties that go into default, as they can't attract any buyers at all. The better ones can still be sold, if perhaps not at prices that will cover the seller's financing costs. Mortgage holders and banks are now feeling the stress and financial institutions are forced to put on the breaks as they are at risk of illiquidity; especially for properties that are less desirable.

## PARALYSIS

After panic and distress comes the deep freeze. Subdivision of land has now ceased completely; there is virtually no new lending, and also very limited trading of existing property. Build-out property market values may now have declined substantially below replacement costs. Those who hold on to their real estate are burdened by the continued losses and are thus unable to buy new property, let alone start new construction, until their balance sheets have been repaired. Much new or renovated property is difficult to sell because it is in default with lenders. Property sold at foreclosures attracts few bidders since financing is impossible. It will often go to mortgagees, who bid up to the value of their mortgages. Bargain hunters will buy distressed mortgage bonds at great discounts and then foreclose upon the titleholder and freeze out remaining bondholders at the foreclosure sale. This continues until foreclosures have run their course and old obligations have been cleared out.

The deep freeze phase may become extended considerably if it leads to systemic weakness in financial institutions, and even more if this is followed by exchange rate crises. Some of these symptoms were, for instance, present in the 1997 Asian financial crisis (especially in Indonesia and Thailand) and in the Japanese meltdown after 1990. Crises in financial institutions as a consequence of real estate collapses are most likely in countries where property is financed by banks – less so when it is financed by mortgage institutions.

The cleansing process, which takes 4–5 years and sometimes much more, moves property from weak to strong hands while natural demand slowly can catch up with static supply. Much property is now in the hands of mortgage owners who are willing to sell it for the amount of their mortgage or less – and perhaps adding a limited rental guarantee to the package. Meanwhile, the economy is recovering and skilled investors are picking up real estate for a song. Vacancies begin to decline; rents stabilize. And then they begin to advance. Furthermore, construction costs are now low and renovation and new construction begins to make sense.

The least ugly real estate categories in this stage are those servicing consumers with tight budgets. This means 2nd tier regional malls and factory outlets. Figure 23.3 shows the sector rotation in property markets over the full property cycle.

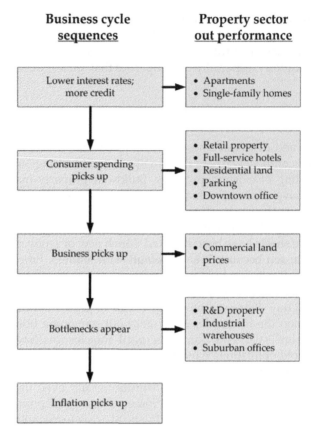

**Figure 23.3**   Property sector rotation over the property cycle.

## RELATIVE VOLATILITY

No description of this real estate sector rotation is complete, however, without considering volatility. In 1976, the British National Economic Development Office published a study where they concluded:

> Within the broad heading of investment, investment in private dwellings can be seen to be the most unstable, more unstable even than investment in the manufacturing sector of industry.

Private property is volatile, but office space is the most unstable category, whereas industrial is less so, and retail space least volatile. Volatility in building activity is small, in prices larger, and in trading volume huge. The latter is especially clear in residential real estate, where trading

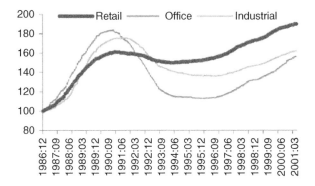

**Figure 23.4** Relative volatility in retail, office and industrial property markets. The graph shows that retail is the most stable, and office the most volatile.

volume can vary 25 times as much as prices (which makes residential real estate agency business a real rollercoaster!). And finally, land plots are about twice as volatile as build-out properties. Homer Hoyt found, for example, a rather striking case of how much land prices can fluctuate: Chicago land purchased for $11 000 an acre in 1836 sold for less than $100 in 1840. That's a drop of more than 99% in four years! Much of this land was, in fact, converted back into cultivation as people finally gave up hope of seeing new metropolises shooting up in the cornfields. What all of this means is, of course, that the ultimate killing in real estate is this:

- Purchase of downtown office space (for a potential quick return) . . .
- . . . or of land (for a possibly huge return) . . .
- . . . from a distressed seller or a credit holder
- . . . at the bottom of a property cycle

This may sound easy in theory, and going short REITs (real estate investment trusts or listed real estate brokers) at the top wouldn't be bad either. The key challenge here is, however, to predict when the real estate cycle will turn. This brings us to the leading indicators for property.

## FORECASTING PROPERTY CYCLES

One of the best leading indicators for property markets is simply a previous property boom or bust. A study from the Bank of International Settlement in Basel (BIS Papers no. 21 from 2005) found that 40% of real estate booms had ended in busts, whereas another by Bordo and Jeanne from 2002 found the number to be 55% (the difference depends on samples and definitions of "booms" and "busts"). Whether the number is 40 or 55%, it is clearly much higher for real estate than for equities, where the BIS paper found that only 16% of booms were followed by busts. But what is a "boom" or a "bust"? For residential property, we would primarily look at long-term trend deviations in these three indicators:

- Affordability, which is monthly mortgage payments as part of disposable income
- Ratio of house prices to employee compensation
- Ratio of house prices to GDP

For commercial property, we would primarily study:

- Ratio of ROIs and CAP rates to interest rates
- Ratio of rental costs to mortgage costs

---

### PROPERTY BUSTS AND FINANCIAL CRISES

The Bank of International Settlements has investigated house price busts and their effect on the financial system. Some of their findings are:

- BIS analyzed 75 long- and short-term property cycles and found that the average bull phase lasted just under 3 years and led to price increases of 11%, whereas the decline phase was one year and led to losses of 6%
- Average house price bursts are associated with an 8% drawdown in GDP, whereas average equity busts only correlate with 4% GDP drawdowns
- The probability of boom ending in bust is just under 40%. A bust is just as likely after a weak bull market as after a strong bull market
- All major banking in developed countries since World War II had been associated with housing price busts

Source: Helbling, 2005.

---

We have already seen that most turning points in commercial property follow turning points in residential property with a lag. The most important category of leading indicators for commercial real estate is monetary conditions, where real interest rates and money supply are particularly useful. A significant fall in real interest rates and/or an increase in money

**Table 23.1** Leading indicators for UK commercial property, 1986–2002, in months. Source: Krystaloyianni, Matysiak and Tsolacos, 2004.

|  | Retail property | Industrial property | Office property |
| --- | --- | --- | --- |
| M0 money supply | 0 | 4 | 6 |
| M4 money supply | 6 | 5 | 9 |
| Press recruitment ads | 6 | 2 | 4 |
| Gross trading profits | 0 | 4 | 5 |
| House building starts | 1 | 5 | 5 |
| New car registrations | 6 | 8 | 5 |
| Retail sales | 10 | 12 | 12 |
| Industrial production | 0 | 4 | 6 |
| Consumer confidence | 0 | 5 | 4 |
| Gilt yields | 5 | 2 | 2 |

supply will, for instance, be powerful forewarnings on a pick-up in property – and vice versa. This is illustrated by a fairly recent study, *Forecasting UK Commercial Real Estate Cycle Phases With Leading Indicators: A Probit Approach* by Krystaloyianni, Matysiak and Tsolacos, 2004. These three economists tested a number of potential leading indicators for commercial property in the UK during 1986–2002. Table 23.1 shows that retail property moved first, as one would expect in upswings led by consumer spending.

Industrial and office properties turned a few months later. The study had the following conclusion:

> Our study is helpful in determining which particular indicators of the UK economy are worth monitoring in predicting the direction in UK commercial property capital values. Two indicators, the gilt yield and broad money supply (M4), enter the vector of explanatory variables for all three real estate sectors analysed. For the office and industrial sectors, industrial production is also significant. For retail capital values the car registrations series is significant.

This all makes good sense. Improvement in monetary conditions *is* good for the economy, puts downward pressure on CAP rates, enhances DCR rates and corresponds with improved financing conditions. It's also logical that industrial production is a strong predictor for industrial property. Rising industrial production means rising capacity utilization, which again means demand for new industrial space. And car registrations for retail property? Well, car registrations are a very variable part of consumer spending, so this should be a good predictor.

Our final question may be whether there exist leading indicators that can warn of an *imminent* top in property prices. The following six warning signs tend to be useful:

- Increasing number of days on the market
- Increasing number of unsold homes in a city
- Decreasing ratio of asking price/transaction price
- Increasing number of homes on the market more than 120 days
- Increasing percentage of properties bought for investment
- Decreasing number of mortgage applications

## DURATION OF CYCLES

We have already seen that Homer Hoyt found a cycle with an average duration of 18 years. However, he didn't emphasize that aspect of his findings at all. Rather, on the contrary, he expressed severe doubts that it would persist, and stated later in his life that he thought it had stopped. This is interesting, and it is also sort of odd that Kuznets, whose name the cycle often bears, never related it to property markets. His book, *Secular Movements in Production and Prices* (1930) contains 536 pages with no lack of detail, and a summary of relevant business cycle theories at the end. None of the theories he mentions are about property markets. The words are not even mentioned: the index contains references to numerous obscure factors such as sewing machines, locomotives, potatoes and silk, but the words "land," "property," "building" or "construction" are simply not there. Nor is there any reference to Homer Hoyt for that matter. So is it really fair to state that the 18–20-year cycle is driven by property markets?

It certainly seems so. Let's call in our first witness: Mr Roy Wenzlick, an American real estate broker and founder of Roy Wenzlick Research Corporation, which, over the years, created a number of widely used appraisal manuals. His company did over 475 000 actual appraisals, numerous site surveys and over 60 studies of major real estate redevelopment projects. He was also editor and publisher of *The Real Estate Analyst* from 1932 and of a book, which, in 1936, correctly forecast a coming real estate boom. However, what we need from him is a look into a study he published in 1974. This work covered US real estate at the national level for the period 1795 to 1973 – which means no less than 178 years. He found that the average duration of property cycles was 18 1/3 years. Another study, *Building Cycles and the Theory of Investments* by Clarence Long, found 18-year urban building cycles in the US for the period 1868–1935.

A more recent study of UK markets commissioned by The Royal Institution of Chartered Surveyors (RICS, 1999) and covering UK cycles from 1921 to 1997 found some indication of overlapping cycles of roughly five years and nine years in duration, which are rough multiples of 18 years. The UK market was also studied by Barras, who, in 1994, published a study of UK construction activity (*Property and the Economic Cycle: Build-*

*ing Cycles Revisited*), where he found a series of overlapping fluctuations with 4–5 year, 9–10 year, 20-year and 50-year durations. An interesting aspect was that he found that the 20-year cycles were associated with *major* speculation episodes before their peaks. Finally, a study by Helbling and Terrones included in IMF's *2003 Economic Outlook Report* provided a detailed analysis of equity and house prices in 14 developed countries (equity prices for 1959–2002 and house prices from 1970–2002). What they were looking for were "busts," which they identified as follows:

> Drawing on business cycle analysis, peaks and troughs in asset prices are first identified. Then, a bust is defined as a peak-to-trough decline where the price change fell into the top quartile of all declines during bear markets; similarly, a boom is defined as a trough-to-peak rise where the price increase was in the top quartile of all increases.

This meant that they were not looking for each and every oscillation; only for the real "busts." So how often did these occur?

> To qualify as a bust, a housing price contraction had to exceed 14 percent, compared with 37 percent for equities. Housing price busts were slightly less frequent than equity price crashes. In 14 countries with real residential housing prices between 1970:Q1 and 2002:Q3, 20 housing price crashes were recorded (compared with 25 equity price crashes). This corresponds to roughly one bust a country every 20 years.

So, whereas Hoyt had found the average interval between busts to be 18 years, Barras's UK-based study, as well as the IMF study from 14 countries, found bust-to-bust intervals of some 20 years – about the same as Hoyt. The RICS study also found a 20-year interval between major speculation episodes.

The impression from these studies is that there are short-term fluctuations in property markets, but that *major busts* appear every 18 (or perhaps 20) years *on average* (the fact that some studies find shorter cycles can be explained easily by a more lenient definition of how large a fluctuation should be in order to be called a "cycle," as previously mentioned). However, all of this leads us to a good question: is it the economy that leads property markets in the 18-year cycle, or vice versa? The answer to this is that it is property that leads in this long cycle. Let's consider why.

## WHY PROPERTY CYCLES EXIST

In his book *The Power in the Land*, Fred Harrison mentions a study by G. Shirk of US construction cycles, which he compares to Hoyt's cycles in land values and the timing of economic recessions. The results are shown in Table 23.2.

**Table 23.2**   Timing sequence of property markets and recessions, 1818–1929. Source: Harrison, 1983.

| Peaks in land values | Building cycle peaks | Economic recessions |
|---|---|---|
| 1818 | — | 1819 |
| 1836 | 1836 | 1837 |
| 1854 | 1856 | 1857 |
| 1872 | 1871 | 1873 |
| 1890 | 1892 | 1893 |
| — | 1916 | 1918 |
| 1925 | 1927 | 1929 |

**Table 23.3**   Distribution of British national income 1920–1939. Sources: Harrison, 1983 and Deane and Cole, 1962.

| | Average decadal percentages of total income | |
|---|---|---|
| | Rents | Profits, interest and mixed incomes |
| 1920–29 | 6.6 | 33.7 |
| 1925–34 | 8.1 | 31.2 |
| 1930–39 | 8.7 | 29.2 |

Table 23.2 shows that land prices and construction activities slowed down *before* the economy in general, and that land prices in most cases peaked *before* construction activity. Harrison provides a good explanation for this: the upswing phase of property cycles has been associated with increasing returns on property (rents) and decreasing returns on other business. He mentioned several studies, including the numbers in Table 23.3 from the years 1920–29.

He also found numbers to clarify what had happened during a later cycle (Table 23.4).

The fact that housing starts provide the best economic leading index for the economy in general, and that, when they crash, property markets mostly have turned before the economy as a whole, are strong indicators that property markets drive the turning point of business cycles every 18 years on average.

## CYCLICAL DRIVERS

We have already discussed why the property cycle is so slow, but perhaps we should examine this a bit closer. Time lags play an important role in

**Table 23.4** Leading indicators for land prices.

| Land type | Leading indicators | Cyclical behavior |
|---|---|---|
| Construction land<br><br>• Residential<br>• Commercial | • Money supply<br>• Interest rates (inverted)<br>• Housing starts (for residential)<br>• New office construction (for office)<br>• Capacity utilization (for industrial) | • Residential lands move strongly towards the middle of the cycle and commercial land towards its end<br>• Volatility can be extremely high |
| Agricultural land<br><br>• Forest<br>• Farming | • Money supply<br>• Interest rates (inverted)<br>• Inflation and inflation expectations<br>• Soft commodity prices | • Moves late in cycle<br>• Moderate volatility |

**Table 23.5** Income shares as a percentage of GNP at factor cost, UK, 1955–1973. Source: Harrison, 1983.

| | Rent | Corporate profits |
|---|---|---|
| 1955–59 | 4.5 | 18.0 |
| 1960–63 | 5.1 | 17.9 |
| 1964–68 | 6.4 | 16.8 |
| 1969–73 | 7.6 | 13.2 |

business cycles, and there are plenty of them in real property as well. Let's start with rentals. Residential contracts are often fixed on a 6–12 month basis or longer; office and retail rents may be fixed for many years.

There are also very long lags in construction, and especially in development of commercial property because of its size. A report ("Land into Cities") from The Lincoln Institute of Land Policy from 1980 illustrated one aspect of this. The study was based on interviews with 700 owners of undeveloped land at the outskirts of six metropolitan areas in the USA from 1977 to 1979. It showed how slow the early process of construction may be: the investors and developers interviewed had often acquired and held on to their land for more than 15 years before anything actually was built on it. Real estate development involves zoning, infrastructure development, third party financing, planning, construction and marketing. An example: International Place Two in Boston was conceived in 1981, announced in 1983, approved by the city in 1985, broke ground in 1988, and opened in 1993. This meant 12 years from idea to reality, and when the building finally opened, things had turned sour, with 14% of all office space in Boston vacant.

Property markets may also be slow to react to changes in interest rates. Some countries, such as Australia, Canada, Finland, Ireland, Luxembourg, Norway, Portugal, Spain and the UK, have financing based predominantly on variable (short-term) rates, and they will react quickly to changes in money rates. However, others, including Belgium, Denmark, France, Germany, Italy, Japan, the Netherlands and the United States, have a higher proportion of long term fixed rates, which makes them more resilient to money rates.

Another category of cyclical drivers of property markets is a sort of positive feed-back loop. Much of the collateral directly or indirectly used for purchase of new real estate is . . . well . . . real estate. As real estate prices go up, the value of real estate collateral rises and new funding is released. This is a positive feedback loop, but a slow one. A similar *acceleration* process happens when owners of commercial property enjoy declining vacancy rates. This leads to disproportional increases in their profitability, which again multiplies the perceived value of their companies.

A third pro-cyclical accelerator effect in property markets is psychological. People considering purchase of a house may watch prices rise and conclude that they have to buy quickly before they can't afford it any more (regret theory). Others will be attracted by rising prices and buy for expected re-sale – thus also contributing to further price increases. This emotional accelerator is most effective if people have forgotten the last real estate bust, which is likely to be the case if a generation or so (approximately 20 years) has passed. So, yes, there are very good reasons why real estate must be inherently cyclical, and the core of the matter seems to be this:

- Property markets tend to decline when the general business cycles turn down for reasons that are unrelated to property markets. Such declines in property markets are lagged *responses* to falling demand and tighter monetary conditions, and may be mild and brief. Property markets may even continue a climb during an inventory- or capital spending-induced recession
- The behavior of residential property can be very helpful for central bankers who want to pull an economy out of recession. Housing starts is one of the first significant responses the central banks get when they ease. Property is yet again *responding* to other events in the cycle. However, whereas residential property markets *trail* GDP at they cycle's peaks, they *lead* it during revivals

- Whereas residential property amplifies the effect of central banking policies immediately, the commercial property market picks up at a later stage, and acts thereby as a kind of rather late echo to the initial, monetary stimulus. This revival of commercial property markets will often happen at a time when central bankers no longer wish to see additional economic expansion
- While property in most cases simply responds to changes in demand and interest rates, there is, in fact, also an inherent property cycle that relates to instability in its *supply*
- The inherent property cycle evolves slowly and averages some 18 to 20 years from peak to peak. When this inherent cycle reaches its apex, then it tends to level off before the rest of the economy and thereby contribute as a trigger of the subsequent decline. These episodes will, in most cases, evolve into serious and longer lasting recessions/depressions
- There are three major impacts when property cycles turn down. First, the wealth effect (which is around 4%, whereas typical property values are 2.5–3.5 times GDP) of falling prices is negative. Secondly, falling prices mean declining building construction. Building construction averages a little over 10% of GDP. Finally, many property cycle downturns lead to banking crises, and in some cases even exchange rate crises, which can amplify the negative impact

This means, in other words, that the inherent, 18-year (on average) property cycle essentially is *supply-driven*, whereas shorter and smaller property fluctuations simply are passive responses to changes in aggregate demand and financing costs created by inventory and capital spending cycles.

### PROPERTY CYCLES AND BUSINESS CYCLE THEORY

Property cycles contain many drivers that can be recognized from general business cycle theory. Their response to changes in aggregate demand and interest rates caused by other cycles reminds, for instance, of Ragnar Frisch's *"rocking horse."* There is also a *hog cycle*, whereby developers try to adapt to increased demand but end up overshooting. There is a concept of entrepreneurs acting in Schumpeter's *"swarms"* following an initial impulse, and there are *overinvestments* (Tugan-Baranovsky) or Austrian *malinvestments* choking the expansion and

**Table 23.6**   Leading indicators and cyclical behavior for residential property.

| Property categories | Leading indicators | Cyclical behavior |
| --- | --- | --- |
| • Single family (Owner occupied)<br>• Apartment renters | • Money supply<br>• Interest rates<br>• Affordability<br>• House price to employee compensation<br>• House price to GDP index<br>• Number of days on the market<br>• Number of unsold homes in a city<br>• Ratio of asking price/ transaction price<br>• Number of homes on the market more than 120 days<br>• Percentage of properties bought for investment<br>• Number of mortgage applications | • The first category to turn<br>• Apartments overperform single family in recessions and early growth<br>• Price volatility is limited for residents, but high for second homes.<br>• Trade volatility is very high |

leading to *capital misallocation* and *declining marginal efficiency* of capital (Keynes). When property development goes through the roof, we are reminded again of what John Stuart Mill wrote in *Paper Currency and Commercial Distress* from 1826.

> Every one calculating upon being before-hand with all his competitors, provides himself with as large a stock as he thinks that the market will take off; not reflecting that others, equally with himself, are engaged in adding to the supply; not calculating upon the fall of price which must take place as soon as this increased quantity is brought to the market. The deficiency is soon changed into excess.

We have also elements of the so-called *financial accelerator*, where real estate is used as collateral (Bernanke), and this contributes to *financial instability* (Minsky and Kindleberger). Rising property prices can attract new *speculators* (Marshall), and real estate downturns can be brutal and lead to *debt deflation* (Fisher), excessive *cash preferences* (the Austrians) and *liquidity traps* (Keynes again). Real estate cycles are, in other words, a permutation of what business cycles generally are about (and most of all a hog cycle), but because of the sector's huge size, their economic and financial impact may be very ugly indeed.

**Table 23.7** Leading indicators and cyclical behavior for commercial property.

| Property type | Leading indicators | Cyclical behavior |
|---|---|---|
| Retail<br>• 1st tier regional malls<br>• 2nd tier regional malls<br>• Factory outlet centers<br>• Neighborhood and community centers<br>• Power centers | • Money supply<br>• Interest rates<br>• GDP<br>• Inflation expectations<br>• Aggregate disposable income<br>• Aggregate household wealth<br>• Retail sector expenditure<br>• Retail sales<br>• Car registrations<br>• Vacancy rates<br>• Ratio of Cap rates to interest rates<br>• Ratio of rental costs to mortgage costs | • Lags residential property, but leads (together with hotels) the other commercial sectors<br>• Neighborhood and community centers move first, power centers and 1st tier malls follow during early decline, whilst factory outlets and 2nd tier malls outperform during late decline |
| Office<br>• Office downtown<br>• Office suburban | • Money supply<br>• Interest rates<br>• GDP<br>• White collar employment<br>• Ratio of Cap rates to interest rates<br>• Ratio of rental costs to mortgage costs | • Follows approximately one year after retail<br>• Downtown gets filled first and is thus cycle leader<br>• Volatility is high, especially for less desirable property |
| Industrial<br>• R&D flex<br>• Industrial warehouse | • Money supply<br>• Interest rates<br>• GDP<br>• Industrial production<br>• Retail sales<br>• Capacity utilization<br>• Manufacturing employment<br>• Transportation employment<br>• Airfreight volume<br>• Rail and truck volume<br>• Vacancy rates<br>• Ratio of Cap rates to interest rates<br>• Ratio of rental costs to mortgage costs | • Moves simultaneously with, or slightly after, office market |
| Hotel and convention<br>• Hotel (full service)<br>• Hotel (limited service) | • Money supply<br>• Interest rates<br>• Air passenger volume<br>• Tourism receipts or number visitors<br>• Vacancy rates<br>• Ratio of Cap rates to interest rates | • Moves early, with full-service hotels as market leader and limited-service hotels outperforming during downturns<br>• Limited volatility in prices for prime location hotels, but room prices vary continuously |
| Parking | • Money supply<br>• Interest rates<br>• New car sales<br>• Cap rates versus interest rates | • Moves early as response to consumer spending<br>• Limited volatility |

> ## REAL ESTATE AND THE WEALTH EFFECT
>
> Case, Quigley and Shiller made a study in 2001, where they compared wealth effects (whereby loss of wealth leads to diminished spending from busts in stock markets and in real estate). They couldn't detect a stock market wealth effect, but for real estate, the matter was clear and ugly:
>
> > The evidence of a stock market wealth effect is weak; the common presumption that there is strong evidence for the wealth effect is not supported in our results. However, we do find strong evidence that variations in housing market wealth have important effects upon consumption.

## THE LAND OF THE RISING SUMS

How bad is ugly? Well, we have already seen that the total value of real estate tends to equal 2–3 times annual GDP in a typical country, that it constitutes around 50% of total variable-price gross wealth. We have also seen that it fluctuates a lot. A brilliant example of these fluctuations played out in Japan during the 1990s, which saw the build-up of one of the most absurd asset inflations in modern history. The combined value of commercial land in Tokyo doubled between 1986 and 1988, where total real estate values in this city exceeded the cost of all real estate in the United States. By the end of 1989, the value of all property in Japan exceeded the value of US real estate by a factor of no less than five, and the value of the entire global equity market by a factor of two. That wasn't the end of it, though: by 1990, the total Japanese land values reached levels that were 50% higher than all land in the rest of the world, as a single family house in Tokyo could cost 30 or 40 million dollars, and a golf club membership 300 000.

These prices made them feel very rich. Many Japanese felt so wealthy that they would gladly take out huge loans and use them to outbid just about everyone else in just about any other market.

Our next chapter is about collectibles, and we shall here meet a few very eager bidders from Japan who had just made a fortune on property markets. Or, well, at least they thought they had . . .

Chapter **24**

# When Art was In

I had reservations about making art a business, but I got over it.

*Mary Boone*

The year was 1987, and the markets for fine art and other collectibles, such as classic and sports cars and collector watches, were on the boil. Since 1985, the prices and trading volumes of most of these fine objects had risen steeply, and Christie's, Sotheby's and thousands of galleries, dealers and auction houses were thriving.

Many felt that this golden era had begun with the sale of the "Jay Gould Collection." Before his death, Jay Gould had invested some of the money from his famous railroad and gold speculations in art, but in April 1985, 175 pictures from this collection were auctioned on behalf of his heirs by Sotheby's in New York. At that time, there were perhaps some 400 000 active art collectors worldwide (people spending at least USD 10 000 a year on art), and maybe 250–350 "very big" collectors (people with collections worth millions of dollars). But the audience at the auctions had always been very narrow, and the large majority of the people who could afford expensive art had never set foot in an auction house. However, the sale of the Gould collection had attracted a much wider audience than normal. It was not only the audience that grew, however. It was also the amount of money that the buyers had at their disposal. Buyers at Sotheby's auctions could now borrow the purchase sum for 12 months, and the sellers could receive some of the expected sales sum in advance. But the biggest change was the new presence of numerous ultra-rich Japanese buyers.

## THE SALE OF SUNFLOWERS

It was in this environment that Christie's in January 1987 announced that it had been entrusted to sell one of the world's most famous masterpieces, van Gogh's *Sunflowers* on his birthday, March 30. When the auction house first received the painting, it estimated its value at GBP 5–6 million. On second thoughts, they raised it to almost double that figure. Then, a few weeks before the auction was due to take place, the British government bought *Stratford Mill* by John Constable for GBP 10 million. This made the staff at Christie's think again. If *that* picture could sell to *that* buyer for *that* price, what would museums not be willing to pay for *Sunflowers*? This thought was at the same time encouraging and scary; encouraging because it confirmed a very strong market, but scary because, due to tax regulations, *Sunflowers* had to fetch 15–18 million pounds at an auction in order to give the seller the same after-tax revenue as a sale to a museum for 10 million. So, either the picture had to reach that level, or people might consider the sellers ill advised by not making a private sale to a museum. A few weeks before the auction, Christie's estimate was expressed at "GBP 10 million, maybe more – and maybe a lot more."

On the night of the auction, the rooms were absolutely packed and the atmosphere tense. Would this van Gogh set a new record? Charles Allsopp opened the bidding at GBP 5 million, close to the first estimates. The next bid came quickly after. It was for 5.5 million. Then 6 million. Then 6.5. The price was now over the initial estimate, and there were many bidders, some in the main hall, some in the side room and some giving their bids via telephone.

The next bid was 7 million pounds. Then 7.5

Then 8

Then 8.5

Then 9

Then 9.5 . . .

It just went on, and spontaneous applause broke out when 20 million pounds was bid for the painting. Twenty million, and there were still two bidders! The bids from these two anonymous investors were received via telephone by two of Christie's employees. Finally, as the price reached 22.5 million pounds, one bidder gave up, and the picture was sold at the highest price ever paid for a piece of art: 22.5 million pounds in hammer price, plus 10% commission, or 24.75 million pounds in total. A few days later, it was disclosed that the buyer was Yasuda Fire and Marine Insurance, Japan. The other bidder had been Alan Bond, the Australian real estate tycoon.

The successful sale of *Sunflowers* had a strong effect on the market. Three months later, a less famous van Gogh, *Le Pont de Trinquetaille*, was sold for GBP 12.6 million, again with Alan Bond as the underbidder. People were already beginning to wonder which picture would set the next record.

A candidate appeared during the summer, when Christie's announced that they would sell van Gogh's *Irises*, a picture that most people would rate higher than *Sunflowers*. The sale would take place in November 1987, and if all went well, this could perhaps take the new world record. Then came the great stock market crash on Black Monday, and if professionals in the art business had been slightly nervous about these prices before, they were deeply concerned now. Would art markets crash as well, or would their much smaller audience simply ignore the crash on Black Monday and keep bidding?

## BULL MARKET

The first clue came on Wednesday, when Christie's held a jewelry auction, which, to most people's surprise, went well. This was followed by a book sale on Friday, where a Gutenberg Bible went for USD 5.9 million – the highest price ever paid for a printed book. So when van Gogh's *Irises* was due for its sale on November 1, there was fear, but also hope. Maybe it would break the record after all. There were more than 2000 people present for the auction, where *Irises* appeared about a third of the way down the list. Although everyone expected it to be something special, one could almost sense the collective gasp as the opening bid for it was given:

"15 million dollars"

From this level, which was about twice as much as ever paid for a picture before *Sunflowers*, the price jumped one million dollars at a time. No one in the hall could know that the reserve (the set minimum price) was as high as 34 million dollars, well above the world record. But the bidding soon passed this level, went to 40 million and kept rising, until the last bidder pulled out at 49 million dollars hammer price, which made 53.9 million USD commission included, according to Artprice. Again, as

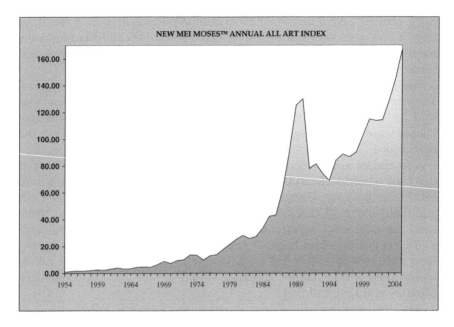

**Figure 24.1**  Mei Moses All Art Index by Professors Jianping Mei and Michael Moses, New York University. Source: Beautifulassetadvisors.com. Reproduced by permission of Mei Moses Annual Art Index.

at the sale of *Sunflowers*, the hall exploded in a massive round of applause. It was later confirmed that the buyer was Alan Bond.

## Two Remarkable Months

The bull market in art was still very much intact two years later, when Sotheby's was holding an auction in which lot sixteen, Willem de Kooning's *Interchange*, had an estimate of USD 4–6 million. The bidding for this lot was supposed to be in units of USD 200 000. As it reached 1.7 million, however, a voice suddenly cried out:

"Six million dollars!"

The auctioneer frowned for a second before resuming his task. Who would jump straight from 1.7 million to six? Well, Mr Kamayama from Japan apparently would. The next bid was supposed to be 6.2 million, but again the system was broken as a new bid was given via phone:

"Seven million."

After that, the bidding continued with the regular 200 000 dollar jumps, edging up to 15.8 million. Mr Kamayama's competitor was Mr Alveryd, a Swede. The next bid broke the order again:

"17 million."

This was a mistake, however – Mr Kamayama had not been concentrating. The auctioneer recognized this and accepted the bid as 16 million. But at 16.8 million it jumped again:

"18 million."

Mr Kamayama had apparently lost his concentration again, so the bid was corrected to 17 million. Finally, the Swede gave up and Mr Kamayama got the picture for USD 20.7 million, including commission. This episode was symptomatic of the events during November and December 1989, when art markets reached frenzy. Many Japanese banks,

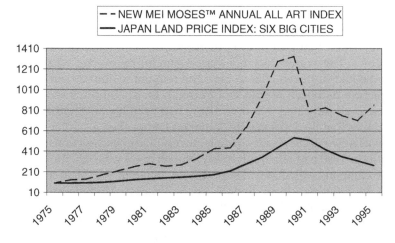

**Figure 24.2**   Mei Moses All Art Index and Japanese land prices for six cities, 1975–1996, indexed. The graph shows a remarkable correlation between the prices of Japanese land and the global art prices. Source: Beautifulassetadvisors.com and Datastream. Reproduced by permission of Mei Moses Annual Art Index.

including Fuji Bank, Mitsubishi Bank, Daiichi Kangyo Bank and Mitsui-Taiyo Kobe Bank, would now offer financing for paintings, typically at up to 50% of their estimates.

These two months were perhaps the most remarkable in the history of the art business. More than 300 pictures were sold at prices exceeding 1 million dollars, and 58 at prices above 5 million dollars. The art index was now up about 580% since the beginning of 1985, according to Artprice. An increase of 580% in four years. What a market! What a trend!

## AN EXPENSIVE PORTRAIT

It was no surprise that Christopher Burge, the Chief Executive Officer of Christie's in the United States, had reason to be satisfied when he packed for the Christmas holiday at the end of 1989. Business was great and he carried with him a draft press release about the sale of another van Gogh. One which might very well set the third world record in four years! It was the famous *Portrait du Dr Gachet*.

Christie's had estimated the sale price at 40–50 million dollars, and the sellers had set the secret "reserve" at USD 35 million. There were perhaps 10–20 people in the world that might be interested and able to pay that sort of amount. Five in the USA, three in London, but none of them English, three in Switzerland, one in Germany and five to ten in Japan. Alan Bond, the Australian, was no longer in the game. After he bought *Irises* it had been revealed that part of the purchasing amount had been financed by Sotheby's. This was, in fact, not a good sign for the market, and especially since he had not been able to raise the remaining amount either, so that the picture had been re-sold to a museum for an "undisclosed" amount. Undisclosed indicated that it probably had been lower. Another negative factor was that the Japanese stock market had peaked just after Christmas and was now falling rapidly. Finally, several European auctions in the first months of 1990 had failed miserably. Not all news was bad, though. A real estate company called Maruko Inc. began, in January 1990, to sell partnerships in paintings from Renoir, Pablo Picasso, Modigliani and Marc Chagall to the public. Each shareholder would then get a proportion of the proceeds when the paintings were re-sold after some years.

The boom in collectibles was now broad and global. Everything that you could characterize as a collectible seemed to be gripped by the frenzy. Consider classic and sports cars, for instance. Keith Martin, the founder of *Sports Car Magazine*, experienced the unusual state of the market as he bought a Ferrari Daytona in New York in 1990. It wasn't really a car, though, rather the . . . er . . . remains of one. The thing was completely

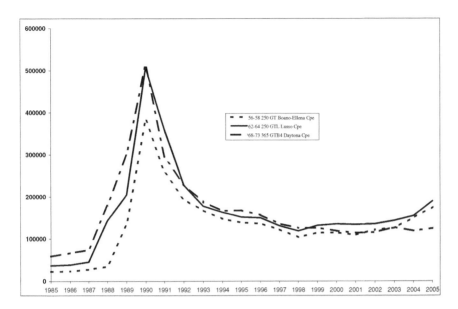

**Figure 24.3** Ferrari prices 1985–2005. The prices of vintage Ferraris mirrored (but exceeded) the price gains of other collectibles during the 1987–1990 bubble, where they rose about 1000%. Source: Cars of Particular Interest. Reproduced by permission of Black Book National Auto Research.

burned out – so much so that the carburetors had melted. He sold it for 115 000 dollars. And then there was the pile of disintegrating rust, which had once been an Alfa 6C2500. He found it in a barn, bought it for 25 000 dollars and had it pulled out by a tractor – and watched in horror as the rusty remains of its trunk caved in. Never mind, he sold the wreck to a friend the same day for 50 000, and this friend re-sold half an hour later for 85 000, thus more than tripling its price in a single day.

## TOWARDS THE PEAK

But let's get back to the sale of *Portrait du Dr Gachet*. It was scheduled for sale on May 15th, and at six-thirty on that day, the audience began to arrive. Before the doors closed, 1700 people had been let in and shown to their places. There were 20 lots before "Dr Gachet" on the list, and these sold reasonably well. Finally, when lot 21 was next, the television lights were turned on. Now was the time!

The auctioneer opened the bidding at a cool 20 million dollars, and thereafter it started climbing rapidly with one million dollar jumps. As it reached 35 million, the reserve price, the auctioneer pushed back his spectacles: the sale was at least secured now. The price kept rising, however, until at 40 million there was a pause. A bidder had apparently dropped out, so was this the final offer?

It wasn't. Suddenly a Japanese dealer in the back of the hall raised his hand. The next bid came from Maria Reinshagen, an employee of Christie's, Zurich, who was on the phone with a client. Applause broke out as the price reached 50 million dollars. But the battle continued as the price rose steadily to 60 million, then 70, 71, 72, and then 73 million dollars. It was Maria's turn now, and she whispered for a long time on the phone. Then she raised her arm.

"74 million dollars."

But Kobayashi wasn't quite finished. As he bid 75 million, the audience could see that Maria was listening more than talking on the phone, and finally she looked up and shook her head. The bidder, whoever it was, had had enough, and the picture went to Mr Kobayashi for 75 million plus commission, or 82.5 million dollars in total. Only two days later, he bought Renoir's *Au Moulent de la Galette* for 71 million dollars in hammer price plus commission.

It would later be revealed that the real buyer had been Ryoei Saito, the chairman of Daishowa Paper Manufacturing, who estimated his fortune (at the time) to be some 770 million dollars. When he received the painting, he looked at it once before sending it to a store room, where it remained in a cloth-covered plywood box for most of the time. He did look at it at least one other time, though: he once had it sent to Kiccho, a famous restaurant, where he entertained a visitor from Sotheby's with an exclusive viewing.

## COLLAPSE

*That* purchase marked the peak of the market. Prices and trading volume in the collectibles markets began contracting soon after, and within the next two years, the ArtPrice index dropped by about 50% – a huge fall by any measure. As the cleaning process played out, it became clear how important Japanese buyers really had been. *Sunflowers, Interchange* and *Dr Gachet* had not been the only paintings bought by Japanese investors at astonishing prices. There had also been Yasumichi Morishita, the owner of Aska International, who had invested 384 million dollars in impressionists and postimpressionists like Renoir and Monet, including some 100 million dollars invested in about 100 pictures at a single New York auction during the fall of 1989. And there had been Mitsukohi Department Stores' purchase of Picasso's *Acrobat* and *Acrobat et Jeune Arlequin* (37.5 million dollars), and Nippon Autopolis's purchase of *Les Noces de Pierette* for 52 million dollars. It was, in fact, estimated that more than 10 000 paintings bought by Japanese were now stored away in bank vaults as collateral as the crash unfolded.

Things didn't only turn sour in the art markets. Alan Bond (the buyer of *Irises*) had recorded a loss for his company of USD 980 million in 1989 before sending it to receivership. He was subsequently charged with criminal dishonesty in 1992 and sent to prison. One year later, Mr Ryoei Saito, the buyer of *Dr Gachet* and *Au Moulent de la Galette* was charged as well – in his case for trying to bribe an official. Mr Saito went bankrupt too.

## DEFINING COLLECTIBLES

The story of the rise and crash in collectibles markets from 1987 to 1991 illustrates that these can behave every bit as irrationally as those of stocks and real estate. However, before we get to why this is so, we should perhaps define what these markets really consist of, and how they are tracked.

### DEFINING COLLECTIBLES

The market for collectibles is not easy to define, but here is one way to classify it:

- Ancient art (antiquities)
- American Indian and African Oceanic and pre-Columbian art
- Asian and Islamic art
- Books and manuscripts
- Varia
- Fine art
- Furniture and decorative arts
- Watches and wristwatches
- Motor cars
- Stamps
- Numismatics

The numbers referred to in this chapter exclude jewelry and precious metals, which are treated separately later on.

Collectibles are often simply called "art," even if this definition includes items such as collectible cars and arms, which may or may not be artistic. The best recorded collectibles are pure art, though, which is tracked by several individuals and institutions. The best known sources of art price indices are probably *Mei Moses All Art Annual Index, Art Market Research, Kusine Company* and *Gabrius*.

The market for collectibles is tiny compared to real estate or financial assets. A study by The European Fine Art Foundation in 2002 concluded that global sales of art totaled approximately some 26 billion dollars in that year (the amount was about the same in euros). The United States carried approximately 45% of that, whilst the UK was responsible for some 20%. Add fine collector wine, cars, etc. to this and we probably arrive at a total traded volume of auction-class collectibles of USD 30 billion (excluding jewelry). We may now make a very simple piece of guesswork to get to a very rough estimate of the size of the total collectibles stock. Let's say that fine art and other high-grade collectibles, on average, are traded once every 15 years. This would mean that total volume of collectibles would be some 450 billion dollars in 2002, which we could express as "0.3–0.6 trillion." That's a lot, of course, but not when compared to real estate or bonds and equities. The bottom line seems to be that collectibles amount to some 0.7–2.5% of GDP, and around 0.3% of all global gross variable-price assets.

## CYCLICAL DRIVERS

One fairly obvious conclusion from this should be that whereas the economy may influence collectibles markets, the reverse couldn't be the case. So how do collectibles markets respond to business cycles?

First, we know that it's *wealthy* people that drive collectibles markets. You are very likely to be wealthy if you show up at an auction and bid for a painting of any financial significance. Cap Gemini and Merrill Lynch have jointly made a series of annual studies of this population segment, and concluded in 2003 that there were 8.3 million people worldwide with more than one million in financial assets, and this segment controlled a total of 31 trillion dollars. This estimate did not include their real estate or any other non-financial assets. These people are called HNWI (high net worth individuals) and it seems very fair to assume that they are the dominant drivers of collectibles markets.

Collectibles markets have different layers, and we shall see later that the top tier behaves somewhat differently than the rest. This exclusive part of the market is driven by what the Cap Gemini/Merrill Lynch report in one place calls the "uber-wealthymulti-decamillionaires" (also called "Ultra-HNWIs"), by which they mean people with at least 30 million dollars to invest. There should be some 77 500 in this category by 2004. So what drives an uber-wealthymulti-decamillionaire, such as Japanese tycoons before 1991, to invest in expensive art? There seem to be three economic motives:

- Potential financial gain
- Safety of tangible assets
- Diversification

The other, obvious drivers for investment in collectibles are related to the *emotional dividend* and *utility*:

- Esthetic pleasure/emotional dividend
- Social prestige

These motives belong in the upper end of Maslow's so-called Hierarchy of Needs Pyramid, which is what people make a priority when all else has been fulfilled. The first assets people seem to buy are basic utilities: refrigerators, radios, MP3s and televisions, followed by nice clothes, and then vehicles. These are assets in a sense, but also highly practical. Typical consumers will then consider pension plans and then, if they continue to gather wealth, save up for their own residence. Further wealth seems to be diverted into more speculative investments, better residences and perhaps second homes. The highest level of assets in the hierarchy to most people would be premium assets such as very expensive utilities (boats, private planes, etc.) and also premium collector items such as expensive paintings. We can imagine how people will feel free to move faster up such a hierarchy if they feel that their previous investments have gained considerable value (Figure 24.4).

## COLLECTIBLES AS ASSET CLASSES

Collectibles can be a reasonable asset class if held over very long periods (in particular, if one ignores the high transaction, insurance and perhaps storage costs), and the most profitable segments are low- to mid-priced art, according to Professors Jianping Mei and Michael Moses of New York University. Furthermore, it looks good in a portfolio perspective in as

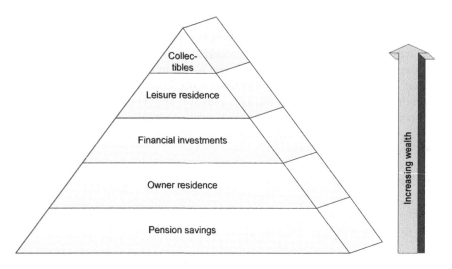

**Figure 24.4** A hierarchy of asset purchases. It is possible to imagine how investors will move up through the levels of investment priorities faster as the values of previous investments increase.

**Table 24.1** Performance correlation between art and other asset classes, 1978–2003. Source: Fernwood Art Investments.

| Asset class | Correlation with art 100 index, 1978–2003 |
| --- | --- |
| S&P 500 (US equities): | −0.029 |
| US 10-year government bonds | −0.037 |
| S&P Gold Index | 0.035 |
| UK FTSE 100 (UK equities) | 0.055 |

much as it has limited statistical correlation with financial assets. Fernwood Investments calculated the correlation coefficients between an art index and other asset classes for a 25-year period; these are shown in Table 24.1.

Art is also tangible, and may be preferred at times when investors distrust other asset classes. Some examples: US and UK equity markets both fell 6% during 1913–20 (WWI), whereas the Mei/Moses Art Index climbed 125%. US equity markets rose just 7% and UK 0% during 1937–46 (WWII), while art markets rose 30% during the same period. The US stock market rose 67% during 1949–54 (Korean War), but art markets spurted 108% ahead during the same period. And the Vietnam War? American equities fell 27% from 1966 to 1975, whereas art prices went up no less than 108% during this period. Art markets have also behaved well when equity markets endured rapid shakeouts. The Art 100 index rose 2.86% in October 1987, when S&P 500 fell 31.54%.

## COLLECTIBLES AND BUSINESS CYCLES

So how do collectibles markets relate to business cycles? A study by Olivier Chanel, *Is Art Market Behavior Predictable?*, found that art prices in England, Japan and America tended to lag equity prices by one to four quarters. He concluded:

> It would appear, then, that financial markets react quickly to economic shocks, and that the profits generated on these markets may be invested in art, so that stock exchanges may be considered as advanced indicators to predict what happens on the art market.

This study was published in 1995, though, and it didn't fit at all with the fact that art markets did very well during the equity markets meltdown from 2000 to 2002. The core of the matter seems to be that collectibles do well whenever the rich get richer, which they did during the years 2000–2002. Not only did real estate prices advance strongly during these years, but HNWI financial wealth, as measured in *The World Wealth Report*, managed to advance as well. When the rich get richer, there are also a disproportionate number of people that can move up through the pyramid of needs. This is reflected by findings in Jianping Mei and Michael Moses's study *Art as an Investment and the Underperformance of Masterpieces* from 2002, which showed that when art markets rise, it's the lower- and mid-priced pieces that appreciate fastest, while it is also those that fall most rapidly during downturns.

Net wealth was obviously increasing rapidly during the collectibles mania in the late 1980s, especially in Japan, as the value of properties exceeded the value of all other property in the world by a significant margin. It is natural that people that have accumulated huge wealth in one asset class (in this case property) will have the confidence to invest in other assets as well, perhaps for diversification reasons and perhaps just because they think they can afford it. So, our conclusions are:

- Collectibles will perform well when global HNWI wealth grows fast . . .
- . . . which tends to be in times of falling interest rates and at least reasonable economic growth

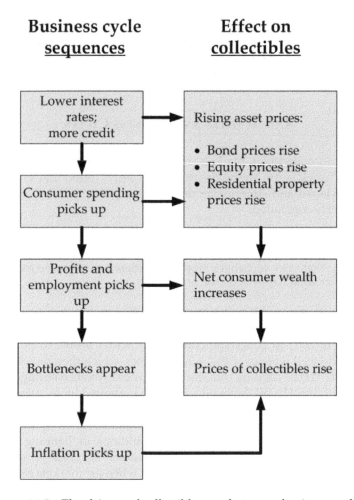

## Business cycle sequences

## Effect on collectibles

| Business cycle sequences | Effect on collectibles |
|---|---|
| Lower interest rates; more credit | Rising asset prices:<br><br>• Bond prices rise<br>• Equity prices rise<br>• Residential property prices rise |
| Consumer spending picks up | |
| Profits and employment picks up | Net consumer wealth increases |
| Bottlenecks appear | Prices of collectibles rise |
| Inflation picks up | |

**Figure 24.5** The drivers of collectibles markets over business cycles.

• Collectibles are, like other asset markets, prone to being caught in speculative fever if they have risen for some time
• They have high correlation with property prices, partly because these are the main determinants of HNWI growth
• They have low correlation with equities, but may lag them at turning points
• They overperform fixed interest rate markets over the very long term

- They underperform equities markets over the very long term
- Mid- and lower-priced segments are most sensitive to business cycles

   Collectibles is a small market, as already discussed, but it is interesting because it illustrates an interesting aspect of Newcomb's equation: a rise in net asset values at the right side of the equation will give many the sense that their wealth has increased, and this will lead to more activity and then a higher velocity of money, enabling, as in 1990, a huge bubble in collectibles. The same happened ten years before, but here the object of collective madness wasn't paintings or sports cars; it was gold and diamonds. These are two fascinating markets, and we shall start our story about them in a dusty marketplace several thousand years ago. But that's for the next chapter.

# Chapter 25

# All That Glitters

There is a big difference between prospecting for gold and prospecting for spinach.

*Will Rogers*

I was just trying to make some money.

*Bunker Hunt*

I never hated a man enough to give him his diamonds back.

*Zsa Zsa Gabor*

Imagine the scene: we are somewhere on the Arabian Peninsula around 500 BC, and in front of us sit two men who want to trade a bag of gold dust. The men have to agree on how much gold there is in the bag, so one of them loads the gold dust on the left weight of an equal arm balance scale. Then the other opens a little bag and pours out a number of small seeds from the carob tree on the right, until the weight finds a balance: the gold and the seeds weigh the same now. And then they count the carob seeds to determine how much gold there is. Carob seeds are a perfect unit for that, since they have this special quality that they all weigh almost exactly the same.

The use of carob seeds as a weight measure seems to have been invented in the eastern Mediterranean, but it soon spread. The Greeks were among those who adapted it, and they brought the tree to other areas, where it was valued for its beans and pods, but also for these uniform little seeds, which the Greeks called "keration." Time passed, and keration became "carat," and this is still the unit that we use today to describe two of our most precious possessions: gold and diamonds. If we say today that a diamond weighs "one carat," then it weighs as much as a seed of the carob tree, or, as we define it now, 0.2 grams. And whereas that unit still describes the *weight* of diamonds, it is now an expression for purity when used for gold. Gold of 24 carats is almost 100% pure, and lower carats such as 22, 18, 14 or 9 have been mixed with some alloy or combination of silver, copper and/or palladium, and perhaps platinum. Gold of 24 carats is rather soft and very stretchable. So much so, in fact, that it can be made into sheets that have 1/1000 the thickness of a page of this book.

## THE DISCOVERY OF GOLD

Gold was probably first used in central and eastern Europe about 6000 years ago, and mainly for making simple tools. The oldest gold jewelry ever discovered was placed inside the Sumerian Royal Tombs at Ur approximately 5000 years ago. Then came the magnificent works in the Egyptian pyramids, including the gold mask of King Tutankamen, which still looks as brilliant and beautiful as it was when it was created 3500 years ago. Gold was also used for fine art by the Chavin civilization in Peru about 3200 years ago, and these remains are also in good condition today. This illustrates one of the reasons for man's fascination with this metal: it doesn't react with air, water or most solvents. It seems to last forever.

That is a good sales argument for the jewelry industry. Around 80% of annual gold demand today is for jewelry, whereas some 8% goes to retail investment, and the remaining 12% is used in electronics and for other industrial purposes.

## THE GOLD BUSINESS

The metal's durability is also the reason that almost all the gold that has ever been mined is still around. Some has been lost to tooth fillings, of course, or to glass coatings and electronics, and there are sunken gold treasures at the bottom of the seas. However, virtually all the rest is still here, and mankind is probably sitting on a pile (so-called "above ground stock") of some 130–140 million kilos by now, an amount which grows by around 2.6 million kilos every year. We can translate this to per capita numbers: the existing pile of gold amounts to 20 grams per capita in the world. The annual production is 0.4 grams per head; not a lot when compared to a steel production of 150 kilos per capita, or the production of aluminum (4.3 kilos) or copper (2.1 kilos).

A golf ball made of gold would weigh about one kilo (and would be sort of hard to use), and this high density means that all the gold in the world could be stored in a container of 18 by 18 by 18 meters (or 60 by 60 by 60 feet). So what would that container be worth? Baron von Rothschild once said that he only knew of two men who really understood the true value of gold – an obscure clerk in the basement vault of the Banque de Paris, and one of the directors of the Bank of England – but, unfortunately, they disagreed. Value is always subject to discussion, but at least the price of gold seems clear. We know that the market price of gold hovered around 440 dollars per troy ounce during much of 2005, which equated to some 14 000 dollars per kilo. Multiply that by 130 million kilos and we get 1.8 trillion dollars, or 285 dollars per capita. Let's make that 1.6–2.0 trillion. We can put that number into perspective by comparing it to the other asset values we have described before (2004):

- Global property market: 90–130 trillion
- Bonds: 45–55 trillion
- Equities: 35–40 trillion
- Collectibles: 0.3–0.6 trillion

So, 1.6–2.0 trillion puts gold at around 5% of equities, but at around eight times the value of collectibles. The market cap of all the gold companies was around 100 billion (and of silver companies around two billion). Who owns the world's gold, by the way? About 30 000 tons, or around 23%, is owned by central banks; mainly the United States, Germany, IMF, France, Italy and Switzerland (in roughly that order). The rest is mainly privately owned jewelry; anything from bracelets to gold watches, bars and coins. So let's guess where it is – 80% in America, Europe and Japan, perhaps?

Actually not at all. India is the world's biggest buyer of gold, followed by the US and China. The Muslim world buys a lot too; especially Arab countries plus Turkey and Pakistan. The surprising bottom line is, in fact, that the Middle East plus emerging markets account for approximately 80% of global demand for gold, and that just India uses more than the USA, Europe and Japan combined.

## SILVER AND PLATINUM

Silver and platinum are both serving dual use in jewelry and for industrial purposes. A little over 7% of silver is used for collectibles (jewelry, sterling ware and silver plate), whereas the rest is used for photographic material, electronics, batteries, catalysts and many other purposes. Around 50% of all platinum is used for jewelry, around 20% for automotive catalysts and the rest for a number of industrial uses, according to *The CRB Commodity Yearbook 2005*.

Annual production of silver in 2003 was 18700 tons and of platinum just 205 tons, corresponding to around 3 and 0.03 grams per capita worldwide, respectively. Stocks of above-ground silver fell steadily during the 1980s and 90s, reaching a consensus estimate of approximately 600 million troy ounces (a bit less than 20000 tons) by mid 2004, equal to a value of some 3.5–4 billion dollars.

## GOLD AND SILVER AS MONEY

Why are the Middle East plus emerging markets such great consumers of gold? The first suspicion is that they regard jewelry, gold bars and gold coins as safe alternatives for storing wealth. It has most definitely served that role in the past. The ancient Egyptians used it as such, and the gold coin called a "shekel," which evolved in Mesopotamia around 3000 BC, became a standard medium of exchange in the Middle East. The concept then spread rapidly, and gold became the world's premiere form of money until first the Chinese and later John Law made attempts to replace it with paper, and we will recall that it still served as monetary anchor when Jay Gould and Jim Fisk tried to manipulate its price against the dollar. Silver has also been used for coins since around 500 BC, beginning in Turkey and later spreading to Greece, Persia, Macedonia, and finally the mighty Roman empire.

It seems that silver and, in particular, gold is still viewed as a sort of money, and sometimes for good reasons. The developed world experienced its embarrassing episodes of inflation during the 1970s, and many citizens in emerging markets can recall how it feels when hapless politicians do like the Duke of Orleans – just recall Chile in the 1970s, or the South American currency crises from 1992 to 1994, the South East Asia currency crisis of 1997, the Russian currency crisis in 1998 or Argentina in 2002.

Gold and silver may be a form of money, but it can never again become the only one. We could relate the value of gold to a global GDP (41 trillion) or global assets (170–220 trillion) and conclude that the gold price would have to go up by several orders of magnitude if the world should go back to the gold standard. This would transfer a huge amount of wealth from countries without gold mines or gold stocks to those fortunate enough to have them, it would lead to absurd efforts to find new gold (and pollution; gold mining is not good news for the environment), and it would leave central banks incapable of dealing with business cycles and shocks. We have long ago passed the time where gold was a realistic alternative to paper credit. Gold is money, but only in a complementary sense. It is also an asset class. We shall consider this question further, but first we will look at the objects that often accompany gold and silver in jewelry: diamonds.

## THE BIRTH OF A GIRL'S BEST FRIEND

The earth beneath our feet is full of carbon atoms; some of it in the form of natural gas, some as oil, coal or stone. However, sometimes, very deep down, the conditions get so hot and heavy that carbon takes a new and very dense configuration: a diamond has been created. This can happen when temperatures reach 1000–2000 degrees Celsius, and pressure perhaps 700 000 tons per square meter.

Then it just lies there for millions of years until suddenly there is an eruption that spews it out of the mouth of a volcano under an inferno of smoke and fire. This is where most diamonds get destroyed. Some sink deep into the magma, where they just melt and dissolve into free carbon atoms again. Others cool too slowly and become graphite, and others still reach oxygen at the surface while they are still burning hot – that will vaporize them into the carbon dioxide that plants breathe. But some get it just right; they reach the surface, but not the air, and then they cool rapidly, not slowly. Such an intact diamond may then just lie there like an ugly duckling among all this ash and lava and wait to be found by a human being.

It is estimated that the first time people started picking up diamonds and using them for jewelry was around 5000 years ago. The first time people actually mined for them was in India, probably around 2400 years go. However, no one in Europe had heard about them until around the 1300s, when people occasionally picked them up and used them in octahedral crystals without cutting them first. These stones would look a bit like milky glass, and that was all. All this changed in the 1600s, when gem merchant Jean Baptiste Tavernier made six trips to India, where he saw something that astonished him: the Mogul emperor collection of cut diamonds. He returned to Europe with no less than 44 large cut diamonds and 1122 smaller ones. This was the time of our famous Sun King, so guess who was Tavernier's best client? Correct. The Sun King bought 14 of the 44 large and several small diamonds. One of these stones was exceptional; it weighed as much as 112 seeds of the carob tree, but its cut had been made in so-called Indian style, which emphasized the size, rather than the sparkle. The Sun King had it re-cut in 1668 to a more beautiful 67 carat stone. This has since been re-cut one more time and the result, which is called the Hope Diamond, is now sitting in the crown of the Queen of England, where it shines a lot.

---

### THREE IMPORTANT DIAMONDS

The Koh-i-noor (Mountain of Light) is the world's most famous diamond. It weighs 108.93 carats and was first described in 1304. The largest one on Earth was the Cullinan, which was found in South Africa in 1905. It weighed 3106.75 carats when found, and was cut into the Great Star of Africa, weighing 530.2 carats, the Lesser Star of Africa, which weighs 317.40 carats, and 104 other diamonds.

The largest diamond known in the *universe* is of another scale, though. It is the heart of the burned-out star "BPM 37093," which seems to be a diamond that weighs 10 billion trillion trillion carats. That's one followed by 34 zeros. It is estimated to be 2500 miles, or some 4000 kilometers, wide. Don't expect to see it sold at Christie's, though. It is 50 light years away and as heavy as our sun.

---

## THE MODERN DIAMOND DISTRIBUTION SYSTEM

Most diamonds are today found in Africa, Australia or Canada. After discovery, they are sent to classification and evaluation centers and sorted into numerous categories – De Beers uses 16 000 categories. All diamonds look like dull glass pebbles at this stage, and only one in a million exceed one carat. Even out of those that make it to jewelry instead of industrial use, it is only one out of 20 that exceed the weight of one carob seed.

After the sorting comes the first sale. About half of all the world's stones are sold through the De Beers controlled Central Selling Organization (CSO) in London to four brokers, who re-sell them at "sights." Boxes with mixed stones are here presented to pre-invited "sightholders" at events that take place every five weeks. The negotiation follows a time-honored principle: you can take it or you can leave it. Sightholders who start arguing about the price, or don't buy, are not invited again. Sightholders re-sell the stones to a much broader network of dealers. Around 80% of these sales take place at four diamond bourses in Antwerp.

The dealers will now arrange for the cutting of the stones, which mostly happens in India (the cheapest and most plentiful stones), in China, Israel and Belgium (medium range) or in New York (mainly "specials," which means the best stones). The cut stones are subsequently passed through several additional levels of dealers as they find their way to the final user. All of this adds to the price, but it also serves the function of matching stones to each other and to the wishes of final buyers. A stone can change hands several times a day, and may have had ten owners before it reaches the consumer. The state of this intermediary market is tracked constantly by the so-called Rapaport service, which lists high prices where almost all sellers would be willing to sell (actual prices tend to be 10–40% below Rapaport prices).

## STONES BY NUMBERS

There is an old rule of thumb in marketing, which says that 20% of sales in most businesses represent 80% of the value. This is true for diamonds too, where only about 20% of the stones can be considered of gem quality, but these represent – well, you guessed it. Another 45% are what is called "near-gem," and would typically not be used for jewelry before 1970. However, Indian polishers today are so cost effective, that many of these also can be used profitably in less expensive gems. The global market for diamond jewelry in 2004 was approximately 70 billion dollars at the retail level, with the value of the stones themselves constituting some 18 billion. Nearly half of the world's $60 billion diamond jewelry sales are in the United States, 50th and 47th Street merchants handle over 95% of the diamonds imported.

These same stones were valued at approximately 16 billion dollars when polished but not yet set, and around 12 billion as roughs bought for polishing by traders. The value ex mines was just over 10 billion. Diamonds constitute only one of many precious/semi-precious stones for jewelry. We can compare this with colored gemstones such as emeralds, rubies and sapphires. The US Bureau of Mines estimated in 2004 that the annual world retail market for all colored stones was worth between 10 and 12 billion dollars at the retail level. That's 0.01 trillion, so we shan't bother with it.

Global production of diamonds was just 12.6 million carats just after World War II, rose to around 40 million in the late 1960s and exceeded 145 million carats (or close to 30 tons) by 2004. If 20% of that was gem quality and 45% near-gem, then there would be almost 20 tons cut for gem use. Stones lose around 50% of their weight through the cutting, which means that around 10 tons would reach the market in the form of gem-stones. Diamonds are, like gold, "forever," but it is very difficult to esti-mate the value of all gem quality diamonds that exist (diamonds will actually decay, but it may take a million years. It is gold that truly is forever). We could guess that average annual production of final gem-stones from the end of WWII until 2004 was 4–5 tons/year. That would amount to 200–250 tons of gem quality diamonds in circulation, equaling around 350–450 billion dollars. There are numerous uncertainties sur-rounding that number (the quality of cuts have changed over time, for instance), so let's round it up further and say that it is in the order of mag-nitude of 0.3 to 0.5 trillion dollars, which we can compare to gold stock of 1.6 to 2.0 trillion. We can also, just for fun, estimate how much space all these diamonds would take up if we gathered then together. Since solid diamonds weigh 3.5 tons per $m^3$ they would need a container of 70–100 $m^3$ if there were no empty spaces between them, or perhaps 150–200 $m^3$ given their actual shapes. The higher number is a container of just 6 * 6 * 6 meters (20 * 20 * 20 feet).

Who buy diamonds? The picture here is rather different from what we saw with gold. Around 50% of all diamond sales are in the US, followed by Europe and Japan (China and India should soon catch up, though).

## THE GREAT BOOM

What drives the prices of gold, silver and diamonds? De Beers has attempted to control pricing in the diamond market for decades, and has been largely successful in achieving a smooth and stable environment for the sector by managing large buffer stocks and dictating wholesale prices. However, there was a major episode between 1977 and 1982, where some underlying forces became so powerful that they could no longer contain price movements. The result was that the Antwerp Diamond Price Index suddenly broke out of the narrow range targeted by De Beers in 1977 to rise no less than 400% over three years. The last part of the run-up was the fastest. A flawless diamond, which in January 1979 cost 20000 dollars in Antwerp, had risen to 60000 dollars at the peak 13 months later – up

300% in just over a year. The subsequent crash was fast too – our flawless diamond was back to 20 000 again as soon as January 1982. This episode was followed by new stability and De Beers seemed clearly back in control after that. However, this cartel has gradually lost market share, and it is possible that the future will bring more natural volatility to diamond prices.

The 1980 diamond bubble happened at the same time that Nelson Bunker Hunt made his famous attempt to corner the global silver market. The episode seems to have begun in 1970, when Nelson Bunker Hunt, one of the heirs to an oil empire, was visited by a friend at his ranch in Texas. The friend, Alvin Brodsky, pointed out to Bunker Hunt that everything he saw around him in the kitchen, where the discussion took place, would be more expensive the next year. The world was at the early stages of its great inflationary spell, as central banks made the mistake of believing in a long-run Phillips curve relationship. Brodsky suggested that since the value of money was falling every year, one should consider changing it to silver. Bunker Hunt, who had a steady stream of approximately 30 million dollars a year of oil revenues from Libya, warmed to the idea and began, after a while, to buy the metal.

The silver price remained fairly steady for several years, but eventually, towards the end of the decade, it started to advance. Normally, if you want to make a good investment, you try to hide your intentions so that you don't have to compete with others, but Hunt had meanwhile changed his attitude. Now, he wanted not only to buy silver in anticipation of increasing prices, it seems that he wanted to engineer these price rises by forming a consortium of buyers. He found his allies in Saudi Arabia. A joint group of investors would now buy up huge amounts of silver future and then take physical delivery as contracts expired.

Hunt didn't trust the American authorities much, so he decided to ship no less than around 125 tons (40 000 000 troy ounces) of silver to Switzerland. He held a shooting competition amongst the cowboys at his farm, and the winners were given the task of flying with the piles to Europe. Hunt chartered three Boeing 707 airplanes, loaded the silver and the cowboys one night, and had the planes flown across the Atlantic and unloaded in Zurich. And then he and his partners resumed their buying, where they would later take delivery of at least as much again as Hunt already had in store in Switzerland. Silver prices were now going through the roof, but the consortium was finally hit by a squeeze between exchange authorities, who disallowed new long positions, and an aggressive central bank, which had started raising interest rates to squeeze out inflation. The whole scheme collapsed in 1980, and Bunker Hunt was forced into bankruptcy in 1988.

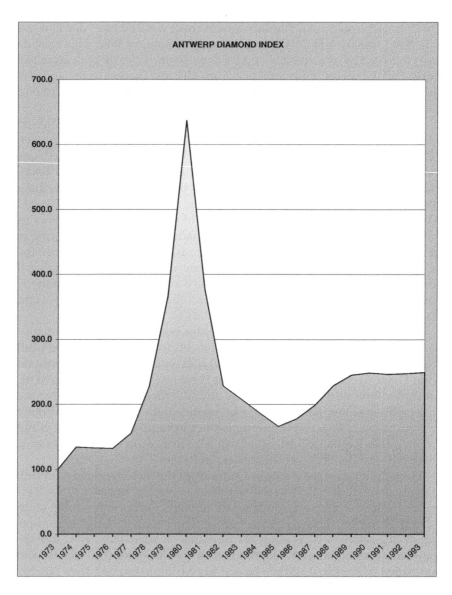

**Figure 25.1** The 1980 diamond bubble. The prices are from the Antwerp Diamond Index. Reproduced by permission of Antwerp World Diamond Cent.

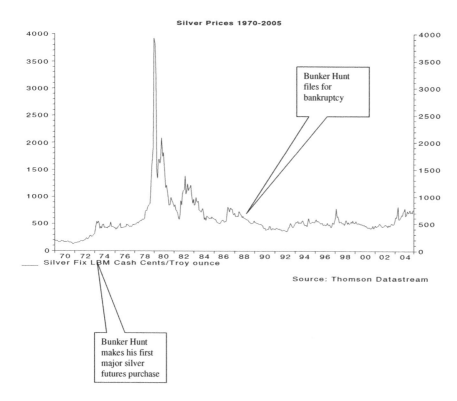

**Figure 25.2** The silver bubble and Nelson Bunker Hunt. Many would relate the bubble to Bunker Hunt and his partner's aggressive purchases, but there were similar, if less dramatic, spikes in prices of gold, platinum and diamonds. Reproduced by permission of Datastream.

## PRECIOUS METALS, DIAMONDS AND BUSINESS CYCLES

The bubble of 1980 engulfed gold, silver, platinum and diamonds (Figure 25.2). Whatever caused it, the bubble wasn't specific to factors like supply disturbances in any of these four markets – it was of a more general nature; a brief, but massive, spike of speculative *demand*. Let's look at what is known about cyclical drivers of demand for these materials.

Because gold is a large and liquid market, it is here that we find the best studies of the impact of business cycles. We can start with a study made by Irwin and Landa, with tests of correlations between, amongst others, T-bills (short-term bonds), T-bonds (long-term bonds), stocks, real estate and gold. Their core findings are summarized in Table 25.1.

**Figure 25.3** Correlation between gold, silver and platinum prices. The graph shows the coordination between the bubbles in the three precious metals in 1980.

A positive number in Table 25.1 means positive correlation, and this study showed that gold movements were *inversely* related to movements in bonds and stocks, which is well known in the trading community. However, the study also showed a positive correlation between gold and property markets, which is a fact that we shall return to. Another study, *Facts and Fantasies about Commodity Futures* by Gorton and Rouwenhorst from 2004 examined how commodity prices fluctuated over US business cycles, based on NBER's official business cycle stage classification from 1959 to 2004. Commodity prices are global, of course, whereas the US business cycle is local, so there could be periods where different economies pulled in different directions. However, there is a considerable synchronization, and the US economy averaged around one-third of the global economy over the period. Table 25.2 shows how precious metals performed in this context. The table illustrates a rather clear difference between the behavior of gold on one side, and that of silver and platinum on the other. Silver and platinum are largely industrial metals and have relatively small above-ground stocks – this should explain why they do so well during late stages of expansion and badly (especially platinum) at late stages of recessions. The price of gold, on the other hand, should be almost completely independent of the supply flow and industrial

**Table 25.1**  Return correlation between gold and other asset classes. Source: Irwin and Landa, 1987.

|  | T-bills | T-bonds | Stock markets | Real estate |
|---|---|---|---|---|
| Correlation coefficient | −0.53 | −0.23 | −0.15 | +0.41 |

**Table 25.2**  Behavior of precious metals over business cycles. Source: Gorton and Rouwenhorst, 2004.

|  | Early expansion | Late expansion | Early recession | Late recession |
|---|---|---|---|---|
| Gold | −1.2 | 4.1 | −2.5 | 14 |
| Silver | −2.0 | 13.9 | −1.1 | −0.2 |
| Platinum | 5.0 | 16.3 | −2.5 | −20.2 |

demand. It is an asset and a store of wealth and as such performs best when interest rates are low.

## CYCLE DURATION

We saw in Chapter 16 that it is possible to use Hurst's rescaled range approach to test a time series for cyclicality. Edgar Peters used this approach in his book *Fractal Markets Analysis, Applying Chaos Theory to Investment and Economics* from 1994, for gold prices during the 25 years from January 1968 to December 1992, and found modest signs of two gold cycles, one averaging 48 weeks and another of 248 weeks. The latter was interesting, since 248 weeks is 4.8 years, which is close to the average duration of the inventory cycle. Hamish Tweedie made a similar study in his thesis *An Investigation into Forecasting Methods to Derive Gold Price Movements* from 1994, where he studied gold markets from 1966 to 1994, when there had been six bull markets and five bear markets in gold prices. His conclusion:

> In summary it appears that potential exists for the conclusion that 80–100-day and 240-week cycles or long term memory/dependence exists in gold prices over the past 15 years.

**Table 25.3**   Leading indicators for gold. Source: Gold Fields Mineral Services Ltd.

| Global | India | Japan | USA | European Union |
|---|---|---|---|---|
| • GDP<br>• Industrial countries production | • GDP<br>• Consumer expenditure | • GDP | • GDP<br>• Industrial production | • Industrial production |

We note here that 240 weeks is 4.3 years, which brings us even closer to the average of the inventory cycle. How about leading indicators for gold? Tweedie tested a number of time series from the American, Japanese and Swiss economies, as well as some commodity prices, and found that many of them acted as good leading indicators for the two first gold cycles during the 28 years, but that only four seemed useful for the entire period:

• US help wanted advertisements (average lead: 14 months)
• US industrial production (11 months)
• US prime interest rates, inverted (28 months)
• US loans and investments (18 months)

Another approach, which seems more promising, has been taken by Gold Fields Mineral Services Ltd, which has developed forecasting models for gold using the indicators shown in Table 25.3.

This approach makes sense in as much as it includes India plus the four largest economic blocks.

So where does all this lead us? Before we draw a conclusion, we should consider why people might buy precious metals and diamonds. We have already seen that the total above-ground stocks of gold are somewhere around five times as big as the value of existing gem quality diamonds, and almost 50 times the stock of silver. Furthermore, gold can be traded as futures and options at very low transaction costs, as it is a clearly defined commodity. The global trading of gold through derivative markets is more than 50 times as large as the trade of the physical material, which means that gold trading probably is several hundred times as large as trading in diamonds.

Diamonds are not a clearly defined commodity at all. We have already seen that De Beers divides them into 16 000 categories, and it takes a thorough investigation of each single stone by an expert to classify it with reasonable certainty. It gets worse when the stones have been set in jewelry, which most of them have. Good second-hand diamond jewelry is largely traded via auctions, where the hammer price shouldn't go over 75% of the Rapaport price of the stone plus setting costs – many will actually go for 35–50%. Seller and buyer will then pay a commission, which means that the seller often ends up receiving only one-third of the Rapaport price, and an even smaller fraction of the high street price. Gold is atoms from our periodic system – well defined, cheap to trade and a great investment tool. Diamonds are, rather, atoms of pleasure, and provide a great way to display love, beauty or perhaps wealth. However, investments they are not.

## ATOMS OF PLEASURE

When discussing collectibles we saw that people buy objects of pleasure when they can afford them, and that an *increase in wealth* is the main driver. The market for diamonds is broader than the market for auction-class collectibles; De Beers announced, for instance, that 80% of Shanghai brides received diamond wedding rings in 2005 (it is safe to say that far fewer than these 80% would ever buy auction-class collectibles). So diamonds have a fairly broad market, but how much is bought should depend largely on wealth growth. This brings us to four potential demand drivers for precious metals and diamonds:

- Falling interest rates
- Rising equity prices
- At least reasonable economic growth
- Rising property markets

Property markets seem likely to be the best candidate of these to create broad-based wealth growth, so let's see how these assets behaved up to the great diamond bubble in 1979–1980. The answer is simple: many countries, including the UK and the US, had a very significant run-up in real home prices from 1975 to 1978. It seems plausible that net wealth growth triggered by this property boom was the key driver of the diamond bubble, and a contributing driver of demand for gold, silver and platinum. However, gold prices cannot be explained exclusively by wealth effects, since purchase of gold can have another motive: distrust of money.

It is often said that gold investors reach their decision through a process of elimination, which would explain why the metal tends to go up when bonds and stocks go down – and vice versa. They also consider it in its old-fashioned role as a sort of money. Gold goes up when people think short-term interest rates are too low compared to expected future inflation. This means in praxis that they like gold when short-term interest rates are low compared to long-term interest rates – the latter being an indicator of expected future inflation. Gold tends to be strong, in other words, when the so-called "yield curve" gets steep. (This expression covers a line that plots the interest rates, at a set point in time, of bonds having equal credit quality, but differing maturity dates. It is steep when short-term rates are much lower than long-term rates. It flattens when central banks raise rates, and it may get "inverted" towards the end of such a tightening). The conclusion of all this is that the strongest underlying cyclical forces driving precious metals and diamonds in the future most likely will be:

- Economic growth (high growth is positive)
- Property cycles (rising prices are positive)
- Real short-term yields (low yields are positive)
- Yield curves (steep yield curves are positive)

*Economic growth* means reasonable employment security and thus confidence. The *property cycle* is the dominant long-time driver of wealth, and thus particularly important for diamonds. *Real short-term yields* are major drivers for gold, since much gold is traded as futures and/or as a substitute for interest rate bearing money. The opportunity loss of not getting interest from gold is small when real short-term yields are low. And finally, the *yield curve* compares present money rates to future inflation expectations, and a steep curve should therefore speak for gold as an alternative to paper money. The yield curve is typically steepening when the

**Table 25.4** Behavior of precious metals and diamonds in relation to their demand drivers.

|  | Precious metals | Diamonds |
| --- | --- | --- |
| Economic growth | Leader, especially economic growth in OECD | Leader, especially economic growth in India, Muslim and other emerging markets |
| Property cycle | Leader, especially OECD property cycles | Leader, especially property cycles in India, Muslim and other emerging markets |
| Real short-term yields | Low yields are bullish | Weak correlation |
| Yield curve | Rising yield curve is leader, especially in OECD | Weak correlation |

economy enters cyclical decline. Early cyclical decline often coincides with rising inflation and rising long-term bond yields, whereas central banks will begin reducing short-term yields. This is partly the explanation of why gold often rises when equities and bonds are falling. We can sum it up as in Table 25.4.

It should be added that exposure to gold need not be direct. Alternative forms of exposure are gold mining shares. These will tend to overperform the gold in periods of low inflation, but underperform if structural inflation is high.

### COMPARING CYCLES IN PROPERTY, COLLECTIBLES, PRECIOUS METALS AND DIAMONDS

- Property cycles are best described as inherent, supply-driven "hog-cycles" that can drive the economy as a whole
- Cycles in collectibles, precious metals and diamonds are demand-driven "real cycles" that mainly reflect changes in private wealth. These markets are too small to have meaningful effect on business cycles.
- Monetary conditions, and in particular *changes* in nominal rates and in *absolute levels* of real interest rates are *direct* drivers of all of these markets.
- Monetary conditions are also *indirect* drivers of cycles in collectibles, precious metals and diamonds through their effect on property prices and thus wealth
- Bubbles in any single of these markets are typically separated by at least 15 years, as people need time to forget the previous collapse. There is thus a tendency towards "bubble-rotation" so that, for instance, a bubble in precious metals/diamonds is followed by a bubble in collectibles which may again be followed by a bubble in property or precious metals/diamonds.

# Chapter 26

# What Things are Made of: Commodities

A mine is a hole in the ground with a liar standing over it.

*Mark Twain*

The art of creating an ideal portfolio is not just about seeking high average returns; it's also about stability. Many large investors achieve this by combining some very different asset classes. Here, for instance, is how the famous Yale Endowment's target asset allocation looked by June 2004:

| | |
|---|---|
| Equity | 30.0% |
| Bonds | 7.5% |
| Hedge funds | 25.0% |
| Private equity | 17.5% |
| Real assets | 20.0% |
| Total | 100.0% |

Such a portfolio model is interesting, because stocks and bonds, the traditional investment categories, amounted to only 37.5%. It is also interesting because this endowment has achieved excellent and stable returns through thick and thin. These results are partly achieved because hedge funds (which accounted for a significant part of their exposure) tend to weather economic crises well, but also because a sizeable part was in real assets. Real assets can be property, or farm- and timberland, as they mostly were in this case. They could also be commodity futures.

Commodities are everywhere in our lives, of course. Table 26.1 shows some examples of how much is produced globally per year per capita in the world.

**Table 26.1**  Average global per capita consumption of selected commodities in kilos, 2004 (est.). Source: Commodity Research Bureau, 2005.

| Energy | Textiles, Grains, Softs | | Industrials | |
|---|---|---|---|---|
| Crude petroleum: 562 | Corn and maize: | 110 | Cement: | 277 |
| Coal: 13 | Rice: | 93 | Raw steel: | 150 |
| | Wheat: | 97 | Aluminum: | 4.3 |
| | Soybeans: | 36 | Copper: | 2.1 |
| | Sugar: | 22 | Zinc: | 1.5 |
| | Oranges: | 7.8 | Lead: | 1.1 |
| | Cotton: | 3.3 | Nickel: | 0.2 |
| | Coffee: | 1.1 | | |
| | Olive oil: | 0.5 | | |

These numbers tell us where the bulk of commodities are: it's what we eat, it's energy, and it's all that steel and cement that you see everywhere in a city. However, the story changes somewhat when we move to the dollar value of traded commodity futures. First, steel and cement are very small in the futures markets – they are predominantly traded outside financial markets. The most traded commodity groups in futures markets can be listed as:

- Energy (oil and gas)
- Industrials (lumber, etc.)
- Textiles (cotton, wool, etc.)
- Livestock (cattle, hogs, pork bellies)
- Grains (corn, wheat, feed grains, rice, soybean, etc.)
- Softs (cocoa, coffee, orange juice, etc.)
- Industrial metals (aluminum, copper, etc.)
- Precious metals (gold, silver, platinum, palladium)

### TRACKING COMMODITY MARKETS

The most popular commodity indices are Reuters-CRB, Goldman Sachs Commodity Index, Dow Jones-AIG Commodity Price Index and Rogers International Commodity Index.

## WHAT KEYNES FOUND

One of the most famous early commodity speculators was none other than John Maynard Keynes. In 1923 he published an article in the *Manchester Guardian*, "Some Aspects of Commodity Markets," where he explained one of his reasons for dabbling in this market. Let's say you want to buy a commodity that costs 100 dollars here and now. However, you buy it in the futures market for delivery in 12 months. You would then (obviously) expect the seller to charge warehousing/financing costs for holding it for you for 12 months – let's say 5%. So you would expect the price to be 105 dollars for the 12-month future. That 5% premium would be called a "contango." However, there are many times where the forward price is *lower* than the actual spot price, and this is called "backwardation."

What Keynes described was a systematic tendency towards this backwardation. The reason was that most of the sellers in the market were commodity producers, who wanted to hedge their risks by selling forward, which meant that most of the buyers had to be speculators. The backwardation occurred because speculators on average wanted a risk premium for taking a chance. This was so normal that Keynes called it, well, "normal backwardation," and it illustrated what the ideal role of good speculators in a market should be: people who act as insurance companies by taking over risk and providing liquidity.

A study by Gorton and Rouwenhorst from Yale International Center for Finance (*Facts and Fantasies about Commodity Futures*) from 2004 showed that normal backwardation existed and made a huge contribution to the returns of commodity futures over time. So big, in fact, that a portfolio of commodity futures, continuously rolled over to new maturity dates, not only beat bonds, but on average over a 43-year period did about as well as US equities. This was far better than cash commodities, which had not even beaten inflation. However, there are three issues about backwardation that need to be mentioned. The first is that it has primarily been the norm in energy. Backwardation in industrial commodities has tended to occur mainly when there was a real supply shortage in the market, which meant that backwardated markets often were right in forecasting future price falls.

The second issue is that it can change to a contango at any time. The German company Metallgesellschaft booked a loss in 1993 of 1.33 billion dollars on that account. Its US subsidiary, MGRM, had sold 160 million barrels of oil forward on five and ten-year fixed price contracts. They would then try to hedge their risk through purchase of short-term futures contracts, where they would cash in the backwardation advantage as they rolled each contract over before it expired. However, the market turned against their hedge position in late 1993, as spot prices fell and the market moved into contango. This forced them to make huge margin payments on their futures contracts, which had also exceeded the amounts they were supposed to hedge.

The third aspect of backwardation to mention is that there has been an increasing presence of hedge funds speculating in commodity markets since around 1995. These may contribute to reducing the normal backwardation, as this is largely what they are chasing.

## CYCLICAL TIMING

Backwardation is one reason to trade the long side ("long" means buy, whereas "short" is sell) of commodity futures. Another is that their prices tend to peak later than equities, which means that a combination of equities and commodities is more stable than any of the two in isolation. Gorton and Rouwenhorst investigated what an average of commodity futures had done during periods where equities got hammered. First, they selected the 5% worst months in equity markets, where stocks had dropped an average of 9.18% and found that commodities had *risen*, on average, 1.43% during these months. That commodity performance was pretty good. It was, in fact, *more* than the average commodity return for all months, which was 0.88%. However, the story got even better when the two economists narrowed their focus to the 1% most awful months in the stock markets. Equities had, on average, fallen 13.87% during these months, but commodities had, in those cases, *risen* by an average of 2.32%.

This leads us to another characteristic aspect of commodities. We will recall how Mandelbrot in 1960 had found a bell-shaped drawing with two fat tails on a blackboard in Harvard University, and discovered that it illustrated the distribution of monthly returns of cotton. Gorton and Rouwenhorst analyzed such fat tails for the combined commodity indices and compared these to the tails of equity performance distributions – they found something interesting. The equity fat tails, they discovered, were eschewed to the *left* and the commodity tails to the *right*. This means that extraordinarily strong movements in equity prices tended to be to the downside, whereas unusual movements in commodity prices were to the upside. Surprises tended, in other words, to be negative for the equity investor but positive for the (long) commodity investor.

So we can conclude that there are three good reasons to include commodity futures in an investment portfolio: normal backwardation, low

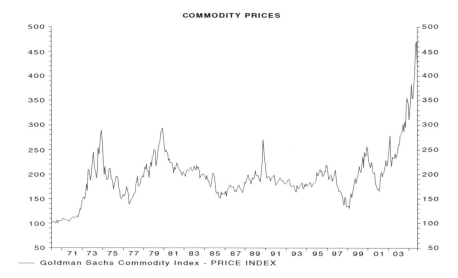

**Figure 26.1** CRB Commodity Index 1970–2004. Source: Thomson Datastream. Reproduced by permission.

correlation with bonds and stocks and a volatility that is skewed towards the upside. However, commodities should not constitute a huge part of portfolios. Commodities now account for some 2.5% of global GDP, and while that percentage can rise during major capital investment spurts, the number is likely to stay limited. The good question now is whether exposure to commodities can be timed successfully over business cycles. Many commodities, like cereals, livestock and textiles, relate to non-durable consumer goods, and are therefore not strongly tied to business cycles. The commodities that *do* relate to business cycles are those that go into the large, cyclical sectors: property construction, capital spending and cars. Let's take property construction first and look at how it acts as a cyclical demand driver for some commodities.

## CYCLICAL DEMAND DRIVERS

We have already seen (in Chapter 21) that the building construction market normally constitutes a bit over 10% of GDP. This is partly made by the public sector (airports, railroads, hospitals, schools, administration buildings, etc.), but the vast majority is private. This makes it an important element in the cyclical demand for many commodities. Just think about what buildings are made of: there is wood, there is steel, and there is cement, zinc, copper, aluminum, and much more – tons of it. It is normally estimated that global building construction accounts for some 25% of the virgin wood harvested, and 40% of the raw stone, gravel and sand used in the world each year. Worldwatch Institute claims that the construction and operation of buildings is responsible for 40% of the world's total energy use, and 30% of raw materials consumption. We have already seen that property construction moves in slow cycles (of 18 years' average duration) with high amplitude. It is reasonable to expect that this stimulates similar slow cycles in the relevant commodities.

Then there is corporate *capital spending* on machinery and equipment, which is mainly done by companies in manufacturing, transportation, communications, wholesale, retail, finance, utilities and insurance and real estate sectors. Some of the big blocks here are machines and machine tools (mainly in manufacturing), trucks, airplanes, corporate car fleets (mainly in the transportation and finance/insurance sectors) and information technology (mainly communications, manufacturing, finance and insurance). An overall breakdown in a country will often show some 30% of this spending going into information technology, and 20% into transportation equipment. It can vary a lot, but the average is around 10% of a modern economy.

Our third important demand driver of commodities is *inventories*. These fluctuate a lot, and a bit less than a third of them in many countries is accounted for by cars.

So which listed commodities go into property construction, capital spending in machinery and equipment and in inventories? There are three categories: industrial metals, lumber and energy. Let's take the industrial metals first. Two of them are particularly related to building construction:

- *Copper* is used primarily for electrical applications, such as wires (50%), general and industrial engineering applications (20%), architectural building and construction parts, such as rooftops, lighting fixtures, plumbing fixtures and plumbing (15%), and transportation, such as radiators and intercoolers/heat exchangers (11%). These numbers do not paint the full picture, though, because a substantial part of the electrical applications mentioned first are also part of building and construction – they are just not what is called "architectural." This means that *almost half of all copper consumption is linked to property construction*. There are also many electrical applications in *cars*. US-built cars have, on average, more than 50 pounds (23 kilos) of copper, 80% of which is in electrical components. The average single-family home in the United

States requires 439 pounds (200 kilos) of copper. The global production of raw copper in 2002 was 13.6 billion kilos. Divide that into a global population of 8.9 billion and we get to 2.1 kilos per capita. Approximately 40% is recycled.

- *Zinc*: approximately 57% is used in *construction*, 23% in *transportation*, 10% in *machinery and equipment* and 10% in consumer goods. Global production in 2003 was 1.5 kilos per capita. Around one-third of global zinc production is recycled.

---

**AVERAGE COPPER CONTENT IN AN AMERICAN SINGLE-FAMILY HOME**

In an average single-family home, you will find about:

195 pounds/88 kilos of building wire
151 pounds/68 kilos of plumbing tube, fillings, valves
24 pounds/11 kilos of plumbers' brass goods
47 pounds/21 kilos of built-in appliances
12 pounds/5 kilos of builders' hardware
10 pounds/4.5 kilos of other wire and tube

Source: Copper.org

---

The next one, nickel, is largely related to capital spending:

- *Nickel*: some 92% of nickel is used in alloys, such as stainless steel. These are again used in kitchen appliances, wires, chemical industry plumbing, etc. Nickel is thus mainly tied to *capital investment* and *building construction*. Global production per capita in 2002 was 0.2 kilos per capita, and 40–50% is recycled.

The two last ones are tied largely to cars and other transportation equipment:

- *Aluminum*: approximately 41% is used in transportation (cars, airplanes, trucks, etc.), where it is used primarily for making fuel-efficient engines in cars and trucks. Its low weight reduces fuel consumption and emissions during transportation, etc. 18% is used in construction, 16% in packaging (mainly cans), 9% in electrical equipment and 9% in

**Table 26.2**   Cyclical behavior of selected industrial metal futures. Source: Gorton and Rouwenhorst, 2004.

| Metal | Early expansion | Late expansion | Early recession | Late recession |
|---|---|---|---|---|
| Copper | 2.3% | 18.8% | 11.3% | –21.6% |
| Zinc | 3.3% | 11.9% | –8.6% | –1.7% |
| Nickel | 3.4% | 14.1% | 6.9% | –11.2% |
| Aluminum | –0.6% | 4.6% | 5.6% | –3.8% |
| Lead | 2.6% | 11.6% | –16% | –9.7% |

**Table 26.3**   Cyclical behavior of stock and bond futures. Source: Gorton and Rouwenhorst, 2004.

| | Early expansion | Late expansion | Early recession | Late recession |
|---|---|---|---|---|
| Corporate bonds | 11.5% | 3.6% | –2.9% | 25.7% |
| S&P total return | 18.1% | 10.4% | –15.5% | 17.3% |

machinery/equipment. This links aluminum primarily to the car cycle (and thus to the short *inventory cycle*), but also to the longer building construction and capital investment. Global production in 2003 was 4.3 kilos per capita. Over 25% of aluminum is recycled.

- *Lead*: approximately 76% of lead goes into lead–acid batteries (especially car batteries), and it is thus closely associated with the *inventory cycle* and private consumption of cars. Global production is 1.1 kilo per capita (a very large proportion of lead is recycled, as it is poisonous).

Gorton and Rouwenhorst's *Facts and Fantasies about Commodity Futures*, which we also mentioned in the last chapter, summarized how each of these (and other) commodities fluctuated over US business cycles from 1959 to 2004. Table 26.2 shows their average price performance numbers.

Let's just compare this to how corporate bonds and equities performed in the study to get a perspective (Table 26.3). The difference is clear. Corporate bonds explode upwards even during late recession and continue into the recovery, as inflation melts away, liquidity expands and a better future is discounted. Equities follow closely after for the same reason, and because the discount rate of futures earnings (which is bond yields) is dropping. Both fall during early recession. Commodities are a different matter, though. Copper and zinc perform extremely well late in the expansion, when construction activity peaks. Copper even stays high into early recession, as most construction projects are continued until their completion, even if the economy has fallen out of bed meanwhile. But the metal gets hammered in late recession, as previously planned building construction projects are finally completed.

Nickel behaves much as copper and zinc, since capital spending projects also take time to finish. Finally, aluminum and lead are more stable, as they are tied to the somewhat less volatile car market. Car production is consumer driven, and production of cars can be cut down quickly. This is, in particular, reflected by the rapid decline in lead prices during early recession. It seems that you can diversify an equity portfolio with copper, but not with lead.

## LEADING INDICATORS FOR INDUSTRIAL METALS

In the 1990s, Geoffrey Moore designed a series of leading indicators for primary metals in general, as well as specific leaders for copper and scrap steel (scrap steel is not traded as large futures contracts). Moore's indicators provide forewarning of "industry activity" in the metals sectors, which means their production, prices and employment. The list in Table 26.4 shows these with a distinction between the effect of general economic conditions, development in sectors that create demand for metals and telltale clues from the supply side.

It is interesting to note here that these indicators focus on housing starts as leading indicators for all groups, which illustrates the importance of the property cycle. The indicators are published by the US Geological Survey on a monthly basis.

## LUMBER, ENERGY AND BUSINESS CYCLES

So much for industrial metals – let's move on to lumber. This is largely used in housing construction, so how does it perform over the cycle? The answer, it seems, is largely like copper, but with an earlier decline, which may be because a lot of wood is also used for furniture, which should turn earlier in the cycles.

The final group of commodities that relates strongly to property, capital spending and cars is energy. Table 26.6 shows the performance statistics.

We see that oil performs well in early recession, which may have two explanations: first, a lot of oil goes into building construction, which is

**Table 26.4**   Geoffrey Moore's leading indicators for metals. Source: US Geological Survey.

| | Category of indicator | Leading index all industrial metals | Leading index for steel | Leading index for copper |
|---|---|---|---|---|
| **General economic conditions** | Monetary stimulus | US M2 growth | US M2 growth | Yield curve |
| | General health of the manufacturing sector | Purchasing managers' index (PMI) | Purchasing managers' index (PMI) | |
| | General leading indicator of growth and profitability | Ratio of price to unit labor cost | | |
| **Specific sector demand** | Residential housing market | Housing starts | Housing starts | Housing starts |
| | Shipment of final products | | Shipment of household appliances; | |
| | | | Retail sales of US passenger cars and light trucks | |
| **State of the metals industry sector** | Directly related stock prices | Weighted S&P index, machinery, construction and farm and industrial | Weighted S&P index, steel companies | Weighted S&P index, building product companies |
| | Specific new metals orders | New orders, primary metal products | New orders, iron and steel mills | New orders, non-ferrous metal products |
| | Bottlenecks in metals business | Average weekly hours, primary metals | Average weekly hours, iron and steel mills | Average weekly overtime hours, copper rolling, drawing, extruding and alloying |
| | Metals prices | JOC-ECRI metals price index growth rate | Growth rate in the price of scrap | LME spot price of primary copper |

**Table 26.5** Cyclical behavior of lumber futures. Source: Gorton and Rouwenhorst, 2004.

|  | Early expansion | Late expansion | Early recession | Late recession |
|---|---|---|---|---|
| Lumber | 0.0% | 15.5% | –7.0% | –23.6% |

**Table 26.6** Cyclical behavior of energy futures. Source: Gorton and Rouwenhorst, 2004.

|  | Early expansion | Late expansion | Early recession | Late recession |
|---|---|---|---|---|
| Crude oil futures | 4.4% | 12.1% | 26.3% | –21.3% |
| Natural gas futures | 5.2% | 10.3% | –15.3% | –21.5% |

not the case for natural gas. Secondly, there are cases where spikes in oil prices have, in fact, been the triggers of recessions. An increase in oil prices will have its maximum impact with a 12-month delay. Having said this, the table illustrates that energy prices behave much like copper – they perform well late in the expansion and early in the recession – and then they get squashed.

## COMMODITIES VERSUS COMMODITY COMPANIES

It would seem intuitive to assume that an investment in a range of commodity-producing companies should give a better return than investing in commodity futures. Commodity companies are profitable, whereas commodities produce no direct yield. Gorton and Rouwenhorst investigated this question but concluded that commodity futures – over a 41-year period – had been far more profitable than a basket of commodity companies.

## THE SUPPLY SIDE

One good question to ask is why commodity pricing isn't more effective over the business cycle. The answer is two-fold. First, the demand is, as we have just seen, cyclical. However, the other aspect is that supply is inflexible and characterized by large, fixed costs. There is normally a very long time lag – often some seven to 15 years – from the time that a deposit of metals or energy is discovered, until its exploitation commences. It took, for instance, 11 years from the time when oil was discovered in the North Sea until any of it reached the market. The same is true for metals mining. Even increasing the production of lumber takes time: trees don't grow up overnight. However, once the infrastructure is in place, the commodity producer is inclined to keep producing, even if prices are falling. Whereas a producer of finished goods may be unable to sell his products during recessions, the commodity producer will always find a market, but not necessarily at a good price. These supply lags on the way up and down are, in themselves, sufficient to create hog-cycle phenomena.

# Chapter 27

# Bonds, Stocks and Funds

But what I'm saying, I guess, is that anybody who thinks that they're smarter than the market, they're the guys who bought Iomega 40 points ago.

*Jim Cramer*

Few other subjects in business have been investigated more closely than how the prices of stocks, bonds and funds behave. It was even a subject of considerable scrutiny by the first economists; we will recall that Law, Cantillon, Thornton and Ricardo all were very active in the market, and with success – Richard Cantillon could perhaps even challenge Warren Buffet for the title of the most financially successful investor of all time. Keynes and Fisher had their ups and downs in the market, but they were certainly very familiar with the subject. And then we had Babson, with his market sequence from *Business Barometers used in the Accumulation of Money*, which is worth repeating here:

1. Increasing money rates
2. Declining bond prices
3. Declining stock prices
4. Declining commodity prices
5. Declining real estate prices
6. Low money rates
7. Increasing bond prices
8. Increasing stock prices
9. Increasing commodity prices
10. Increasing real estate prices

These are the words that Roger Ward Babson wrote *in 1910*, which makes them rather impressive considering that he actually got it very right. But there is much more to these sequences, and neither Babson nor the first economists could know quite as much as we do by now. So let's take a closer look.

---

### FRICTION IN DIFFERENT MARKETS

Carl von Clausewitz used the term "friction" in his *Von Kriege* to describe the complications of executing the generals' plans in the field.

Friction is also present in business, but to very different degrees. One end of the spectrum is financial markets, where dealers and brokers experience very little friction. If you have the necessary trading lines, then you may execute a trade of perhaps USD 100 million in less than one minute. But other markets have much more friction. When a retailer orders his goods, it will usually take days or weeks before they are delivered. Reselling them may take longer. Buying real estate can take months, and selling it in a bad market can take years. Getting capital goods delivered may take years. The differences in friction have an effect on how different markets relate to the business cycle. Having virtually no friction, the financial markets forecast it. Capital goods markets, on the other hand, tend to lag aggregate output.

---

## BONDS

We can start with bonds. There are bonds with short-term maturity (such as three months to three years) and longer-dated bonds (three to 30 years). And then there is the specter from investment grade and junk bonds, where investment grade bonds carry the lower yield, but are issued by more solid institutions. Gold has no yield, but it is, like bonds, a sort of transnational money supply.

There are two good reasons why bond yields fall (and bond prices rise) at the beginning of the cycle: first, there is still much excess capacity after the slowdown, so price competition is fierce, which means little inflation; secondly, central bankers are reducing rates and pumping out money. Junk bonds outperform investment grade in the early to mid cycle because they are perceived as relatively safe when profits are up and economies are firm. Finally, bond yields pick up late in the cycle in anticipation of inflation and monetary contraction.

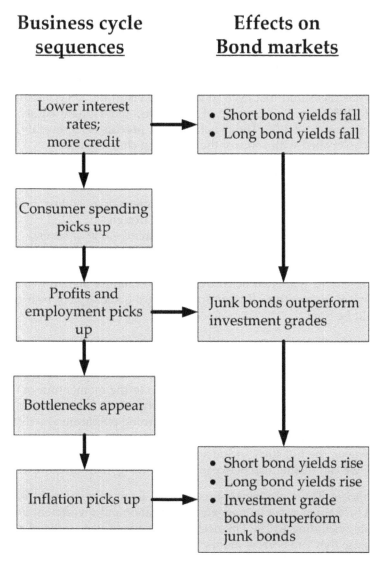

## Business cycle sequences

## Effects on Bond markets

Lower interest rates; more credit

- Short bond yields fall
- Long bond yields fall

Consumer spending picks up

Profits and employment picks up

Junk bonds outperform investment grades

Bottlenecks appear

Inflation picks up

- Short bond yields rise
- Long bond yields rise
- Investment grade bonds outperform junk bonds

**Figure 27.1** Bond market behavior over business cycles.

### EQUITIES

Let's now look at equities, which normally lag bonds on the way up as well as down, as Babson observed. During a cycle of central bank rate tightening, the equity markets tend to start rising rapidly around the time when there is just one tightening left. This will often be close to a phase where there is a financial accident somewhere, which convinces the central bank that enough is enough (or too much). Equities have, on average, peaked some *nine months before a peak in the economy*, and then normally have either gone into a trading range or turned down. Goldman Sachs has measured that cyclical bear markets in the US economy from 1847 to 1982 lasted an average of *23 months*, and brought equity prices *down an average of 30%*. The usual peaking process lasts several months and is associated with some of the following characteristics:

- Prior to the peak there is an acceleration in the upwards trend under large trading volume
- The price pattern violates its previous pattern of ascending peaks and troughs by making a lower peak and/or trough
- There are shock movements against the trend – one or several
- There is lack of breadth as mid and small capitalization equities under-perform the larger ones
- These events will often occur over several months, and all will lead to a loss of momentum. If they don't, then the subsequent bear market could be brief

The behavior is somewhat different at troughs, where equity markets on average turn back up some *five months before the economic trough*. So they are leading indicators at peaks as well as at troughs, but their lead-time is longer at peaks, which may be due to the momentum of capital spending and property construction activity, which can't be terminated very quickly. The price patterns at lower turning points are also different, since they often come as abrupt u-turns that are more difficult to time.

However, the full story includes sector rotation within this asset class, where we can distinguish between the following main categories:

- *Financials*. These are banking, consumer finance, investment banking and brokerage, asset management, insurance and investment and real estate, including REITs. Financials react very early to signs of revival, because they can borrow money at low rates and place it in bonds with a higher yield (this is what we have called a "steep yield curve"). The early signs of revival also see lending activity about to pick up, and non-performing loans peaking
- *Consumer discretionary*. This includes automobiles and components, consumer durables and apparel, hotels, restaurants and leisure, as well as media and retailing. These equities follow on the heels of financials, as consumers are the first to spend in the cycle, since they enjoy low borrowing/mortgage costs. Refinancing of mortgages to lower rates

may be a considerable factor here. Furthermore, they have pent-up savings and desires after an economic slow-down, which can now be released. Finally, many consumer durables seem cheap at this stage

- *Information technology.* This includes software, hardware, IT services and telecommunications. It picks up fairly early in the cycle, lead by consumer electronics and because commercial IT dates and needs replacement even if there is no need yet to increase capacity
- *Industrials.* These are capital goods, commercial services and supplies and transportation. Information technology and industry will initially respond to accelerating consumer demand by running down their inventories, but will later rebuild these, leading to an internal multiplier effect. Furthermore, industrial companies experience increased pricing power as capacity utilization reaches its limits and order backlogs increase
- *Resources.* This category covers chemicals, construction materials, containers and packaging, metals and mining, paper and forest products. Resources outperform late as industry needs to increase its capacity; a process which requires many basic resources
- *Consumer stables.* These are food, drugs, beverages, tobacco, plus household and personal products. These start outperforming late in the cycle almost by default: it's the only sector where demand is reasonably steady. This sector is thus considered defensive, and its most stable parts are those with limited fixed costs, which often are service oriented
- *Utilities.* These are gas, electricity and water. Utilities have (like consumer stables) fairly stable demand for their output. However, utilities have massive financing costs, and they can discount a decrease in these from the time that central banks stop raising rates, which means that they outperform towards the end of the cycle

Common to all equities is that they *discount* future events, which is why most of the arrows in Figure 27.2 point upwards.

## SIZE AND VOLATILITY

Another aspect of equities is the size of the companies. These are normally divided into "small cap" (300 million–2 billion USD market capitalization), "mid cap" (2–10 billion) and "large cap." Small and mid cap perform best during recoveries and expansion, as this brings an appetitite (and room) for new players. Large cap companies overperform during declines, as this squeezes many smaller operators out and forces market consolidation.

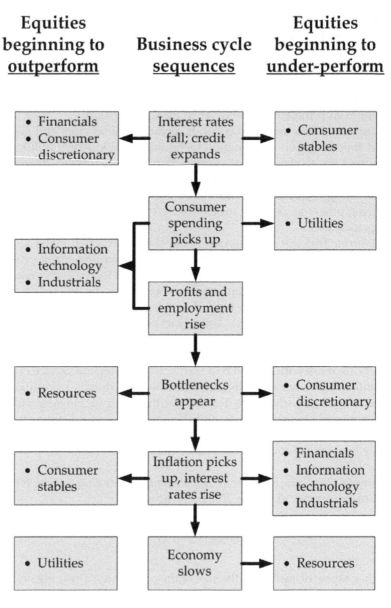

**Figure 27.2**   Equity market behavior over business cycles.

A final aspect about equities is that companies with high fixed costs, or produce capital goods, are small, are associated with commercial real estate or are suppliers for capital spending are particularly volatile.

## HEDGE FUNDS AND PRIVATE EQUITY

The final financial markets to consider are the so-called "alternative investments," which are often subdivided into the categories shown in Table 27.1.

This subdivision of the hedge funds is taken from the *Managed Account Report*, as this structure has been used as the basis for several studies of hedge fund performance in different environments.

## ALTERNATIVE INVESTMENTS AND BUSINESS CYCLES

In 2001, Franklin Edwards and Mustafa Caglayan published a study of how hedge funds had performed during bull and bear markets, and concluded that only three hedge fund categories had given investors protection during bear markets: macro, market neutral and event driven. It makes intuitive sense that macro funds should do well in bear markets, since their managers should maintain a high focus on business cycles and early signs of overall deterioration in market conditions. It also seems logical that market neutral funds perform fine in bear markets: these tend to reveal weaknesses of many companies which can be utilized by short selling. As for event-driven hedge funds, it is clear that bear markets provide many investment opportunities, but performance will obviously depend on whether they go into the decline with a portfolio full of cash or full of distress assets.

Another, more recent, study from 2003 (Capocci, Corhay and Hübner), was interesting because it included performance during the great meltdown from the spring of 2000. Their study, which covered the performance of 2894 hedge funds from 1994 to 2002, showed the average returns listed in Table 27.2.

The best performance numbers are highlighted in bold. A general observation is that the average of all funds did far better in the bull market than in the bear market, but most made money in both market phases, which is the whole point of hedge funds.

A third interesting study is a Masters thesis by Isariya Sinlapapreechar from 2003, which found that equity hedge funds and market neutral funds

**Table 27.1** Overview of categories of hedge funds and private equity funds.

| Hedge funds | Private equity |
|---|---|
| • *Event-driven funds* follow strategies that are independent of overall market direction. The events might, for instance, be mergers, takeovers, bankruptcies or the issuance of securities<br>• *Distressed securities* funds buy distressed equities and/or bonds. They will usually participate actively in restructuring, and may convert debt to equity<br>• *Risk arbitrage funds* mainly attempt to exploit pricing discounts arising from takeover bids<br>• *Global emerging funds* specialize in emerging markets. Short selling is often difficult in these markets, which means that the exposure mainly tends to be long<br>• *Global international funds* concentrate on economic change around the world and pick stocks in favored markets. They make less use of derivatives than macro funds<br>• *Global established funds* look for opportunities in established markets. They may specialize in growth, small cap or value, for instance<br>• *Global macro funds* trade in a wide range of derivative instruments in reflection of global economic changes<br>• *Market neutral funds* trade long and short positions to achieve an average position that is close to market neutral. They may specialize in pure arbitrage, diverse long/short exposure or mortgage backed securities<br>• *Sector funds* specialize in specific sectors<br>• *Short-seller funds* short overvalued equities<br>• *Funds of funds* invest in multiple hedge funds. Some have a diversified approach, while other specialize | • *Venture capital* invests in start-up companies anywhere from initial financing to last financing before an exit is in sight. Most start-ups have mediocre or poor performance, but those that succeed may provide outstanding returns<br>• *Buy-out funds* buy all or controlling parts of companies. These may be private or listed companies. The funds will often rationalize, strip or merge these companies before seeking an exit. Purchase motives may be that the companies are mismanaged, have unrealized potential or are grossly undervalued<br>• *Mezzanine funds* will typically provide loans to companies that are too small to issue bonds and too risky to obtain the necessary bank financing. The mezzanine loan provider will normally have an equity "kicker", which gives them an opportunity to purchase shares in the lender. This means that they receive current income and may get an upside |

**Table 27.2** Hedge fund behavior over business cycles. Source: Capocci, Corhay and Hübner, 2003.

| Hedge fund category | Mean monthly return | |
|---|---|---|
| | Bull market | Bear market |
| Event-driven; distressed securities | 1.23 | 0.25 |
| Event-driven; risk arbitrage | 1.27 | 0.37 |
| Global established | 1.96 | −0.21 |
| Global international | 1.30 | −0.08 |
| Global emerging | 1.57 | 0.27 |
| Macro | 1.10 | 0.19 |
| Market neutral | 1.18 | 0.71 |
| Long only leveraged | 1.83 | −1.17 |
| Sector | 2.56 | 0.38 |
| Short sales | 0.39 | 1.99 |

did particularly well during bullish months, whereas market neutral and arbitrage-oriented funds did well during bearish months. And, of course, short sellers got hammered in bull markets and made bundles when markets went down.

The overall impression of these studies has to be tempered a bit by the knowledge of what really happened over these years. A brilliant performance of emerging market hedge funds after 2000 can be explained easily by specific market factors, for instance. What seems most clear is that the following hedge fund categories are likely to do best during *equity bull markets*, in order of performance:

- Sector-specific funds (that capture the specific key theme of any given bull market)
- Long only hedge funds
- Equity hedge funds (global, emerging market, international, established)
- Event-driven funds
- Market neutral funds

As for *equity bear markets*, the best performers seem to be:

- Short sellers (no surprise here!)
- Market neutral funds
- Event-driven funds
- Macro funds

Private equity funds are more difficult to study than hedge funds; partly because there are less of them, and partly because they tend to disclose NAV on a quarterly, rather than monthly, basis, and these numbers may be rather subjective, since they invest in non-listed entities. However, what does seem clear from various studies is that private equity companies generally perform best if they have been founded during periods of economic weakness, when these investments were rare. There can be four good reasons for this:

- Less competition for good deals
- More time to perform due diligence
- Lack of immediate exit opportunities would force them to be more selective with their investment choices
- Lower valuations at entry point

There may be a slight difference in the optimal market timing, though. Buy-out funds tend to thrive during crises, where they can make investments at attractive valuations and perhaps buy from distressed sellers. Mezzanine funds have a balanced exposure to fixed income, equity kickers and default risks, and their performance is less tied to the business cycle. And finally, venture capital funds will typically hope that other investors will follow their lead, but at gradually higher valuation levels. This means that their optimal entry point may be at the beginning of economic revival.

Exits are another matter. All three fund categories will be able to seek exits at high prices during booms. We can summarize their relative performance using Table 27.3.

It should be noted that investors can't jump in and out of existing private equity funds at will. Most of these funds will require approval of their investors, and an investor who wants to enter an existing private equity fund during an emerging bull market may only be able to do so if he can find someone else who wants to leave, and if the fund approves the change of ownership of the shares.

**Table 27.3**   Private equity fund performance over business cycles.

|                  | Best entry point | Best exit point |
| ---------------- | ---------------- | --------------- |
| Venture capital  | Early revival    | Boom            |
| Buy-out          | Recession        | Boom            |
| Mezzanine        | Neutral          | Boom            |

### EFFECTS OF A RISE IN OIL PRICES ON DIFFERENT BUSINESS SECTORS

Significant changes in oil prices can hurt the earnings of some companies while helping others. Table 27.4 shows which companies typically will benefit and which will suffer from higher oil prices.

**Table 27.4**  The winners and losers when oil prices rise.

| Positive effects | Negative effects |
|---|---|
| • Crude oil producers | • Airlines |
| • Oil services and equipment | • Aluminum smelters |
| • Coal mines | • Amusement parks |
| • Natural gas suppliers | • Boat manufacturers |
| • Railroads | • Car leasing |
| • Solar power providers | • Car manufacturers |
| • Nuclear power providers | • Cement manufacturers |
| • Biomass energy providers | • Ceramic manufacturers |
| • Hydro power companies | • Fast food operators |
| • Energy conservation companies | • Glass manufacturers |
| • Public transportation companies | • Home builders |
| | • Hotels |
| | • Land developers |
| | • Petrochemical plants |
| | • Plane makers |
| | • Tire manufacturers |
| | • Truck manufacturers |
| | • Toll highways |

### FINANCIAL LIQUIDITY AND BULL MARKETS

A bull market is often preceded by an increase in financial liquidity. Some of the early indicators can be:

• High or increasing time saving deposits
• High or increasing broker's cash accounts
• High or increasing broker's security loans
• High or increasing mutual funds' cash/asset ratio
• High or rising debit/loan ratio
• High net free bank reserves
• Falling velocity of money

Interestingly, the financial bull markets do not absorb liquidity; it would be more correct to say that they create it. Whenever someone buys a financial asset, someone else has sold it, and as prices go up, the perception of wealth increases, which will drive acceleration of velocity of money.

*Chapter* **28**

# The World's Biggest Market: Foreign Exchange

Blaming speculators as a response to financial crises goes back at least to the Greeks. It's almost always the wrong response.

*Larry Summers*

While bonds and stocks are huge markets, they are dwarfed by currencies. Foreign exchange ("forex") trades can normally be executed within 10–15 seconds, even if the amount is 100 million dollars or more. There have been numerous studies of this market, and most indicate that the global volume had reached two trillion dollars a day by 2005, equaling some 770 trillion dollars a year. That's rather a lot, of course, since most people in the world hardly trade a single dollar in their entire lives. Divide two trillion by a global population of 6.5 billion, and we get just over 300 dollars *a day* in foreign exchange trading. That's just over 110 000 dollars a year per capita. Compare that to a global GDP per capita of 6300 dollars, and we get the picture: forex trading is almost 20 times bigger than GDP.

It takes many forms. The most common is swaps, where you can trade any two of a very large number of currencies against each other intraday or with maturity at just about any date in the future – at least up to a few years out. Other forms of forex trading can be futures and options. The positions taken can be based on an expected change in exchange rates, and this is often called a *spot trade* (even though the term also means an intraday trade). It can also be to enjoy a difference between a low interest rate in the currency that is being sold and a high one on the bought currency; this is called a *carry trade*. There are also numerous ways to trade for anticipated changes in volatility, even if you don't have an idea which direction your exchange rate movements will take; this is called *trading volatility*.

The academic community has made numerous studies to make sense of currency price movements, and while they may find some traces of system to it, many end up scratching their heads quite a lot. The reason is that relative movements in two currencies can reflect a very wide range of variables, such as differentials in:

- Productivity
- Government spending
- Current account balances
- Interest rates
- Purchasing power parities
- Economic growth rates
- Direct investments
- Portfolio flows
- Psychology
- Risk hedging activity
- Import prices
- Export prices
- Central bank interventions

Some of this can seem very messy to a statistical analyst. Central banks, for example, will often try to be as unpredictable as they can when they intervene. There is also a fair amount of psychology involved, and this just doesn't behave well in quantitative academic research. However, there are two aspects of foreign exchange behavior that we can identify clearly, and which are related closely to business cycles:

- Central banks raise rates late in expansion phases of cycles, and this tends to pull the currency upwards against others that are not in the same situation. This is an inflation/interest link
- Some countries with large commodity production have currencies that tend to fluctuate with the global commodity cycles – some of which are linked directly to business cycles

These are core observations. Let's study the inflation/interest rate link first.

### THE INFLATION/INTEREST LINK

Swap agreements in the forex market have a spot price and a forward price. The spot is the relationship between the prices of the two currencies traded here and now. However, the forward rate is adjusted for the differences in the interest rates of the two currencies, and this rate is virtually always different from the spot. Let's say that you sell a low interest rate currency against another which has higher rates. You may, for instance, sell 10 million US dollars (USD) against Brazilian real (BRL). This may appear as "–10 USD/BRL" on a trading slip. The forward price would then appear as what a commodity trader would call "contango", because it would be higher than the spot price. The structure of forward rates in forex swaps is not really in contango or backwardation, though, because there is no special risk assessment and estimate of future prices built into the forward price. It is much more mechanical: the forward price adjustment is simply a precise reflection of differences in interest rates of the two currencies – nothing else.

Let's take the example with our trader again. He has sold dollars forward and gets a forward price that is higher than the spot price. Perhaps substantially higher if the difference in interest rates is large. This means that he is certain that he will make money if the currency prices don't move until his swap matures. He will make even more money if the Brazilian real rises. And he may make money if it falls too, as long as it doesn't fall more than what he earns on the interest rate differentials. These odds are so compelling that traders have a considerable urge to buy currencies with unusually high interest rates.

That is actually what central bankers mostly hope for. Whilst long-term interest rates are fixed by the market, the short-term rates are controlled by central banks. If a central bank raises short rates, then it is because it is concerned about inflation. Now, if speculators enter the scene and buy the currency, then it will tend to appreciate, which will make import prices fall and dampen activity in the export sector. Both effects will help central bankers achieve what they want, which is to flush out inflation.

So how strongly do forex markets react to changes in monetary policy? In 2005, Jonathan Kearns and Phil Manners of Reserve Bank of Australia published a study of this question (*The Impact of Monetary Policy on the Exchange Rate: A Study Using Intraday Data*). The report, which covered data that spanned from 1993 to 2004 for Australia, Canada, New Zealand and the United Kingdom, led to the following conclusion:

> The results indicate that the exchange rate appreciates on average by around $1\frac{1}{2}$ per cent in response to an unanticipated 100 basis point increase in the policy interest rate. The estimates for individual countries range from 1.0–1.8 per cent. For a 25 basis point surprise this equates to an average appreciation of 0.35 per cent ($\frac{1}{4}$–$\frac{1}{2}$ of a per cent for individual countries).

Numerous other studies have confirmed this general relationship between interest rates and forex prices. Forex markets discount many interest rate changes in advance, but when they are caught by surprise, they react immediately by bidding up currency prices when interest rates go up, and vice versa. The result is that a local currency becomes a lagger in the local business cycle: it tends to rise late in its cycle and often also for a time after activity has peaked. Exchange rate movements are consequently closely tied to business cycles.

## COMMODITY CURRENCIES IN BUSINESS CYCLES

The second very strong link between currencies and business cycles relates to commodity-producing economies. The three main so-called "commodity currencies" are Australian dollars (AUD), New Zealand dollars (NZD) and Canadian dollars (CAD). Table 28.1 is a list of the

**Table 28.1** Selected contributors to composition of non-energy price indices for Australia, New Zealand and Canada, based on average world market prices in USD 1972–2001 (calculation of Canadian numbers begins from 1972, Australian from 1983 and New Zealand from 1986; all end in Q2, 2001). These selected numbers show that Australia specializes primarily in soft commodities and metals, whereas New Zealand is particularly strong in foods and Canada in wood products. Source: Chen and Rogoff, 2002.

|  |  | Australia | New Zealand | Canada |
|---|---|---|---|---|
| Soft | Cotton | 3.4 | | |
| commodities | Rice | 0.8 | | |
| | Sugar | 5.9 | | |
| | Wheat | 13.5 | | 8.9 |
| | Wool | 18.3 | | |
| | Beef | 9.2 | 9.4 | 9.8 |
| | Dairy products | | 21.5 | |
| | Lamb | | 12.5 | |
| Industrials | Aluminum | 9.1 | 8.3 | 4.8 |
| | Copper | 3.2 | | 4.7 |
| | Lead | 1.3 | | |
| | Zinc | 1.8 | | 4.4 |
| | Iron ore | 10.9 | | |
| | Nickel | 2.6 | | 3.9 |
| | Lumber, logs, sawn timber, pulp, newsprint | | 11.2 | 47.5 |

average percentage value of some of the most important non-energy production items from each of these countries from 1972 to 2001.

These numbers show that New Zealand is heavily geared towards *agricultural products*, whereas Australia and Canada are fairly strong on *industrial commodities*, which we know relate to the business cycle. Another area is energy production, where Australia and (in particular) Canada are both large producers, whereas New Zealand absolutely is not. Since we now have a feel for what these countries do in terms of commodities, we can move on to the conclusion from the study:

> The world prices of commodity exports, measured in real US dollars, do appear to have a strong and stable influence on the real exchange rates of New Zealand and Australia. For Canada the relationship is less robust...

Two comments are relevant here. The first is that there is a close currency link between Australia and New Zealand, and it is possible that the latter's currency simply is being dragged around by the former. The second comment is that this study was completed in 2002, and the Canadian dollar advanced aggressively (as did Australian and New Zealand

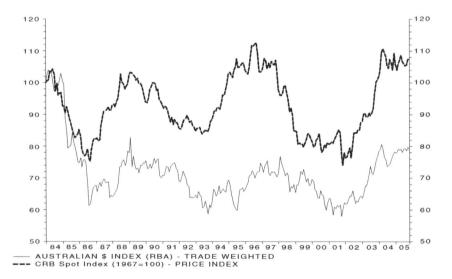

**Figure 28.1** Correlation between the Australian dollar exchange rate index and CRB commodity price index 1984–2005. The chart shows a clear correlation between the prices of the Australian dollar and this index of commodity prices. Source: Thomson Datastream. Reproduced by permission.

NEW ZEALAND $ INDEX 1990=100 (BOE) - TRADE WEIGHTED
CRB Spot Index (1967=100) - PRICE INDEX

**Figure 28.2**   Correlation between the New Zealand dollar exchange rate index and CRB commodity price index 1985–2005. The correlation seems even more clear than that for Australian dollars in Figure 28.1. Source: Thomson Datastream. Reproduced by permission.

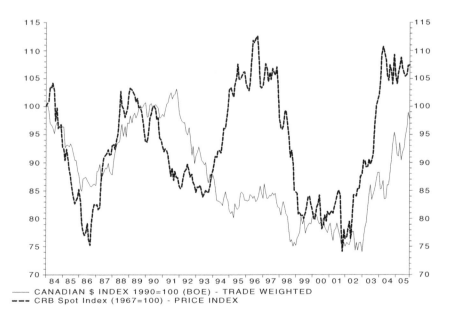

CANADIAN $ INDEX 1990=100 (BOE) - TRADE WEIGHTED
CRB Spot Index (1967=100) - PRICE INDEX

**Figure 28.3**   Correlation between the Canadian dollar exchange rate index and CRB commodity price index 1984–2005. The correlation was weak during 1995–97, but otherwise very strong. Source: Thomson Datastream. Reproduced by permission.

dollars) as commodity prices rose after 2002. A study including these years would have shown a stronger correlation for Canadian dollars.

There are two more studies that we should mention. In 2002, Cashin, Cěspedes and Sahay from the International Monetary Fund published a working paper with investigation of how the currencies from 58 countries with large commodity exports related to commodity prices. They applied fairly restrictive criteria for defining a relationship, but found nevertheless that 22 countries had strong, statistical correlation with commodity prices. So strong, in fact, that more than 80% of their movements could be linked to fluctuations in commodity prices. The 22 currencies included Australia, but the rest were currencies of small countries that are rarely traded by speculators. Neither Canada nor New Zealand was included. However, this study was also completed before the great run-up in commodity prices and commodity producers' currencies after 2002.

We can perhaps fill a bit of this gap by looking at a study conducted by RBC Capital Markets for the period 2002 to November 2004. It concluded that the New Zealand dollar had a particularly high correlation with the ANZ commodity index, which is very focused on agricultural products and has no energy component, whereas Australian and Canadian dollars were mainly tied to base metals, which of course makes them interesting from a business cycle perspective. Table 28.2 shows some of the specific correlation coefficients for the two-year period, where positive correlations over 0.70 are highlighted in italics.

The table shows high correlations between NZD and the agriculturally focused ANZ index. Furthermore, all currencies have very high correlation with copper, nickel and the CRB base metals index, which ties them firmly to capital spending and property cycles. The correlation with aluminum is a bit weaker, which may be explained by the fact that a fair amount of aluminum consumption is for cans and other consumer stable packaging, which isn't particularly cyclical.

**Table 28.2** Correlations between commodity currency performance and selected commodities and commodity indices. Source: RBC Capital Markets, 2004.

|  | Australian dollars (AUD/USD) | New Zealand dollars (NZD/USD) | Canadian dollars (CAD/USD) |
|---|---|---|---|
| ANZ index | 0.52 | *0.82* | 0.64 |
| CRB base metals index | *0.83* | *0.83* | *0.81* |
| Copper | *0.77* | *0.76* | *0.73* |
| Aluminum | 0.67 | *0.71* | 0.64 |
| Nickel | *0.90* | *0.89* | *0.88* |

## TRADING FOREX

There exist an abundance of forex trading strategies, of course, but two are very closely related to longer-term business cycle movements. The first is to shift focus to commodity currencies as capital spending- and property-driven business cycles move towards the late stages of expansion. The second is an approach to forex, bonds and equities. It will often make sense to take the following rotation:

- Early expansion: buy bonds and equities, hedge (sell) the currency
- Late expansion: sell bonds, keep equity, and then sell that too. Close currency hedge and buy the currency when central bank starts raising rates
- Early decline: stay out of bonds and equities (or trade the short side). Stay long the currency for as long as the central bank is raising rates or until you think there is only one hike left
- Late decline: short the currency; buy bonds and then also equities

This sounds simple, of course, so perhaps it is appropriate to quote what Warren Buffet once said:

"Investment is simple, but not easy."

# Chapter 29

# Business Cycles and Market Rotation

Finance is the art of passing money around from hand to hand until it finally disappears

*Robert W. Sarnoff*

We have now studied each of the major asset classes and their behavior over business cycles, and also how business cycles in themselves play out. We have looked at inventory cycles, capital investment cycles and property cycles, and concluded that these are the three phenomena that matter most. So now is the time to add it all together. This is complex, so here is what we will do: we will make a few gross simplifications of business cycle theory and of financial markets, and then describe a perfect scenario where all dynamics follow their historical averages. They won't, of course, so what we will aim for is a *reference model*, not a forecast.

## SEVEN DRIVERS OF CYCLES

Our first simplification is particularly gross. We will simply bundle all business cycle models that ever made sense into just seven groups, which we will give our own names. The first group of these seven is the central bank action that triggers strategic change:

- *Monetary accelerator.* A monetary expansion happens when real rates go below natural rates (Wicksell) and/or money supply increases above trend. This leads to optimism, activity, asset appreciation, and therefore also (after a delay) to acceleration in the velocity of money (Cantillon, Thornton, Friedman, etc.)

We are now calling this an "accelerator" because it contains the seeds of its own amplification, as expansion of money supply leads to events that drive up velocity of money and perceptions of wealth. The next four groups, which we will also call "accelerators", are those major, non-monetary phenomena that can drive economies forward in cyclical movements:

- *Inventory accelerator.* Low inventories induce companies to order more. This creates increased overall growth, which means more sales, which further depletes inventories (Metzler, Abramowitz, Kitchin, etc.)
- *Capital spending accelerator.* Bottlenecks in mature expansions force companies to build more capacity (Aftalion, Clark, Juglar, etc.). This creates more growth, which means that they have to build even more capacity
- *Collateral accelerator.* Rising asset prices (von Mises, von Hayek, Schumpeter, Minsky, Kindleberger, etc.) create added collateral value. This enables more borrowing, which stimulates business, which is good for asset prices (Bernanke, Gertler and Gilchrist, etc.). This has the largest impact when it happens in property markets (Hoyt, Burns, etc.), but is also significant in equities
- *Emotional accelerator.* Rising asset prices will, at a given stage, capture the imagination of unskilled investors, which leads to momentum investments and bubbles (Tversky, Kahneman, Shiller, Thaler, Staman, etc.)

The sixth of our phenomena is the inherent tendency for the economy to finally reach turning points:

- *Exhaustion phenomena.* A boom creates bottlenecks in labor, physical resources and credit, which eventually make further growth in private spending impossible and new business unprofitable (Hawtrey, Tugan-Baranovsky, Kassel, Hobson, Catchings, Foster, Pigou, Keynes, etc.)

All of the six clusters of phenomena described above can work in reverse as well. However, we need to add one final cluster of phenomena, which only plays out during deep recessions/depressions, and this one is nasty:

- *Credit crunch.* Significant contractions may lead to debt deflation and/or liquidity traps (Fisher, Minsky, Kindleberger, Keynes, etc.)

So this is it; a grossly simplified model driven by just seven economic phenomena – incomplete, but not *entirely* without merit.

## CYCLE DURATION

Our next assumption is that business cycles always behave like they do on average:

- Each and every inventory cycle lasts 4.5 years
- Every capital spending cycle takes nine years
- Every property cycle is completed in 18 years
- These cycles synchronize into a neat pattern with four inventory cycles and two capital spending cycles within each real estate cycle . . .
- . . . so that peaks and troughs coincide when possible

This is crude too, but not completely insane, since the *average* length of these cycles has actually been remarkably robust over time and across economies, and since there really is an inherent tendency for peaks and troughs to align (Schumpeter, Forrester, Mosekilde, etc.).

These are simple assumptions about the economy. We also need to make a few simple statements about how and why people invest, because that will lead us to one significant conclusion about almost all investment.

## WHY PEOPLE INVEST

Let's take the motives first, beginning with assets that are predominantly bought for *commercial reasons*, as shown in Table 29.1.

Let's take the pecuniary motives first, beginning with assets that are predominantly bought for *commercial returns*, as shown in Table 29.1. These motives are, as we can see from the table, combinations of currents yields, commercial scarcity and backwardation.

The rest of the assets in our inquiry, residential property, collectibles, precious metals and diamonds in jewelry, are mainly bought for none-commercial reasons; they are meant for *personal pleasure*. The predominant investment motive seems here to be affordability. People will buy these items when they think they can afford them.

## THE ROLE OF INTEREST RATES

So if some assets are bought to make money and others for personal pleasure, is there any common theme in how they all are priced? There is one: Interest rates have a unique role in determining the price across all of these

**Table 29.1** Commercial motives for investing in different asset classes/investment vehicles.

| Investment category | Motives for buying | Main investment criteria |
|---|---|---|
| Bonds | Net income | Ratio of yield to expected inflation |
| Currency deposits/ forwards | Net income | Ratio of yield to expected inflation, expected relative growth, balance of payments |
| Equities | Net income | Ratio of forward P/E (price to earnings) ratios to bond yields |
| Hedge funds | Net income | Ratio of expected yield to equity yields and/or inflation |
| Private equity | Net income | Ratio of expected yield to equity yields and/or inflation |
| Commercial property | Net income, utility | Ratio of CAP rates to bond yields |
| Industrial metals | Utility, scarcity | Estimate future scarcity and inflation, add normal backwardation and compare it all to bond and equity yields |
| Precious metals futures | Security, hedge of unanticipated inflation | Backwardation and ratio of interest rates to expected inflation |

asset classes. Falling interest rates and low real interest rates have a strong, positive influence of the pricing of each and every of these asset classes. Money rates and bond yields drive residential property markets, because they drive their affordability, and this leads to private wealth gains, which again drive prices in jewelry and collectibles. Furthermore, bonds drives equity markets because interest rates are used as the discount factors for future earnings. Bonds also drive economic activity, which drives everything. All of this is illustrated in Figure 29.1.

## THE PRINCIPLE OF BUBBLE ROTATION

There is one further common aspect of all these asset classes. We have seen that business cycles from time to time create monetary environments that are conductive to asset bubbles. However, people will recall past crashes for a while, and this means that whatever asset people bought in the last bubble will rarely be chosen for the next. This leads to a systematic bubble rotation. There was bubble in precious metals/diamonds in 1980, for instance, and then in collectibles (and Japanese land) in 1990, and then in equities in 2000.

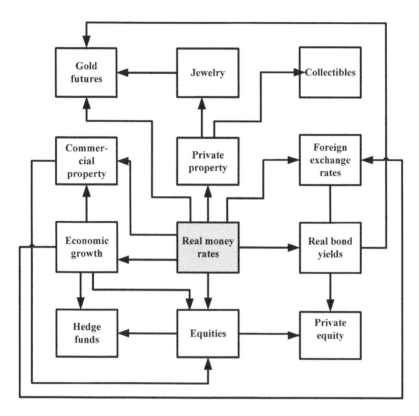

**Figure 29.1** The role of real money rates in asset valuation.

PERFORMANCE OF VARIOUS ASSET CLASSES IN DIFFERENT
GROWTH/INFLATION SCENARIOS

In 2005, Barclays published a study of how different asset classes had
performed in the UK market from WWII to 2004, dividing these 60
years into four categories as shown in Table 29.2. They then measured
how different asset classes had performed in each of the different
scenarios. Here are the results (where the performance for property
and commodities is measured from 1970 to 2004); the best categories
within each scenario are highlighted with *italics*:

This study showed, as one would expect, that the performance of
physical assets (art, property and commodities) depended mainly on
economic growth, whereas the performance of equities depended
strongly on the absence of inflation.

**Table 29.2** Performance of different asset classes in the UK to 2004. Source: Barclay's Bank, 2004.

|  | High inflation | | Low inflation | |
|---|---|---|---|---|
| **High growth** | | | | |
|  | Equities: | 4.4% | *Equities:* | *13.4%* |
|  | Bonds: | −0.2% | Bonds: | 0.1% |
|  | Cash: | −0.4% | Cash: | 2.0% |
|  | *Art:* | *9.2%* | *Art:* | *7.5%* |
|  | *Property:* | *8.1%* | *Property:* | *11.0%* |
|  | *Commodities:* | *6.1%* | *Commodities:* | *15.1%* |
| **Low growth** | | | | |
|  | *Equities:* | *4.1%* | *Equities:* | *11.1%* |
|  | Bonds: | −0.8% | Bonds: | 0.0% |
|  | Cash: | 0.7% | Cash: | 2.2% |
|  | Art: | 0.3% | Art: | 0.9% |
|  | Property: | −4.2% | Property: | 4.7% |
|  | *Commodities:* | *2.8%* | Commodities: | 3.2% |

That's it. So here we are with our super-simple model, like the economic steam machine we talked about in Chapter 21: a machine that follows a few easy rules, screams and squeaks, and sends different assets up and down in a never-ending pattern. Let's now imagine that we fill the boiler with coal, fire it up and set it to start at the point, where the positions of its pistons and rising and falling weights would correspond to the bottom of a depression. Where it would correspond, in other words, to the situation where cycles in inventory, capital spending and properties have all reached their troughs simultaneously. Clonk, squeak, clonk . . . here we go.

## New Dawn

The expansion has just begun, but there have actually been early fore-warnings. Remember the four "long leading indicators" in Chapter 22? These were bond prices, real money supply, new building permits and the ratio of prices to unit labor costs, and they began rising some eight months before our first pick-up in GDP. The other leading indicators have also turned up, but some of them just a few months before activity.

We are now still at the very early phase of expansion, and people have been concerned about employment for a while, so they have held back their spending. Unemployment is high, but the overwhelming majority is still working, and their savings are actually piling up. So there is lots of cash on the sidelines, loans have gotten cheaper, and some are therefore beginning to spend a bit again. Sales volume of residential real estate is rising rapidly, and property prices start ticking gently upwards soon after.

The equity markets are also rising, and much faster than property prices. They had been hammered at the beginning of the downturn, and it is now dawning on the smartest investors that many of these shares are completely underpriced. Some of the listed companies are running losses, partly because they are talking huge write-offs, but you can calculate how they will do when their revenues pick up ("normalized earnings"), and the result would justify much, much higher share prices. So smart investors buy; chasing up, in particular, consumer discretionary, financials and information technology. Our *monetary accelerator* is clearly kicking in now, as velocity of money rises.

Property prices, meanwhile, are continuing upwards, and homeowners refinance their mortgages at lower rates, while booking profits on the financial portfolios. Consumer confidence rises and more people head for the shops – and for the car dealers. Prices of aluminum and lead – two

**Table 29.3** Economic characteristics of a typical inventory cycle (Kitchin cycle).

*Duration and amplitude:*
- Average duration is 4.5 years and has fairly high regularity
- Decline phase averages 6–9 months
- Amplitude is limited. Many of the declines do not become recessions, only "growth cycle" downturns

*Main drivers:*
- Inventories, which average around 6% of annual GDP
- A disproportionate part of inventories is durable goods, which fluctuate more than services and stables. Inventories of cars and car parts play a significant role

*Key theoretical concepts:*
- Inventory cycles
- Beer-game phenomena
- Hog cycle/cobweb/ship-building cycles

*Disruptive effects:*
- Very limited

*Positive effects:*
- Eliminate inflation problems

*Key indicators:*
- General: composite leading indicators, short- and long-term interest rates, yield curve
- Specific: inventories

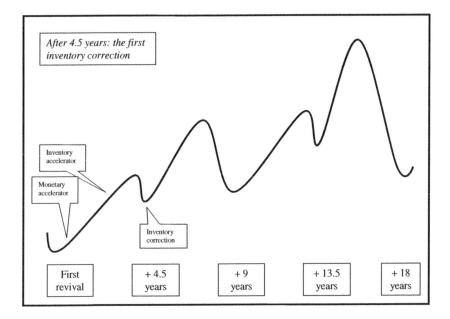

**Figure 29.2**   The first inventory cycle in the multi-cycle reference model.

metals widely used in cars – pick up. This is also a golden opportunity for most hedge fund managers, as they see that value propositions abound and can trade with the strong momentum.

## THE FIRST PROBLEMS

The surge in demand takes some companies by surprise, as their inventories dwindle. They respond by ordering more to rebuild normal inventory levels, and this activity feeds yet more growth: our *inventory accelerator* is coming into play. Companies are still sitting on considerable spare capacity, and can meet this new demand with their existing workforce. This enables them to boost revenues without adding much cost; their profits surge dramatically. Furthermore, companies that have been suffering throughout the recession finally feel that they have a bit of pricing power, and so a wave of price hikes hits the economy. The central bank watches this with considerable concern, however, so they decide to take the foot off the speeder. And then they hit the brakes: they raise rates and our *monetary accelerator* goes into reverse after a while.

Some investors get concerned too. Bonds peak out and start falling modestly. This happens at approximately the same time that companies reach satisfactory inventory levels, and the deceleration of inventory creates ripples through the economy, which slows down for a while: our *inventory accelerator* has gone into reverse.

It has now been 4.5 years since the expansion started. Hedge funds are struggling, since the market is correcting in a complicated, choppy fashion and refusing to settle into a clear bear market trend.

## NEW REVIVAL

All of this has one very positive effect, though: it brings inflation back under control within a matter of months. Central banks see that core CPI (consumer price inflation) is falling below their target rate, and as the PMI (purchasing managers' index) goes below the neutral reading of 50, they decide that enough is enough and go on hold. Six months later they start easing. Bonds turn up again, with equities following right on their tail, and we haven't even seen proof of the new, economic revival before stock markets reach new highs. Residential property prices rise again as people take advantage of the new fall in mortgage rates. Our first *inventory cycle* is complete.

## THE CAPITAL INVESTMENT CYCLE

The inventory cycle is real enough, but it doesn't amount to very much when compared to the *capital investment* cycle. Pure inventory cycles leave, for instance, very little impact on gold, diamonds, private equity and collectibles, which is why they are not included in Table 29.4. However, our steam machine is still running, and while the first inventory cycle has played out, there has been a slow, but significant, change in one key indicator: *capacity utilization* has gradually been moving upwards.

This is important. Although capacity utilization stalled during the brief decline of the inventory cycle, companies have largely been able to meet demand by using their existing capacity plus asking their staff to run faster – or by hiring more. They have used much of what they have earned to improve their balance sheets after the deep recession that ended 4.5 years before. Banks have written down all their bad debts, and companies have paid down their loans to levels that are now better than safe.

**Table 29.4** Typical asset price behavior over inventory cycles.

| | Early expansion | Late expansion | Early decline | Late decline |
|---|---|---|---|---|
| Bond yields | Falling (bond prices rising). Junk bonds outperform | Reaching trough and then rising modestly | Rising. Investment grade outperforms | Declining modestly |
| Currency | Stable or modestly falling | Begins to rise modestly | Rises modestly | Falls |
| Equities overall | Rise rapidly, but with a time lag after bonds | Rise steadily, then peak and fall modestly | Fall briefly, then rise again as inflation declines and long leading indicators rise | Rise |
| Equity sectors | *Overperformers:* Financials, consumer, information technology, small caps | *Overperformers:* Industrials | *Overperformers:* Consumer stables, utilities, large caps | *Overperformers:* Financials, consumer, information technology, small caps |
| | *Underperformers:* Consumer stables and utilities, large caps | *Underperformers:* Financials | *Underperformers:* Consumer discretionary, information technology, small caps | *Underperformers:* Consumer stables, utilities and industrials |

| | Perform very well | Perform well | Perform relatively poorly | Perform modestly |
|---|---|---|---|---|
| Hedge funds overall | | | | |
| Best performing hedge funds | Sector-specific funds, long only, equity hedge, event-driven and market neutral | Sector-specific funds, long only, equity hedge, event-driven, market neutral | Short sellers, market neutral, event-driven, macro | Sector-specific funds, long only, equity hedge, event-driven and market neutral |
| Property overall | Rises | Rises | Stagnates | Rises |
| Property overperformance | Apartments, Single-family homes | Retail property, full-service hotels, residential land, parking, downtown office, commercial land | Suburban office, R&D flex, industrial warehouses, | 2nd tier regional malls, factory outlets |
| Commodities overall | Stagnating | Rising modestly | Rising | Falling |
| Commodity outperformance | Lead | Copper, zinc, nickel, aluminum, lead | Copper | |

Perhaps so safe, in fact, that shareholders start asking why they don't invest more in their future. And so more and more companies decide to do exactly that: they begin to invest more in R&D, and also in new production capacity. This wave of investments triggers the *capital spending accelerator*, as companies sell production capacity to each other.

The increase in capital spending is extremely welcome in the commercial real estate sector, which has hitherto remained stubbornly slow. Rentals are now improving, and vacancy rates in the best offices (downtown) fall from medium to almost nothing, and some new tenants have to settle for the less attractive suburban offices. Industrial property is also picking up now, as new capacity is being built.

Capacity building is at this point taking over from consumer spending as the main driver of overall growth, and shares in companies providing the latest technology are rising smartly. Then they accelerate upwards into more determined buying, and then frenzy, and then perhaps mania: the *emotional accelerator* has kicked in. Wealth is now growing rapidly and assets are used as collateral for loans: our *collateral accelerator* is at work. And so is the *monetary accelerator*, as velocity of money accelerates and business invents new forms of credit to meet soaring demand.

Market share is now the key priority in most companies, and a wave of mergers and acquisitions follows. Meanwhile, metals and mining producers find it hard to keep up the pace and react by raising their prices, whilst they prepare for new production capacity. It will take several years before most of that capacity is effective, though. Copper, aluminum and lead do well here, and zinc and nickel may do even better; there is, after all, a lot of this stuff in engineering applications, wires, chemical industry plumbing, etc. Hedge fund managers thrive, since they see soaring earnings and firm, tradable trends. So do private equity funds, which can exit many of their investments at excellent, if not exorbitant, prices. And gold, diamonds and collectibles? They are doing very well indeed, thank you.

Business is generally very good now, and our inventory accelerator is again contributing to the party. But a problem is gradually emerging: costs seem to be spiraling everywhere. Commercial property rental is getting more expensive, for instance, as lease agreements come up for renegotiation. Companies are also, for the first time, experiencing serious wage pressure for many categories of skilled labor, as they steal the best people from each other by offering them ever more additional benefits. Demand is high, but supply is tight, so whereas corporate top line growth is fine, the bottom line begins to lag behind: our *exhaustion phenomena* are emerging. This is the point where central bankers get worried and start raising rates. Bonds go into decline. Industrial metals are still rising for a while longer, though.

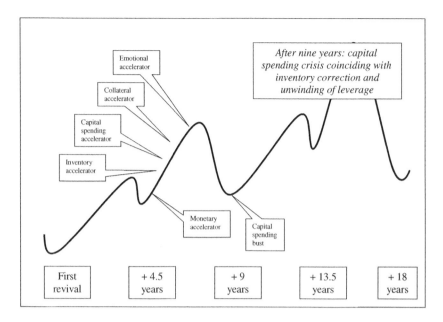

**Figure 29.3** The first capital spending cycle in the multi-cycle reference model.

Some corporate managers are also getting worried now, as they can't see how further expansion could add to their income at these cost levels. Also, their economists have told them that long leading indicators tend to turn approximately 14 months before the peak of activity. And, well, they have already turned! So they stop investing. This is the inflection point that leads to the first, serious recession in nine years; one that combines a collapse in capital spending with a serious correction in inventory levels. Property markets are also hurt, but not as badly, because while demand is leveling off, there isn't any problem with over-building. Supply is reasonable.

Our *inventory, capital spending, collateral* and *emotional* accelerators are now all working in reverse. Equity markets drop like rocks, and in particular sectors related to the recent wave of capital spending. Industrial commodities follow somewhat later. Many hedge fund managers miss the last part of the bull market because they know that momentum isn't backed by value, and they may also bungle their timing of the turning point. However, once the bear market is firmly in place, they jump on the bandwagon and start making money again. Private equity funds that didn't manage to make exits during the previous bull market are in for a hard time. It's typically not a part of their mandate to go short, so some go bust instead.

**Table 29.5**  Economic characteristics of a typical capital spending cycle (Juglar cycle).

*Duration and amplitude:*
- Average duration is nine years. Frequency varies somewhat and is influenced by specific innovations, trade liberalization, etc.
- Decline phase typically lasts some 2–2.5 years
- Amplitude can be large

*Main drivers:*
- Capital spending, which tends to average some 10% of GDP in developed economies and more in rapidly growing emerging markets. It is associated with specific stages of development and technological innovation

*Key theoretical concepts:*

| General | During expansion phase | During decline phase |
|---|---|---|
| • Capital spending cycles | • Natural rate versus real rate | • Monetary accelerator (in reverse) |
| • Capital investment accelerator | • Asset inflation | • Emotional accelerator (in reverse) |
| • Multiplier | • Emotional accelerator | • Collateral accelerator (in reverse) |
| • Hog cycle/cobweb/ ship-building cycles | • Collateral accelerator | • Credit crunch |
| | • Exhaustion phenomena | |

*Disruptive effects:*
- May be substantial, as the decline in investments may lead to rampant debt deflation, exorbitant cash preference and liquidity traps

*Positive effects*
- Eliminates inflation
- Reins in exorbitant employee compensation pressure
- Leads to necessary consolidation and balance sheet rebuilding process

*Key indicators:*
General: composite leading indicators, short- and long-term interest rates, yield curve
Specific: capacity utilization, trailing and forward earnings of listed equities

The economy is now at risk of falling into a liquidity trap, and urgent attention from central banks is required. However, as most of the decline in assets concerns equities, which largely were bought cash, the debt deflation problem is not insurmountable, and central bankers' tasks thus not too hard.

## TOWARDS A PROPERTY BOOM

The next 4.5 years evolve pretty much like the first 4.5 years in our story, as the economy recovers from the crisis while companies still hold back

**Table 29.6** Typical asset price behavior over capital spending cycles.

| | Early expansion | Late expansion | Early decline | Late decline |
|---|---|---|---|---|
| Bond yields | Falling (bond prices rising). Junk bonds outperform | Reaching trough and then rising | Rising. Investment grade outperforms | Declining |
| Currency | Stable or modestly falling | Begins to rise modestly, commodity currencies overperform | Peaks | Falls or crashes, commodity currencies underperform |
| Equities overall | Rise rapidly, but with a time lag after bonds | Rise rapidly and perhaps culminate in a blow-off top. Then reverse and fall rapidly | Fall substantially, then reverse ahead of the economy | Rise |
| Equity sectors | *Outperformers:* Financials, consumer discretionary, information technology, small caps  *Underperformers:* Consumer stables and utilities, large caps | *Outperformers:* Industrials, information technology, small caps  *Underperformers:* Financials | *Outperformers:* Consumer stables, utilities  *Underperformers:* Consumer discretionary, information technology, small caps | *Outperformers:* Financials, consumer, information technology, small caps  *Underperformers:* Consumer stables, utilities and industrials |
| Hedge funds overall | Perform well | Perform spectacularly | Perform relatively poorly | Perform well |

**Table 29.6** *Continued*

| | Early expansion | Late expansion | Early decline | Late decline |
|---|---|---|---|---|
| Best performing hedge funds | Sector-specific funds, long only, equity hedge, event-driven and market neutral | Sector-specific funds, long only, equity hedge, event-driven and market neutral | Short sellers, market neutral, event-driven, macro | Sector-specific funds, long only, equity hedge, event-driven and market neutral |
| Private equity | Does well, especially buy-out and venture capital funds | Does well, especially buy-out and venture capital funds | May make great exits | Many funds suffer greatly, especially venture capital |
| Property overall | Rises | Rises | Stagnates or falls modestly | Rises |
| Property overperformance | Apartments, Single-family homes | Retail property, full-service hotels, residential land, parking, downtown office, commercial land | Suburban office, R&D flex, industrial warehouses | 2nd tier regional malls, factory outlets |
| Commodities overall | Stagnating | Rising modestly | Rising | Falling |
| Commodity outperformance | Lead | Copper, zinc, nickel, aluminum, lead | Copper | |
| Gold, diamonds and collectibles | Rise | Rise very rapidly, perhaps creating a bubble | Peak, then fall | Fall, then level out |

with new capital spending after the shock they have just been through. The revival starts about 18 months later, which is some nine years after the trough of the last, serious crisis. Consumers have been badly hurt, and business sectors that provide capital equipment have been absolutely hammered; many are, in fact, bankrupt. However, while the property sector may be stirred, it isn't really shaken. And as economic growth comes back, it becomes clear that the wheels of the huge, slow property cycle have begun to turn a bit faster, even though they haven't reached anywhere near their maximum speed. Our imaginary economic time machine has now been ticking for 13.5 years, and we are getting ready for the wildest part.

## THE PROPERTY CYCLE KICKS IN

The wildest part comes from the property cycle. There hasn't been any severe shortage of property until recently, but now it's there. The economy has, after all, expanded a lot over the last many years, and while most investors chased capital spending projects, they just didn't pay enough attention to real estate.

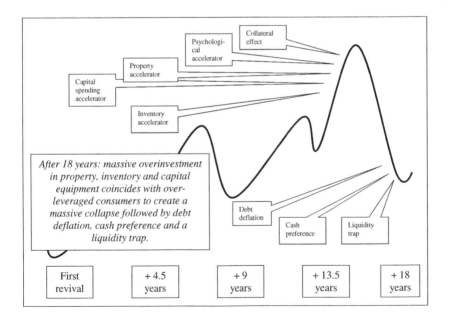

**Figure 29.4** Property cycle in the multi-cycle reference model.

**Table 29.7**   Economic characteristics of a typical property cycle (Kuznets cycle).

*Duration and amplitude:*
- Average duration is 18 years. Frequency varies somewhat and is influenced by the structural trends in interest rates (which again depend on trade liberalization and central banking policies, etc.)
- Decline phase typically lasts some 3–3.5 years
- Amplitude can be very large

*Main drivers:*
- Property construction activity, which is some 8% of global GDP (but very volatile) plus the wealth effect of property prices (which tends to be valued at around 250% of global GDP). Property construction constitutes a higher proportion of GDP in developed countries than in emerging markets

*Key theoretical concepts:*

| *General* | *During expansion phase* | *During decline phase* |
|---|---|---|
| • Property cycles<br>• Multiplier hog cycle/cobweb/ ship-building cycles | • Natural rate versus real rate<br>• Asset inflation<br>• Emotional accelerator<br>• Collateral accelerator<br>• Exhaustion phenomena | • Monetary accelerator (in reverse)<br>• Emotional accelerator (in reverse)<br>• Collateral accelerator (in reverse)<br>• Credit crunch |

*Disruptive effects:*
- Collapses in property prices are almost always followed by long and serious slowdowns, which also lead to problems in the financial sectors.

*Positive effects:*
- Eliminates inflation
- Increases savings rates
- Allows demand for property to catch up with supply

*Key indicators:*
- General: composite leading indicators, short- and long-term interest rates, yield curve
- Specific: housing affordability, ratio of house prices to employee compensation, ratio of house prices to GDP, ratio of commercial property CAP rates to bond yields, ratio of rental costs to mortgage rates

Tight property markets mean that rentals and selling prices now are firming up considerably, and CAP rates and ROIs are looking increasingly attractive when compared to interest rates. Skilled property developers have smelled money for a while, and there are many construction projects in the pipeline, but more will soon go into the planning process. Businessmen develop new concepts, secure financing and commence

**Table 29.8** Typical asset price behavior over property cycles.

|  | Early expansion | Late expansion | Early decline | Late decline |
|---|---|---|---|---|
| Bond yields | Falling (bond prices rising). Junk bonds outperform | Reaching trough and then rising | Rising rapidly, investment grade outperforms | Staying low for sustained period |
| Currency | Stable or modestly falling | Begins to rise modestly, commodity currencies overperform | Falls | Falls or crashes, commodity currencies underperform |
| Equities overall | Rise rapidly | Rise steadily, then peak and fall modestly | Fall rapidly or crash | Rise |
| Equities; | *Overperforming:* Financials, consumer, information technology, small caps, REITs | *Overperforming:* Industrials, REITs, consumer discretionary | *Overperforming:* Consumer stables, utilities | *Overperforming:* Financials, consumer, information technology, small caps |
|  | *Underperforming:* Consumer stables and utilities, large caps | *Underperforming:* Financials | *Underperforming:* Consumer discretionary, information technology, small caps, REITs | *Underperforming:* Consumer stables, utilities and industrials, REITs |
| Hedge funds overall | Perform well | Perform well | Perform relatively poorly | Perform well |

**Table 29.8** *Continued*

| | Early expansion | Late expansion | Early decline | Late decline |
|---|---|---|---|---|
| Hedge funds overperformance | Sector-specific funds, long only, equity hedge, event-driven and market neutral | Sector-specific funds, long only, equity hedge, event-driven and market neutral | Short sellers, market neutral, event-driven, macro | Sector-specific funds, long only, equity hedge, event-driven and market neutral |
| Property overall | Rises | Rises, but trading volume declines late in expansion | Crashes | Stabilizes with minimal trading volume |
| Property overperformance | Apartments, Single-family homes | Retail property, full-service hotels, residential land, parking, downtown office, commercial land | Suburban office, R&D flex, industrial warehouses | 2nd tier regional malls, factory outlets |
| Commodities overall | Stagnating | Rising rapidly | Rising | Crash |
| Commodity outperformance | Lead | Copper, zinc, nickel, aluminum, lead | Copper | |
| Gold, diamonds and collectibles | Rise | Rise very rapidly, perhaps creating a bubble | Peak, then fall | Fall, then level out |

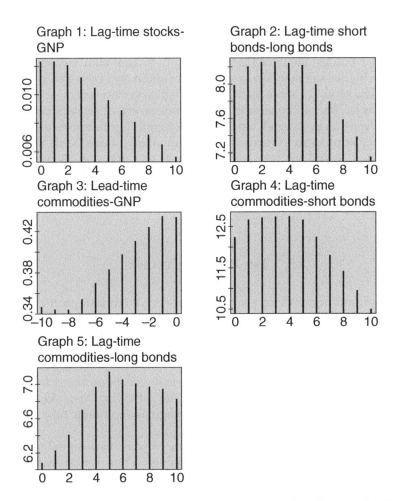

**Figure 29.5** Financial sequences around business cycles. The graphs illustrate cross-covariance analysis in between the movements of short bonds, long bonds, the stock market, GNP, and commodity prices in the USA for the years 1900–1983. The statistics used are based on quarterly figures, and each diagram illustrates the covariance between two time series. A lag is detected if covariance peaks after one or more quarters. The first graph illustrates that GNP turns, on average, at the same time or one month after the stock market: there is a high correlation, but a short lag time. The second illustrates the clear four-quarter time lag from short bonds to long bonds. The third illustrates a one-quarter lag from GNP to commodity prices. The fourth illustrates a two to four-quarter lag from commodities to short bonds. The last illustrates a five-quarter lag from commodities to long bonds. Together, the graphs illustrate the traditional short bond – long bond – stock market – GDP – commodities cycle sequence. Source: Klock, 1992.

construction. New land is being zoned and subdivided, selling is brisk, and a mania in building starts as consumers join the party and snap up summer houses. Some of them are simply buying with the intention of selling higher and others because they are afraid they can't afford it if they wait. The property boom leads to overall growth, and several accelerators are now in effect at the same time: *monetary, inventory, capital spending* and *property accelerators* are all working their magic. Furthermore, the gathering pace of property construction and capital investment leads to rapidly growing demand for base metals, and miners can't cope. They invest to increase their capacity. And this is where mania takes hold. A frenzy of speculators gobble up stocks, real estate and collectibles as if the sky was the limit. Art markets have a field day.

## The Final Meltdown

It is not until some 15–16 years after the end of our last, great crisis that the frenzy finally loses steam. Real estate is now severely overbuilt, capacity is excessive, consumers are stretched beyond their limits, inflation is rising and central bankers are raising rates to stop it all. Everything stalls, and then collapses, leading to debt deflation, banking crises and paralysis as the central bank tries in vain to revive the economy for several years – it's time for our *credit crunch*. This is the Big One, and it culminates 18 years after the last time. Our imaginary economic time machine has gone full circle.

We have passed through four inventory cycles, two capital spending cycles and one property cycle. And pending on how we positioned ourselves for them, we will now be either very well off, "still standing", as they say, or perhaps very poor. We may in any case be a bit wiser.

# Afterword: The Beat of the Heart

I had been outside for about ten seconds earlier in the morning, so I knew that it was cold. Now I was back inside, sitting comfortably by the fireplace, eating my breakfast and reading the newspaper.

I put the paper down and looked out of the windows to enjoy the sight of millions of ice crystals blinking like tiny blitz lights in the air. Suddenly I noticed two round bears coming up from the garden. A big black one, and a very small white one. Whenever they had taken a few steps forward, the small one would stop to investigate something in the snow, and the big one would then turn around and wait patiently. Finally they appeared under the balcony, right in front of the windows. The big one opened the terrace door, letting frosty air into the room. It was my wife Itziar, dressed in her long, black coat. Little Sophie was with her and ran over to my chair so that I could take off her white coat and tiny boots. Both of them had red chins and I saw that their eyes were shining.

"You seem to be enjoying yourself," Itziar said ". . . You have been eating breakfast for four hours now, do you know that?"

Sure. I could eat breakfast the whole day.

"Let me guess," she said, "You have been reading the newspapers or books about business cycles?"

"Both."

"So what have you found out – I mean about business cycles?"

"No cure. But interesting. You can modify the fluctuations, but it is impossible to avoid them completely. If you try that, then they will just get worse."

She poured out some coffee and looked at Sophie, who was now playing with an apple on the floor. I looked out of the window. Small ripples rolled very slowly towards the lake shore. Maybe the water would start to freeze over along the shore this week? Itziar was looking out the windows as well. She was thinking. Then she pulled a crumpled note in my handwriting out of her pocket.

"I have been looking for that . . . ," I said ". . . where did you find it?"

"Down in the garden house," she answered. "Now I know why you bothered to write it down."

And then she read it aloud:

"Cycles are not like tonsils, separable things that might be treated by themselves, but are, like the beat of the heart, of the essence of the organ that displays them."
Joseph Schumpeter, 1939

# Appendix 1

# List of Important Events in Business Cycle Theory

1705    John Law publishes *Money and Trade with a Proposal for Supplying the Nation with Money*, where he calls for the establishment of a landbank.

1716    Law & Company is founded.

1734    Cantillon dies and leaves behind him the manuscript for *Essai sur la Nature du Commerce en General*. The manuscript includes an analysis of the effects of velocity of money.

1759    Adam Smith publishes *The Theory of Moral Sentiments*.

1764    Adam Smith sails to France, where he meets Quesnay.

1773    Adam Smith publishes *The Wealth of Nations*, which includes the concept of the "Invisible Hand".

1788    Jean Babtiste Say reads *The Wealth of Nations*.

1797    The British House of Commons invites Henry Thornton to testify about the causes of a panic.

1799    David Ricardo reads *The Wealth of Nations*.

1802    Henry Thornton publishes *Paper Credit of Great Britain*, which is a detailed account of how monetary policy works. He proposes stabilization through active monetary policy.

1803    Jean Babtiste Say publishes *Traite d'Economie Politique*, which includes "Say's Law", suggesting that supply creates its own demand.

1808    James Mill meets David Ricardo and starts to persuade him to write about economics.

1809 David Ricardo publishes *The High Price of Bullion, a Proof of the Depreciation of Bank Notes.*

1816 David Ricardo publishes *Proposals for an Economical and Secure Currency.* He suggests that use of paper money that is convertible to gold will stabilize the economy.

1819 James Mill's son John Stuart Mill publishes *Elements of Political Economy* at the age of 13.

1822 Charles Babbage publishes *Observations on the Application of Machinery to the Computation of Mathematical Tables.*

1826 John Stuart Mill introduces the concept of competitive investment in his *Paper Currency and Commercial Distress.*

1848 John Stuart Mill publishes *Principles of Political Economy,* where he relates velocity of money to economic upswings and speculation, and emphasizes the importance of confidence. Karl Marx writes the first draft texts for *Das Kapital,* which contain descriptions of business cycles.

1862 Clement Juglar publishes *Les Crises Commerciales et leur Retour Periodique en France, en Angleterre et aux Etats Unis;* the first clear description of business cycles as caused by inherent instability phenomena.

1867 The first volume of Karl Marx's *Das Kapital* is published.

1871 William Stanley Jevons publishes *The Theory of Political Economy,* which contains the first formal description of "Rational Man".

1873 Walter Bagehot (the editor of *The Economist*) publishes *Lombard Street: A Description of the Money Market,* which describes the roles and main economic consequences of banking.

1875– William Stanley Jevons writes a series of articles about business
1882 cycles, which he tries to explain as the consequence of sunspots, or of expectations of sunspots.

1885 Simon Newcomb introduces what is later called the "Quantity Theory of Money" in his *Principles of Political Economy.*

1889 Leon Walras publishes *Elements of Pure Economics,* where he attempts to describe the economy in mathematical terms. John Atkinson Hobson publishes *The Physiology of Industry,* where he introduces an underconsumption theory of business cycles.

1890 Marshall publishes *Principles of Economics,* where he describes positive feedback processes in the economy.

1894 Mikhail Tugan-Baranovsky publishes *The Industrial Crises in England* with an overinvestment/exhaustion model of business cycles.

1896 Irving Fisher distinguishes between natural and real interest rates in his *Appreciation and Interest.*

1902　Arthur Spiethoff publishes *Vorbemerkungen zu einer Theorie der Überproducktion*, with an overproduction/technology theory of cycles.

1903　Arthur Spiethoff publishes *Die Krisentheorien von M. v. Tugan-Baranovsky und L. Pohle.*

1907　Knut Wicksell publishes *The Influence of the Rate of Interest on Prices*, where he introduces the concepts of real rate and natural rate.

1910　Roger Ward Babson publishes *Business Barometers Used in the Accumulation of Money.* The book describes how money rates, stocks, bonds, commodity prices and real estate fluctuate in relation to business cycles. Nikolai Kondratieff describes a long-term cycle in *Archiv fur Sozialwissenshaft.*

1911　Irving Fisher publishes *The Purchasing Power of Money.* The main theme is the destabilizing effects of inflation and fluctuations in money supply. Joseph Schumpeter publishes *The Theory of Economic Development*, where he introduces the theory that innovations arrive in clusters and that these can explain business cycles. He also introduces the concept of "creative destruction."

1913　Ralph George Hawtrey publishes *Good and Bad Trade*, which focuses on monetary instability and an explanation of business cycles. Wesley Mitchell publishes *Business Cycles.*

1915　Dennis Holme Robertson publishes *A Study of Industrial Fluctuations*, which emphasizes fluctuating capital investments as a key driver behind business cycles.

1920　Irving Fisher publishes *Stabilizing the Dollar*, where he suggests initiatives to stabilize inflation and money supply. Wesley Mitchell cofounds the National Bureau of Economic Research (NBER).

1923　Joseph Kitchin publishes *Cycles and Trends in Economic Factors*, where he describes a short-term business cycle phenomenon. Catchings and Foster publish *Money* with an underconsumption theory.

1925　Catchings and Foster publish *Profits.*

1926　Irving Fisher publishes *A Statistical Relationship between Unemployment and Price Changes.* This describes what is later known as the "Phillips curve".

1927　Pigou publishes *Industrial Fluctuations.* Catchings and Foster publish *Business Without a Buyer.* Mitchell publishes *Business Cycles: The Problem and its Setting.*

1929　Babson predicts a stock market crash, Fisher disagrees.

1930　Ragnar Frisch founds "The Econometric Society" together with Joseph Schumpeter, Irving Fisher and others. Kuznets publishes

*Secular Movements in Production and Prices,* where he describes a medium-term cycle.

1931   R.F. Kahn introduces the concept of the multiplier in *The Relationship of Home Investment to Unemployment.*

1933   Friedrick von Hayek publishes *Monetary Theory and the Trade Cycle.* He suggests that the monetary system in itself is unstable and that monetary inflation can go on for some years without leading to inflation. Homer Hoyt publishes *One Hundred Years of Land Values in Chicago* with the first theories of property cycles. The first issue of *Econometrica* is published. Ragnar Frisch publishes *Propagation Problems and Impulse Problems in Dynamic Economies,* where he shows how random shocks can generate cyclical fluctuations in the economy. Joseph Schumpeter starts to write a book about business cycles. Robert Bryce visits the USA and gives a speech about John Maynard Keynes's new ideas.

1936   John Maynard Keynes publishes *The General Theory of Employment, Interest and Money* in which he suggests that the state should use fiscal policy to stabilize the economy. The book also describes "propensity to consume" and "propensity to save", "liquidity preference" and the "multiplier". Jan Tinbergen develops a 24-equation model of the American economy.

1937   Von Haberler publishes *Prosperity and Depression* on the initiative of The League of Nations. The book examines all the existing business cycle theories.

1938   Einarsen publishes *Reinvestment Cycles,* a book that describes some "echoes" in investments in the Norwegian shipping industry. Ezekiel publishes *The Cobweb Theorem.*

1939   Jan Tinbergen publishes two articles where he tests the theories in von Haberler's book. One of his conclusions is that fluctuations in aggregate profit are by far the most important explanation of fluctuations in aggregate investment. Paul Samuelson publishes an article where he examines the combined effect of the accelerator and the multiplier. He finds a complicated pattern where several completely different effects are possible, depending on parameter values. Joseph Schumpeter publishes *Business Cycles,* where he suggests that there are three dominant fluctuations: Kitchin, Juglar and Kondratieff, and that depressions can be the result of synchronized downturns.

1941   Lloyd Appleton Metzler publishes *The Nature and Stability of Inventory Cycles,* which explains how fluctuations in inventory can generate short-term business cycles.

1943 A.C. Pigou publishes *The Classical Stationary State*, where he suggests that deflation under a recession increases the purchasing power of the circulating cash, which is a negative feedback loop. This is later called the "Pigou Effect".

1946 ENIAC, the world's first computer is formally introduced to the public. Jay Forrester gets approval for his Whirlwind project.

1948 Milton Friedman joins the NBER.

1951 H.E. Hurst publishes *Long Term Storage Capacity of Reservoirs*, where he introduces the Hurst Exponent.

1953 Von Mises publishes his *Theory of Money and Credit*.

1954 Kenneth Arrow and Gerard Debreu publish *Existence of an Equilibrium for a Competitive Economy*, which provides a mathematical demonstration of how an economy may become inherently stable.

1956 Jay Forrester joins the Sloan School of Management, where he later introduces the concept of "system dynamics".

1957 Hyman Minsky publishes *Central Banking and Money Market Changes*, which is the first of a series of publications where he describes instability in capital markets as key aspects of business fluctuations.

1958 The Phillips curve is rediscovered by Phillips, who publishes *The Relationship between Unemployment and the Rate of Change of Money Wages in the United Kingdom, 1861–1957*.

1961 Edward Lorenz discovers the butterfly effect in a simulation of a weather system. Muth publishes *Rational Expectations and the Theory of Price Movements*. This is the forerunner of the "Rational Expectations" hypothesis.

1963 Milton Friedman publishes *A Monetary History of the United States* with Anna J. Schwartz. They conclude that over the short term, money growth is reflected in activity, and over the long term, it is reflected in inflation.

1967 Hamilton Bolton publishes *Money and Investment Profits*, where he describes the effects of financial liquidity.

1969 Ragnar Frisch and Jan Tinbergen receive the Nobel Prize for "having developed and applied dynamic models for the analysis of economic processes."

1970 Paul A. Samuelson receives the Nobel Prize for "the scientific work through which he has developed static and dynamic economic theory and actively contributed to raising the level of economic analysis in economic science."

1971 Simon Kuznets receives the Nobel Prize for "his empirically founded interpretation of economic growth, which has led to new and deepened insight into the economic and social structure and process of development." Robert May discovers Feigenbaum cascades in the simulation of a fish population. Friedrich A. von Hayek and Gunnan Nyrdal receive the Nobel Prize for "their pioneering work in the theory of money and economic fluctuations and for their penetrating analysis of the interdependence of economic, social and institutional phenomena."

1975    James Yorke and Tien-Yien Li publish *Period Three Implies Chaos*, which introduces the term "deterministic chaos".

1976    Jay Forrester publishes *Business Structure, Economic Cycles and National Policy*. Milton Friedman receives the Nobel Prize for "his achievements in the fields of consumption analysis, monetary history and theory, and for his demonstration of the complexity of stabilization policy."

1979    Edward Lorenz publishes *Predictability: Does the Flap of a Butterfly's Wings in Brazil Set Off a Tornado in Texas?*

1980    Lawrence R. Klein receives the Nobel Prize for "the creation of econometric models and the application to the analysis of economic fluctuations and economic policies."

1981    Lucas and Sargent publish *Rational Expectations and Economic Practice*, where they apply the rational expectations hypothesis to econometric models.

1982    Finn Kydland and Edward Prescott publish *Time to Build and Aggregate Fluctuations*, which introduces the modern concept of "real business cycles".

1986    Mosekilde and Aracil receive the Jay Forrester Award for their system dynamics research.

1989    Sterman publishes *Deterministic Chaos in an Experimental Economic System*.

1990    Sterman, Mosekilde and partners study the M.I.T. System Dynamics National Model and find hyperchaos in it.

1991    Edgar Peters publishes *Chaos and Order in the Capital Markets*, where he demonstrates the presence of fat tails (indications of positive feedback) in a number of markets.

1995    Robert E. Lucas Jr receives the Nobel Prize for "having developed and applied the hyphothesis of rational expectations."

# Appendix 2

# List of the Largest Financial Crises in History

| Year | Country | Speculation in: | Peak | Acute crisis |
|------|---------|-----------------|------|--------------|
| 1557 | France, Austria, Spain (Habsburg Empire) | Bonds | 1557 | |
| 1636 | Holland | Primarily tulips | Summer 1636 | November 1636 |
| 1720 | France | Compagnie d'Occident, Banque General, Banque Royale | December 1719 | May 1720 |
| 1720 | England | South Sea Company | July 1720 | September 1720 |
| 1763 | Holland | Commodities, based on kite flying | January 1763 | September 1763 |
| 1773 | England | Real estate, canals, roads | June 1772 | January 1773 |
| 1773 | Holland | East India Company | June 1772 | January 1773 |
| 1793 | England | Canals | November 1792 | February 1793 |
| 1797 | England | Securities, canals | 1796 | February–June 1797 |
| 1799 | Germany | Commodities, financed by kite flying | August–November 1799 | 1799 |

| Year | Country | Speculation in: | Peak | Acute crisis |
|------|---------|-----------------|------|--------------|
| 1811 | England | Export projects | 1809 | January 1811 |
| 1815 | England | Exports, commodities | 1815 | 1816 |
| 1819 | USA | Production enterprises generally | August 1818 | June 1819 |
| 1825 | England | Latin American bonds, mines, wool | Beginning of 1825 | December 1825 |
| 1836 | England | Wool, railroads | April 1836 | December 1836 |
| 1837 | USA | Wool, land | November 1836 | September 1837 |
| 1837 | France | Wool, building sites | November 1836 | June 1837 |
| 1847 | England | Railroads, wheat | January 1847 | October 1847 |
| 1848 | European continent | Railroads, wheat, real estate | April 1848 | March 1848 |
| 1857 | USA | Railroads, land | End 1856 | August 1857 |
| 1857 | England | Railroads, wheat | End 1856 | October 1857 |
| 1857 | European continent | Railroads, heavy industry | March 1857 | October 1857 |
| 1864 | France | Wool, shipping, new enterprises | 1863 | January 1864 |
| 1866 | England, Italy | Wool, shipping, new enterprises | July 1865 | May 1866 |
| 1873 | Germany, Austria | Building sites, railroads, stocks, commodities | Fall 1872 | May 1873 |
| 1873 | USA | Railroads | March 1873 | September 1873 |
| 1882 | France | Bank stock | December 1881 | January 1882 |
| 1890 | England | Argentinian stock, stock flotation | August 1890 | November 1890 |
| 1893 | USA | Silver and gold | December 1892 | May 1893 |
| 1895 | England, Continental Europe | South African and Rhodesian gold mine stock | Summer 1895 | End of 1895 |
| 1907 | USA | Coffee, Union Pacific | Beginning of 1907 | October 1907 |
| 1921 | USA | Stocks, ships, commodities, inventories | Summer 1920 | Spring 1921 |
| 1929 | USA | Stocks | September 1929 | October 1929 |

| Year | Country | Speculation in: | Peak | Acute crisis |
|---|---|---|---|---|
| 1931 | Austria, Germany, England, Japan | Miscellaneous | 1929 | May–December 1931 |
| 1974 | International | Stocks, office buildings, tankers, aircraft | 1969 | 1974–75 |
| 1980 | International | Gold, silver, platinum, diamonds | January–February 1980 | March–April 1980 |
| 1985 | International | Dollars | February–March 1985 | February–March 1985 |
| 1987 | International | Stock | August 1987 | October 1987 |
| 1990 | Japan | Stock, real estate | December 1989 | February 1990 |
| 1990 | International | Art and collectibles | March 1990 | 1991 |
| 1997 | Asia/Pacific | Real estate, general overinvestment | June 1996 | October 1997 |
| 1997 | Russia | General overinvestment, undercapitalized banks | 1996 | August 1997 |
| 1999 | Brazil | Government spending | 1998 | January 1999 |
| 2000 | International | Internet and technology shares | March 2000 | 2001 |
| 2001 | Argentina | Government spending | August 2000 | March 2001–June 2002 |

# Chapter Notes

When you write a factual book, you have to decide whether you want to pursue a strictly scientific format or not. This one is not; it is rather what you might call "popular science" (even if it might not be very popular). This means that I have been selective with sources and have felt free to choose what I think makes sense. Because of the selection of this format I have also chosen not to use footnotes. Almost every sentence in this book has one or several sources, and a format which constantly referenced these would be irritating. I have instead chosen to make notes for each chapter, in which I describe how and where I found the information, and then give a traditional bibliography, where the exact written sources can be found.

It should be noted that the process of finding data has changed completely over the last few years. A very substantial number of the studies used for this book can now be downloaded in full from the Internet. It took me, for instance, less than a minute to find and download the full text of John Law's pamphlet from 1705 (it turned up on a URL called http://socserv2.socsci.mcmaster.ca/~econ/ugcm/3ll3/law/mon.txt). Much of the older material, which is beyond copyright, is now available as PDFs or Word documents at university websites. However, I very rarely list specific websites (other than the example above), as URLs change all the time. Just try, and you will, in most cases, find that a search on Google (or another search engine) will lead you to the current ways of down-loading sources. Many are free, others require a credit card. As for books, I found that almost all could be bought on Amazon – including those out of print.

Most of the structure of the book follows a chronological narrative, and there are a few books that I have found particularly helpful in understanding the history of economic thought and crises. The most important is Schumpeter's *The History of Economic Analysis*. My copy has 1260 pages, and it wasn't an easy read, but it certainly contains a lot of information. Much more accessible was Staley's little *A History of Economic Thought: From Aristotle to Arrow*. It has 280 pages, but like my first car, it seems bigger inside than from the outside: I recommend it highly. Heilbroner's *The Worldly Philosophers* focuses on a few economists, but it does it brilliantly. Breit and Spencer's *The Life of the Laureates* was also useful. As for the academic debate after WWII, I wish to highlight two excellent sources: Beaud and Dostaler's *Economic Thought since Keynes* and Warsh's *Economic Principals*. And then there are the historical crashes. I guess the first reference book of choice must be Kindleberger's *Manias, Panics and Crashes*. I also enjoyed Sobel's *Panic on Wall Street* and Beckman's *Crashes*.

As for reference books about business cycles, I can strongly recommend *Business Cycles and Depressions*, which is edited by Glasner. It ignores property markets but covers most other relevant subjects very well. There are also a couple of good websites. One is called *The History of Economic Thought Website*, and I will contradict myself by giving the link: http://cepa.newschool.edu/het/home.htm. The other is www.investopedia.com. Oops, that was another link – sorry.

Finally, I am using a number of charts. Those without external sources have been made with Datastream, BCView and CQG.

## CHAPTER 1 GAMBLING MAN, AND CHAPTER 2 CASH PAYMENT

• The most widely read source on this episode is probably Mackay's *Extraordinary Popular Delusions and the Madness of Crowds*, which was originally published in 1844. I think this is a wonderful book that every citizen on this planet should read, but its 45 pages dedicated to John Law do not always seem to be entirely accurate. He writes, for instance, that Law shot Mr Wilson, whereas it seems that he actually killed him with a sword. The book that I have used as my primary sources for these two chapters is *The Moneymaker* by Janet Gleeson from 1999. This has 272 pages and is extremely well researched. It lists, of course, numerous sources of its own. It must be the definitive source, and it is highly readable on top.

- Cantillon's original work is Cantillon, 1892.
- Law & Company is often described as Europe's first central bank, but government sponsored banks with more limited responsibilities had existed before in Sweden (from 1668), England (1694) and Scotland (1695).
- I use the term "junk bonds" to describe a part of Law's scheme. That is a more recent expression, however, as is my "debt-for-equity swap."
- The term "payment at sights" means that your paper money can be exchanged for more tangible values, like, for instance, gold.
- The daily stock prices of the Mississippi Company are available at *Banqueroute de Law* by Edgar Faure, which is available in Biblioteque de l'Arsenal in Paris.
- My best sources on the South Sea Company are Sperling, 1962 and Ashton, 1959. I also described it previously in my own book Tvede, 2002.
- I made the graph of the South Sea Company stock prices from original stock price lists. There is a technical analysis of it in Tvede, 2002.

## CHAPTER 3  THE DREAM TEAM OF MONEY

- I have used the following sources for the life of Adam Smith: Buchholz, 1989; Heilbroner, 1999; Schumpeter, 1954; Scott, 1937; Spiegel, 1983; Staley, 1989; and Warsh, 1993. It should be mentioned that much of Adam Smith's original text now can be downloaded from numerous sources on the Internet.
- Jsaac Newton was Master of the Mint until 1727, see Staley, 1989.
- I refer to cutting off material from coins. This phenomenon is called "sweating." See Friedman, 1992.
- Schumpeter's reference to Quesnay as one of the four most important economists ever appeared in Schumpeter, 1954.
- I write that many Members of Parliament referred to Adam Smith's work. This is described in Willis, 1979.
- Thornton's life is described in Hetzel, 1987; Peake, 1978; Schumpeter, 1954; Spiegel, 1983; Staley, 1989; and Thornton, 1939 (reprint).
- I refer to the active attempts by banks to force each other into trouble. Ashton, 1959, contains a description of an event where the old East India Company in the year 1700 tried to force the Bank of England into bankruptcy. See also Trevelyan, 1960.

- The description of English road acts and economic fluctuations in 1700–1800 is from Ashton, 1959 and Thornton, 1939.
- Thornton's speech is reprinted in Thornton, 1939.
- There are life sketches of Thornton in Schumpeter, 1954; Spiegel, 1983; and Staley, 1989.

## Chapter 4  The Napoleon of Finance

- Jevons's reference to the dinners in the Political Economy Club appears in Jevons, 1876. The forum is also described in Staley, 1989.
- There are good descriptions of John Stuart Mill's life in Buchholz, 1989; Schumpeter, 1954; Spiegel, 1983; and Staley, 1989.
- The crash in 1837 is best described in Sobel, 1999.
- There are many references to Overstone in Schumpeter, 1954, and also in Glasner, 1997.

## Chapter 5  Jay and the Phantom Gold

- My source for the crash of 1847 is Kindleberger, 2000.
- There are descriptions of the life and work of Karl Marx in Schumpeter, 1954; Staley, 1989; and Heilbroner, 1999.
- The descriptions of the railroad crash in 1857 are from Beckman, 1990.
- The gold speculation is described in Beckman, 1990; Klein, 1986; O'Connor, 1962; and Sharp, 1989. I found that the daily close prices for gold in the relevant period as they appear in the stock lists do not always correspond exactly to the prices quoted by the authors, but this may be due to very large intraday price moves, which are not recorded in the stock lists.

## Chapter 6  Seven Pioneers

- There is a short description of Babbage's life in Slater, 1987.
- Juglar's life is described in Beauregard, 1909 and Schumpeter, 1954.
- Jevons, Edgeworth and Newcomb are described in Glasner 1997; Heilbroner, 1999; Robbins, 1998; Schumpeter, 1954; and Staley, 1989.

- The life and contributions of Walras and Pareto are described in Robbins, 1998; and Staley, 1989.
- Detailed descriptions of the meetings in the Political Economy Club appears in Mallet, 1921. Another source is Political Economy Club, 1876.

## CHAPTER 7 THE GOLDEN ERA

- Marshall is often considered the last of the Classical Economists.
- The more colorful parts of my description of the panic from 1907 are mainly taken from Sobel, 1999, but I have also used Glasner, 1997 and Kindleberger, 2000.
- The best description of Foster and Catchings I have found is written in my (almost) mother tongue – Norwegian (I am Danish). It is Munthe, 1977.
- Descriptions of the other authors described in this chapter are plentiful. I found them in Buchholz, 1989; Glasner 1997; Heilbroner, 1999; Schumpeter, 1954; Staley, 1989; and Warsh, 1993.

## CHAPTER 8 THE ARCHEOLOGISTS

- Burns, Mitchell, Kondratieff, Kuznets and Kitchin are described in Schumpeter, 1954. There are references to Burns's life and work in Burns and Mitchell, 1946 and Allen, 1991. There is also a chapter on Kuznets's life in Spiegel and Samuels, 1984.
- Mager, 1987 describes Kondratieff's life in some detail.
- Abramowitz, 1950, is a good source on inventory cycles.
- Mitchell's analysis of the business cycle was based on a method in which he first determined for each cycle the beginning and end of nine phases by marking troughs and peaks in the aggregate indicators. He then expressed the value of any time series of a given phase as a percentage of its value through all the nine phases. In this way, he reduced the effect of the long-term trend, so that he could isolate the deviations around it. Having done this, he calculated average fluctuations of a large number of cycles to identify a prototype of the development through a cycle. Mitchell lived to see that his indicators were successful but not to see whether they would work in other countries. That test was not initiated until NBER many years later – in 1973 – decided to try to develop an international economic indicator system (called "IEI").

The Americans cooperated with scientists from leading OECD countries to duplicate, as far as possible, Mitchell's warning system in these other countries. Again, the indicators worked, confirming Juglar's old notion that business cycles are indeed an independent phenomenon.

## CHAPTER 9  FISHER AND BABSON

- There is an excellent description of Fisher's life and work in Fisher, 1956.
- Babson's methods are explained in his own book, Babson, 1909, and his life in another of his works, Babson, 1937.
- There are descriptions of the German hyperinflation in Beckman, 1990 and Kindleberger, 2000 as well as Kindleberger and Laffargue, 1982.

## CHAPTER 10  KEYNES AND THE AUSTRIANS

- For information about von Mises's life and work, see Mises, 1981.
- The Mises statement about credit expansions and collapses is from Mises, 1981.
- The reference to the "Treasury View" White Paper is from Patinkin, 1978.
- The life and work of Keynes is obviously described extremely well in numerous sources. I have used Buchholz, 1989; Burkett and Wohar, 1987; Glasner 1997; Heilbroner, 1999; Robinson, 1972; Schumpeter, 1954 (although he is very brief about Keynes!); Spiegel, 1983; Staley, 1989; and Warsh, 1993. If I could recommend just one among these, then I would choose Heilbroner.
- Descriptions of Keynes's investment performance are from Chua and Woodward, 1983.
- The economic statistics are from Datastream.
- The stories about Somary and Keynes are from Somary, 1963.

## CHAPTER 11  THE GREAT DEPRESSION

- There exist numerous descriptions of the Great Crash, and I have used those of Beckman, 1990; Bose, 1988; Fisher, 1930; Galbraith, 1955;

Kindleberger, 1986; Patterson, 1956; and Thomas and Morgan-Witts, 1979. The latter is a particularly excellent historical account of the crash.

- The stories about Jesse Livermore are from Lefevre, 1964 and Thomas and Morgan-Witts, 1979.
- The story about the fuse that blew is from Patterson, 1956.
- The references to Fisher's stock market losses are from Allen, 1991, and those to Keynes's investment performance are from Chua and Woodward, 1983
- The descriptions of art sales are from Watson, 1992.
- The reference to bankers as parasites by Pomerene is from Grant, 1992.
- The economic statistics are from Datastream.
- The reference that Keynes and Roosevelt each doubted the sanity of the other is from Galbraith, 1971.
- The literature about Keynes's General Theory is overwhelming. Some that I have used, other than the original work, are: Bernstein, 1985; Burkett and Wohar, 1987; Garrison, 1984; Heilbroner, 1999; Nenties, 1988; O'Donnel, 1990; Patinkin, 1976, 1978; Patinkin and Leith, 1977; Pesaran and Smith, 1985; Staley, 1989; and Sylos-Labini, 1984.
- The multiplier was not Keynes's theory, but Kahn's. Keynes popularized it, however. See Patinkin, 1978.

## CHAPTER 12  LOVER, HORSEMAN, ECONOMIST

- Robert Bryce later became Deputy Minister of Finance in Canada.
- Allen, 1991, is an excellent source on Schumpeter's life and work. Another good source is Spiegel, 1983.
- References to Somary are from Somary, 1963.

## CHAPTER 13  THE PROBLEM WITH MONEY

- One of the best sources on Minsky and his works is Fazzari and Papadimitriou, 1992.
- There is an excellent record on Friedman's life and work in Frazer, 1988.
- Interesting literature about money supply and velocity of money includes Cogley, 1999; Fisher, 1923; Friedman, 1986, 1992; Friedman and Schwartz, 1963a, 1963b; Garrison, 1984; Gordon, 1952; Holtrop, 1929; Humphrey, 1990; Kydland and Prescott, 1990; Nenties, 1988; Scheide, 1989; von Haberler, 1937; von Hayek, 1933; von Mises, 1953; Wicksell, 1907; and Woodford, 1989.

- Duck, 1985, contains a study of monetary conditions and business cycles in 33 countries over the years 1962 to 1982. Among his results were:
  - For most major Western countries, a change in the rate of monetary growth produces a change in the rate of growth of nominal income about six to nine months later. Inflation is hardly affected at all within this timeframe, however.
  - The effect on prices of a changed rate of monetary growth is distributed over time, but typically shows up some two years later. That is why you cannot stop inflation overnight.
  - Velocity of money tends to rise in the expansion phase of the business cycle and to fall in the contraction phase.
- Robert E. Lucas received the Nobel Prize in 1995 for the development of his theory of rational expectations.

## CHAPTER 14 THE SIMULATORS

- The magazine where the three cobweb theories appeared in 1930 was *Zeitschrift fur Nationalkonomi*, Wien, 1(5).
- For information about the life and work of Tinbergen, see De Wolff, 1970; Spiegel and Samuels, 1984; and Van der Linden, 1988.
- The ship-building cycles are described in Einarsen, 1938.
- Keynes was often called "the winning economist, but the losing gentleman". But in his debate with Tinbergen, there has since been large agreement that he was also the losing economist; it is difficult to imagine the subsequent development of economic theory without the use of econometrics. Since Tinbergen's pioneering work, enormous amounts of money have been poured into ever-larger econometric models. One such example was Lawrence Klein's giant model of the American economy (later "Klein–Golberger") in the early 1980s, which contained over 1000 equations, and which was combined via "Project Link" with other national models to form a several-thousand-equation multinational model. The critique of Keynes is described in Hansen and Clemence, 1959.
- Tinbergen's study of business cycles from 1919–1932 appeared in *Business Cycles in the U.S.A., 1919–1937*, printed in 1938, which later evolved into *A Method and its Application to Investment Activity*, 1939.
- Keynes's discussions with Tinbergen are examined in Hansen and Clemence, 1959.
- Samuelson's original study of the accelerator is in Samuelson, 1939.

- There are a number of articles about real business cycles in Hartley, Hoover and Salyer, 1998.
- The original work by Kydland and Prescott appeared in Kydland and Prescott, 1982. The response from Summers was published in Summers, 1986.

## CHAPTER 15  BRAINS OF STEEL

- The description of the ENIAC project and the people involved in it, is from Slater, 1987.
- Metzler's pioneering work on inventory cycles appears in Metzler, 1947.
- The beer game was made in such a way that beer could only flow from the brewery down the chain; orders could only flow up the chain. So the point was to minimize your inventory and backlogs. Each player could place new orders if desired, but had to receive what he had ordered, and ship what had been ordered from him. Unfilled orders were listed as backlog (with a two-dollar penalty) until they could be filled.
- The beer game simulations are described in Mosekilde and Larsen, 1988 and Mosekilde, Larsen, Sterman and Thomsen, 1992.
- Forrester's comments on business cycles appear in Forrester, 1976.
- There is a good autobiography by Forrester in Forrester, 1992.

## CHAPTER 16  FAT TAILS AND ALL THAT

- Science has known about fat tails at least since 1897, when Pareto discovered them in income distribution. Such fat-tail distributions are today often called "Pareto" or "Pareto–Levy" distributions.
- The problem in Hurst's card game is described in Hurst, 1951 and Hurst *et al.*, 1965.
- I believe it was Mandelbrot who rediscovered the Rescaled Range technique, see Mandelbrot, 1972 and Mandelbrot and Wallis, 1969. There is a good explanation of the phenomenon in Peters, 1991.
- Mandelbrot worked in the IBM Thomas J. Watson Research Center, N.Y.
- My main source on Mandelbrot, Lorenz and May is Gleich, 1987.
- Lorenz's experiments are described in Lorenz, 1963, 1964 and 1979.
- May's model is described in May, 1976.

- Bifurcations such as in Feigenbaum trees have been found in climatology. When you let a computer simulate weather development day in and day out, hundreds or even thousands of years into the future, then it can suddenly, completely unprovoked, swing into a global ice age, stay there for many years, and then swing back again. There seem to be two equilibria in the simulation system, much as there might be in the real climate.
- Andersen, 1988 contains a good description of chaos in system dynamics simulations.

## CHAPTER 17   MONKEY SEE, MONKEY DO

- The description of Peter Lynch is from Lynch, 2000.
- The story about the crash in 1987 is from Tvede, 2002.
- The results of Shiller's questionnaires are summarized in Shiller, 1987b.
- The generally accepted standard reference on personality disorders is American Psychiatric Association, 1994 (updated reprints continue to appear from time to time).
- The following references are the most relevant for the subject of mass psychology in asset markets: Benartzi and Thaler, 1995; Berger, 1994; Bowman, Minehart, Rabin, 1993; Darkes and Blumer, 1985; Festinger 1957, Gilovich, Medvec and Kahneman, 1998; Hawkins and Hastie, 1990; Jegadeesh and Titman, 1993; Kahneman, 1970; Kahneman and Riepe, 1998; Kahneman and Tversky, 1973, 1979, 1982 and 1984; Kahneman, Knetsch and Thaler, 1991; Kahneman, Slovic and Tversky, 1974; Loomes and Sugden, 1982; Martin and Clark, 1990; McGuire, 1969; Odean, 1998; Ruysso and Schoemaker, 1990; Shefrin and Statman, 1985; Shiller, 1989 and 1990.

## CHAPTER 18   DOT BOMB

- There is a detailed description of the drivers of the Internet boom in Tvede and Ohnemus, 2001.
- The warnings from Perkins were given in Perkins and Perkins, 1999. Another classic from this episode is Shiller, 2000.
- There are numerous good descriptions of this bubble written after the crash – I haven't read many, as I was a first hand witness myself, but

one of the better ones is Lowenstein, 2004. And as for the go-go culture, I think Lewis, 2001 beats everything.

## CHAPTER 19  THE STATE OF THE ART

- The entire Part IV is more a reflection of personal opinion and less of hard data than the other four sections, and there are, for that reason, less specific sources.
- I have three main sources for Chapter 19. The first is Beaud and Dostaler, 1995, and especially its Chapters 3, 4, 5 and 8. The second is Warsh, 1993, and the third one Ormerod, 1994.

## CHAPTER 20  THREE QUESTIONS

- There are obviously no direct sources for this chapter.
- Both Erik Mosekilde and Edgar Peters have told me in individual conversations in the mid 1990s that they believed that you would need around nine cycles before you would have strong, statistical evidence of a Kondratieff cycle. Neither NBER nor most other scientifically based authorities seem enthusiastic about the theory of a Kondratieff cycle. It is often described in the more popular investment literature, however.

## CHAPTER 21  THE FIVE MAIN DRIVERS OF CYCLES

- The numbers I provide in this chapter are meant to describe orders of magnitude only. I took the global population count from US Census and United Nations websites. This figure is obviously the easiest of them all.
- The numbers for global GDP are from the World Bank website, using, as I wrote, the "Atlas" method. There is another way, the "PPP" method, which gives a modestly higher result by taking cost of living differences into account, but as I want to compare GDP numbers with other nominal numbers, I think the Atlas method is most correct.
- My estimate of property prices is based on the report *UBS Research Focus – Real Estate*, UBS, April 2005. This report contains estimates of OECD

property markets, and I used these as a basis to estimate emerging market property, where I just used the proportional relationship of GDP in developed versus emerging markets as a basis.

- My estimates for equity and bond valuation are in line with what appears on the Bloomberg trading screens.
- The estimates for values of existing/above-ground gold and collectibles were taken from Chapters 24 and 25 in this book (see below).
- For the estimate of the orders of magnitude of economic variables, I did my own estimates and then consulted with Fernando Irausquin and Stan Shipley from ISI, the famous US broker, as well as with George Magnus, Senior Economic Advisor of UBS Investment Bank, and Dr Daniel Kalt, Director, UBS Wealth Management Research. Each provided valuable input, for which I am very grateful. I tried to incorporate this input, but my final result would not necessarily be endorsed by any of them.
- I looked at OECD data for gross fixed capital formation, which includes inventories, capex and construction, and then studied each of the subcomponents individually. Interest payments were found in domestic national income tables (not GDP).
- I was, like many others, brought up with the idea that property construction, investment in machinery and equipment and inventories each are in the range of 10% of GDP, leaving around 70% for consumption. However, inventories have been falling as a proportion of GDP due to Enterprise Resource Management systems and other IT technologies, and because of a gradual shift towards service economies. Inventories are now around 6%, as stated.
- There is a good explanation of the role of financial versus nonfinancial debt in Reid and Schreft, 1993.


### CHAPTER 22  THE TEN CHALLENGES OF CENTRAL BANKING

- The four books that I found particularly helpful for preparation of this chapter were Fazzari and Papadimitriou, 1992; Lahiri and Moore, 1991; Oyen, 1991; and Zarnowitz, 1992. Apart from that, I have used a large number of academic papers, most of them produced by central bank research staff, and the large majority recent. There seems to have been an increased production of such papers after the Japanese bubble and the 2000–2003 stock market crash, partly because of the magnitudes of these episodes, and partly because there is a sense that inventories have had declining destabilizing effects, whereas variable-price gross assets

have grown in value as inflation has been tamed during the 1980s and 1990s.
- The most important of the papers I used were:
  — On inflation and forecasting: Batini and Nelson, 2001; Cecchetti, Chu and Steindel, 2000; Fisher, 2000; Garner, 1995; and Stock and Watson, 1999.
  — On crashes and liquidity traps: Blanchard, 2000 and Hoggarth, Reis and Saporta, 2001.
  — On asset prices versus monetary policy: Bernanke and Gertler, 2000 and 2002; Bordo and Jeanne, 2001, 2002; Browne, Hellerstem and Little, 1998; Bullard and Schaling, 2002; Cogley, 1999; Fair, 2000; Ferguson, 2005; Filardo, 2000, 2001; Hayford and Malliaris, 2001; Rigobon and Sack, 2001; Smets, 1997; Tarhan, 1995; Trichet, 2005; and Vickers, 2000.
  — Specifically on the asset price bubble in Japan: Shiratsuka, 2005 and Takatoshi and Mishkin, 2004.

### CHAPTER 23 THE MOTHER OF ALL CYCLES: PROPERTY

- I found two books about property markets that give a good introduction to the area. The first is the old classic Hoyt, 1933, which is perhaps more a historic relic than a state-of-the art piece of research. It is, however, my source for the first part of the chapter, where I describe his observations. The book had a very high standard for its time. The other is Harrison, 1983. Harrison has a tendency to think very little of decision makers, but his books do contain some interesting data.
- Heath, 2005, provides a good list of warnings of overheating in property markets.
- Pyhr, Roulac and Born, 1999 provides a good general introduction to property cycles and subcycles.
- My best sources about property market crashes and their consequences are Helbling 2003 and Helbling and Terrones 2005.
- The best sources on leading indicators for property markets are Heath, 2005 and Krystaloyianni, Matysiak and Tsolacos, 2004.
- Other than the sources mentioned above, the chapter builds on the sources on asset markets and business cycles mentioned in Chapter 22, as well as the following specific sources: Berger-Thomson and Ellis, 2004; Case, Quigley and Shiller, 2001; Chinley, 1996; Foldvary, 1991;

Janssen, Kruijt and Needham, 1993; Katz, 2004; Key, Firoozeh and Haq, 1999; Long, 1940; Matysiak and Tsolacos, 2003; and Quigley, 1999.
- The example of International Place Two is taken from Katz, 2004.

## CHAPTER 24  WHEN ART WAS IN

- I made a draft of this chapter and asked two art experts from UBS, Mr Adrien Iynedjian and Mr Céderic Courtil, for comments. They gave me valuable comments, but this is no guarantee that they would endorse the final result.
- *The World Wealth Report* from Cap Gemini and Merrill Lynch can normally be downloaded from various sites on the Internet.
- The stories about Japanese buyers of art during the bubble period are partly from Watson, 1992, but mainly from Shibata, 1999.
- Olivier Chanel's study is Chanel, 1995.
- Fernwood Art Investments provide various updated statistics on their website http://www.fernwood.com/home.cfm. So do www.kusin.com, www.artprice.com and Mei-Moses at http://s107117993.onlinehome.us/login.cgi.
- Regarding Maslow's Hierarchy of Needs Pyramid, see Maslow, 1943.
- Several major banks have in-house art specialists. UBS has an art department in Basel, and Dresdner Bank also have special expertise. Wilke, 2000 was published by Dresdner Bank, and it provides a good introductory overview of the art business. This study suggests that the boom in art prices by the late 1980s was derived from soaring Japanese stock markets. I would think that property markets played an even more important role.
- The fact that lower-priced art is more volatile, but also performs best price-wise over the long run is documented in Mei and Moses, 2002.
- The study by The European Fine Art Foundation is *The European Art Market in 2002: A Survey*.

## CHAPTER 25  ALL THAT GLITTERS

- My best general resources on gold were Green, 1981 and Gotthelf, 2005, on diamonds, Harlow, 1998 and Balazik, 1997, and for precious metals in general, the surveys from the two leading precious metals survey groups, CPM and GFMS, CPM, 2005 and GFMS, 2005. The websites are http://www.gfms.co.uk/index.htm and http://www.cpmgroup.

com/. Statistics for usage and production have also been obtained from *CRB Commodity Yearbook* and the World Gold Counsel website (gold) and Diamonds.net (diamonds). The latter is provided by Rapaport.
- The Edgar Peters source is Peters, 1994.
- The forecasting system used by Gold Fields Mineral Services Ltd is described in Klapwijk, 2003.

## CHAPTER 26  WHAT THINGS ARE MADE OF: COMMODITIES

- Mr Telis Mistakides, division manager for Copper, Zinc and Lead divisions at Glencore, one of the world's largest mining companies, read a draft of this chapter and gave valuable input.
- Keynes's description of backwardation was introduced in Keynes, 1965 (which is a reprint of a 1930 edition).
- My source for all usage statistics was *The CRB Commodity Yearbook*, 2005.
- Schneeweis, Spugin and Georgiev, 2000, provide a good overview of base metals cycles, including nice graphs. Bernstein, 1981, Fama and French, 1988 and Murphy, 1991 are also useful.
- The basic resource for the tables of cyclical behavior was Gorton and Rouwenhorst, 2004. It was a living document at the time of my writing. I found one version on the Internet, and they sent me another via e-mail.
- US Geological Survey's metals forecasts can be found on http:// minerals.usgs.gov/minerals/pubs/mii/.

## CHAPTER 27  BONDS, STOCKS AND FUNDS

- There exists a huge amount of literature about the cyclical performance and market rotation of equities and bonds. I think Murphy, 1991, Pring, 1992 and Taylor, 1998 all have good input. However, the single best sources I have found were two subscriber-only studies from The International Bank Credit Analyst, *Forecasting Sector Performance: A Cycle Approach* from January 2004 and *Global Equity Market Cycles* from March 2005.
- The best studies on hedge fund performance in different environments are Capocci, Corhay and Hübner, 2003; Schneeweis, Kazemi and Martin, 2001; and Sinlapapreechar, 2003. As for private equity, I used Kaplan and Schoar, 2003 as the primary resource.

## CHAPTER 28  THE WORLD'S BIGGEST MARKET: FOREIGN EXCHANGE

- I chose to focus on commodity currencies in this chapter, but if I had given forex more space in the book, then it would have made sense to deal with defensive currencies as well. These include Swiss francs and yen.
- The IMF study on a broad specter of commodity currencies is Cashin, Cěspedes and Sahay, 2002 and 2003.
- There is a good study of how currencies react to unexpected interest changes in Kearns and Manners, 2005.
- Fan, 2004 gives a good study of the behavior of commodity currencies in relationship to various commodity indices.
- Other useful sources were Chen and Rogoff, 2002 and Cashin, Cěspedes and Sahay, 2003.

## CHAPTER 29  BUSINESS CYCLES AND MARKET ROTATION

- The only two specific sources for this chapter are Klock, 1992 and Barclays Bank, 2004. All the rest is really a summary of findings from across the book, and I haven't been able to find a single source that tried to link all assets to all categories in this way (I wish I had).

# Bibliography

Abramovitz, M. (1950) *Inventories and Business Cycles*, New York: NBER.

Adelman, I. (1965) 'Long Cycles: Fact or Artefact?,' *American Economic Review*, 55, 444–463.

Adelman, I. and Adelman, F. (1959) 'The Dynamic Properties of the Klein–Golberger model', *Econometrica*, 4, 596–625.

Aiyagari, S.R. (1988) 'Economic Fluctuations Without Shocks to Fundamentals; Or, Does the Stock Market Dance to its Own Music? Federal Reserve Bank of Minneapolis', *Quarterly Review*.

Allen, R.K. (1991) *Opening Doors*, Transaction Publishers, USA.

American Psychiatric Association (1994) *Diagnostic and Statistical Manual of Mental Disorders*, 4th edition. Washington, DC: American Psychiatric Association.

Andersen, D.F. (1988) 'Foreword: Chaos in System Dynamics Models,' *System Dynamics Review*, 4(1–2).

Anderson, J.R. (1985) *Cognitive Psychology and Its Implications*, 2nd edition, New York: W.H. Freeman.

Arrow, K. and Debreu, G. (1954) 'Existence of an Equilibrium for a Competitive Economy,' *Econometrica*, 22, 265–290.

Ashton, T.S. (1959) *Economic Fluctuations in England 1700–1800*, Oxford: Clarendon Press.

Azariadis, C. (1981) 'Self-fulfilling Prophecies,' *Journal of Economic Theory*, 25, 380–396.

Babbage, C. (1822) 'Observations on the Application of Machinery to the Computation of Mathematical Tables,' *Memoirs of the Astronomical Society*, 1, 311–314.

Babson, R.W. (1909) *Business Barometers Used in the Accumulation of Money*, Massachusetts: Babson Institute.

Babson, R.W. (1937) *Actions and Reactions*, Harper & Brothers.

Bagehot, W. (1873) *Lombard Street: A Description of the Money Market*, New York: Scriber, Armstrong & Co.

Balazik, R.F. (1997) 'Gemstones,' *Prospecting and Mining Journal.*

Bank of International Settlements (1998) *The Role of Asset Prices in the Formulation of Monetary Policy*, BIS conference paper no. 5, Basle, March.

Bannerjee, A.V. (1992) 'A Simple Model of Herd Behavior,' *Quarterly Journal of Economics*, 107(3).

Barclays Bank (2004) *Barclays Equity Gilt Study 2004.*

Barras, R. (1994) 'Property and the Economic Cycle: Building Cycles Revisited,' *Journal of Property Research*, 11, 183–197.

Batini, N. and Nelson, E. (2001) *The Lag from Monetary Policy to Inflation: Friedman Revisited*, Bank of England.

Baum, A. (2004) *Evidence of Cycles in European Commercial Real Estate Markets – and Some Hyphotheses*, Henderson Investors.

Beaud, M. and Dostaler, G. (1995) *Economic Thought since Keynes*, London: Routledge.

Beauregard, P. (1909) *Notice sur la Vie et les Travaux de M. Clement Juglar, Compte Rendu*, L'Academie des Sciences Morales et Politiques, February.

Beckman, R. (1990) *Crashes*, London: Grafton Books.

Bell, D.E. (1982) 'Regret in Decision Making Under Uncertainty,' *Operations Research*, 30(5), 961–981.

Belsky, G. and Gilovich, T. (1999) *Why Smart People Make Big Money Mistakes – and How to Correct Them*, New York: Simon and Schuster.

Benartzi, S. and Thaler, R.H. (1995) 'Myopic Loss Aversion and the Equity Premium Puzzle,' *Quarterly Journal of Economics*, 110(1), 73–92.

Berger, L.A. (1994) 'Mutual Understanding, the State of Attention and the Ground for Interaction in Economic Systems,' *Business and Ethics Quarterly.*

Berger-Thomson, L. and Ellis, L. (2004) *Housing Construction Cycles and Interest Rates*, Economic Group, Reserve Bank of Australia.

Bernanke, B. and Gertler, M. (2000) *Monetary policy and asset price volatility*, NBER Working Paper no. 7559.

Bernanke, B. and Gertler, M. (2002) 'Should Central Banks Respond to Movements in Asset Prices?' *American Economic Review: Papers and Proceedings*, 91, 253–257.

Bernstein, J. (1981) *The Handbook of Commodity Cycles*, New York: John Wiley & Sons, Inc.

Bernstein, P.L. (1985) 'Wall Street's View of Keynes and Keynes's View of Wall Street,' in H.L. Wattel (ed.) *The Political Consequences of John Maynard Keynes*, New York: Sharpe, pp. 22–29.

Blanchard, O. (2000) *Bubbles, Liquidity Traps, and Monetary Policy: Comments on Jinushi et al, and on Bernanke*, working paper, Department of Economics, MIT.

Bolton, A.H. (1967) *Money and Investment Profits*, Homewood, Illinois: Dow Jones–Irwin.

Bordo, M. and Jeanne, O. (2001) *Asset Prices, Reversals, Economic Instability and Monetary Policy*, Paper presented at the Allied Social Science Association Meetings in New Orleans, Louisiana.

Bordo, M. and Jeanne, O. (2002) 'Monetary Policy and Asset Prices: Does "Benign Neglect" Make Sense?,' *International Finance*, 5(2), 139–164.

Borio, C. and Lowe, P. (2002) 'Asset prices, financial and monetary stability: exploring the nexus,' presented at the 2002 Asset Price Bubbles Conference in Chicago, *BIS Working Papers*, no. 114, July.

Bose, M. (1988) *The Crash*, London: Bloomsbury.

Bowman, D., Minehart, D. and Rabin, M. (1993) *Loss Aversion in a Savings Model*, University of California working paper in economics 93–12.

Brayton, F. and Tinsley, P. (1996) *A Guide to FRB/US*, Board of Governors of the Federal Reserve System, Finance and Economics Discussion Papers #1996-42.

Breit, W.S. and Spencer, R.W. (1986) *The Life of the Laureates: Seven Nobel Economists*, Cambridge, Mass.: MIT Press.

Brock, W.A. (1988) 'Is the Business Cycle Characterized by Deterministic Chaos?,' *Journal of Monetary Economics*, 22, 71–90.

Brock, W.A. (1990) *Chaos and Complexity in Economic and Financial Science*, Social Systems Research Institute, University of Wisconsin-Madison, paper no. 382, pp. 423–450.

Brown, H.J., Philips, R.S. and Roberts, N.A. (1980) *Land Into Cities*, The Lincoln Institute of Land Policy, Mass.

Browne, L.E., Hellerstem, R. and Little, J.S. (1998) 'Inflation, asset markets, and economic stabilisation: lessons from Asia,' *New England Economic Review*, September/October.

Buchholz, T.G. (1989) *New Ideas from Dead Economists: An Introduction to Modern Economic Thought*, New American Library Trade.

Buckle, T.H. (1872) *History of Civilisation in England*, London.

Bullard, J. and Schaling E. (2002) 'Why the Fed Should Ignore the Stock Market,' *Review of the Federal Reserve Bank of St. Louis*, 84, March/April, 35–41.

Burkett, P. and Wohar, M. (1987) 'Keynes on Investment and the Business Cycle,' *Review of Radical Political Economy*, 19(4), 39–54.

Burns, A.F. (1935) 'Long Cycles in Residential Construction,' in *Economic Essays in Honor of Wesley Clair Mitchell*, New York: Columbia University Press, pp. 63–104.

Burns, A.F. and Mitchell, W.C. (1946) *Measuring Business Cycles*, New York: NBER.

Cagan, P. (1966) *Changes in the Cyclical Behavior of Interest Rates*, NBER occasional paper 100.

Camerer, C. (1995) 'Individual Decision Making,' in J.H. Kagel and A.E. Roth (eds), *Handbook of Experimental Economics*, Princeton, NJ: Princeton University Press, pp. 587–703.

Campbell, J.D. and Tesser, A. (1983) 'Motivational Interpretations of Hindsight Bias: An Individual Difference Analysis,' *Journal of Personality*, 51, 605–620.

Cantillon, R. (1892) *Essai sur la Nature du Commerce en General*, reprint, Boston: Harvard University Press.

CapGemini and Merrill Lynch (2005) *World Wealth Report 2005*.

Capocci, D., Corhay, A. and Hübner, G. (2003) *Hedge Fund Performance and Persistence in Bull and Bear Markets*, Department of Management, University of Liege.

Caporale, G. and Williams, G. (1997) *Revisiting Forward Looking Consumption and Financial Liberalization in the United Kingdom*, London Business School, Discussion Papers, #20.

Case, K.E., Quigley, J.M. and Shiller, R. (2001) *Comparing Wealth Effects: The Stock Market Versus the Housing Market*, NBER.

Cashin, P., Céspedes, L. and Sahay R. (2002) *Keynes, Cocoa, and Copper: In Search of Commodity Currencies*, IMF Working Paper 02/223.

Cashin, P., Céspedes, L. and Sahay, R. (2003) 'Commodity Currencies,' *Finance and Development*, 40(1), IMF.

Cecchetti, S.G., Chu, R.S. and Steindel C. (2000) 'The Unreliability of Inflation "Indicators",' *Current Issues in Economics and Finance*, Federal Reserve Bank of New York, April.

Chan, L., Jegadeesh, N. and Lekonishok, J. (1996) 'Momentum Strategies,' NBER Working Paper 5375, *Journal of Finance*.

Chanel, O. (1995) 'Is Art Market Behaviour Predictable?' *European Economic Review*, 39.

Chen, P. (1986) *Mode Locking to Chaos in Delayed Feedback Systems*, Center for Studies in Statistical Mechanics, University of Texas at Austin.

Chen, P. (1988) 'Empirical and Theoretical Evidence of Economic Chaos,' *System Dynamics Review*, 4.

Chen, Y.C. and Rogoff, K. (2002) *Commodity Currencies and Empirical Exchange Rate Puzzles*, IMF working papers 02/27.

Chiarella, C. (1986) *The Elements of Non-linear Theory of Economic Dynamics*, PhD Thesis, University of South Wales.

Chinley, P. (1996) 'Real Estate Cycles: Theory and Empirical Evidence,' *Journal of Housing Research*, 7(2).

Chua, J.H. and Woodward, R.S. (1983) 'J.M. Keynes's Investment Performance: A Note,' *Journal of Finance*, 38(1), 232–235.

Clark, J.M. (1917) 'Business Acceleration and the Law of Demand,' *Journal of Political Economy*, xxv(3), 217–235.

Cogley, T. (1999) 'Should the Fed Take Deliberate Steps to Deflate Asset Price Bubbles?,' *Economic Review of the Federal Reserve Bank of San Francisco*, Number 1, pp.42–52.

Collard, D.A. (1983) 'Pigou on Expectations and the Cycle,' *Economic Journal*, 93(379), 411–414.

Commodity Research Bureau (2005) *The CRB Commodity Yearbook 2005*, New Jersey: John, Wiley & Sons, Inc.

CPM Group (2005) *Silver Survey 2005*.

Damasion, A.R. (1994) *Descartes' Error*, New York: Grosset/Putnam.

Darkes, H.R. and Blumer, C. (1985), 'The Psychology of Sunk Cost,' *Organizational Behavior and Human Decision Processes*, 35, 124–140. Reprinted in T. Connolly *et al.* (eds), *Judgment and Decision Making: An Interdisciplinary Reader*, Cambridge: Cambridge University Press.

Deane, P. and Cole, W.A. (1962) *British Economic Growth 1688–1959*, Cambridge: Cambridge University Press.

Desnoyers, Y. (2001) *L'effet de la Richesse sur la Consummation aux Etats-Unis*, Banque du Canada, Document de Travail #2001-14.

Deutscher, P. (1990) *R.G. Hawtrey and the Development of Macroeconomics*, London: Macmillan.

De Wolff, P. (1970) 'Tinbergen's Contribution to Business-Cycle Theory and Policy,' *The Economist*, 118(2), 112–125.

Dowall, D.E. (ed.) (2003) *Land Into Cities*, Lincoln Institute of Land Policy.

Duck, N.W. (1985) *Money, Output and Prices: An Empirical Study using Long Term Cross Country Data*, Working Paper, University of Bristol, September.

Eachus, P. (1988) 'The Psychology of the Stock Market,' *The Psychologist*, March.

Edgeworth, F. (1881) *Mathematical Physics*, Kegan Paul.

Edwards, F.R. and Caglayan, M.O. (2001) 'Hedge Funds and Commodity Fund Investments in Bull and Bear Markets,' *Journal of Portfolio Management*, 27(4), 97–108.

Eichner, A. (ed.) (1983) *Why Economics is not a Science*, London: Macmillan.

Einarsen, J. (1938) 'Reinvestment Cycles and their Manifestation in the Norwegian Shipping Industry,' *Review of Economic Statistics*, February.

Ezekiel, M. (1938) 'The Cobweb Theorem,' *Quarterly Journal of Economics*.

Fair, R. (2000) Fed Policy and the Effects of a Stock Market Crash on the Economy,' *Business Economics*, April, 7–14.

Fama, E.F. and French, K.R. (1988) Business Cycles and the Behaviour of Metals Prices,' *Journal of Finance*, 43(5), 1075–1093.

Fan, M. (2004) 'Are Commodities Proxies for Commodity Currencies?' *RCB Capital Markets*, Global FX Strategy, November.

Fazzari, S. and Papadimitriou, D.B. (eds) (1992) *Financial Conditions and Macroeconomic Performance*, M.E. Sharpe.

Federal Reserve Bank (1997), *Humphrey-Hawkins Report*, 22 July.

Ferguson, R.W. Jr (2005) *Recessions and Recoveries Associated with Asset-Price Movements – What do We Know?* Stanford Institute for Economic Policy Research, Stanford, California, 12 January.

Festinger, L. (1957) *A Theory of Cognitive Dissonance*, Stanford, California: Stanford University Press.

Filardo, A.J. (2000) 'Monetary policy and asset prices,' *Federal Reserve Bank of Kansas City Economic Review*, 85(3), 11–37.

Filardo, A. (2001) 'Should Monetary Policy Respond to Asset Price Bubbles? Some Experimental Results' in G. Kaufman (ed.) *Asset Price Bubbles: Implications for Monetary Policy and Regulatory Policies*, New York: JAI Press, pp. 99–118.

Fischhoff, B. (1975) 'Hindsight is Not Foresight: The Effect of Outcome Knowledge on Judgment under Uncertainty,' *Journal of Experimental Psychology: Human Perception and Performance*, 1, 288–299.

Fisher, I. (1896) *Appreciation and Interest*, New York: American Economic Association.

Fisher, I. (1920) *Stabilizing the Dollar*, New York: Macmillan.

Fisher, I. (1922a) *The Purchasing Power of Money*, New York: Macmillan. First published in 1911.

Fisher, I. (1922b) *The Making of Index Numbers: A study of their varieties, tests and reliability*, New York: Sentry Press.

Fisher, I. (1923) 'The Business Cycle Largely a Dance of the Dollar,' *Journal of the American Statistical Association*, December, 1024–1028.

Fisher, I. (1926) 'A Statistical Relation between Unemployment and Price Changes,' *International Labour Review*, 13(6), 785–792.

Fisher, I. (1930) *The Stock Market Crash – and After*, New York: Macmillan.

Fisher, I. (1933) 'The Debt-Deflation Theory of Great Depressions,' *Econometrica*, October.

Fisher, J. (2000) 'Forecasting Inflation with a Lot of Data,' Federal Reserve Bank of Chicago, *Chicago Fed Letter*, March.

Fisher, N. (1956) *My Father Irwin Fisher*, New York: Comet Press.

Foldvary, F.E. (1991) *Real Estate and Business Cycles: Henry George's Theory of the Trade Cycle*, Latvia University of Agriculture.

Forget, E.L. (1990) 'John Stuart Mill's Business Cycle,' *History of Political Economy*, 22(4), 629–642.

Forrester, J.W. (1976) 'Business Structure, Economic Cycles and National Policy,' *Business Economics*, January.

Forrester, J.W. (1992) 'From the Ranch to System Dynamics: An Autobiography,' in A.G. Bedeian (ed.) *A Collection of Autobiographical Essays*, Vol. 1, JAI Press.

Foster, W.T. and Catchings, W. (1923) *Money*, Boston: Houghton Mifflin Company.

Foster, W.T. and Catchings, W. (1925) *Profits*, Boston: Houghton Mifflin Company.

Foster, W.T. and Catchings, W. (1927) *Business Without a Buyer*, Boston: Houghton Mifflin Company.

Frazer, W.J. (1988) *Power and Ideas: Milton Friedman and the Big U-turn*, Gainsville, Florida: Gulf/Atlantic.

Friedman, B.M. (1986) 'Money, Credit, and Interest Rates in the Business Cycle,' in R.J. Gordon (ed.) *The American Business Cycle: Continuity and Change*, NBER, University of Chicago Press, pp. 395–438.

Friedman, B.M. (1992) *Money Mischief*, London: Harcourt.

Friedman, M. and Schwartz, A.J. (1963a) 'Money and Business Cycles,' *Review of Economics and Statistics*, 45, 32–78.

Friedman, M. and Schwartz, A.J. (1963b) *A Monetary History of the United States, 1867–1960*, Princeton University Press.

Frisch, R. (1933) 'Propagation Problems and Impulse Problems in Dynamic Economics,' in *Economic Essays in Honor of Gustav Cassel*, New York: George Allen & Unwin.

Galbraith, J.K. (1955) *The Great Crash 1929*, New York: Houghton Mifflin.

Galbraith, J.K. (1971) *Economics, Peace and Laughter*, New York: Houghton Mifflin.

Garner, A.C. (1995) 'How useful are leading indicators of inflation?' *Federal Reserve Bank of Kansas City Economic Review*, 80(2), 5–18.

Garrison, C.B. (1984) 'Friedman versus Keynes on the Theory of Employment,' *Journal of Post Keynesian Economics*, 7(1), 114–127.

George, H. (1975) *Progress and Poverty*, Robert Schalkenback Foundation.

GFMS (2005) *World Silver Study 2005*.

Gilovich, T., Medvec, V.H. and Kahneman, D. (1998) 'Varieties of Regret: A Debate and Partial Resolution,' *Psychological Review*, 105, 602–605.

Glasner, D. (1997) *Business Cycles and Depressions*, Garland.

Gleeson, J. (1999) *The Moneymaker*, Bantam Books.

Gleich, J. (1987) *Chaos – Making a New Science*, Viking, USA.

Goetzmann, W.N. and Peles, N. (1993) *Cognitive Dissonance and Mutual Fund Investors*, Yale School of Management.

Gordon, R.A. (1952) *Business Fluctuations*, New York: Harper and Row.

Gorton, G. and Rouwenhorst, K.G. (2004) *Facts and Fantasies About Commodity Futures*, Yale IFC Working Paper No. 04–20.

Gotthelf, P. (2005) *Precious Metals Trading: How To Forecast and Profit from Major Market Moves*, New Jersey: John Wiley & Sons, Inc.

Grant, J. (1992) *Money of the Mind*, New York: Farra Straus Giroux.

Green, T. (1981) *The New World of Gold: The Inside Story of the Mines, the Markets, the Politics, the Investors*, Walker & Company.

Grissom, T. and DeLisle, J.R. (1999) 'A Multiple Index Analysis of Real Estate Cycles and Structural Change,' *Journal of Real Estate Finance*, 18(1), 97–129.

Hadady, R.E. (1983) *Contrary Opinion, How to Use It for Profit in Commodity Futures*, Hadady Publications, USA.

Hamish, T. (1994) *An Investigation into Forecasting Methods to Derive Gold Price Movements*, 78.499 Research Report, Massey University.

Hansen, A. and Clemence, R.V. (1959) *Readings in Business Cycles and National Income*, 2nd edition, London: George Allen & Unwin.

Harlow, G.E. (ed.) (1998) *The Nature of Diamonds*, Cambridge: Cambridge University Press.

Harrison, F. (1983) *The Power in the Land*, New York: Universe Books.

Hartley, J., Hoover, K.D. and Salyer, K.D. (1998) *Real Business Cycles: A Reader*, Routledge.

Havrilevski, T. (1972) 'The Money Supply Theory of J.S. Mill,' *South African Journal of Economics*, 40(1), 72–76.

Hawkins, S.A. and Hastie, R. (1990) 'Hindsight: Biased Judgements of Past Events after the Outcomes Are Known,' *Psychological Bulletin*, 107, 311–327.

Hawtrey, R. (1913) *Good and Bad Trade: An Inquiry into the Causes of Trade Fluctuations*, London: Constable & Co.

Hayford, M. and Malliaris, A.G. (2001) 'Is the Federal Reserve Stock Market Bubble-Neutral?' in G. Kaufman (ed.) *Asset Price Bubbles: Implications for Monetary Policy and Regulatory Policies*, New York: JAI Press, pp. 229–243.

Heath, R. (2005) *Real Estate as Financial Soundness Indicators*, BIS Papers 21, Bank of International Settlements.

Heilbroner, R.L. (1999) *The Worldly Philosophers: The lives, times and ideas of the great economic thinkers*, 7th edition, Pocket Books. First published in 1953.

Helbling, T.H. (2005) *Housing Price Bubbles – a Tale Based on Housing Price Booms and Busts*, BIS Papers 21, Bank of International Settlements.

Helbling, T.H. and Terrones, M. (2003) 'When Bubbles Burst,' in *World Economic Outlook 2003*, IMF.

Hetzel, R.L. (1987) 'Henry Thornton: Seminal Monetary Theorist and Father of the Modern Central Bank,' *Federal Reserve Bank of Richmond Economic Review*, 73(4), 3–16.

Hicks, J.R. (1969) 'Automatists, Hawtreyans, and Keynesians,' *Journal of Money, Credit and Banking*, 1(3), 307–317.

Hobson, J.A. (1988) *The Physiology of Industry: Being an exposure of certain fallacies in existing theories of economics*, A.M. Kelley. First published in 1889.

Hoggarth, G., Reis, R. and Saporta, V. (2001) 'Costs of banking system instability: some empirical evidence,' *Financial Stability Review*, Bank of England, issue 10, article 5, June.

Holtrop, M.W. (1929) 'Theories of the Velocity of Circulation of Money in Earlier Economic Literature,' *The Economic Journal*, January.

Hoyt, H. (1933) *One Hundred Years of Land Values in Chicago*, Chicago: Chicago University Press.

Humphrey, T.M. (1990) 'Ricardo versus Thornton on the Appropriate Monetary Response to Supply Shocks,' *Federal Reserve Bank of Richmond Economic Review*, 76(6), 18–24.

Hurst, H.E. (1951) 'Long-term Storage Capacity of Reservoirs,' *Transactions of the American Society of Civil Engineers*, 116, 770–808.

Hurst, H.E., Black, R.P. and Simaika, Y.M. (1965) *Long Term Storage: An Experimental Study*, London: Constable.

IMF (2003) *World Economic Outlook*, April.

IMF (2005) *Global Financial Stability Report: Market Developments and Issues*, September.

Irwin, S.H. and Landa, D. (1987) 'Real Estate, Futures and Gold as Portfolio Assets,' *The Journal of Portfolio Management*.

Janis, I. (1972) *Victims of Groupthink*, Houston: Boston.

Janssen, J., Kruijt, B. and Needham, B. (1993) 'The Honeycomb Cycle in Real Estate,' *The Journal of Real Estate Research*, 9(2).

Jegadeesh, N. and Titman, S. (1993) 'Return to Buying Winners and Selling Losers: Implications for Stock Market Efficiency,' *Journal of Finance*, 48(1).

Jevons, W.S. (1871) *The Theory of Political Economy*, London: Macmillan.

Jevons, W.S. (1875) *Money and the Mechanism of Exchange*, London: H.S. King.

Jevons, W.S. (1876) 'The Future of Political Economy,' *Fortnightly Review*, November.

Jevons, W.S. (1884) *Investigations in Currency and Finance*, London: Macmillan.

Joint Center for Housing Studies of Harvard University (2004) *The State of the Nation's Housing 2004*.

Juglar, C. (1862) *Les Crises Commerciales et leur Retour Periodique en France, en Angleterre et aux Etats Unis*.

Juster, F.T., Lupton, J.P., Smith, J.P. and Stafford, F. (2004) *The Decline in Household Saving and the Wealth Effect*, Board of Governors of the Federal Reserve System.

Kahn, R. (1972) 'The Relationship of Home Investment to Unemployment,' in R. Kahn (ed.) *Selected Essays on Employment and Growth*, Cambridge: Cambridge University Press.

Kahneman, D. (1970) 'Remarks on Attention Control,' in A.F. Sanders (ed.), *Attention and Performance III*, pp. 118–131.

Kahneman, D. (1991) 'Judgment and Decision Making: A Personal View,' *Psychological Science*, 2, 142–145.

Kahneman, D. (1994) 'New Challenges to the Rationality Assumption,' *Journal of Institutional and Theoretical Economics*, 150, 18–36.

Kahneman, D. and Henik, A. (1981), 'Perceptual Organization and Attention,' in M. Kubovy and J. Pomerantz (eds) *PerceptualOrganization*, Hillsdale, NJ: Lawrence Erlbaum.

Kahneman, D. and Riepe, M. (1998) 'Aspects of Investor Psychology,' *The Journal of Portfolio Management*, 24, 52–65.

Kahneman, D. and Tversky, A. (1973) 'On the Psychology of Prediction,' *Psychological Review*, 80, 237–251.

Kahneman, D. and Tversky, A. (1979a) 'Prospect Theory: An Analysis of Decisions under Risk,' *Econometrica*, 263–291.

Kahneman, D. and Tversky, A. (1979b) 'Intuitive Prediction: Biases and Corrective Procedures,' *Management Science*, 12, 313–327.

Kahneman, D. and Tversky, A. (1982) 'The Psychology of Preferences,' *Scientific American*, 246, 160–173.

Kahneman, D. and Tversky, A. (1984) 'Choices, Values and Frames,' *American Psychologist*, 39, 341–350.

Kahneman, D., Knetsch, J. and Thaler, R. (1991) 'The Endowment Effect, Loss Aversion, and Status Quo Bias,' *Journal of Economic Perspectives*, 5, 193–206.

Kahneman, D., Slovic, P. and Tversky, A. (1974) *Judgement under Uncertainty: Heuristics and Biases*, Cambridge: Cambridge University Press.

Kahneman, D., Slovic, P. and Tversky, A. (eds) (1982) *Judgment under Uncertainty: Heuristics and Biases*, New York: Cambridge University Press.

Kahneman, D., Tursky, B., Shapiro, D. and Crider, A. (1969) 'Pupillary Heart Rate and Skin Resistance Changes During a Mental Task,' *Journal of Experimental Psychology*, 79, 164–167.

Kaldor, N. (1972) 'The Irrelevance of Equilibrium Economics,' *Economic Journal*, 82(328), 1237–1255.

Kaplan, S. and Schoar, A. (2003) *Private Equity Performance: Returns Persistence and Capital*, NBER Working Paper 9807.

Katona, G. (1975) *Psychological Economics*, New York: Elsevier.

Katz, J. (2004) 'Running in Cycles – Ups and Downs in the Market for Downtown Office Space,' *Regional Review Q2/Q3*, Federal Reserve Bank of Boston.

Kearns, J. and Manners, P. (2005) *The Impact of Monetary Policy on the Exchange Rate: A Study Using Intraday Data*, Research Discussion Paper, Economic Research Department, Reserve Bank of Australia.

Key, T., Firoozeh, Z. and Haq, N. (1999) *The UK Property Cycle – a History from 1921 to 1997*, The Royal Institute of Chartered Surveyors.

Keynes, J.M. (1936) *The General Theory of Employment, Interest and Money*, London: Macmillan.

Keynes, J.M. (1965) *A Treatise on Money*, London: Macmillan & Co. First published in 1930.

Kindleberger, C.P. (1986) *The World in Depression, 1929–1939*, Berkeley: University of California Press.

Kindleberger, C.P. (1995) 'Asset inflation and monetary policy,' *BNL Quarterly Review*, no. 192.

Kindleberger, C.P. (2000) *Manias, Panics, and Crashes*, 4th edition, Macmillan, USA.

Kindleberger, C.P. and Laffargue, J-E. (1982) *Financial Crises*, Cambridge: Cambridge University Press.

Kitchin, J. (1923) 'Cycles and Trends in Economic Factors,' *The Review of Economic Statistics*, January, 10–16.

Klapwijk, P. (2003) *Medium- to Long-Term Outlook for Gold and Silver*, Presentation Paper, The LMBA Precious Metals Conference 2003, Lisbon.

Klein, L. (1946) 'Macroeconomics and the Theory of Rational Behavior,' *Econometrica*, 14.

Klein, M. (1986) *The Life and Legend of Jay Gould*, Baltimore: Johns Hopkins Press.

Klock, C.P. (1992) *Konjunkturteori*, Masters Thesis (unpublished), Copenhagen Business School.

Kondratieff, N. (1926) 'Die Langen Wellen der Konjunktur,' *Archiv für Sozialwissenschaft und Sozialpolitik*, 56, 573–609.

Kondratieff, N. (1984) *The Long Wave Cycle*, reprint, Richardson and Snyder, USA.

Krystaloyianni, A., Matysiak, G. and Tsolacos, S. (2004) 'Forecasting UK Commercial Real Estate Cycle Phases With Leading Indicators: A Probit Approach.' *Working Papers in Real Estate and Planning* 15/04, Department of Real Estate and Planning: The University of Reading.

Kuznets, S.S. (1930) *Secular Movements in Production and Prices*, New York: Houghton Mifflin Company.

Kydland, F. and Prescott, E.C. (1982) 'Time to Build and Aggregate Fluctuations,' *Econometrica*, 50, 1345–1370.

Kydland, F.E. and Prescott, E.C. (1990) 'Business Cycles: Real Facts and Monetary Myths,' *The Federal Reserve Bank of Minneapolis Quarterly Review*, Fall.

Lahiri, K. and Moore, G.H. (1991) *Leading Economic Indicators*, Cambridge: Cambridge University Press.

LeBaron, B. (1988) *Stock Return Nonlinearities: Comparing Tests and Finding Structure*, University of Wisconsin-Madison, November.

LeBaron, D. (1983) 'Some Reflections on Market Efficiency,' *Financial Analysts Journal*, May/June.

Lefevre, E. (1964) *Reminiscences of a Stock Operator*, reprint, New York: American Research Council.

Lewis, M. (2001) *The New New Thing*, Penguin.

Long, C.D. (1939) 'Long Cycles in the Building Industry,' *Quarterly Journal of Economics*, 53, 371–403.

Long, C.D. (1940) *Building Cycles and the Theory of Investment*, Princeton University Press.

Loomes, G. and Sugden, R. (1982) 'Regret Theory: An Alternative Theory of Rational Choice under Uncertainty,' *The Economic Journal*, 92, 805–824.

Lorenz, E. (1963) 'Deterministic Nonperiodic Flow,' *Journal of Atmospheric Sciences*, 20.

Lorenz, E. (1964) 'The Problem of Deducing the Climate from the Governing Equations,' *Tellus*, 16.

Lorenz, E. (1979) *Predictability: Does the Flap of a Butterfly's Wings in Brazil set off a Tornado in Texas?*, Washington: American Association for the Advancement of Science.

Lorenz, H.W. (1987) *Can Keynesian Demand Policy Imply Chaos?*, Georg-August-Universitat Göttingen.

Lowenstein, R. (2004) *Origins of the Crash*, The Penguin Press.

Lucas, R.E. (1972) 'Expectations and the Rationality of Money,' *Journal of Economic Theory*, 4.

Lucas, R.E. (1975) 'Econometric Policy Evaluation: A Critique,' in K. Brunner and A.H. Meltzer (eds) *The Phillips Curve and Labour Markets*, Carnegie-Rochester Conference Series on Public Policy 1, North-Holland, pp. 19–46.

Lucas, R.E. (1981) *Studies in Business Cycle Theory*, Cambridge, Mass.: The MIT Press.

Lucas, R.E. and Sargent, T.J. (eds) (1981) *Rational Expectations and Economic Practise*, Minneapolis: University of Minnesota Press.

Ludvigson, S. and Steindel, C. (1999) 'How Important is the Stock Market Effect on Consumption?' *Economic Policy Review*, Federal Reserve Bank of New York, 5.

Lynch, P. (2000) *One Up On Wall Street: How To Use What You Already Know To Make Money In The Market*, New York: Simon & Schuster.

Macaulay, F.R. (1938) *The Movements of Interest Rates, Bond Yields and Stock Prices in the United States since 1856*, New York: NBER.

Mackay, C. (1980) *Extraordinary Popular Delusions and the Madness of Crowds*, reprint, New York: Harmony Books.

Mager, N.H. (1987) *The Kondratieff Waves*, New York: Praeger.

Mallet, J.L. (1921) *Minutes of Proceedings Roll of Members, and Questions Discussed of the Political Economy Club*.

Mandelbrot, B.B. (1966) 'Forecasts of Future Prices, Unbiased Markets, and "Martingale" Models,' *Journal of Business*, 242–255.

Mandelbrot, B.B. (1966) 'The Variation of Some Other Speculative Prices,' *Journal of Business*.

Mandelbrot, B.B. (1971) 'When Can Price be Arbitraged Efficiently? A Limit to the Validity of the Random Walk and Martingale Models,' *The Review of Economics and Statistics*, 53, 225–236.

Mandelbrot, B.B. (1972) 'Statistical Methods for Nonperiodic Cycles: From the Covariance to R/S Analysis,' *Annals of Economic and Social Measurement*, 1/3, 259–290.

Mandelbrot, B.B. and Wallis, J.R. (1968) 'Noah, Joseph and Operational Hydrology,' *Water Resources Research*, IV, 909–918.

Mandelbrot, B.B. and Wallis, J.R. (1969) 'Robustness of the Rescaled Range R/S in the Measurement of Noncyclic Long Run Statistical Dependence,' *Water Resources Research*, 5.

March, J.G. (1994) *A Primer on Decision Making. How Decisions Happen*, New York: Free Press.

Marshall, A. (1947) *Principles of Economics*, 8th edition, London: MacMillan.

Marshall, A. (2003) *Money, Credit and Commerce*, Prometheus Books. First published in 1923.

Martellaro, J.A. (1985) 'From Say's Law to Supply-side Economics,' *Rivista Internazionale di Science Economiche e Commerciali*, 32.

Martin, L.L. and Clark, L.F. (1990) 'Social Cognition: Exploring the Mental Processes Involved in Human Social Interaction,' in M.W. Eysenck (ed.) *Cognitive Psychology, An International Review*, New York: John Wiley & Sons, Inc.

Marx, K. (1867) *Das Kapital*.

Maslow, A.H. (1943) 'A Theory of Human Motivation,' *Psychological Review*, 50.

Mass, N.J. (1975) *Economic Cycles: An Analysis of Underlying Causes*, Cambridge, Mass.: Wright-Allen Press.

Matlin, M. (1994) *Cognition*, 3rd edition, New York: Harcourt Brace.

Matysiak, G. and Tsolacos, S. (2003) 'Identifying short-term leading indicators for real estate rental performance,' *Journal of Property Investment and Finance*, 21(3).

May, R. (1976) 'Simple Mathematical Models with Very Complicated Dynamics,' *Nature*, 261, 459–467.

May, R. and Oster, G.F. (1976) 'Bifurcations and Dynamic Complexity in Simple Ecological Models,' *The American Naturalist*, 110, 573–599.

Mayer, C. and Simons, K. (1994) 'International Evidence on the Determinants of Saving,' *Journal of American Real Estate and Urban Economics*, 22(2).

Mazursky, D. and Ofir, C. (1990) 'I Could Never Have Expected It to Happen: The Reversal of the Hindsight Bias,' *Organizational Behavior and Human Decision Processes*, 46, 20–33.

McGuire, W.J. (1969) 'Attitudes and Attitude Change,' in G. Lindzey and E. Aronson (eds) *Handbook of Social Psychology*, Reading, Mass.: Addison-Wesley, pp. 233–246.

McKinsey Global Institute (2005) *$118 Trillion and Counting: Taking Stock of the World's Capital Markets*.

Mehra (2001) 'The Wealth Effects in Empirical Life Cycle Aggregates Consumption Equations,' *Federal Reserve Bank of Richmond Quarterly Review*, 87.

Mei, J. and Moses, M. (2002) 'Art as an investment and the underperformance of masterpieces,' *The American Economic Review*, Bd. 92, 5.

Meltzer, A.H. (1967) 'Money Supply Revisited: A Review Article,' *Journal of Political Economy*, 2.

Merrill Lynch (2004) *Size and Structure of the World Bond Market 2004*.

Metzler, L.A. (1941) 'The Nature and Stability of Inventory Cycles,' *Review of Economics and Statistics*, 23.

Metzler, L.A. (1947) 'Factors Governing the Length of Inventory Cycles,' *Review of Economics and Statistics*, 29, 1–15.

Mill, J. (1821) *Elements of Political Economy*.

Mill, J.S. (1826) *Paper Currency and Commercial Distress*.

Mill, J.S. (1920) *The Principles of Political Economy with Some of their Applications to Social Philosophy*, London: Longmans Green.

Millman, G.J. (1995) *Around the World on a Trillion Dollars a Day*, London: Transworld Publishers Ltd.

Minsky, H. (1957) 'Central Banking and Money Market Changes,' *Quarterly Journal of Economics*, 71(2), 171–187.

Minsky, H. (1975) *John Maynard Keynes*, New York: Columbia University Press.

Minsky, H.P. (1982) *Can 'It' Happen Again?*, New York: Armonk.

Minsky, H.P. (1986) *Stabilizing an Unstable Economy*, New Haven: Yale University Press.

Mischel, W. (1986) *Introduction to Personality*, Fort Worth, Chicago: Holt, Rinehart and Winston.

Mises, M. (1981) *Ludwig von Mises, der Mensch and sein Werk*, Philosophia Verlag.

Mitchell, W.C. (1913) *Business Cycles*, Berkeley: University of California Press.

Mitchell, W.C. (1927) *Business Cycles – The Problem and its Setting*, New York: NBER.

Mitchell, W.C. (1941) *Business Cycles and their Causes*, University of California Press.

Mitchell, W.C. (1951) *What Happens During Business Cycles?*, New York: NBER.

Modigliani, F. and Tarantelli, E. (1975) 'The Consumption Function in a Developing Country and the Italian Experience,' *American Economic Review*, 65.

Moore, G.H. (ed.) (1965) *Business Cycle Indicators*, Books on Demand.

Moore, G.H. (1969) 'Generating Leading Indicators from Lagging Indicators,' *Western Economic Journal*, 7(2), June.

Moore, G.H. (1980) *Business Cycles, Inflation, and Forecasting*, Cambridge, Mass.: Ballinger Publishing Company.

Moore, G.H. and Cullity, J.P. (1988) 'Little-known Facts about Stock Prices and Business Cycles,' *Challenge*, 31(2), 49–50.

Moore, G.H. and Shiskin, J. (1967) *Indicators of Business Expansions and Contractions*, NBER.

Mosekilde, E. and Larsen, E.R. (1988) 'Deterministic Chaos in the Beer Production-Distribution Model,' *System Dynamics Review*, 4(1–2), 131–147.

Mosekilde, E., Larsen, E.R., Sterman, J.D. and Thomsen, J.S. (1992) 'Non-linear Mode Interaction in the Macroeconomy,' *Annals of Operations Research*, 37.

Munthe, P. (1977) 'Foster and Catchings – Amerikanske Underkonsumptionister,' *Ekonomisk Debatt*, 2.

Murphy, J.J. (1991) *Intermarket Technical Analysis*, New York: John Wiley & Sons, Inc.

Muth, J.A. (1961) 'Rational Expectations and the Theory of Price Movements,' *Econometrica*, 29(3), 315–335.

Neisser, U. (1967) *Cognitive Psychology*, New York: Appleton-Century-Crofts.

Nenties, A. (1988) 'Hayek and Keynes: A Comparative Analysis of their Monetary Views,' *Journal of Economic Studies*, 15(3–4), 136–151.

Newcomb, S. (1885) *Principles of Political Economy*, New York: Harper & Brothers.

Nordhaus, W. (1975) 'The Political Business Cycle,' *Review of Economic Studies*, 42, 169–190.

O'Brian, D.P. (1971) *The Correspondence of Lord Overstone*, Cambridge: Cambridge University Press.

O'Connor, R. (1962) *Gould's Millions*, New York: Doubleday.

Odean, T. (1998) 'Are Investors Reluctant to Realize Their Losses?,' *Journal of Finance*, LIII(5), October, 1775–1798.

Odean, T. and Barber, B. (1999) 'The Courage of Misguided Convictions: The Trading Behavior of Individual Investors,' *Financial Analysts Journal*, Nov/Dec, 41–55.

Odean, T. and Barber, B. (2000) 'Too Many Cooks Spoil the Profits: The Performance of Investment Clubs,' *Financial Analysts Journal*, Jan/Feb, 17–25.

Odean, T. and Gervais, S. (2001) 'Learning to be Overconfident,' *Review of Financial Studies*, 14(1), 1–27.

O'Donnel, R.M. (1990) 'Keynes on Mathematics: Philosophical Foundations and Economic Applications,' *Cambridge Journal of Economics*, 14(1), 29–47.

Ogawe, K. (1992) 'An Econometric Analysis of Japanese Households' Behavior,' *Financial Review*, 25.

Ormerod, P. (1994) *The Death of Economics*, Faber and Faber.

Oyen, D.B. (1991) *Business Fluctuations and Forecasting*, Dearborne.

Patinkin, D. (1976) 'Keynes and Econometrics: On the Interaction Between the Macroeconomic Revolutions of the Interwar Period,' *Econometrica*, 44(6), 1091–1123.

Patinkin, D. (1978) *Keynes and the Multiplier*, The Manchester School, pp. 209–223.

Patinkin, D. and Leith, J.C. (1977) *Keynes, Cambridge and the General Theory*, London: The Macmillan Press.

Patterson, R.T. (1956) *The Great Boom and Panic 1921–1929*, Chicago: Henry Regnery Co.

Peake, C.F. (1978) 'Henry Thornton and the Development of Ricardo's Economic Thought,' *History of Political Economy*, 10(2), 193–212.

Perkins, A.B. and Perkins, M.C. (1999) *The Internet Bubble: Inside the Overvalued World of High-Tech Stocks – And What You Need to Know to Avoid the Coming Shakeout*, HarperCollins Publishers.

Persons, W.M. and Frickey, E. (1926) 'Money Rates and Security Prices,' *The Review of Economic Statistics*, January 29–46.

Pesaran, H. and Smith, R. (1985) 'Keynes on Econometrics,' in T. Lawson and H. Pesaran (eds) *Keynes's Economics: Methodological Issues*, New York: Armonk pp. 134–150.

Peters, E. (1991) *Chaos and Order in the Capital Markets*, New York: John Wiley & Sons, Inc.

Peters, E. (1994) *Fractal Markets Analysis, Applying Chaos Theory to Investment and Economics*, New York: John Wiley & Sons, Inc.

Phillips, A.W. (1958) 'The Relationship between Unemployment and the Rate of Change of Money Wage Rates in the United Kingdom, 1861–1957,' *Economica*, 25, 283–289.

Pigou, A.C. (1927) *Industrial Fluctuations*, Macmillan.

Pigou, A.C. (1943) 'The Classical Stationary State,' *Economic Journal*, 53.

Poincaré, H. (1992) *New Methods of Celestial Mechanics*, American Institute of Physics.

Political Economy Club (1876) *Revised Report of the Proceedings at the Dinner of 31st May, 1876, held in Celebration of the Hundredth Year of the Publication of the 'Wealth of Nations'*, London, p. 88.

Pring, M. (1992) *The All-season Investor: Successful strategies for every stage in the business cycle*, New York: John Wiley & Sons, Inc.

Pudney, S. (1989) *Modelling Individual Choice*, Oxford, New York: Basil Blackwell.

Pyhr, S.A., Roulac, S.E. and Born, W.L. (1999) 'Real Estate Cycles and Their Strategic Implications for Investors and Portfolio Managers in the Global Economy,' *Journal of Real Estate Research*, 18(2).

Quattrone, G.A. and Tversky, A. (1984) 'Causal versus Diagnostic Contingencies: On Self-Deception and on the Voter's Illusion,' *Journal of Personality and Social Psychology*, 46(2), 237–248.

Quigley, J.M. (1999) 'Real Estate Prices and Economic Cycles,' *International Real Estate Review*, 2(1).

Rasmussen, D.R. and Mosekilde, E. (1988) 'Bifurcations and Chaos in a Generic Management Model,' *North European Journal of Operational Research*, 35, 80–88.

Rasmussen, S., Mosekilde, E. and Sterman, J.D. (1985) 'Bifurcations and Chaos in a Simple Model of the Economic Long Wave,' *System Dynamics Review*, 1.

RBC Capital Markets (2004) *Are Commodities Proxies for Commodity Currencies?* Global FX Strategy, November.

Reid, P.R. and Schreft, S.L. (1993) 'Credit Aggregates from the Flow of Funds Accounts,' *Federal Reserve Bank of Richmond Economic Quarterly*, 79/3, summer.

Ricardo, D. (1810) *The High Price of Bullion: A Proof of the Depreciation of Bank Notes*.

Ricardo, D. (1816) *Proposals for an Economical and Secure Currency*.

Rigobon, R. and Sack, B. (2001) *Measuring the Reaction of Monetary Policy to the Stock Market*, NBER working paper 8350.

Robbins, L. (1998) *A History of Economic Thought*, Princeton, NJ: Princeton University Press.

Robertson, D.H. (1915) *A Study of Industrial Fluctuations*, Westminster: P.S. King and Son.

Robertson, D. (1922) *Money*, Nisbet & Co.

Robertson, D. (1926) *Banking Policy and the Price Level*, London: Macmillan.

Robinson, A. (1972) 'John Maynard Keynes: Economist, Author, Statesman,' *The Economic Journal*, June.

Rossi, N. and Visco, I. (1995) 'National Savings and Social Security in Italy,' *Recierce Economiche*, 49.

Rousseau, P.L. (2001) *Jacksonian Monetary Policy, Specie Flow, and the Panic of 1837*, working paper no. 00-W04R, Vanderbilt University.

Routh, G. (1989) *The Origins of Economic Ideas*, London: Macmillan.

Ruysso, J.E. and Schoemaker, J.H. (1990) *Decision Traps: Ten Barriers to Brilliant Decision-Making and How to Overcome Them*, New York: Simon & Schuster.

Samuelson, P. (1939) *Interaction Between the Multiplier Analysis and the Principle of Acceleration*, RES.

Samuelson, P. (1955) *Economics*, 3rd edition, New York: McGraw Hill.

Samuelson, P. and Solow, R.M. (1960) 'Analytical Aspects of Anti-Inflation Policy,' *American Economic Review*, 50, 177–184.

Sargent, T.J. and Wallace, N. (1976) 'Rational Expectations and the Theory of Economic Policy,' *Journal of Monetary Economics*, 2.

Say, J-B. (1803) *Traite d'Economie Politique*.

Say, J.B. (1827) *A Treatise on Political Economy on the Production, Distribution, and Consumption of Wealth*, Philadelphia: John Grigg.

Sayers, C.L. (1989) *Chaos and the Business Cycle*, Department of Economics, University of Houston, May.

Scheide, J. (1989) 'On Real and Monetary Causes for Business Cycles in West Germany,' *Schweizerische Zeitsehrift fur Wolswirtscaft and Statistik*, 125(4).

Schneeweis, T., Kazemi, H. and Martin, G. (2001) *Understanding Hedge Fund Performance*, Lehman Brothers.

Schneeweis, T., Spugin, R. and Georgiev, G. (2000) *The LMEX And Asset Allocation: The Economic Foundations For Investment Into Base Metals*, Center for International Securities and Derivatives Markets.

Schumpeter, J. (1939) *Business Cycles*, New York: McGraw-Hill.

Schumpeter, J. (1951) *Ten Great Economists*, London: George Allen & Unwin.

Schumpeter, J. (1954) *The History of Economic Analysis*, London: Allen and Unwin.

Schumpeter, J. (1961) *The Theory of Economic Development* (reprint), Harvard University Press, Mass. First published in 1911 (in German).

Scinasi, G.J. and Hargraves, M. (1993) *Boom and Bust in Asset Markets in the 1980s: Causes and Consequences*, Washington DC: International Monetary Fund, Staff Studies for the Economic Outlook.

Scotland, F. (ed.) (2004) 'Forecasting Sector Performance: A Cycle Approach,' *Bank Credit Analyst*.

Scotland, F. (ed.) (2005) 'Global Equity Market Cycles,' *Bank Credit Analyst*.

Scott, W.R. (1937) *Adam Smith as Student and Professor*, Glasgow: Jackson, Son & Co.

Shaffer, S. (1991) 'Structural Shifts and the Volatility of Chaotic Markets,' *Journal of Economic Behaviour and Organisation*, 15, 201–214.

Sharp, M.S. (1989) *The Lore and Legends of Wall Street*, Dow Jones-Irwin.
Shefold, B. (1986) 'Schumpeter as a Walrasian Austrian and Keynes as a Classical Marshallian,' in H.J. Wagener and J.W. Drukker, (eds) *The Economic Law of Motion of Modern Society: a Marx–Schumpeter Centential*, Cambridge: Cambridge University Press, pp. 93–111.
Shefrin, H. and Statman, M. (1985) 'The Disposition to Sell Winners Too Early and Ride Losers Too Long: Theory and Evidence,' *Journal of Finance*, XL, 777–792.
Sherif, M. (1937) 'An Experimental Approach to the Study of Attitudes,' *Sociometry*, 1.
Shibata, Y. (1999) *The Art of a Failed Economy*, Japan.inc, December.
Shiller, R.J. (1984) *Stock Prices and Social Dynamics*, Brookings.
Shiller, R.J. (1986) *Survey Evidence Regarding the September 11–12 Stock Market Drop*, Yale University, November.
Shiller, R.J. (1987a) 'Fashions, Fads and Bubbles in Financial Markets,' in J. Coffee (ed.) *Knights, Raiders and Targets. The Impact of the Hostile Takeover*, Oxford: Oxford University Press.
Shiller, R.J. (1987b) 'Investor Behaviour in the October 1987 Stock Market Crash: Survey Evidence,' NBER working paper 2446, reprinted in Robert Shiller, *Market Volatility* (1989).
Shiller, R.J. (1989) *Market Volatility*, Cambridge, Mass.: MIT Press.
Shiller, R.J. (1990) 'Market Volatility and Investor Behavior,' *American Economic Review*, 80(2), 58–62.
Shiller, R.J. (1995) 'Conversation, Information, and Herd Behavior,' *American Economic Review*.
Shiller, R.J. (1997a) 'Public Resistance to Indexation: A Puzzle,' *Brookings Papers on Economic Activity*, I, 159–228.
Shiller, R.J. (1997b) 'Human Behavior and the Efficiency of the Financial System,' working paper, Yale University.
Shiller, R.J. (2000) *Irrational Exuberance*, Princeton University Press.
Shiller, R.J., Kon-Ya, F. and Tsuitsui, Y. (1996) 'Why Did the Nikkei Crash? Expanding the Scope of Expectations Data Collection,' *Review of Economics and Statistics*, 78, 156–164.
Shiratsuka, S. (2005) 'The Asset Price Bubble in Japan in the 1980s: Lessons for Financial and Macroeconomic Stability,' in *BIS Papers No. 21 – Real Estate Indicators and Financial Stability*.
Shleifer, A. (1986) 'Do Demand Curves for Stocks Slope Down?' *Journal of Finance*, 41, 579–589.
Siegel, J.J. (1991) 'Does it Pay Stock Investors to Forecast the Business Cycle?,' *Journal of Portfolio Management*, 18, 27–34.
Silberman, J. and Klock, M. (1989) 'The Behavior of Respondents in Contingent Valuation: Evidence on Starting Bids,' *Journal of Behavioral Economics*, 18, 51–60.
Simon, H.A. (1955) 'A Behavioral Model of Rational Choice,' *Quarterly Journal of Economics*, 69, 99–118.
Simon, H.A. (1987) 'Behavioral Economics,' in J. Eatwell, M. Millgate and P. Newman (eds) *The New Palgrave: A Dictionary of Economics*, London and Basingstoke: Macmillan.
Sinlapapreechar, I. (2003) *Hedge Fund Returns and Market Factors*, Masters thesis, Johns Hopkins University.

Sirkin, G.W. (1976) 'Business Structure, Business Cycles and National Policy, Comment,' *Business Economics*, March.

Skinner, B.F. (1938) *The Behaviour of Organisms*, New York: Appleton-Century.

Slater, R. (1987) *Portraits in Silicon*, Massachusets: MIT.

Slater, R. (1996) *Soros*, New York: Irwin.

Slovic, P. (1972) 'Psychological Study of Human Judgment: Implications for Investment Decision Making under Uncertainty,' *Journal of Finance*, 27(4), 779–799.

Smets, F. (1997) *Financial asset prices and monetary policy: theory and evidence*, BIS working Paper no. 47, September.

Smith, A. (1937) *An Inquiry into the Nature and Causes of the Wealth of Nations*, New York: Modern Library Edition.

Smith, A. (1976) *The Theory of Moral Sentiments*, Indianapolis: Liberty Classics. First published in 1759.

Smith, W.B. and Cole, A.H. (1935) *Fluctuations in American Business, 1790–1860*, Harvard University Press.

Sobel, R. (1999) *Panic on Wall Street: A History of America's Financial Disasters*, Beard Books. First published in 1968.

Solnik, B. (1984) 'Stock Prices and Monetary Variables: The International Evidence,' *Financial Analysts Journal*, March–April.

Somary, F. (1963) *Erinnerung Aus Meinen Leben*, Manesse Verlag.

Soros, G. (1987) *The Alchemy of Finance*, Simon & Schuster, USA.

Sowards, J.K. (1965) *Western Civilisation to 1660*, St Martin's Press, USA.

Sperling, J.G. (1962) *The South Sea Company*, Boston, Mass.: Baker Library.

Spiegel, H.W. (1983) *The Growth of Economic Thought*, Durham, North Carolina: Duke University Press.

Spiegel, H.W. and Samuels, W.J. (1984) *Contemporary Economists in Perspective*, Greenwich, Connecticut, JAI Press, Inc.

Spiethoff, A. (1902) 'Vorbemerkungen zu einer Theorie der Überproduktion,' in *Jahrbuch für Gesetzgebung, Verwaltung und Volkswirtschaft im Deutschen Reich*, 26, 721–759.

Spiethoff, A. (1903) 'Die Krisentheorien von M. Tugan-Baranowsky und L. Pohle,' in *Jahrbuch für Gesetzgebung, Verwaltung und Volkswirtschaft im Deutschen Reich*, 27, 679–708.

St. John-Stevas, N. (1965–1986) The Collected Works of Walter Bagehot, *The Economist*, 9.

Staley, C.E. (1989) *A History of Economic Thought: From Aristotle to Arrow*, Cambridge, Mass.: Basil Blackwell.

Statman, M. (1988) 'Investor Psychology and Market Inefficiencies,' in K.F. Sherrerd (ed.) *Equity Markets and Valuation Methods*, Charlottesville, VA: The Institute of Chartered Financial Analysts.

Statman, M. (1989) 'Cognitive Biases,' *Intermarket*, July.

Statman, M. (1994a) 'Behavioral Capital Asset Pricing Theory,' *Journal of Financial and Quantitaive Analysis*, September.

Statman, M. (1994b) 'Tracking Errors, Regret, and Tactical Asset Allocation,' *Journal of Portfolio Management*.

Statman, M. (1997a) 'Behavioral Finance,' *Contemporary Finance Digest*.

Statman, M. (1997b) 'Investment Advice from Mutual Fund Companies,' *Journal of Portfolio Management*.

Statman, M. and Bowen, J (1997) 'Performance Games,' *Journal of Portfolio Management*.

Statman, M. and Shefrin, H. (1986) 'How Not to Make Money in the Stock Market,' *Psychology Today*, 20(2), February.

Statman, M. and Shefrin, H. (1994) 'Behavioral Capital Asset Pricing Theory,' *Journal of Financial and Quantitative Analysis*, September.

Statman, M., Brick, I. and Weaver, D. (1989) 'Event Studies and Model Misspecification: Another Look at the Benefits to Outsiders from Public Information About Insider Trading,' *Journal of Business Finance and Accounting*, 16, Summer.

Sterman, J.D. (1989a) 'Deterministic Chaos in an Experimental Economic System,' *Journal of Economic Behaviour and Organisation*, 12, 1–28.

Sterman, J.D. (1989b) 'Modeling Managerial Behavior: Misperceptions of Feedback in Dynamic Decision Making Experiment,' *Management Science*, 35(3) 321–339.

Stigler, G.J. (1976) 'The Successes and Failures of Professor Smith,' *Journal of Political Economy*, December, 1199–1213.

Stock, J.H. and Watson, M.W. (1999) 'Forecasting Inflation,' *Journal of Monetary Economics* 44(2).

Summers, L.H. (1986) 'Some Skeptical Observations on Real Business Cycle Theory,' *Federal Reserve Bank of Minneapolis Quarterly Review*, 10, Fall.

Svenson, O. (1981) 'Are We All Less Risky and More Skillful than Our Fellow Drivers?,' *Acta Psychologica*, 47, 143–148.

Svenson, O. and Maule, J.A. (eds) (1993) *Time Pressure and Stress in Human Judgement and Decision Making*, New York and London: Plenum Press.

Sylos-Labini, P. (1984) 'Keynes's General Theory and the Great Depression,' in P. Sylos-Labini (ed.) *The Forces of Economic Growth and Decline*, MIT Press, pp. 227–243.

Takatoshi, I. and Mishkin, F.S. (2004) *Two Decades of Japanese Monetary Policy and the Deflation Problem*, NBER working paper 10878.

Tarhan, V. (1995) 'Does the Federal Reserve Affect Asset Prices?,' *Journal of Economic Dynamics and Control*, 19, 1199–1222.

Taylor, J. (1993) 'Discretion versus Policy Rules in Practice,' *Carnegie-Rochester Conference Series on Public Policy*, 15, 151–200.

Taylor, J.G. (1998) *Investment Timing and the Business Cycle*, New York: John Wiley & Sons, Inc.

Taylor, J. (1999) 'A Historical Analysis of Monetary Policy Rules' in J.B. Taylor (ed.) *Monetary Policy Rules*, Chicago: The University of Chicago Press.

Thaler, R.H. (1980) 'Judgment and Decision Making Under Uncertainty: What Economists Can Learn from Psychology,' *Risk Analysis in Agriculture: Research and Educational Developments*, Proceedings of a seminar sponsored by the Western Regional Research Project W-149, Tucson, Arizona, June.

Thaler, R.J. (1990) 'Gambling with the House Money and Trying to Break Even: The Effects of Prior Outcomes in Risky Choice,' *Management Science*, June.

Thaler, R.H. (1992) *The Winner's Curse*, Princeton, NJ: Princeton University Press.

Thaler, R.H. (1993) *Advances in Behavioral Finance*, New York: Russell Sage Foundation.

Thaler, R.H., Tversky, A., Kahneman, D. and Schwartz, A. (1997) 'The Effect of Myopia and Loss Aversion on Risk Taking: An Experimental Test,' *Quarterly Journal of Economics.*

The American Economic Association (1944) *Readings in Business Cycle Theory*, London: George Allen & Unwin.

The European Fine Art Foundation (2002) *The European Art Market in 2002: A Survey.*

Thomas, G. and Morgan-Witts, M. (1979) *The Day the Bubble Burst*, London: Hamish Hamilton.

Thomas, H. (1995) *An Unfinished History of the World*, London: Papermac.

Thorndike, E.L. (1898) *Animal Intelligence: An Experimental Study of the Association Process.*

Thornton, H. (1939) *An Enquiry into the Nature and Effects of the Paper Credits in Great Britain*, London: Library of Economics.

Tiger, L. (1979) *The Biology of Hope*, New York: Simon & Schuster.

Titchener, E.B. (1905) *Experimental Psychology: A Manual of Laboratory Practice*, London: Macmillan.

Tobin, J. (1975) 'Keynesian Models of Recession and Depression,' *American Economic Review*, 65.

Tobin, J. (1989) 'Review of Stabilizing an Unstable Economy by H.P. Minsky,' *Journal of Economic Literature*, 27.

Tolman, E.C. (1922) 'A New Formula for Behaviorism,' *Psychological Review*, 29.

Train, J. (1989) *The New Money Masters*, New York: Harper and Row.

Trevelyan, G.M. (1960) *Illustrated English Social History*, Middlesex: Penguin Books.

Triandis, H.C. (1977) *Interpersonal Behavior*, Monterey, California: Brooks/Cole Publishing Company.

Trichet, J-C. (2005) *Asset Price Bubbles and Monetary Policy*, Mas lecture, 8 June 2005, Singapore.

Tufte, E.R. (1978) *Political Control of the Economy*, Princeton, NJ: Princeton University Press.

Tugan-Baranovsky, M. (1894) *The Industrial Crises in England.*

Tvede, L. (1992) 'Reasons Trends may be Predictable in Financial Markets,' *The Journal of International Securities Markets*, 6, spring.

Tvede, L. (2002) *The Psychology of Finance, revised edition*, Chichester: John Wiley & Sons, Ltd.

Tvede, L. and Ohnemus, P. (2001) *Marketing Strategies for the New Economy*, Chichester: John Wiley & Sons, Ltd.

Tversky, A. (1972) 'Elimination by Aspects: A Theory of Choice,' *Psychological Review*, 79, 281–299.

Tversky, A. (1977) 'Intransitivity of Preferences,' *Psychological Review*, 84, 327–352.

Tversky, A. and Kahneman, D. (1973) 'Availability: A Heuristic for Judging Frequency and Probability,' *Cognitive Psychology*, 5, 207–232.

Tversky, A. and Kahneman, D. (1974) 'Judgment under Uncertainty: Heuristics and Biases,' *Science*, 185, 1124–1131.

Tversky, A. and Kahneman, D. (1980) 'Causal Schemata in Judgments under Uncertainty,' in M. Fishbein (ed.) *Progress in Social Psychology*, Hillsdale, NJ: Lawrence Erlbaum, pp. 49–72.

Tversky, A. and Kahneman, D. (1981) 'The Framing of Decisions and the Psychology of Choice,' *Science*, 211, 453–458.

Tversky, A. and Kahneman, D. (1986) 'Rational Choice and The Framing of Decisions,' *Journal of Business*, 59, 251–278.

Tversky, A. and Kahneman, D. (1991) 'Loss Aversion in Risk-less Choice: A Reference-Dependent Model,' *Quarterly Journal of Economics*, November, 1039–1061.

Tversky, A. and Kahneman, D. (1992) 'Advances in Prospect Theory: Cumulative Representation of Uncertainty,' *Journal of Risk and Uncertainty*, 5, 297–323.

Tversky, A. and Shafir, E. (1992) 'The Disjunction Effect in Choice Under Uncertainty,' *Psychological Science*, 3(5), 305–309.

Tweedie, H. (1994) *An Investigation into Forecasting Methods to Derive Gold Price Movements*.

UBS (2005) *Research Focus – Real Estate*, April.

Van der Linden, J. (1988) 'Economic Thought in the Netherlands: The Contribution of Professor Jan Tinbergen,' *Review of Social Economy*, 46(3), 270–288.

Van der Ploeg, F. (1985) 'Rational Expectations, Risk and Chaos in Financial Markets,' *Economic Journal*, 96.

Van Raijn, W.F. (1981) 'Economic Psychology,' *Journal of Economic Psychology*.

Van Raijn, W.F., van Veldhoven, G.M. and Warneryd, K.E. (1988) *Handbook of Economic Psychology*, Dordrecht: Kluwer Academic Publishers.

Vickers, J. (2000) 'Monetary policy and asset prices,' *The Manchester School* (Supplement), pp. 1–22.

Von Clausewitz, C. (1998) *Von Kriege*, Philipp Reclam jun Verlag GmbH.

Von Haberler, G. (1937) *Prosperity and Depression: A theoretical analysis of cyclical movements*, London: George Allen & Unwin.

Von Hayek, F.A. (1933) *Monetary Theory and the Trade Cycle*, Harcourt, Brace & Co.

Von Mises, L. (1922) Socialism: An Economic and Sociological Analysis.

Von Mises, L. (1981) *Human Action: A Treatise on Economics*, Fox & Wilkes.

Von Mises, L.W. (1953) *Theory of Money and Credit*, Yale University Press.

Walras, L. (1874) *Elements of Pure Economics*.

Warburton, C. (1966) *Depression, Inflation and Monetary Policy*, Johns Hopkins University Press.

Warsh, D. (1993) *Economic Principals: The Masters of Modern Economics*, The Free Press.

Watson, J.B. (1913) 'Psychology as the Behaviorist Sees It,' *Psychological Review*, 20.

Watson, P. (1992) *From Monet to Manhattan*, New York: Random House.

Weblen, T.B. and Volker, P.A. (1978) *The Rediscovery of the Business Cycle*, New York: Free Press.

Weimer, A. and Hoyt, H. (1939) *Principles of Real Estate*, New York: Ronald Press.

West, K.D. (1988) 'Bubbles, Fads, and Stock Price Volatility: A Partial Evaluation,' *Journal of Finance*, 43, 639–655.

Wicksell, K. (1907) 'The Influence of the Rate of Interest on Prices,' *Economic Journal*, 17, 213–220.

Wicksell, K. (1936) *Interest and Prices: A study of the causes regulating the value of money*, London: Macmillan. First published in 1898.

Wilke, W. (2000) *Investing in Art*, Dresdner Bank.

Willis, K. (1979) 'The Role in Parliament of the Economic Ideas of Adam Smith 1776–1800,' *History of Political Economy*, 11(4), 505–544.

Wolfe, J.N. (1956) 'Marshall and the Trade Cycle,' *Oxford Economic Papers*, 8, 90–101.

Wolfson, M.H. (1989) 'Theories of Financial Crises,' in W. Semmler (ed.) *Financial Dynamics and Business Cycles*, New York: M.E. Sharpe, Inc., pp. 221–227.

Woodford, M. (1989) 'Finance, Instability, and Cycles,' in W. Semmler, (ed.) *Financial Dynamics and Business Cycles*, New York: M.E. Sharpe, Inc., pp. 18–37.

Yorke, J. and Tien-Yien Li (1975) 'Period Three Implies Chaos,' *American Mathematical Monthly*, 82.

Zarnowitz, V. (1992) *Business Cycles, Theory, History, Indicators and Forecasting*, Chicago: University of Chicago Press.

# Index

Printed and bound by CPI Group (UK) Ltd, Croydon, CR0 4YY

23/04/2025

14660956-0004